MAN ALL IMMORTAL;

OR, THE

NATURE AND DESTINATION OF MAN

AS TAUGHT BY

REASON AND REVELATION.

BY

REV. D. W. CLARK, D. D.

CINCINNATI:
PUBLISHED BY POE & HITCHCOCK,
CORNER OF MAIN AND EIGHTH STREETS.

R. P. THOMPSON, PRINTER.
1866.

PREFACE.

THE germ of this volume was a series of lectures delivered, some years ago, to the students of Amenia Seminary. The purpose of the author was to present, in a popular and yet in a sufficiently scientific manner, certain topics concerning the Nature and Destination of Man, not usually treated upon in ordinary sermonizing, but which are ever rife in the young intelligence. The interest they awakened, *as delivered*, we hope may be taken as giving some assurance that they will not be wholly without interest *written*. To the young gentlemen and ladies, who listened to them in the day of their student life with kindly approbation, and who are now with manly and womanly vigor bearing the burdens and discharging the duties of life, for which they then received nurture and training—these thoughts will come as living souvenirs of the past.

The main design of these lectures was to guard the minds of especially the young, against the materialistic tendencies of the age, and to confirm them in the faith that has been with us from the beginning. They comprise topics of the highest moment, showing that "our great immortality" entered into all the plans of the Creator in relation to man. They show that *spirit* is as really and truly a substance as *matter*, and that our individuality is to remain unimpaired forever. In the line of these discussions, skepticism is met at some of the points where its most insidious efforts are now being put forth to remove the very foundations of Christianity. Among these is the assumption that the soul or spirit is nothing more than a result of the bodily organism, by which it is begotten, and with which it dies. Also that still more subtile figment, which resolves both soul and body into "force." So of the theories that would spread the pall of unconsciousness over the dead, that would annihilate personality, deny recognition, and dissolve the very heaven of glory into an airy, unsubstantial dream, by denying our essential humanity in the future state. Against these and kindred skeptical notions we have sought to furnish an antidote, recognizing, at all times, that there can be no true Philosophy of Human Nature, without the recognition of the Bible as the true interpreter of the suggestions of reason and the teachings of nature.

At the outset we found it impossible to turn aside to discuss the theories of modern speculatists, without becoming too prolix. The same reasons have kept us to the original plan in the volume. The form of address, and the style of composition, in some portions of the work, still bear the impress of the occasion and purpose for which those parts were written. We trust it will not prove any less valuable to the reader on that account. From a wide field of reading and study we have gathered our material, and then wrought it up so as to make it our own. To how many authors we are indebted, and in what proportions, it is impossible to say. We have endeavored to acknowledge, in the appropriate places, our indebtedness to each.

The preparation of this work has been a soul-nurture to the author. May it become such to the reader!

D. W. C.

CONTENTS.

IV.

THE HUMAN SOUL AND THE ANIMAL SENSES.

V.

THE HUMAN SOUL DISTINGUISHED FROM ANIMAL INSTINCT.

VI.

MIND IS INDESTRUCTIBLE AND IMMORTAL.

VII.

DEATH AND RESULTS.

VIII.

THE INTERMEDIATE STATE OF THE DEAD.

XIII.

RECOGNITION OF FRIENDS IN HEAVEN—CONTINUED.

XIV.

DURATION OF MEMORY AND ITS RELATION TO THE FUTURE LIFE.

MAN ALL IMMORTAL.

I.

THE DOUBLE NATURE OF MAN; OR, SOUL AND BODY.

"And the Lord God formed man of the dust of the ground and breathed into his nostrils the breath of life, and man became a living soul." GENESIS ii, 7.

"There is a spirit in man; and the inspiration of the Almighty giveth them understanding." JOB xxxii, 8.

WHENCE came I? what am I? and whither am I bound? are questions which have ever excited in the human mind an intensity of thought and feeling awakened by no other subject. They are questions of transcendent importance. For all that can elevate us in the scale of being; all that can direct to noble and virtuous purpose the energies of our nature; in fine, all that can give permanency to our hopes of an eternal being, or satisfy our longings after immortality, are centered in the solution which reason and religion give of them. The very rules of life, the maxims of society, the ultimate purposes and aims of a social and immortal being, are dependent upon them. For, unless we know what man is, unless we know what are the present objects of his being, and what is to be his final destiny, how can we prescribe rules for his conduct or lay before him proper motives of action? how can we still the disquietude of his heart or prevent the soul from falling back, discomfited and distressed, in its unsatisfied longings to solve the mysterious problem of its own being? Any effort, then, however feeble and unsatisfactory it may be, looking toward the solution of this problem of humanity is not unworthy of considerate attention and thought.

But how little does man know of himself! After all the researches of science, from the time that "know thyself" was first inscribed upon the temple of reason till the present hour, what has been the result? How little do we know of even our physical economy—the curious mechanism of the human body! The coarser appurtenances of the grand machinery are known; but the finer integuments of our being, which are essential to our existence, which give energy and power to the elastic springs of life, have, as yet, eluded the ken of science and the skill of human ingenuity. New discoveries have perpetually evolved new mysteries, displaying more, and still more, the surpassingly-wonderful organism of our bodies. What complexity of parts, and yet what unity of design! What mysterious interweaving of machinery, what delicate, what wonderful processes, and yet how harmonious the combination, and what simplicity in the result! Who can look upon this organism without feeling that he is indeed "fearfully and wonderfully made!"

But if the investigation of our physical nature is attended with so many difficulties, and involves mysteries so inscrutable to the unaided intellect, can we wonder that the mind—the immaterial and thinking principle—should involve questions still more subtile and inexplicable? Can we wonder that the undying spirit—that emanation of light and glory from the bosom of the Eternal—should rise above our comprehension, and elude the research of our unaided powers? Nothing can be more striking than the impotent efforts of heathen philosophers to solve the mystery of this intangible, subtile, conscious element of our nature; unless, indeed, it be the equally-important efforts of those who, though favored with the light of Divine

Revelation, have chosen to conduct their inquiries independently of it. Such are the men who prefer to wander in the barren deserts of speculation, and to bewilder themselves with the mirages of their own imagination, than to draw water from the Fountain of Truth, or to sit beneath the shade and take of the fruit of the Tree of Life. Philosophy, eagle-eyed, has never, unaided, been able to solve the far-reaching mysteries that center in our nature. What a mystery is man!

> "I tremble at myself,
> And in myself am lost. How reason reels!
> O, what a miracle to man is man!"

I remember to have stood once, in the evening twilight, upon the edge of a towering precipice, from whose base the boundless ocean stretched away in solemn grandeur. What sublime emotions, what burnings of insatiable curiosity thrilled the soul, deepening and still deepening as Night was gradually drawing her sable curtain over the scene! Just then a solitary star, rising in the east, sent streaming up through the surrounding darkness its pencil of light. From its distant home in the heavens it seemed to say, "Mortal man, beyond the narrow bounds of thy vision, beyond the gloom and darkness that envelop thee, there is a world of light, a creation of glory." So often do we, in imagination, stand upon the outer verge of mortal life and send our anxious thought into the dark future! What yearning desire takes hold upon us to solve its problem! What restless anxiety to break over and go beyond the narrow limit that bounds our horizon! Happy he upon whose longing, weary soul breaks the rising star of heaven's own most glorious truth, bringing "life and immortality to light!" To this light the soul instinctively responds, recognizing the glorious truth that "God is light, and in him is no darkness at all." In this revelation the great problem of human life, the nature and destination of man, is solved. It is presented, not in the form of mere hypothesis, not in abstruse, metaphysical theories, but in the clear and broad statement of immutable truth—MAN ALL IMMORTAL.

Let us begin with the first elements of this discussion, that we may follow it step by step to the grand conclusion. At the very outset, then, we find the DOUBLE NATURE OF MAN asserted; for, while it was said that man's body was *formed of the dust of the ground*, it is also said that *the Lord God breathed into his nostrils the breath of life, and man became a living soul.* It is also declared that *there is a spirit in man, and the inspiration of the Almighty giveth them understanding.* Man, then, is an embodied spirit. When the Almighty had molded the dust into a form of beauty and majesty fit to become the abode of, and to be animated by, a spirit, it was not left inanimate and dead. A mysterious and sublime emanation from himself was infused into the molded dust while as yet it was lifeless as the clod—a principle of feeling, of thought, and of action, a germ of immortality—and then man became a living soul. The union of these two elements constitutes the sublime mystery of humanity. How body and spirit may cohere; how they are made to blend together, to act in unison, and to depend upon each other, we shall not undertake to explain. We shall confine ourselves to the *fact* of such relationship, which is the only really-essential question in the case. The fact is approachable, demonstrable; but its mysteries branch off and spread out into the illimitable and eternal.

I. MAN POSSESSES A PHYSICAL NATURE.

Both science and Revelation combine to assure us that the entire created universe of God is composed of two distinct and independent substances; namely, matter and spirit.

Each of these possesses peculiar and striking characteristics, which distinguish it from the other.

If it is asked what is meant by matter, or what matter *is*, we must confess that we know not what constitutes its *essence*. In this respect its ontology is beyond our reach; and the only advance we find it possible to make is to point out some of the properties of matter as discerned by our senses, and to exhibit some of the laws by which it is governed. Thus we say it possesses extension, impenetrability, inertia, and form, and that it is subject to the laws of gravitation and cohesive attraction. Behind these properties we can not go to explore the essence of that in which they inhere; for these properties, as addressed to the senses, are the only media through which we become acquainted with its existence.

Matter, thus defined and thus made known, makes up the material universe. And the human body itself, though curiously and wonderfully made, is only one of the modifications under which matter exists. The spirit may claim affinity with the skies, but the body, though its form be erect and stately, its front bold and daring, may say "to corruption, thou art my father; to the worm, thou art my mother and sister;" *for the grave is its home and its bed is made in darkness.*

The gross earth upon which we tread is the first or primal form of matter. The rank luxuriance of vegetation, which clothes the earth with new and living beauty, presents only a modification of the form under which matter exists. And, if we advance still further and observe those bodies which are endowed with the peculiar honor of being the abodes of animal and sentient life—whether it be the body of man or beast—still it is *matter*, changed in form and relations and not in nature. It is matter still, only existing under a new and greatly-modified form. Nor can matter, by any possible transformation, be made to lose its distinctive characteristics, and assume the higher prerogatives of spirit. Change it as you may; condense, attenuate, or refine it as you please, it will be matter still. The essential properties of matter will still remain, while the higher indications of intellect will no where appear.

Man, then, possesses a body composed of matter under the various modifications of bones, flesh, and blood. The limestone that forms his bony substance is not different from that which is found in the mountain ridges of the earth and in the coral beds of the ocean. Then, too, what are the softer elements of the body but a combination of oxygen, hydrogen, nitrogen, and carbonic acid, with a little sulphur, iron, and quartz? From these are formed the fibrin of the muscles, the albumen of the brain and nerves, the gelatinous substances and the fat of the body, and even the blood that circulates in the veins and arteries. Indeed, such are the materials entering into the composition of the human body, and such the proportions in which those materials are combined, that of the whole weight, when its parts are separated, *three-fourths are water.* But, again, what is this wonderful structure, the human body, but a mechanical instrument? The bones are levers, the bloodvessels are hydraulic tubes, and the muscles are the connecting links through which motive power is applied, and even the nerves are only the unconscious wires of telegraphic communication.

Then, too, in his mere physical organization man has little advantage over the brute creation. His symmetry of conformation is no more perfect than that of many species in the animal kingdom. His organs are not better adapted to their ends; his joints have no finer articulation, nor his sinews any firmer texture. Nay, even the organs of sense are often less delicate and acute in man than in the brute. A modern writer puts this point in a very forcible light: "The body of man lacks the massy strength of the elephant and the whale; it can not rival the muscles of the lion; the antelope and the grayhound are far more graceful; man has no pinions to mount on high; he can not live in the deep; the falcon has a keener eye, the grouse a quicker ear, the dog a more discerning smell, and the bat a more susceptible touch; and of all the beasts the most hideous is that which most resembles him in form, gestures, and visage."*

Nor is the body of man any more guarded against liabilities to accident and change. In none of these respects can we claim any advantage for poor human nature. The beasts of the field perish, and so does man. Indeed, in whatever form matter exists it is liable to change. Even the granite bulwarks of the everlasting hills crumble away in the lapse of time. Can it then be wonderful that the fine and delicate workmanship of the human frame should wear out by the common friction of use? or, when long exposed to the action of the elements, should fall into decay? How little honor, then, is to be attached to the mere material organic body! This is not *the man.*

Did we stop here, much as we might admire the beautiful organism of our bodies, interested as we might be in our investigation of its complicated machinery, and important as might be the scientific theories evolved, still it would be but a sad account we could give of the nature and destination of man. The purposes of his animal existence here may be accomplished in a few years, and then the worn-out machinery is laid aside and forgotten; it wastes away in the charnel-house of the dead. "I said in mine heart concerning the estate of the sons of men, that God might manifest them, and that they might see that they

* Burgess's Last Enemy, p. 10.

themselves are beasts. For that which befalleth the sons of men befalleth beasts; even one thing befalleth them; as the one dieth, so dieth the other; yea, they have all one breath; so that a man hath no preëminence above a beast; for all is vanity. All go unto one place; all are of the dust, and all turn to dust again." (Eccl. iii, 19, 20.) But yet there is a wide and eternal distinction between man and the brute: "Who knoweth the spirit of man that goeth *upward*, and the spirit of the beast that goeth *downward* to the earth." (Eccl. iii, 21.)

II. Man Possesses a Living Soul.

As the crowning work of creation was the production of man, so the crowning work in the formation of man was the imparting from the living God of a soul or spirit that was to animate the material temple. The Temple of old was not left without the indwelling glory of God; so also this fair structure of the human body received its complement in an indwelling soul. "And the Lord God formed man of the dust of the ground and *breathed into his nostrils the breath of life; and man became a living soul.*" This is a distinct announcement that the soul of man is something different in its origin and distinct in its character from the body. The one is formed from "the dust of the ground," the other emanated from the breath of the Almighty. The one is "dust," the other "*a living soul.*" The soul is not a part of the physical structure, does not grow out of it, but is superadded to it. The mysterious combination of these two elements in man completed the work of his creation.

Breathed into his nostrils the breath of life. The Hebrew has the plural, *breath of lives.* Whether, as some have supposed, this implies that man is endowed with the vegetative life of plants, the sensitive life of animals, and also the higher life that distinguishes spiritual beings; or, indeed, whether any peculiar force of meaning is to be attached to the mere circumstance of plurality of form, it is difficult to determine. Nor is the determination of the question essential to our present purpose; as it now concerns us only to show that to man was imparted a higher nature than that which is merely animal. In fine, we claim that it was the *intention* of Inspiration to assert for man all that we understand to be implied in the possession of a "living soul" breathed from God, and "a spirit" inspired with understanding from the Almighty.

And man became a living soul. That the Hebrew word *nephesh* is, in other places, applied to living animals, reptiles, creeping creatures upon the earth, and also to other things, does not prove that it can not here be employed to express what we mean by the word *soul*, or *living soul.* Even with us, though the word *soul* has come to have a technical and definite meaning, nothing is more common than to use it outside of that meaning—as when a vessel founders at sea, and we say, *every soul on board perished*, meaning simply that every person on board lost his life. The fact is, there is no single word in Biblical Hebrew, answering in fixed and definite import to either of the English words *soul* and *body*. The same is true of the Greek, and also of the Latin. But both body and soul, as distinguished from each other, and as embodying the *ideas* attached to these words in our current English, are distinctly recognized and taught in the Bible. If, then, the intrinsic nature of the soul is not disclosed by the import of the Hebraic terms used to denote it, it is not because that nature is not recognized, but because human language was then destitute of an appropriate word which might be thus employed. The same remarks, in a greater or less degree, are applicable to the other Hebrew words *ruahh, neshamah*, etc., expressed by the words soul, spirit, etc. And is it not thus also with the English word *soul?* Even the question of its origin is unsettled, much less has its philological import been made to appear. And yet it has come to have a known and acknowledged signification. It may be said to have grown into this signification, or by gradual process come to be appropriated to this use; so that now, whenever used, we take it to mean the spiritual and immortal nature, unless the connections in which it stands determine some other signification.

Whatever, then, may be said of the philological import of the Hebrew term rendered by the words *living soul*, the connections of the term when used in relation to the creation and endowment of man, fully establish the high sense in which it is used. In the creation of unintellectual animals God said, *Let the earth bring them forth.* Nothing is said about breathing into *them* the breath of life. Then, too, man was to be modeled after a higher type. *Let us make man after our own image and likeness.* Higher purposes were to be accomplished in his being. He was to have *dominion* over the animal creation. It was to be a wide dominion, including all animal kind in the sea, upon the earth, and in the air. That dominion, too, was to spread over *every herb bearing seed, and every tree which is upon the face of all the earth.* The circumstances and the objects of man's creation are such as would indicate a new and higher order of endowment. This is still further confirmed by the importance attached to his creation in the councils of the Creator. The persons in the Godhead, and it may be the higher order of angelic beings, seem to have been summoned into council over his creation. Nothing can be more clear than that all this is implied in the expression, "*Let us make.*" If by *the breath of lives* is simply meant that the animal man began then to use his organs of respiration, began to breathe, why is the case mentioned at all in contradistinction from the creation of the unintellectual animals? While, then, man is possessed of the breath of animal life, the plan, the design, the circumstances of his creation, and especially the Divine origin of the higher principle of the life that is within him, render the conclusion inevitable, that superadded to his merely animal life is another life—that of the soul.

It will be seen by the above, that we are not to look exclusively to the philological meaning of the words employed to express soul or spirit, to demonstrate this higher endowment in the life of man; we claim simply that there is nothing, so far as is known, in the philological meaning of the words that would lie in the way of this use; we claim that the terms were actually employed to express this higher endowment; and that the distinction of spirit, as something different from the body; something different from animal life; something more Divine, more nearly allied to God, and with different relations to eternity, is brought to light in a thousand ways all through the Bible. In fact, it is a doctrine that permeates all revelation, and gives to it its sublime applicability and force of teaching. No one can read the Bible without being impressed with the fact that it as fully recognizes the soul as a distinct essence, as it does the body. The inference, then, made by some, that because the term *living soul* is sometimes applied to animals, reptiles, vegetables, etc., therefore each is endowed with intellectual and immortal faculties, or that none are thus endowed, is equally invalid. It no more follows, than it does when you say of a wrecked ship, every soul on board perished, that the spiritual nature of each one was annihilated, rather than their lives lost. The full force and contents of the term "living soul," as applied to man, is seen only when we place it by the side of that declaration of that God who is both "life" and "spirit," "*Let us make man in our image, after our likeness.*" (Gen. i, 26.) This certainly means something more than that man was made an UPRIGHT ANIMAL WALKING ON TWO FEET!

Man became a living soul. The Greek term ψυχη has for its dominant meaning, *life*, as indicated by the act of breathing. It is distinguished from another Greek term, ζωη, which is also rendered *life.* In John xii, 25, we meet those two terms in a connection which goes very far toward determining the original sense in which each was used: "He that hateth his life (ψυχην) in this world shall keep it unto life (ζωην) eternal." It is evident, then, that the former has special reference to the principle of life manifested in connection with bodily organization; the latter to the higher element of spiritual existence. The terms *living soul*—or, as more frequently used, the simple term *soul*—indicate, as applied to man, a higher than mere animal life. This is the term employed by the apostle when he said, speaking of the "first Adam," the type of humanity, that he was made *a living soul* (εἰς ψυχὴν ζῶσαν.) We use the term *soul* to express the spiritual element of our nature—that element which knows, and thinks, and reasons, and possesses a judgment of right and wrong. The operations of the soul are diversified, but its distinct individuality and the unity of its nature rest upon the firmest basis of reason and truth. Sensation, reason, memory, imagination, will, and conscience are expressive of so many different modes of the soul's action. But they leave its unity untouched. They are so many capabilities, properties, or manifestations of the intelligent *substance* whose being and action are made known by them. These are the *phenomena* through which we are introduced to the knowledge of the soul, and in the light of which we must study its character.

It must not be thought amiss, nor awaken surprise, if we confess that we know not in what the *essence* of soul or spirit consists. We readily acknowledged our ignorance of the *essence*, the *subject-being* of matter. We make the same confession—and under the same limitations—concerning the soul. But though we were unable to tell what matter is, yet we found ourselves able to describe or define it by the sensible properties it possesses and the laws by which it is governed. So it is with the soul. Though we are unable to throw aside the vail and gaze upon its essence, yet we may discover its existence, and something of its nature and qualities, from our consciousness of its operations and our knowledge of its effects. Every one is conscious of a principle within him superior to the frame it inhabits. There is something that warms into life and excites to motion the machinery of our bodies, which is beyond the artist's skill or the chemist's power. There is a beauty lit up in the expressions of the human countenance which the painter's skill can never reach, for it is not an attribute of matter. It is the high and indisputable proof of the divinity that dwells within us. "It is a flame from heaven purer than Promethean fire that vivifies and energizes the breathing form. It is an immaterial essence, a being that quickens matter and imparts life, sensation, motion to the intricate frame-work of our bodies, which wills when we act, attends when we perceive, looks into the past when we reflect, and, not content with the present, shoots with all its aims and with all its hopes into the futurity that is forever dawning upon it."

The properties of mind are manifested in perception, thought, feeling, volition, reason, the passions, and the moral judgments. That every one intuitively recognizes a *something* in his breast which puts forth the distinct operations or experiences the distinct feelings indicated by these words the universal testimony of man abundantly proves. They are not the acts, the operations of matter; they can not be predicated concerning the body. Thought is intangible; you can not see it as you can see light; you can not cause it to travel the magnetic wires as you may cause electricity to travel. But just as the magnetic telegraph is only the vehicle of thought, of ideas, which it neither originates nor constitutes, so are our physical organs only the media for the transmission, *the outward expression* of ideas which they have no power to originate. It becomes, then, one of the clearest dictates of reason that, if there is that wide difference between the properties, the characteristics of matter and spirit, these two principles must be essentially different in their nature. No one can prove infidel to what he feels; and he who marks the swellings of human thought, passion, and desire, expanding and enlarging to the grasp of infinity and eternity, can not fail to discern within him the elements of a spiritual and eternal existence:

> "Who reads his bosom reads immortal life;
> Or Nature there, imposing on her sons,
> Has written fables—man was made a lie!"

Thus are we led to the indubitable conviction that *there is a spirit in man* distinct from the body it inhabits, and therefore he has become *a living soul.*

III. Practical Suggestions.

With the mention of a few of the practical suggestions growing out of the subject, we close this discussion:

1. *The possession of a physical nature is not necessarily an evil.* What is said, by inspiration, of the vegetable body is also true of the animal creation, that "God giveth it a body as it hath pleased him." The ancient philosophers were often accustomed to regard the body as an incum-

brance to the soul—a sort of jail in which the spirit was imprisoned, and from which it longed for deliverance. Such also seems to be a too prevalent notion among many religious persons of the present day, especially those whose minds are of a mystical cast. But the fact that God gave us these bodies, and that they, in our resurrection state, are to be the inheritance of the children of God, sufficiently demonstrates that the human body is not an evil in itself. God intended man to be, not a seraph, but a human being; and therefore endowed him with a body as well as a spirit.

2. *This union of soul and body, though mysterious, is by no means incredible.* The combination of material substances, the impenetration of the one by the other, are scarcely less mysterious; and yet they are facts observable every day. How the electricity of thought can find expression in the movement of the tongue or of the hand is no more wondrous than that the electricity of nature, conducted by the metallic wire, shall give expression to its message thousands of miles distant in an instant of time. As with a thousand other things, our inability to comprehend the *mode* is no argument against the *fact.* The endowment or connection of animal life with a material body is of the same sort of mystery, and yet the fact of such connection is too palpable for denial.

3. *This union of soul and body is essential to the objects of our humanity.* A physical organization was necessary to adapt man to the physical world designed to be the theater of his action and the scene of his embryo growth and development. But, without the spiritual element, the higher link that united him to his God, and made him in fact the representative of the image and likeness of the Divine Being in this lower state, would be wanting. Nor is the material body without its uses. It is the inlet of numerous

enjoyments to the soul. It is a source of infinitely-varied knowledge. It brings the soul into visible and tangible connection with the material world, and gives it a wonderful control over the elements of nature. Then, too, our humanity will not reach its ultimate perfection till a reunion of these elements is consummated by the resurrection of the body. Hence, like the apostle, all we "who have the first-fruits of the Spirit, even we ourselves, groan within ourselves, waiting for the adoption, to-wit, the redemption of our body." (Rom. viii, 23.)

4. *In the creation of so august a being as man there must be ends or objects commensurate with his character and endowments.* He was to occupy a preëminent position in the animal creation. In this subdivision of the kingdom of God he was to be the ruler and governor. The sublime mysteries of creation were to be explored by his intellect; the rough limnings of nature were to be molded to forms of beauty by his hand. He was to be at once the representative and the friend of God. The very contemplation of such a being awakens within us the loftiest expectations with regard to his destiny! The poorest and the darkest specimen of humanity upon the face of the earth has yet some glimmering indications of what humanity is capable in its present or future state.

"How poor, how rich, how abject, how august,
How complicate, how wonderful is man!
How passing wonder He who made him such,
Who centered in one make such strange extremes,
From different natures marvelously mixed—
Connection exquisite of distant worlds!
Distinguished link in being's endless chain—
Midway from nothing to the Deity!
A beam ethereal, sullied and absorbed!
Though sullied and dishonored, still divine!
Dim miniature of greatness absolute!
An heir of glory, a frail child of dust!
Helpless immortal! insect infinite!
A worm! a god!"

II.

ORGANISM AND LIFE.

"Spirit, and soul, and body." 1 THESS. v, 23.
"The body without the spirit is dead." JAMES ii, 26.
"Being yourselves also in the body." HEB. xiii, 4.
"God giveth it a body as it hath pleased him, and to every seed his own body." 1 COR. xv, 38.

WE have already seen that man possesses a double nature—the one organized from the dust of the ground, the other imparted directly from the living God. These two natures were necessary, in order to constitute him the connecting link between the spiritual and the material worlds.

Without the former his present relation to the earth and the inferior animal and vegetable creations would have been impossible; without the latter his present relation to the spiritual universe could not have existed, and he would have become one with the brute creation. Without the combination of these two natures, then, there could not have been such a thing as *humanity*.

On the one hand man has organism and life in common with the animal and vegetable creation; but on the other hand he has a soul or spirit in common with angelic or heavenly natures. This question, then, of organism and life is essential to the full understanding of the nature and destination of man. It becomes especially necessary in order to determine his relation to animated beings and his rank among them.

I. What is a Living Organic Body?

It is not our purpose here to show what life is in itself, but to ascertain the nature of organism, and to show its relations to life. A living organic body has these several characteristics:

1. *It is made up of various parts or members connected by concrescence or a common growth.* The parts do not exist before the whole, so that you have only to bring them together, as is the case in building a house or in the construction of a machine. They all have a concurrent formation, and that too by a common process. The parts of a machine are first manufactured, so that each may exist in full perfection long before they are brought together and the machine is made. So in the creation of an edifice—like the building of Solomon's temple—every part may be first formed and fashioned for its place, so that each one is complete, while as yet no two of them have been put together. But in the organization of a living body this can never be. The branches are not made before the trunk, and then brought and attached to it. The limbs of the animal are not made separate from the body, and then fitted to it by mechanical ingenuity. No one part precedes the others. All grow up together into one homogeneous body.

2. *In organic bodies specific forms are produced, with various parts the same in number and function.* Invariableness in form is, in some sort, true in crystallology. The quartz will invariably assume its six-sided prismatic form, with pyramidal ends; the iron pyrites displays its cubes; the garnet will appear in the form of dodecahedrons; and so each mineral, capable of crystallization, will have its specific and unvarying form. But there is here no diversity

of part or of function. The crystallized mass is a simple aggregation of little crystals, each as perfect in itself as the aggregated body; and when separated fiom the mass the particle suffers no change as the result of that separation. There is no life produced, nor is there made the least approximation to it. The crystal has neither organs nor limbs, and even its dimensions are limited by external relations rather than its internal nature. But in the living germ is to be found the form-determining power, which molds and shapes the organic body. The germ in the acorn can, by no possibility of culture or of external influence, be made to develop into an animal. It embodies the parts, roots, trunk, and branches, of the tree, and that too of its own species, the oak; and nothing else can grow out of it. So of the animal germ. The form, while the embryo being is yet in the egg, is as determinate as when it comes forth into life.

3. *The living body is the product of inward forces.* It gathers its material and incorporates it into the organic body by a power within itself. The block of marble, by a gradual transformation, comes, at length, to assume the human form. But this transformation was not a plan, a work, or a result of its own, nor yet of forces within itself. But for the action of the artist upon it, it had remained a sightless block forever. In the living body there is an invisible power, which takes hold of the elements nature has in store for it, and works them up into its own body, by the most wonderful transformation. This power of assimilation is peculiar to the organic body, and must distinguish it from the inorganic forever.

4. *Organized bodies exist in generations.* The plant "hath the seed in itself" for the production of other plants. The organic is not only a vitalized body, but it possesses the power of vitalizing, and thus giving being

to other vitalized bodies that shall be its successors. Not only have the leaves of the forest a time to fall in their successive seasons, but the trees themselves pass through their successive stages of being and pass away, so that the forest is perpetually renewed with new generations of the race. The human race exists, in like manner, in successive generations. "One generation passeth away and another cometh;" and thus the race is preserved. The crystals are the highest efforts of inorganic nature. Curiously are they wrought in her great laboratory, and come forth sparkling in their beauty. But we find no such relation as would indicate successive generations among them. Each is perfect in itself—is without antecedent crystal as a cause, and also without succeeding crystal as a result. Nor is there periodicity in its duration. Every thing is contingent, dependent upon the action of external chemistry, and not upon internal functions. It may be dissolved in a day, or it may last forever.

5. *In the living body the separation of parts can not take place without the death and decay of the part so separated.* The members all differ from each other in character and office, as the roots, trunks, branches, leaves, blossoms, and fruits in vegetables, and the feet, hands, bodies, heads, and hearts in animals. Yet each assists and promotes the life of the whole. Strike off a part—a limb of a tree or the arm of a person—and the part so stricken off changes in its whole character. It has life no longer, but is decomposed and returns to dust. An inorganic body, like a block of granite, may be broken into pieces; still it is granite, each part, however small, retaining the characteristic properties of the whole. A bar of iron may be cut up into the smallest filings, but each atom is still iron and complete in itself. The mast of a vessel may be snapped asunder in a gale, but mechanical skill may splice the pieces, and the

mast perform the same service as before. But does the storm break the towering trunk of the forest pine, the part so severed is dead. Restoration, so that it may perform its former functions, is impossible. The lightning may tear away a fragment from a building, but the fragment is unchanged in character. It is wood, or stone, or brick as before, and has only to be replaced to repair the damage. But does the lightning rend a limb from a man, the man himself, possibly, may survive, but the limb is dead. Its restoration is impossible. No surgical skill can replace it so that it shall again become a part of the living body.

6. *Among all organic living bodies there are certain common functions not found in inorganic bodies.* The vegetable and the animal are widely removed in characteristics from each other; so widely, indeed, that, to the superficial observer, they seem to have scarcely any properties in common. Yet "their living, growing, feeding, reproducing, secreting, transpiring, vascular, diseased, and dying actions are universal instances of a related similitude. In these things all that have life resemble each other, whether animal or vegetable, and however separating their other properties or capacities may be."* But none of these properties are found in the stone or mineral. They may enlarge, but their enlargement is by exterior accretion, by the addition of exterior particles to their surface. *They do not grow.* They have no development from within. The peculiar functional chemistry so manifest in the operation for the support and growth of living bodies is wholly wanting. Crystallization may produce forms of wondrous beauty, but in none of them do we find *life*. So the stone or mineral needs no nutriment in order to its preservation. If not operated upon by the action of elements exterior to itself, it will remain unchanged forever. Or, again, it may be disinte-

* Turner's Sacred History, I, 153.

grated, may return to its original elements; but it suffers no dying agony; it is simply action from without, separating the parts that had been brought together by external force and blended by nature's chemistry.

II. Organization is Produced by life, and not Life by Organization.

Organism is the incarnation of life. The physiologist finds in nature a special *principle* of organization. No where is inorganic matter converted into organic structures, whether in vegetables or in animals, without the influence of this principle. Call this principle what we may—a germ, a vesicle, or a cell—it possesses an innate power, by which it seizes hold of the material within its reach, and suitable to its purpose, regroups it, and thus develops a new organization.*

In this respect there is a wonderful concurrence between the vegetable and the animal world, showing both to be the conceptions of one overruling Mind. The kernel of grain and the egg of the animal alike contain not only the germ of life, but a stock of nutritive material, which is used in the earlier stages of development. The embryo plant first consumes the nutritive material in the seed, incorporating a part of it into the new organic body that is being found, till the shell is bursted and connection established with the material outside. Then the plant gradually weans itself and commences collecting the materials of its life and growth from the earth, the air, and the sun. The process of development in the egg of the animal is after the same general type. A large portion of the contents of the egg-shell is simply nutritive material kindly stored, upon which the embryo animal may feed till its connections with

*Draper's Human Physiology.

the outside world are so established that it can draw from the latter its support. In both cases, the organizing and appropriating power is LIFE.

In view of this remarkable fact, we can hardly wonder that so many have conceived that there is a *plastic* power in nature itself, by which these organizations are effected. But what is meant by plastic power? Is it any thing more than a convenient term under which philosophy may hide its *failure to solve the problem of* LIFE? The idea of plastic power is, that it is an *agent* which takes hold of inorganic physical materials, and organizes them so as to produce life. But what is this agent? Where does it reside? If it is a quality of matter, and inheres in matter, what is it, then, but to say that matter *organizes itself?* If it is not a quality of matter and does not inhere in matter, how does it differ from the living principle or germ ordained by the great Creator of all for the perpetuation of life—each in its appropriate mode and form? The former is sometimes used by the infidel, as an indirect method of ignoring the direct agency of God in the universe. The latter makes full recognition of that agency. The former endues *matter* with power to produce the various forms of life. The latter recognizes every being possessed of life, as originating in an elementary germ; and that this germ of itself determines the species of the being produced. Hence the celebrated maxim of Harvey, *omne animal ex ovo.* Thus all races and orders of living bodies, first created by God, are also endowed by him with reproductive powers for the perpetuation and increase of the several species.

The tenacity of life in the *ovum* is also worthy of notice as tending to show the mysteriousness of the vital element. The old story of the vegetation of wheat found in an Egyptian mummy, and which had probably been entombed with it three thousand years, is familiar to our readers. In addition to this, the North British Agriculturist not long since gave an account of the clearing away of the *debris* from an old Roman camp, upon the soil of which, thus made bare, there sprung up no less than seventy four varieties of oats never seen in that section before. The matter was thoroughly sifted; and the conclusion was that the place was an old cavalry camp, and that the oats now germing had been brought from other climes, and had lain buried 1,500 years under the earth. Yet this seed, when exposed to the action of the sun, and air, and moisture, germed as readily as though it had been the growth of the preceding harvest. The fact is also well known, that the seed entombed for ages in an alluvial soil, when thrown up with the dirt from the bottom of deep excavations, will germ and grow. These facts indicate that no limits in time can be set to durations of life pent up in a kernel of grain. May not the same be true of the germ of life in the ovum of the animal?

III. Antagonisms between Animal and Vegetable Life.

In this discussion we have thus far made no distinction between animal and vegetable life. There is that relationship between the embryo condition of each that indicates one original type. There is unity of design. But we can not advance far in our investigations without discovering radical differences; and what is still more striking, these very differences reveal to us a higher and grander harmony. Animal life and vegetable life are the counterpart of each other. This is seen in their different action upon the atmosphere, and the different relations they sustain to the earth. The plant is constantly consuming the carbonic acid in the atmosphere, and at the same time replenishing that atmosphere with oxygen. On the other hand, animal bodies are constantly consuming oxygen and returning carbonic acid. Thus has the equilibrium of the atmosphere been preserved for ages.

The French chemists group the differences, or antagonisms, between plants and animals in a very clear and striking manner. They make at least six of them, as follows:

THE VEGETABLE,	THE ANIMAL,
1. PRODUCES the neutral, nitrogenized substances, fatty substances, sugar, gum, and starch.	1. CONSUMES the neutral, nitrogenized substances, fatty substances, sugar, gum, and starch.
2. DECOMPOSES carbonic acid, water, and ammoniacal salts.	2. PRODUCES carbonic acid, water, and ammoniacal salts.
3. DISENGAGES oxygen.	3. ABSORBS oxygen.
4. ABSORBS heat and electricity.	4. PRODUCES heat and electricity.
5. Is an apparatus of DEOXIDATION.	5. Is an apparatus of OXIDATION.
6. Is STATIONARY.	6. Is LOCOMOTIVE.

From the above it will be seen that there is, in various and important respects, a distinct antagonism between plants and animals. And yet when taken in their relation to the inorganic world, we see how indispensable they are to each other, and how these very antagonisms minister to the harmony of the universe.

These differences, or, to express the fact more correctly, these antagonisms between the physical structure of plants and of animals, and their relations to inorganic matter, suggest a wide difference, if not an entire dissimilarity, between the principle of *life* in each. But how wide this difference may be, or in what it consists; whether they differ in nature or only in manifestation, are questions that do not concern this discussion. Nor does it seem that human science has yet grasped the elements of knowledge essential to their solution.

We are not, however, inclined, with Professor Draper, to regard a plant as being a mere physical *operation*, originating in some antecedent physical impression, and that, therefore, all the phenomena of plants are mechanical and material.* We see no reason why He who has created such variety in the substances of the inorganic world, might not also have created different kinds of LIFE. We think there is at least ground for inference that two elements which operate in such direct antagonism in their effects upon the material world must be different in their essential nature. But if in this lowest form of life—so low, indeed, that some philosophers have questioned whether it is any thing more than a physical operation—there are to be found no spontaneous organizations; none without the antecedent *germ* from which it springs; then how complete the demonstration that *organization is produced by* LIFE, *and not life by organization!*

IV. Higher Elements of Life in Man.

The animal creation stands out distinct from and superior to the vegetable—holding, indeed, many things in common with it, but at the same time possessing other qualities which place it at an immeasurable remove from it. So man possesses many qualities in common with the animal, but he has also others which place him at a remove almost infinite.

These other qualities are not, as we have already seen, in his physical organization. Take away the higher endowment of a thinking and reasoning spirit, and man would no longer be able to cope with many species of his cotemporary animals. He could not face the lion, the tiger, or the wolf; the buffalo would cease to acknowledge his prowess; the horse would speed away from him, and even the mule would hold him in derision. You may endow him with all

*Human Physiology, pp. 470, 471.

of life that is possessed or implied in mere animal function, and still, from his very physical organization, he would be compelled to yield the dominion to other animals.

In animal organization we have observed that its departure from the type and characteristics of the vegetable is specially designed to adapt it to the function and nature of animal life. The element of life effecting the organization and the building up of the living plant, could no more be transferred to the animal body and be made to work a like function there, than it could be to the crystal-quartz or any other mineral. In fact, were the transfer made, the very element that built up the plant into a living body would work death in the animal. So in the organization of man. His peculiarities of body are not designed to secure animal superiority, but to adapt the animal organization to the spirit with which it was to be endowed.

If any one shall ask me how a living spirit can dwell in a human body, I will ask him first to solve the problem, How *animal life* can dwell in the animal body; or how *vegetable life* is connected with the plant or the tree? When he has solved these two problems, we may be prepared to approach the solution of the higher and more mysterious problem of spiritual life. In the mean time, the fact of man's being endowed with a spirit rests upon the evidence of, and is demonstrated by, the same class of facts that demonstrate *life* in the vegetable and in the animal.

V. The Modern Theory of Force as Constituting the Soul Considered.

The simple position we have taken in regard to the soul is, that it is an independent substance; that it is something different from a general principle of life infused into all matter, as Professor Taylor Lewis seems to imagine was done when "the Spirit of God moved upon the face of the waters;" in fine, that it is a personality—spiritual in its nature and Divine in its origin.

In opposition to this sublime doctrine of soul there is a theory of ancient materialistic philosophers, revived by some modern speculatists, that the essence of matter is *force*, and also that homogeneous with this is the essence of spirit. According to this, in the final result, the substratum of the universe is FORCE.

Leibnitz objected to the theory of Descartes, who made matter consist essentially in *extension*, that it would produce a world of unalterable existence, but instead of this the world exhibits an innumerable number of ever-varying movements and developments. Hence he attributes to all substances an *inherent power* by which their phenomena are generated. Masses being *infinitely* divisible, the process at length eliminates every material property, strictly so called, and all that remains is "the simple and immaterial idea of power, as the essential basis of all existence." This power or force Leibnitz terms a *monad*. The *atomic theory* in physical science regarded the material universe as composed of an aggregate of material atoms—each possessing the essential properties of matter; but outside of this, and differing from it, spirit was regarded as a distinct substance. But the *monadic* theory, in the last analysis, entirely eliminates *materiality* from the universe, and leaves nothing but a self-working, self-developing *force*. This is the fundamental axiom of the vaunted *dynamics* of the present day. Now let us see how Morell, following in the lead of Leibnitz, attempts to establish this fundamental principle. "The monad," says he, "being indivisible, unextended, *immaterial*, can not be exposed to any influences from without; being insoluble, it can never perish. The cause of the perpetual changing of monads, then, not being external, must be internal; that is, *all monads must contain an inward energy, by which they develop themselves spontaneously.*"* To what result this brings us will be noted by and by.

Mr. Morell, who, with much philosophic acumen, attempts to galvanize this old doctrine into a new life, after granting that material phenomena indicate a substratum, claims that the real philosophic analysis of this substratum will bring us to no other result than that of the "*action and reaction of force.*" This mysterious "force" he makes the substratum of soul as well as body. Having thus merged both matter and spirit into "FORCE," he becomes enraptured at the result. "The universe in this light!" he exclaims, "appears far more simple, more harmonious, more beautiful. Instead of a dualism we have a homogeneous creation, together with the activities of which it is composed, rising in perfect gradation from the lowest forms of matter through all the regions of organic life to the highest development of mind itself. On these principles, power, acting unconsciously and blindly, is matter—power, raised to intelligence and volition, is spirit. The substratum of both is identical."† What, then, is this wonderful FORCE? Is it in its nature material or immaterial? Did it exist antecedent to matter—antecedent to spirit? How? What was its origin? Does it exist independently alike of matter and of spirit? Then what is its substratum? What is the fulcrum upon which it plants its lever? But is it eternal? and did it give being to all the phenomena observed in both the material and the spiritual worlds? Then how does it differ from God? Is it not God himself? Till these questions are solved, the pretender of a *new instauration* has not begun to fathom the depths, nor to comprehend the difficulties of his own system.

* Morell's Hist. Mod. Phil., p. 149. † Ibid., p. 333.

Darwin's theory differs from that of Morell in this: He has something tangible, something real for a starting-point; namely, "the primeval monads." It is by the action of these upon each other—"the working of matter upon matter"—that not only the vast machinery of the universe, together with physical bodies and animal life, have been produced, but also the moral and spiritual faculties of the human race. He has an advantage in this, that his "force" is not a mere abstraction; but in nothing more.

Professor Huxley does not hesitate to follow this theory of "force" out to its legitimate result. He says: "The whole analogy of natural operations furnishes so complete and crushing an argument against the intervention of any but what are termed secondary causes, in the production of all the phenomena of the universe, that, in view of the intimate relations between man and the rest of the living world, and between the forces exerted by the latter and all other forces, I can see no excuse for doubting that all are co-ordinated terms of Nature's great progression, from the formless to the formed, from the inorganic to the organic, *from the blind* force to conscious intellect and will."* And again: "Man is, in substance and in structure, one with the brutes."† Thus, according to these modern skeptics, the highest achievements of science are those which exclude a personal God from the universe and unspiritualize man, making him one with the brutes.

"O, star-eyed science, hast thou wandered there,
To bring us back the message of despair?"

No wonder that the author of such sentiments is compelled to confess that the triumph of man's intellect is a defeat. "It is as if Nature herself had foreseen the arrogance of man, and with Roman severity had provided that his intellect, by its very triumphs, should call into promi-

* "Evidence as to Man's Place in Nature," p. 128. † Ibid., p. 135.

nence the slaves—the lower animal creatures—admonishing the conqueror that he is dust."*

As our modern speculatist has presumed to push in his "force" between us and the good old Scripture doctrine that "there is a spirit in man," and especially as he carps at us as an "old-fashioned theologian," at our theology as being "traditional," and most contemptuously at our doctrine, as "the old theory," it may not be amiss to inquire into the origin of his "force." Where does he find it? How far has he comprehended its nature, measured its scope? Is his new philosophy "positive" or merely speculative? Rejecting the "traditional theology," does he confine himself to that which is real, or does he launch out upon a broad sea of endless speculation? Let us uncover his process. His first postulate is, that the ultimate atoms of matter are either absolutely, essentially, and necessarily inert, or they are absolutely, essentially, and necessarily active. Then he proceeds to discover that "a force of resistance," or, to use a familiar term, *impenetrability*, is one of the elementary attributes of matter. His next step is the discovery of "gravitating force," an attraction in matter. Expanding the former a little he draws from it a "repellant force." And hence he claims that all ultimate atoms of matter are endued with this triple force, and hence *with life!* With one gigantic bound he has distanced all the absurdities of the schoolmen and converted the globe itself into a mass of life, each atom of which possesses a distinct individuality! His postulate we might question, and demand from him how he knows that these ultimate atoms do not possess the essential properties of matter; how he knows that the Almighty Artificer has not endowed them with diverse nature and function. The diversity of manifestation in nature strongly intimates this, and no analysis thus far

* "Evidence as to Man's Place in Nature," p. 125.

has afforded even a presumption to the contrary. Indeed, these very speculatists differ among themselves, some claiming that the ponderables only are endowed with the "attractive force," while the imponderables possess the "repellant force;" others claim that all ultimate atoms are endowed with both forces.

If we question the postulate of this materialistic philosophy, as we do with good reason, still more do we question the legitimacy of the process by which its conclusion is reached. Admit a thing which nobody doubts, namely, that God has endowed matter with the attribute of impenetrability or "repellant force," and also with a "gravitative force"—might not the process of endowment be stopped at any stage of progress pleasing to the Divine Mind? It does not follow that, because matter is endowed with "attractive force," it must therefore kindle with the social affinities of life, nor yet because it is endowed with the "repellant force" that it must declare war and fight. It does not follow because God has created innumerable atoms of matter and endowed them with certain attributes, that he must have made each the abode of life. Nature is very prolific in the development of life; but this modern materialistic philosophy is perfectly prodigal, and as reckless as prodigal, for it converts "the whole material cosmos into a stupendous interacting organism." And then how it exults in rapture over its "homogeneous creation," which, rising from the lowest forms of matter, comprehends even "the highest development of mind itself," all looking back to one common origin; namely, "FORCE!"

But in the midst of this pæan of triumph over the demolished "dualism" of "the old theology," we are arrested by the fact that our materialistic philosopher instead of FORCE has got FORCES into his *unifying system*. One of these forces is attractive, the other resistive; therefore they are not only unlike, but antagonistic. Who yokes them together and makes them draw in harmony? Do these forces rest upon their arms, declare an armistice, agree upon terms of peace, and then peacefully work together, "rising in perfect gradation from the lowest forms of matter through all the regions of organic life to the highest development of mind itself?" We confess ourselves unable to see the universe "more simple," or "more harmonious," or "more beautiful," when seen through the optics of this new philosophy. Having tasted of this new wine, we cheerfully go back to the old and believe it better.

Morell seems to have drawn upon the old atomic theory of Democritus, as taught by Leibnitz, for his philosophy. According to this theory, as developed by Dr. Samuel Brown, the *substratum* of material phenomena, that is, the primary atoms are merely centers of force, "mathematical points encircled with powers of repulsion and attraction;" and that, from the endless variety of combinations of repulsive and attractive forces, the whole material universe is constructed. This theory resolves soul as well as body into mere phenomena—an aggregate of mathematical points encircled with powers of attraction and repulsion. The cancellation of these "forces" would *annihilate nature*. "Instantaneously," says Cronhelm, "without an audible crash, without a visible wreck, the glorious fabric of the earth and the heavens would disappear from existence."

VI. Enumeration of Points Established.

Thus far we have gained important points.

1. *We have been led to the true idea of organization.* Its mysterious element is LIFE. We may not comprehend life; its hidden nature may elude all our researches; but of its *being*, in the plant and in the animal, we have the fullest

demonstration. *How* it exists or *how* it coheres with the material body are unsolved problems. But this mystery unknown can not weigh against the facts known. Organization is the formation of a living body. Inorganic matter is the material out of which it is built up, and LIFE *is the artificer.*

2. *We have been led also to a just discrimination between animal and vegetable life.* We have found that the plant is not only destitute of the organs of sight, hearing, and the other senses; also that it is destitute of the nervous matter which constitutes the sensorial structure of animals, and, consequently, there can be no nervous sensibility in the plant. And then, still further, that there are, in other respects, positive dissimilarities and antagonisms that widely separate the vegetable from the animal creation. We have been thus led to conclude that there is a generic difference between *the life* of the plant and the life of the animal. Organism, we have seen, is the product, not of matter, but of life. The character of the organism, too, is determined, not by the character of the inorganic materials out of which it is constructed, but by the specific nature of *the life* which was the artificer. If, then, organisms, so widely different, are wrought out from the same elementary materials, the *life* effecting the organism must be substantially different. If we bring nitrogen into union with oxygen, the result is air, and if we bring hydrogen into union with it, the result is water.* The reaching of these different results from the same element shows that the agencies brought to bear upon it were themselves different. So when we see vegetable life on the vegetable germ, and the animal ovum working upon the same material, and yet invariably bringing forth results so widely different, the

*Air is composed of 22.2 parts oxygen and 77.7 nitrogen; water 88.9 parts oxygen and 11.1 nitrogen.

conclusion is inevitable that the *life* of the plant is widely different from that of the animal.

3. *The fact that animal and vegetable life are so dissimilar in their character affords a reasonable presumption that the "living soul" in man differs widely from either.* What animal or vegetable life may be, how closely it may be allied to material substance, or how far removed from it, it may not be necessary for us to inquire now. The point insisted upon is simply that God has created different kinds of *life.* The gradations, not of development or of organism, but of *life*, so created, rising from the vegetable to the animal, finally culminate in man, who has been endowed with a *living soul.*

4. *This suggests, finally, the possible relations man may sustain to the unknown and the infinite.* To the animal is awarded a higher life, a broader range, and more extended relations to the created universe than to the plant. But still higher in the scale is man. Through his material nature he is allied to all material existences, but through his spiritual he is allied to all spiritual intelligences in the universe of God. This spiritual life within us relates us to the infinite, and lifts us into communion with it. But for that we could no more apprehend spiritual existence or the Divine Being than the blind man can apprehend the beauties of color in nature. This spiritual nature, then, unfolds an infinitude of relations. Does it not, at the same time, give us intimations of a destiny whose breadth and duration surpass all the bounds of our present comprehension?

> "The chain of being is complete in me,
> In me is matter's last gradation lost,
> And the next step is spirit—Deity!
> I can command the lightning, and am dust!
> A monarch and a slave! a worm, a god!"

III.

THE HUMAN SOUL NOT A FUNCTION OF MATTER.

"There is a spirit in man." JOB xxxii, 8.
"And man became a living soul." GEN. ii, 7.
"Fear not them which kill the body, but are not able to kill the soul." MATT. x, 28.
"Then shall the dust return to the earth as it was; and the spirit shall return unto God who gave it." ECCL. xii, 17.

EVERY instinct of our nature, no less than the calm exercise of reason, coincides with the Scripture declaration that "there is a spirit in man." Yet men have not been wanting, who have sought to prove that themselves and all their race are only a higher order of brutes; that, in fact, man is simply *a developed ape.* They have used the spirit, the noble and godlike intellect bestowed upon them, in wicked effort to prove that no such thing as soul or spirit exists.

The doctrine of this class of philosophers is, that the human soul, instead of being a substance in itself, instead of possessing an existence distinct from that of the body, is a mere *result* of the peculiar bodily organization. In other words, that it is a *function of matter.* Their theory is, that "the bones, muscles, bloodvessels, blood, nerves, and brain, constitute a thinking and feeling machine, working on chemical and mechanical principles." Such a machine as here described, when four-footed, is a brute; when a biped, with wings and feathers, a fowl; and when a biped, without wings and feathers, a man! Marvelous discovery! If this is modern science, what is human folly?

It may be stated, as a general fact, that there are but two opinions in relation to the nature of the human soul. Between these two there are no grounds upon which to erect any other. And into one or the other of these opinions, all theories, in the last analysis, resolve themselves. The first—that which we have endeavored to establish—is that the soul is an independent spiritual existence; the other, that it is a function of matter. This latter is the essential doctrine of materialists, whatever may be the form in which they express it.

I. Materialists Assert that the Soul is a Function of Matter—Their Statements Quoted.

To set at rest the possible charge that we have misrepresented them, we propose to let these materialists speak for themselves: D'Holbach says, "If we are asked, what is man? we reply, that he is a material being, organized, or framed, so as to feel, to think, and to be affected in certain ways peculiar to himself, according to his organization."* M. Comte affirms, that "all natural phenomena are the necessary results either of the laws of extension or of the laws of motion."† M. Crouse is quite clear that "intelligence is a property or effect of matter," and ventures on the very singular declaration, that "body and spirit together constitute matter."‡ So, also, the English materialists affirm that "instinct, passion, thought, are effects of organized substances." Or, still more explicitly, "Mind is the consequence or *product of the material man;* it is not a thing having a seat or home in the brain, but it is *the manifestation or expression of the brain in action*, as heat and light are of fire, and fragrance of the flower."||

*System of Nature. † Course. ‡ Des Principles, pp. 84, 86.
|| "Letters on the Laws of Man's Nature and Development."

Even Dr. Priestley teaches that "man does not consist of two principles so essentially different from each other as *matter* and *spirit*, but the whole man is of *one uniform composition;* and that either the material or the immaterial part of the universal system is superfluous."* Having adopted the principle of *uni-substance* in the universe, he seems to have been, for a time, doubtful whether he should *spiritualize* matter, and declare the one substance of the universe to be *spirit;* or whether he should *materialize* mind, and declare the one substance to be *matter*. But in his course toward error, he had already passed the point where "gravitation turns the other way;" and he soon sunk down into materialism. Yet, strangely enough, he still professed to believe the doctrine of man's immortality, and also of retribution in another life. So in the so-called spiritualism of the present day; it is thoroughly materialistic, while, at the same time, it assumes the style and title of *spiritualism*. A. J. Davis says: "Nature proclaims one of her great working principles to be, that *spirit is evolved out of matter*." But this refined nonsense is illuminated by one ray of true light, when it is admitted that *this spirit* "*outlives the body in which it is educated*." †

Less known than those quoted before, yet not less clear in the statement of this form of materialism, was Mr. Thomas Read, of New York. He says that "the manifestations of the soul, of life, of mind, of sight, thought, feeling, love, and envy, and the effects of electricity, sound, heat, and so on, are all alike the effects of physical, or, if you please, of material causes." ‡ Nor does he shrink from the extremest consequences of this materialism: "The soul

* "Disquisitions Relating to Matter and Spirit."
† "The Principles of Nature and Her Divine Revelations."
‡ Immateriality of the Soul, p. 4.

or life has no independent conscious existence, apart from the organs that produce thought, feeling, and action; and, therefore, life, mind, memory, thought, reason, and consciousness are physical phenomena, and cease at death."* What balder or bolder infidelity than this was ever displayed? What of being can be left to man after the extinction of all these? And yet this man *professed* faith in revelation and in a future life!

There is a class of men who conceal their materialism in the mystical formulas of some development theory, which stealthily but studiously excludes a first cause in the creation of man, and also the higher elements of soul from his nature. Like infidels in all ages, they assume to be, *par excellence*, the men of science, of facts, of reason, and of intelligence. Of this class are Darwin, Morell, Huxley, and their minor followers. But we have already devoted sufficient space to the examination of their respective theories.

We repeat, then, that all the theories relating to the nature of mind or soul range themselves, in the final result, under two general heads. The first is that the soul is an independent spiritual existence, mysteriously connected with the human body. The other is that mind or soul is merely an organic state of matter, such as constitutes the human brain; or, in other words, that *the human soul is merely a function of matter*. Into one or the other of these two opinions all these various theories, in the final analysis, resolve themselves. Nor does the subject seem to furnish the least grounds upon which, outside of these two, any other opinions could be erected.

The first has the sanction of Divine Revelation; the purest and soundest philosophy of all ages has recognized it; and it has ever formed a distinct element in the Chris-

*Immateriality of the Soul.

tian creed. We have already presented, to some extent, the facts and arguments by which it is established. We come now to consider the objections to the opposite theory; that theory which regards the human soul as a mere result of physical organization, or, in other words, as a *function of matter*. This summary method of robbing a man of himself we shall subject to a somewhat rigid analysis; and the more so as it seems to be specially revived in the present day. Brought forth under the guise of a new nomenclature, sustained by the most subtile sophistries, and heralded with the most pompous pretension, it has already obtained a foothold among pretentious theologians, and it seems as though it would, were it possible, "deceive the very elect." To us this theory seems not only fraught with pernicious moral effects, tending to degrade the being, character, and destiny of man, but also, in a philosophical point of view, to be unwarranted by any sound induction of facts. We shall go further, and undertake to show that it is irreconcilable with the phenomena of mental action, and also with well-attested facts in the psychological history of man.

II. The Function-Theory Fails to Solve any Mystery in the Human Organization; nor does it Relieve any Philosophical Difficulty.

Our first objection to the theory that soul or spirit is merely a function of matter is, that it fails to accomplish the end proposed. It solves no mystery, and removes no difficulty. At most it only changes the ground of difficulty. The acknowledged fact for which we seek a solution—that is, the existing spiritual phenomena—is left as mysterious and inexplicable as ever.

If the declaration that "there is a spirit in man" is to

be rejected because it is mysterious and above our comprehension, the assumption that these phenomena originate in the physical condition of our bodies involves a mystery equally inexplicable, and on the same ground must also be rejected. If we can not, upon philosophical principles, explain the origin and nature of mind, still more difficult shall we find the task of explaining by what process matter may become endowed with such transcendent, such surprising power.

The opinion that even *organic matter* could, by any possibility, be made to exhibit such power, can not be received without the most clear and indubitable evidence. What is there to be found in the composition of the brain and nervous system, or in their organization, that would lead us to look for the development of thought, feeling, or conscience in them? The brain has been analyzed, and more than eight-tenths of its substance has been found to be water. Indeed this, mixed up with a little albumen, a still less quantity of fat, osmazome, phosphorus, acids, salts, and sulphur constitute its material elements.* In all cases water largely predominates. Take even the *pineal gland*—that interior and mysterious organ of the brain, supposed by Descartes, and by many philosophers after him, to be the peculiar seat of the soul—even this has been analyzed.

* One hundred parts of the brain, according to Vaugnelin, consist of water, 80; albumen, 7; acids, salts, and sulphur, 5.15; phosphorus, 1.5; osmazome, 1.12; white fatty matter, 4.53; and red fatty matter, 7. According to Gass and Pfaff, who separated the water into its elements: Carbon, 53.48; hydrogen, 16.89; nitrogen, 6.70; oxygen, 18.44; fixed salts, 3.36; and phosphorus, 1.08. Dr. Draper, in his Human Physiology, gives the following table:

	Infants.	Youths.	Adults.	Aged.
Water	827.90	742.60	725.00	738.50
Albumen	70.00	102.00	94.00	86.50
Fat	34.50	53.00	61.00	43.20
Osmazome and salts	59.60	85.90	101.90	121.80
Phosphorus	8.00	16.50	18.00	10.00
	1000.00	1000.00	1000.00	1000.00

Its principal elements are found to be phosphate of lime, together with a smaller proportion of carbonate of lime and phosphates of ammonia and magnesia.

If the brain at large constitutes the soul, then the soul is only a peculiar combination of oxygen and hydrogen with albumen, acids, salts, sulphur, etc. Or, if the pineal gland constitutes the soul, then the principal element of soul is phosphate of lime! If this wonderful theory is true, it may be safely conceded that we gain *something* by it. We have at last found out *what the soul is.* And when the wise man again inquires, "Who knoweth the spirit of man?" these sage philosophers may respond, "We! it is phosphate of lime!" But, what! has a peculiar combination of a few elemental substances; has *phosphate of lime* been the cause, the *fons et origo*, of all the glorious manifestations of intellect that have been made among men? Is it osmazome that has given origin to the creations of art? Is it oxygen that blazes out in the glowing fires of eloquence? Was it hydrogen that soared in the philosophy of Newton, and sought with all-comprehending grasp to encircle the universe of God? Was it phosphate of lime that wove the garlands of poesy, and thus touched the tender chords of human sympathy, taste, and sentiment?

"To rise in science, as in bliss,
Initiate in the mysteries of the skies;
To read creation, read its mighty plans—
The plan and execution to collate."

III. The Soul exerts a Controlling Influence over the Body, and therefore must be Something more than a mere Result of Bodily Organization.

We have seen that this function-theory assumes that the intellectual power of man results from physical organization, just as mechanical power is acquired by the skillful adaptation of machinery. It should be borne in mind that in mechanics it is the *machinery* which originates and modifies the force or power. The *force*, which is the mere result or effect produced by the machinery, can not exert the least influence over the machinery itself. There is a physical impossibility in the case. And so it must be with man, if this function-theory is true.

If the mental phenomena are the mere result, or force, produced by bodily organization, those phenomena must be entirely subject to the laws which govern the physical nature. Instead of acting upon or exerting any influence over our bodies, the mind, according to the established laws of mechanics, must be acted upon—that is, it is produced, modified, controlled, and in the end will be extinguished by the successive conditions of our physical being. But, we ask, is the mind the mere slave of our bodies? Rather, does it not often force those bodies to action, even against the physical inertia which inheres in matter? nay, often against the strong instincts of our nature? Does not the mind possess a strong and controlling influence over our bodies? How then can it be a mere *result or effect* of bodily organization, unless we are prepared to admit the absurdity that *the effect may control the cause?* He who should claim that the movement of the hands in a clock or watch occasioned the movement of the machinery within, would do no greater violence to philosophy, nor be guilty of a more palpable absurdity.

No fact is more certain or more generally acknowledged than that the soul can and does exert a controlling influence over the bodily functions. "A letter or newspaper is brought by a postman to the individual, he reads it, and the result of reading it has been that the man has dropped down dead. Why this? No physical weapon touched him.

It was purely *a mental cause* that acted upon his brain, and the brain acted upon the nervous system, and the man died because the letter contained some fearful or disastrous tidings." Or, again, the sudden knowledge of some great calamity, or even of some great good fortune, has often affected all the senses, and even palsied the whole system. Now, here was a moral fact, addressed, first, to the intelligence, and resulting in physical effects; a thing clearly impossible on the supposition that mind is the mere result or force produced by the organization of matter. Nay, how often has the soul absolutely triumphed over all that was terrible to nerve and sense!

The history of Christian martyrdom presents us instances almost innumerable, any one of which convincingly demon strates the dominion of the soul over the body. Thus we hear Lambert, while consuming by a slow fire, exclaiming, "None but Christ! none but Christ!" Thus also does Cranmer—the soul triumphing over all that was terrible in bodily suffering—steadily hold his hand in the flame, and exclaim, while it is being consumed, "This hand! this wicked hand!" So also Mrs. Cecily Ormes, who was added to the noble host of martyrs at the early age of twenty-two. Approaching the stake, already charred by the fires that had consumed two martyrs before her, she clasped it with her hands, exclaiming, "Welcome! welcome, Cross of Christ!" But a still more striking instance of the triumph of soul over the body is the case of James Bainham. When his legs and his arms were half-consumed, and his body scorched and seething in the flame, he cried out to the bystanders, "Ye look for miracles! Here, now, ye may see one. *This fire is to me a bed of roses.*" Before being led to the stake, Mr. Hawkes agreed with his friends upon a signal by which to express his feelings when he should be no longer capable of speech. When he was so near consumed that all thought him dead, and when his whole body was crisped with the fire, the skin of his arms drawn up, and his fingers literally consumed, suddenly seeming to recollect the appointed signal, he raised his fingerless hands above his head and clapped them three times in token of triumph.

We have quoted these instances, not with reference to their religious significance, but to show the mysterious energy of the soul which makes its abode in these earthly bodies; and especially to show that its life is distinct from, and its power superior to, the material tabernacle it inhabits.

IV. The Power of the Soul is often Disproportioned to that of the Body, and therefore can not be the Result of Bodily Organization.

The theory we are combating represents the soul of man as the "final result and efflorescence of a continually-refined life of the nerves, so that reason and will are nothing but the organic life of matter, which by a refined process attains the power of thinking and willing." In what this "refined process" consists these sage philosophers have failed to tell us.

But if the soul is thus dependent upon the bodily organization, it must follow that, as the body becomes enfeebled by disease, or age, the mind will suffer a corresponding debility. But this is so far from being the case, that a large number of those distinguished for intellectual power have possessed but feeble and emaciated frames. The history of all men and of all ages confirms the general statement, that the vigor and force of intellect depend in but a slight degree upon the corresponding qualities of body. The deep mysteries of science have been penetrated with long-continued and devoted toil, even while the body was bowed beneath the pressure of infirmity and disease. The Genius of Poetry, even when consumption's pallid hues overspread the dying frame, has tuned those celestial notes and strung those heavenly lays that will never cease to touch for high and holy purpose the chords of human sympathy.

Read the works of Richard Watson; trace the footsteps of his giant intellect on every page. Then tell me, would you have expected to find such a radiant, godlike intellect incased in so sickly and feeble a house of clay! Instances have occurred in which paralysis has unnerved the whole system, and yet the *mind* has remained unscathed. We will quote a single case; that of the celebrated, the witty, and the clever diplomatist, Talleyrand. His body was in the most wretched, diseased, and distressed condition one can conceive, and yet the subtilty, and the wisdom, and the skill, and the talent, and the pen etration of that diplomatist are allowed to have remained to his last moments unequaled. Notice, also, the case of the celebrated Dean Swift. It is said that before he died his body was a moving tomb, and yet his mind was as vigorous as in his earlier years.* How often when the body is prostrated by disease and enfeebled in all its energies has the mind—instead of partaking of the body's weakness—retained all its energy and power! The function of memory has been unaffected; the perceptions have been clear and distinct; and reason has retained undoubted supremacy upon its throne. How often while the body was in the last stages of dissolution—when it possessed not a single capability entire—has the mind blazed up with unwonted luster, and put forth unaccustomed energy! The pious and eloquent Dr. Fisk, while in a dying state, exclaimed, "I now feel a strength of soul and an energy of mind which this

*Bible Evidence, Dr. Cumming.

body, though afflicted and pained, can not impair. *The soul has an energy of its own.* And so far from my body pressing my soul down to the dust, I feel as if my soul had almost power to raise the body upward and bear it away."*

It was by examples such as this that Bishop Butler was led to notice that a mortal disease, which, by degrees, consumes and prostrates the body, and finally destroys it, does not necessarily affect our powers of thought and reflection. While the body is being wasted and consumed, and up to the very instant of death, we can exert those powers as fully as ever. From this the Bishop reaches the just conclusion that the soul, which was unaffected through all the process of dying, could not be supposed at the last moment and suddenly to be destroyed. The same fact must lead us, with still stronger force of conviction, to the conclusion that *soul* has an independent and superior existence.

V. The Human Brain may be Diseased and the Mind Remain Unaffected; therefore, the Latter is not a Function of the Former.

At the very outset, in this line of thought, we are met with well-attested facts, showing that the brain has actually been extensively diseased, while the intellectual capability remained unaffected. The annals of medical experience furnish such cases almost without number. Dr. Moore says of the experiments of M. Flouren, that "they prove that the brain may be destroyed, to a large extent, in any direction, without destroying any of the functions of mind." Morgagni and Haller, distinguished anatomists, claim to have ascertained, by a wide induction of facts, that every part of the brain has been found to be destroyed or disorganized, in one instance or another, while yet the indi-

*Life, by Dr. Holdich.

viduals have not been deprived of mind, or even affected in their intellectual powers.

We do not mean that the whole brain has been destroyed in any one individual, intellectual life still remaining, but that a portion of the brain in one instance, and another portion of it in another instance, and so on till the aggre gate would comprehend every organic portion. As an illustration, Dr. Abercrombie mentions the case of a lady, *one entire half of whose brain* was reduced to a mass of sup puration by disease; and yet she retained her faculties to the last, and had been enjoying herself at a convivial party only a few hours before her sudden death. A man is also mentioned by Dr. Fezrier, who died suddenly, retaining all his faculties till the very moment of dissolution; but, upon examining his head, the whole right hemisphere of the brain was found destroyed by suppuration.

Numerous examples might be brought forward from the mournful catalogue of human accidents and infirmities, but these are sufficient to show us, in the clear light of demonstration, that, though the brain and nervous system generally are the appointed organs through which the mind communicates with the material world, yet that mind possesses an existence and a power of action independent of, and superior to, its earthly habitation.

There is still another absurdity in which this physical theory of mind would involve us. If the brain constitutes the mind, then when a man has lost half of his brain he has lost half of his mind. Is it objected to this that "the brain is a double organ," and that each part is possessed of full and separate power of action? If the objector admits that the brain is an *organ* or instrument, then he must also concede that it is an organ or instrument made for *something else*—that is, for the soul—to use, or he must fall back upon the position that *the organ uses itself.* But does the objector assert that brain and intellect are identical, and yet that the brain is made up of two distinct parts, each fully capable of performing all the functions usually attributed to mind? then must he admit that the person who has both these parts—that is, has a whole brain—possesses two minds! Such are some of the absurdities into which men fall when, refusing the revelation from God, which only can solve the problem and the mystery of human life, they attempt to carve out for themselves something more congenial to their own pride and self-complacency than the simple yet sublime philosophy of the Bible.

VI. The Conscious Individuality of Spirit Demonstrates that it is not a Function of Matter.

No department of our knowledge is more positive than that which is founded in individual consciousness. Indeed, take away or even invalidate the authority of consciousness, and you undermine the foundations of all knowledge.

Nothing that is certain will remain. But the very idea of consciousness is that it is not a function of matter. "I appeal to the consciousness of every individual that he feels a power within him totally distinct from any function of the body. What other conception than this can he form of that power by which he recalls the past and provides for the future; by which he ranges, uncontrolled, from world to world, and from system to system; surveys the works of all-creating power, and rises to the contemplation of the eternal Cause?

"To what function of matter shall he liken that principle by which he loves and fears, joys and sorrows; by which he is elated by hope, excited by enthusiasm, or sunk into the horrors of despair? These changes, also, he feels, in many instances, to be equally independent of impressions from without, and of the condition of his bodily frame. In the most peaceful state of every corporeal function, passion, remorse, or anguish may rage within! And, on the other hand, while the body is racked with the most frightful diseases, the mind may repose in all the tranquillity of hope."* We pause here to inquire, What do all these things teach? Evidently that "there is a spirit in man."

VII. The Failure of any Material and Chemical Combination to Produce Life is Further Evidence that Mind is not a Function of Matter.

It might be reasonably expected that if *life* was a mere function of matter, somewhere in the history of human observation instances of its spontaneous and original production would have occurred. Science records no such instance, and, indeed, is compelled to acknowledge its failure to produce life by any combination of merely material elements. Nay, it is compelled to go further, and, from its best lights, confess that it has found life no where without evidence of its antecedent germ. This is predicated of life even in its lowest forms. How much more certain, then, the failure of every such experiment to produce the higher manifestations of soul or spirit!

The science of chemistry has succeeded in analyzing man's physical nature and ascertaining its composition. It has discovered the elements and the proportions in which each is mixed to form the various parts of the body. It can compound these elements again, but man it has not formed and can not form; nor can it, by even the most refined and delicate process, create the smallest organic existence and impart to it animal life.

*Abercrombie's Intellectual Powers.

In this direction the experiments of philosophy and all its research have been utterly fruitless. Who can snatch from the altar of the living God the Promethean fire that breathes life and animation into the inanimate clod of clay? Let foolhardy infidelity blush at its empty boasting, and cease its clamorous self-applause, till it has solved the mysterious, awful problem—"What is life?"

VIII. The State of the Mind in Dying also affords Proof of the Soul's Superior and Independent Being.

We have already noticed that, often when the body is in the last stages of weakness and decay, the mind is left in full possession of its intellectual and spiritual force. This of itself is a proof of man's spiritual and immortal nature. But our attention here is directed to another point. We have carefully studied the state of the mind in dying by actual observation and intercourse with persons up almost to the last moment of earthly being, and we have uniformly found that instead of any consciousness or expectation of the soul's being actually extinguished, the expectation of its living on was as strong and as invincible as in the morning flush of life and health. The dying and decay of the body are expected events; the premonitions of physical death are calmly observed and conversed upon freely. Yet the idea that the soul is going out of existence never once seems to be entertained. Thus, in the very act of dying, the soul asserts its claim to an independent spiritual being, and snatches from the jaws of death the proofs of its immortality.

Let us notice a few cases in point. The Rev. Alanson Reed, who had been wasting away with consumption several years, said to me, only a half-hour before his last breath,

"I know full well that I am at the point of death, but the idea of the spirit being extinguished in death is utterly inconceivable. The soul is going forth, but it has no consciousness of dying; rather the consciousness of living on rises above every other feeling, and it is impossible for me to doubt." The soul seems to possess a sensation of vitality—correspondent to its nature. Thus Mr. Pope, when in a dying state, said, "I am so certain of the soul's being immortal, that I seem to feel it within me, as it were, by intuition." The celebrated Boerhaave contemplated the perceptible difference between his mind and his body, in his last illness, as being like a philosophical experiment to him, that his intellectual self would not perish with his bodily dissolution. The celebrated Haller, as death advanced to the mastery over his bodily system, could only measure its progress by keeping his fingers upon his own pulse. "The artery, my friend," said he at length, "ceases to beat," and almost instantly expired. The Rev. Mr. Halyburton, when dying, said to a brother minister, "I think my case is a pretty fair demonstration of the immortality of the soul. My bones are rising through my skin. This body is going away to corruption, and yet my intellectuals are so lively, that I can not perceive the least alteration or decay in them."

These and kindred facts are in harmony with the sublime idea that man possesses a "living soul." But they are utterly irreconcilable with the idea that the soul is a function of the material nature. An element that can thus remain unaffected by physical decay, that can triumph amid the very ruins of the material man, gives mysterious and wonderful demonstration that the roots of its being are not planted in material soil, but that it possesses a higher life

IX. Concluding Suggestions.

Germain to the points we have made and the principles we have sought to establish, are suggestions of deep, practical import. But our discussion has already been protracted so far, that we barely glance at a few of them.

1. *The soul and the body are mutually adapted to each other.* They are mutually adapted just as the telegraphic wire and the magnetic fluid. This does not imply sameness, or even similarity in nature, but simply that they are adapted to co-work for the accomplishment of specific ends. The telegraphic wire and the magnetic fluid co-work for the transmission of knowledge to points far remote. The soul and the body are united for the production of humanity, with all its inconceivable relations to the universe and all the varied purposes of its being. For aught we know, the Creator might have invested any other kind of being with a soul as well as man. But had the soul been connected with the material mechanism of a beast or a bird, how limited in number, and how restricted in use, would have been the organs it could have controlled! But, in the human organism, what multitudes of parts, and what diversity of limbs and organs wait to do the bidding of the soul! We can scarcely doubt that the human body was formed with special reference to the soul by which it was to be inhabited and controlled.

2. *It is obvious, also, that man was a special device of the Creator.* He is unlike any other being upon the globe. The worlds that people the amplitude of space are no doubt the abodes of life. But their analogies are so remote to ours; their differences in structure, motions, temperature, and surrounding fluid are so great that their peopling must be by something very different from human

life. Some of the ends to be accomplished by this "special device"—the creation of man—are obvious even here, but more of those purposes shall be unfolded hereafter.

3. *Man is not a dualism.* Two elements—the spiritual and the material—enter into his nature, but man is *one.* We never think of reckoning the air or the water as dualistic, and yet two distinct and widely-different elements enter into the composition of each.

4. *The subject also suggests the dignity of the spirit and the culture demanded for it.* The development of the ingenuity and the uses of domestic animals has been one of the grandest achievements of man in the progress of his civilization and the subjugation of the earth. If the culture of the animal is so connected with the earth's advancement, how much more the cultivation of man, and especially of the spirit that is in man! The cultivation and improvement of the animal is every-where beset with difficulties and hedged around with limitations! Mind presents for culture a boundless field, and one fruitful as it is boundless.

"The mind
Forges from knowledge an archangel's spear,
And with the spirits that compel the world,
Conflicts for empire."

IV.

THE HUMAN SOUL AND THE ANIMAL SENSES.

"Why is light given to a man?" JOB iii, 23.
"Who by reason of use have their senses exercised." HEB. v, 14.
"Now hath God set the members every one of them in the body." 1 COR. xii, 18.
"Is not the life more than meat?" MATT. vi, 25.

1. How beings purely spiritual correspond with each other, or with the material world, we know not. Indeed, it is hardly a subject of rational inquiry. Revelation gives us little light upon it beyond the bare fact that such correspondence is not only possible but actual. As a subject of philosophical inquiry, the elements of its determination seem too recondite and inaccessible to the human mind to give any ground of hope for its immediate solution. It is, probably, one of those mysteries the solution of which will be reached only in our future state.

2. But in animal life, and also in an "embodied spirit," such as we have seen man to be, there are organs of sensation through which the living being holds connection with the outside material world. These organs are fitted to receive impressions from without, as when the image of an external object is painted upon the retina of the eye, affecting the sensorial nerve. The nature of that object is thus perceived by the soul, which, by a mysterious intuition, goes forth, as it were, to grasp it in its intelligence. It is by this process that "we are put in relation to material things, as to their color, sound, odor, weight, resistance,

and all that we learn of time and space by contact with matter."

3. Some transcendental philosophers would, indeed, have us believe that the only real substances are *ideas*, and that the imagined existing material things, and their qualities, have no reality in nature. Against this refined transcendentalism we shall not undertake to reason, but leave it to the common-sense and practical judgment of mankind.

4. We usually enumerate five senses—sight, hearing, taste, smell, and touch—but Dr. Moore intimates that a little reflection will convince us that there are other modes of experiencing sensation, and adds: "There would, indeed, be no impropriety in regarding every part of our bodies as an organ of sense, since every part is endowed with a kind of feeling peculiar to itself and exactly suited to its office. Probably all sensations are but modifications of the same nervous action, and they may all be regarded as the contact of an active agent with the organ, or of something moving, or tending to move, operating on nerve."

Thus light strikes upon the retina, the vibrations of air strike upon the tympanum, the odor-laden air comes in contact with the olfactory nerves, the juices spread over the palate, and thus an effect is produced upon the nerves just as much as when a solid comes in contact with the sense of touch.

Between the sensuous system and the soul there is so intimate a connection; our thoughts, and feelings, and stimulus to action seem so dependent upon it, that many have been led to question whether there is or can be any existence of the human spirit independent of it. We have already seen that soul is not a function of matter. This might cover the present question, as the whole sensuous system, which has its center in the brain, is only a part of the bodily organism, and is, therefore, nothing more than a material structure. But our survey of the ground will be incomplete till we have made a more direct examination of the relations of the soul to the senses, in order to demonstrate its existence independent of them.

The position we propose to maintain in this discussion is that

THE BODILY SENSES, WHETHER IN MAN OR IN THE ANIMAL, ARE MERELY ORGANIC INSTRUMENTS, AND, THEREFORE, ARE NOT TO BE CONFOUNDED WITH EITHER ANIMAL LIFE OR THE INTELLIGENT SOUL.

Among the reasons which go to establish this position may be named the following:

I. *It is evident that the organs of sense are mere instruments of the soul, because the soul has power over them to direct them, and also has power to make a choice among them.*

The living organism, as we have already seen, is a sort of *vehiculum* of the soul—the bond of connection and the medium of communication between the soul and the material world. This organ, therefore, has a twofold function—one relating to the material world, and developing itself in *action;* the other relating to the soul, and developing itself in *sensation.* In both these respects it acts in obedience to the impulse given by the mind. The connection is intimate; the velocity of spiritual action inconceivable. "We will to move a foot," says the author of Man and His Motives, "and it obeys us in the 1-200,000,000th of a second." This may as well be expressed by the algebraic formula $x=o$. It may be safely inferred that impressions upon the senses are received and noted by the mind with equal rapidity.

The power of the mind over the action of the limbs is

illustrated in every voluntary movement of the body. I will to raise the left foot instead of the right, or the arm instead of the foot, and instant action of the member takes place in obedience to the mandate. An obstruction is to be cleared from my path. I elect which shall do it, the hand or the foot, and the member receiving the command executes the commission. Some functions, it is true, can be executed only by the hand; others only by the foot; still others only by the teeth, and so on; but above we have reference to cases where the instruments are interchangeable.

Something akin to this is observed in sensation. In many cases the mind may select from among the organs of sense which it will employ to test the external objects. Some things, like the colors, can be tested only by sight; others, like sound, only by the ear, and so on. But there are objects, like a piece of butcher's meat, or a fish, or a quantity of sugar, or a hogshead of tobacco, in the testing of which more than one of the senses may be employed. In such a case the mind elects which sense, whether the sight, the taste, the touch, or the smell; and, indeed, it may employ the whole of them. Here is a distinct election, made by the soul, among the senses, showing them to be merely the instruments used by the mind for the accomplishment of its purposes. In all this the mind handles the organ of sense just as the optician handles his optical instrument, or as the experimenter in acoustics handles his acoustic tubes.

II. *That the organs of sense are mere instruments is further proved from the fact that attention to the impression made upon the organ is necessary to sensation.*

Sensation is something more than an impression made upon the bodily organ; it implies also a change in the state of that which is conscious in the body—*the soul.* Without this there is really no sensation. "We are accustomed to say the eye sees, the ear hears, the finger feels, and so forth; but such language is used only in accommodation to our ignorance, or from the force of habit. It is incorrect. The eye itself no more sees than the telescope which we hold before it to assist our vision; the ear hears not any more than the trumpet of tin which the deaf man directs toward the speaker to convey the sound of his voice; and so with regard to all the organs of sense. They are but instruments which become the media of intelligence to the absolute mind, which uses them whenever it is inclined or obliged to do so."*

The eye is a most perfect optical instrument, combining, by a most exquisite apparatus, those distinct qualities of the camera-obscura and the telescope. The ear is a most perfect acoustic instrument. Human skill has never been able to equal the divine model. So each organ of sense is an instrument, special in its structure and in its purpose—the whole together bearing glorious attestation to the wonderful skill and wisdom of the Creator.

The working of this machinery is so complete, noiseless, and yet with such inconceivable velocity, that we can hardly wonder it seems self-moved. The organs of sense and of action are so instantaneously respondent to the slightest intimation of the will that the very consciousness of willing is almost lost sight of.

And yet the simple fact is apparent that the soul may become so profoundly absorbed in some mighty thought, or in the solution of some intellectual problem, that, though the chords of every sense should be swept by the corresponding elements in nature from without, no sensation would occur within. The mind is dead to any impression upon the organ. What higher demonstration can be

*Soul and Body, by Dr. Moore, p. 25.

demanded, that the bodily senses are mere organic instruments of the soul?

III. *The mind not only interprets the impression made upon the organs of sense, but has the power of comparing sensations and thus perfecting its knowledge of external things.*

The nerves are the media of communication between the organs of sense and the brain. The impressions made upon the former by an external object, they take up and convey to the latter. Here, so far as science has explored, the physical process ends. The instrument has performed its appointed function. How the mind takes up the process so as to carry the impression forward into the intelligence, is an unsolved mystery. Human reason may never, in this state, be able to solve it. But this fact we do know, that where the physical process ceases, the intellectual begins. The connection is complete. Though the links that bind it are unseen, the physical and the intellectual stand before us in manifest union.

Now, it is evident that these four things are necessary in order to sensation, namely—the presence of an external object having a position and nature adapted to affect the sense, an impression upon the organ, the conveyance of that impression to the brain by the nerves, and the apprehension of that impression by the soul.

This process may be interrupted in any of its successive stages, and thus fail to produce the sensation. First, through some obstruction or defect, the sensorial organ may fail to receive its appropriate impression. If the retina of the eye, for instance, is inflamed, the picture, as in a poor looking-glass, will be defective. This defective impression will be conveyed to the brain, and the corresponding sensation will also partake of the defect. Again, if the optic nerve is diseased, it will, like a defective telegraph wire, fail to transmit its message. In the electrical telegraph, the battery may be good, the appropriate shock may be made, and the careful observer at the other end may watch and wait; but all in vain. The message is lost on the way. It is diverted because the wire is not properly insulated; or it is obstructed in consequence of the wire being broken or an imperfect conductor. In like manner in the use of the senses. Unless the nerve is in a healthy condition it fails to transmit the impression to the brain. Though the impression, clear and distinct, is made upon the receiving organ of sense, and though the soul watches and waits at the other end of this wonderful magnetic line, yet no message comes to it.

Then, finally, the organ of sense may receive its appropriate impression, the connecting nerve may take it up and carry it to the brain. But unless the mind gives attention to it there, no sensation results. This is evident from the instances every day occurring, in which, though the senses are known to be unimpaired, the nervous system sound—all its functions complete—and also all the external causes of sensation existing; and yet no sensation occurs, for the reason that the mind is abstracted in some deep and absorbing reverie, or by some difficult and perplexing question.

As a familiar example, an individual absorbed in some difficult mathematical problem or in an interesting book, may be spoken to two or three times before his attention is arrested. The vibrations of air struck upon the tympanum as usual, and the acoustic nerve bore the impression to the brain; but the operator there was inattentive, and the message was lost.

The relation of the senses to the mind as instruments for the conveyance of impressions, and the relation of the mind to the senses as the interpreter of those impressions, becomes still further apparent when we observe the mind comparing the impressions received from the different senses, in order to the perfecting of the knowledge acquired through those sensations.

A vase stands upon the mantle, containing what appears to be an exquisite bouquet of flowers. That is the intimation of the sense of sight. But I approach, subject them to the test of the sense of smell, and find they have no flavor. I try the sense of touch upon them, and find they are stiff and the surface hard and cold. The mind sits in judgment upon these three classes of sensation, and thus ascertains that this is not a bouquet of real flowers, but a delicate representation of them. Along side of this is what appears to the eye a basket of fruit. Such is the sensation produced by sight. But when I subject it to the touch, it is cold and hard; when I take it into the mouth, it is without taste. Then I discover it is not fruit, but a wax representation, yet so delicate as to deceive the eye.

It will be perceived that, in both these cases, the mind made a comparison between the sensations produced by the different senses, and that its knowledge of the external object was the result of that comparison. Without this internal interpreter of our sensations—this arbiter among them—the senses would be constantly leading us astray. We should be their perpetual dupes. But wisely has the Creator of all ordained the function of this central life of our being. "Try the spirits," is an aphorism of Revelation; "try the sensations," is a correspondent aphorism of science.

This idea of the mind's arbitration among the sensations produced within is more difficult of comprehension, from a common error in regard to the process of perception. Perception constantly carries us without ourselves, and we constantly recognize the objects as being without. And thus we form an idea of the mind—not as inclosed within its small and dark chamber, the *vehiculum* of its present being—and there observing the impressions made by a purely-physical process upon the organs of sense—just as the artist examines the image made in the camera-obscura; but as going forth to the object itself. We are thus, by a very common and almost universal misapprehension, led to mistake the point at which the physical terminates and the spiritual begins, in the process of conception. When this point is clearly apprehended, we are able to grasp more fully the function of mind in its relation to sense, and the wisdom, fitness, and beauty of our wonderful organization dawns upon us in a light never seen before.

IV. *That the senses are mere instruments of the soul is further proved from the fact that the loss of one of the organs of sense—though it may embarrass the operations of the intellect, does not impair either its vitality or power.*

The idea we wish to elaborate here may be, perhaps, more forcibly presented by an illustration. A carpenter plying his trade, finds one of the tools—his plane or his saw—missing from his chest; he may devise various substitutes, but fails in the perfection of his work and also in the facility of its execution. The failure is not owing to any lack of strength or skill on the part of the mechanic, but to the lack of the right tools with which to work.

If a single string in a violin is broken, or can not be keyed up into harmony with the others, the most skillful player will fail to produce the varied harmonies of which the instrument is capable. The general skill of the violinist is not diminished. The defect is in the violin. In like manner, in the loss of one or more of the senses, the action of the soul in its relation to the external world is disturbed, but its native powers remain unimpaired.

The loss of the sense of hearing is a serious embarrassment. It interrupts the intercourse of life; shuts out the glorious harmonies of nature. The soul fails of many ideas and of many enjoyments it would otherwise have possessed. But its general powers are not impaired. The tools it might otherwise have worked with, are lessened in number; but the power of memory, of thought, of reason, and even the ability to interpret such impressions as continue to be made upon the senses, are unimpaired. Nay, they are often quickened; without hearing a syllable, the keen eye of the deaf person will often interpret what is said by closely observing the movement of the lips of the speaker.

There is another fact bearing upon this point that must not escape our observation. It is universally noticed that where one or more of the senses fails, the others become more acute, and thus in a measure make up for the loss The sight is destroyed, and as an effect, or rather by an effort of nature to repair the damage, the sense of touch becomes exceedingly acute. In some blind persons this sense has become so acute that they could determine the denomination of a silver coin by slipping it through their fingers, even when it was so worn that the keenest eye could not determine the characters upon it. So, also, blind persons often determine their approach to any solid body by the pressure of the atmosphere—a pressure so slight as to be inappreciable to one having full possession of all his senses. Of the former case we may cite, as an example, the celebrated blind mathematical professor, Dr. Saunderson, of Cambridge University, in England, and also the pupils in our blind asylums generally. In the books printed for their use, the letters are slightly raised, and so delicate becomes the sense of touch, that the letters and words are ascertained by passing the fingers over them. Of the latter, John Metcalf, the celebrated blind road-surveyor over the Derbyshire peaks, may be cited. Some philosophers have even gone so far as to predict, that by new methods of culture yet to be devised, persons deprived of both sight and hearing, "would so increase the sensibility of touch as to locate the seat of the soul in the tips of the fingers."

Now we come to the point of inquiry, By what process is this increased acuteness of the sense obtained? and where shall the improvement be located? Evidently not in the finger-tips. They are no more delicate than before; perhaps not as delicate. The very excessive use of them tends to render them callous. Nor will any one contend that it is in any increased facility in the nerve for the transmission of the impression to the brain, nor yet in the brain for receiving. It is all resolved, then, into *increased attention to, and closer scrutiny of, the impressions made upon the organs of sense.* This is the work of the intelligent principle within. So far, then, from being impaired by the loss of one of the organs of sense, it seems to have nerved itself to repair the damage, so far as it could lie within the function of the intellect to do so. Here we find illustration of not only the great principle of nature's compensation, but of the wonderful harmony of that divine structure, designed to mirror forth God in the created universe.

V. *Concluding remarks.*

The line of discussion we have employed, and the conclusions we have reached, are fruitful in suggestions, having an important bearing upon the nature and destination of man.

1. *This foregoing argument applies to animal life and sensation as well as to human.* The animal is something more than a mere physical organism. If it does not embody "a living soul," yet it does embody *animal life.* What the interior nature of that animal life may be is as little known to us as the interior nature of the living soul. But it is something that is so near akin to intelligence that

it can observe and interpret the impressions made upon the organs of sense. The hound that scents the game is not doubtful as to the import of the impressions made upon his organ of smell; the eagle that, from his aerial hight, sights his prey in the deep below, darts down upon it with lightning velocity, just as the hunter levels his gun at the game seen in the distance. Is there not a similitude between them in the manner in which they interpret the impression made by the object upon the organ of sight?

This is a highly-suggestive fact. We have already seen that there are radical differences which separate the animal mind from the living soul; that these differences are radical, precluding utterly the confounding of the one with the other. The facts just noticed, however, suggest similitudes as well as differences. They suggest, also—as Mr. Wesley and others have believed—the possibility of a future life for the animal; so that the expectation of the poor Indian—

> "Who thinks, admitted to yon equal sky,
> His faithful dog shall bear him company"—

may possibly be within the scope of creation's grand design. Such a purpose, if it exists, does not disturb the spiritual realm of man's empire; does not lessen the dignity of his character nor the grandeur of his destiny; but it does give us broader views of the plans and purposes of the great Creator.

2. *The views here developed suggest an explanation of the phenomena of disordered sensations.* We have already seen that our perceptions comprise two distinct elements—the sensible sign, and the observing of that sign by the mind. The mind has no higher function in the process than that of observing, or, perhaps, we might say, receiving, the impressions made upon the senses, and interpreting them. In order that this may be done correctly, there must be not

only a perfect correspondence between the soul and the body, but also a sound state of the nervous system. "The nerves being disordered, false impressions are received. Experience may correct them, but it often happens that she is incompetent, or that the defect is congenital. Then the mind manifests itself in a defective manner. The relation between the senses and the soul, the link that connects them, is broken, and the thinking principle continues to act according to the power of the machinery with which it is associated, and according to its innate energy of consciousness." But its action is distorted by the erroneous conveyances of the organs of sense. To those of sound nerves, looking on, the man appears insane. His mind grasps the most incongruous assemblage of old sensations revived, and of new ones distorted by the disordered state of the nerves: hence his wild imaginings, his incoherent expressions, his absurd actions, and even his maniac ravings.

All this may occur from diseases purely nervous and physical. Let the most skillful pianist that ever touched an instrument run his fingers over the keys. No music is produced, but strange, discordant notes break upon the air, splitting the ear and torturing the soul! Why these discordant, unmeaning, and grating, if not ludicrous sounds? The mind of the musician has not lost its knowledge, nor his fingers their skill; but the instrument is out of tune, and all the musicians in the world could not extort music from the crazy, rattling machinery. So, often, the wildest madness results from some derangement of the bodily system—a nervous disease, a fracture of the skull, or a derangement of the fluids in the system. Cure the physical disease, restore the fractured skull to its position, and thus put the instrument in order again, and the apparent mental disorder at once ceases. Even in those cases where the insanity has been induced by moral or mental causes, insanity has never ensued till the mental or moral excitement has deranged the nervous system, from overpressure or too constant exercise of it.

There is evidence, also, that the severest cases of idiocy result from disease in the nervous system, and not in the mind. The organs of sense have lost their sensitiveness, the telegraphic wires their conducting power. Hence, as Dr. Moore says, the soulless countenance, the rude mixture of instinct and passions, the unmeaning mirth, the transient fear, the gusty violence, and, he might have added, the stolid inertness of action. "This confusion of faculties and feelings has sometimes been reduced to order even in hereditary idiotism. Light has touched the chaos into beauty; a slight interference has awakened the apparently-torpid soul; an accident has removed the obstruction between the intellect and the world; a fracture of the skull, a fit of frenzy, a fever has cured the disease, and the idiot has suddenly become an observant and reasoning man."* From all these facts it becomes evident that the indwelling soul is ever ready to act when brought into connection with a properly-organized and healthy nervous system, and the presumption follows that the soul is never insane or idiotic.

The physical causes affecting our mental action are numerous. The luxurious thoughts and feelings of the opium-eater when under the influence of his drug, the uncomfortable feeling and feverish disposition of one whose luxurious living has mingled in his blood a superabundance of lithic acid, the phantasms of delirium occasioned by the ferment of the virus of small-pox in the blood of the system, the frightful dreams begotten by local disease or pain, the muddled intellect produced by too great indulgence of the appetite, and that terrible poison developing itself in

*Soul and Body.

hydrophobia, are so many instances in which the action of mind is reached and disturbed by the derangement of our nervous system from physical causes.

3. *The influence of mind upon the body must be noted in this connection.* Ours is evidently a reactive system. The soul has a power over the body and all its organs, as well as the body over the soul. "It is," says M'Cormac, "a matter of common observation, that excitement will cause the heart to throb and the blood to rush to the face. Many sensations are awakened or rendered intense by directing the attention to them; thus, painful or pleasing emotions, and thrills of horror or delight, dart over the frame, and shocks arise, which occasion instant death. Paralysis, and gray hair, and temporary suspension of the faculties, have been similarly produced; the terms, 'transfixed with terror,' 'rooted to the spot with surprise,' are expressive of such occurrences. Individuals, actuated by strong motives and fixity of purpose, go through exertions to which, under other circumstances, they would be wholly unequal. The soldier will make efforts in the hour of victory of which he would be incapable in the languor of defeat. Maniacs, and those in the delirium of disease, often overpower the most robust, and persons whose strength is apparently exhausted become comparatively vigorous after the receipt of pleasant intelligence. Sportsmen and men of science afford instances of people so pre occupied as to be almost insensible to fatigue. The watching and the toil of which a devoted woman is capable, by the couch of sickness, have been the theme of eulogy in every age. Depression renders disease fatal that might have been otherwise, while recoveries ensue in desperate cases in which the patient has displayed unshaken fortitude."* Each of these points might be illustrated by the

*Philosophy of Human Nature, p. 97.

citation of examples, but to most of our readers such examples will recur without citation.

4. *This subject also suggests that, as the bodily senses are mere instruments to be used by the mind for the time being, death may work but little change in the soul itself.* This thought is so beautifully elaborated by Professor Bush that we adopt his expression of it: "If then," he says, "it be conceded that the bodily senses are the mere organical functionaries of an intelligent percipient power within, we say the conclusion bears down upon us, with commanding urgency, that what man is substantially here that he is substantially hereafter. Must it not be so? Look at the phenomena of death. There is the eye in its perfect integrity, but it does not see; there is the ear in all the completeness of its mechanism, but it does not hear; there is the wondrous apparatus of nerves spread over the whole surface of the body, but it has no feeling. The seeing, hearing, feeling power, or *person*, has gone. The house remains, but the occupant has departed. Yet consider what powers, what faculties, what thoughts, what memories, what affections were comprised within the limits of that existence which had just before animated this living, moving, acting mass! Has that perished? Was it not the true man—the actual person, in all his distinguishing attributes—which has now passed out of sight? That which is left behind, though it was all that was visible to the senses, was the mere temporary envelope of the indwelling spirit, and we never call it *the man.* It is now *the corpse*, and we speak of it not as *he*, but *it.* We lay *it* out, we deposit *it* in the grave, and we say *it* sees corruption. But *the man*—with all his distinctive attributes, his varied powers of thought, affection, and will, his true personality and character—survives this dislodgment from its earthly house, and goes, in all his integrity, into another sphere of being, where he lives, sub-

ject to the same moral and intellectual laws that governed his existence here. *The soul is the man.*"*

5. *Finally, this subject affords intimations of the power the soul shall possess hereafter.* Here the senses may restrict as well as aid the action of the mind. They are constituted, in their present organisms, for this world alone, and hence are "of the earth, earthy." Designed to be vehicles of the soul's action, they may also be clogs and incumbrances. Who has not been conscious of intellectual power restricted because of weak and wearied organs of sense? The eyelid droops and the ear becomes dull of hearing. They demand rest, and no mere requirement of intellect can push them further. Who has not been conscious of heaviness of spirit from mere physical exhaustion? "The spirit indeed is willing, but the flesh is weak." So in the utmost exhaustion of body, the soul will often retain the full consciousness of its strength. The burden that bears it down is material. It is not the skill nor the power of the worker that has failed, but the keenness and the fitness of the tools with which he works. The consciousness of *power* remains. And the very struggles of the soul amid this bodily disorder indicate that the germ of immortality is there. Nay, more; they indicate that that germ shall yet burst forth from the mortal casements that incase it, and unfold itself in a world where its powers shall have ample scope and full development forever.

Life makes the soul dependent on the dust;
Death gives her wings to mount above the spheres.
Through chinks—styled organs—dim life peeps at light;
Death bursts the involving cloud, and all is day;
All eye, all ear, the disembodied power."

*The Soul, by George Bush, p. 111.

V.

THE HUMAN SOUL DISTINGUISHED FROM ANIMAL INSTINCT.

"There is a spirit in man; and the inspiration of the Almighty giveth them understanding." JOB xxxii, 8.

"Who knoweth the spirit of man that goeth upward, and the spirit of the beast that goeth downward to the earth?" ECCL. iii, 21.

WE have demonstrated that, in addition to a bodily organization including animal life, man is endowed with *an intelligent soul.* This is his distinguishing peculiarity—that which gives him preëminence in the animal creation; that which assures him of immortality. This distinction is real and not incidental. It implies a radical difference of elements, which are not therefore interchangeable. Nor can one grow up into the other.

Whatever similarity there may seem to be between some of the manifestations of instinct in the brute creation, and some of the manifestations of mind or soul in the human race, still there is an immeasurable and impassable gulf between an intelligent soul and the apparent semi-intellect of the animal instinct. The spiritual principle in man is more divine in its nature, as it is more glorious in its origin. It was given by the "inspiration of the Almighty." Thus our spiritual nature is peculiarly allied to God—a

"Dim miniature of greatness absolute."

Thus allied to God, and made capable of communing with Him; thus endued and made capable of unlimited improvement in all that can elevate and ennoble it; and with a sphere spread out before and around it—adapted to call out and expand its energies, the progress of intellect, the variety of its discoveries, the richness of its acquisitions, and the grandeur of its aspirations—all claim for it an immeasurable superiority over the animal mind.

I. The Lines of Demarkation Stated.

The line of demarkation between the intelligent soul and the animal instinct is clearly drawn by Sharon Turner. He says that "independently of all metaphysical discrimination, the literature, the history, the arts, the mechanisms, and the manufactures of mankind—all that ennobles, enriches, and delights a cultivated nation, show at once, with an irresistible certainty, the immense superiority of the human soul. It has discovered and acquired the sciences, composed the works, displayed the feelings, performed the actions, and created the buildings, ships, the paintings, the statues, the music, and all the other wonders of civilized society.

"These are sufficient facts to separate the human spirit from the animal mind. That never improves—that, in no age or country, has effected any progression. Though it sees, hears, and feels as we do, and thinks and reasons, wills and judges, on its perceptions, so far as its appetites are concerned, much as we do on ours; yet there is its limit. Beyond that small, though useful circle, it never advances. In our appetites, and in the mental agency which they stimulate and inspire, we have a kindredship and a similitude, but no further. When our moral principles begin, when our improvabilities develop, when we rise beyond our animal wants and desires, when we study nature, when we cultivate literature, when we seek after knowledge, when the reason and the sympathies ascend to their Creator, we distinguish our spirit from the animal mind forever. To none of these things can that attain. It is incapable either of receiving or comprehending them; and these ennobling powers, and their phenomena, express and illustrate the amazing difference that parts us from our fellow-brutes more impressively than any verbal definitions or descriptive particularity. Their faculties, instincts, and powers are admirable for their class of being, and enlarge our notions of the benevolence, as well as the almightiness, of our common Maker. But they bear no comparison with the transcending capacity, qualities, and achievements of their human masters. The soul of man, indeed, exhibits a greatness, a strength, a penetration, an expansibility, and a creative power, which urge us to inquire if any order of being, except the Divine Source of all that exists, is superior to what the human spirit now is in its essential nature, and will become in its most perfect state."*

II. Instinct precedes both Experience and Reasoning.

This is one of the peculiar characteristics of instinct. Take the desire of food. We experience an uneasy sensation which we call hunger, and to remove this seek food. This is common to the infant just born and to the man fully grown. The latter, by the aid of reason, may vary his diet, and to some extent regulate his appetite. The former has neither experience, nor is it capable of receiving instruction; yet, when applied to its mother's breast, all the muscles necessary to obtain food by suction are at once brought into play. No amount of instruction or intelligence could improve upon the process; and yet that process is one of no little difficulty, involving a very complicated use of the muscles of the mouth and throat. Who taught

*Sacred History of the World, I, p. 411.

the infant that process? Who informed it that the uneasy sensation of hunger would be thus appeased? How did it learn that food was necessary to support life?

This peculiarity of instinct is the same in the brute as in the human. The new-born calf needs no instruction to enable him to balance himself on four legs, and to seek the food supplied by his mother. It is said that when a sow is delivered of a litter, each pig as it is born runs at once to take possession of one of his mother's nipples, which he considers as his peculiar property ever afterward.* A brood of ducklings hatched by a hen, as soon as their muscular powers are sufficiently developed, will break away from the hen that acts as mother to them, plunge into the water, and then, without example or instruction, commence swimming about. Who taught them what classes of muscles to use, and how they were to be used in this process?

The turtle deposits its eggs in a hole in the sand, where they are hatched by the warmth of the sun. No sooner is the young one hatched than it crawls up through the thin covering of sand spread over it by its mother, and makes in a straight line for the sea,† no matter whether in sight or not. Every obstacle is surmounted. The shore once reached, the young turtle dashes into the new element, and disports itself in the waves as though a veteran. There seems to be a double object in this great haste—escape from the birds of prey that haunt the coast, and an innate desire for its native element. Who taught it the peril of remaining upon land? Who instructed the young turtle in its adaptations to the watery element, and how to use its powers then? Its mother left it to its fate while yet a new-laid egg. Nor had it ever seen one of its tribe to be instructed by it, or to take example from it.

*Mind and Matter, by Benjamin Brodie, Bart., D. C. L., p. 198.
† Buffon's Nat. Hist., IV, p. 218.

On the bank of a river in Ceylon, Dr. Davy found a young alligator just escaping from its egg, and placed his cane before it to prevent its progress toward the water. The young animal at once assumed an attitude of defense, and bit the stick, manifesting all the wrath and venom of its kind.* In the selection of their food there is the same definiteness of action, antecedent to experience and clearly without instruction. Each graminivorous animal makes the selection adapted to its peculiar organization; does it without hesitation; and all the individuals of a species, without concert of agreement and, as it is known to be in many cases, without knowledge of each other's action, selects precisely the same kinds of vegetables. So definite is this, that Linnæus undertakes to give the precise number selected and rejected by the different animal species. He says the cow eats 276 plants, and rejects 218; the goat eats 449, and rejects 126; the sheep eats 387, and rejects 141; the horse likes 262, and avoids 212. We will not vouch for the entire accuracy of this. But something like it is undoubtedly true. And yet it is done without the study of botany, without an analysis of the properties of plants, and also in many cases it is known to be without experience and without observation of the plants eaten by other individuals of the species.

The theory adopted by Mr. Darwin and others, that actions, called instinctive, may be traced to experience acquired by various trials and testings, becomes absolutely untenable in the light of these facts. There are indeed facts of this kind, almost without number, that can be explained only on the supposition that "certain feelings exist which lead to the voluntary exercise of certain muscles, and to the performance of certain acts, without any reference at the time to the ultimate object for which these acts

*Brodie's Mind and Matter, p. 219.

are required."* This is the true function of instinct as distinguished from intellect.

We would not underrate the value of instinct, nor lessen its achievements. This is not necessary to the end we have in view. Our point is that, so far as the animal is concerned, it acts antecedent to experience and without reasoning. It lacks that essential quality of the human soul which improves its knowledge from experience, and then makes that knowledge the pathway of its reason as it ascends to higher and broader conclusions. The more curious and complicated the processes of instinct, the higher the capabilities it evolves and the more complex the results it secures—while yet it acts antecedently to experience and without reasoning—the more wonderful is the display of the wisdom and skill of the Great Architect by whom its nature has been determined and its functions appointed.

III. Instinct is not Incipient Reason.

Animal instinct, upon a superficial view, seems to be a sort of incipient reason, and one is often led to wonder whether, in a new state, and under a different order of things, it will not be developed into an intelligent soul. The idea that prevailed extensively among the ancients that the soul of man existed in the body of some animal, before it entered into its human body and began its permanent life, unquestionably had its origin in this feeling.

In this discussion we are to take the animal instinct as it now appears, and to consider its relationship to mind as illustrated by the manifestations of each. Instinct never increases its stock of knowledge, and never improves upon its processes. The beaver builds a no more perfect dam,

*Brodie's Mind and Matter, p. 199.

nor the bee any more perfect cell, than was constructed by the earliest generations of the same.

Instinct will not depart from its usual course even to save from destruction. It therefore often, if not always, acts with a blind disregard of actual results. These obvious and acknowledged facts also distinguish it from the reasoning soul. Water will obey its natural laws, though it deluge a country; so will fire, though it consume a city. There is an unthinking adherence to natural tendency—an inability, in fact, to depart from it, whatever may be the consequences. So it is with the animal instinct; and, in this respect, it seems more nearly allied to the properties of matter than to the faculties of soul.

There are, indeed, some things in the history of animal instinct that suggest intelligence and reason. On the part of birds, the building of nests, in which to deposit their eggs; the contrivance to preserve the warmth of the eggs, in order to hatching, as seen in the brooding of the bird over them, and, also, as is affirmed, in changing them alternately from the outer circle to the center, and *vice versa*, to equalize the proportion of heat to each. In the efforts to protect their young, as when the quail feigns a broken wing, fluttering and bouncing about almost at one's feet, and yet ever out of one's reach, and all the while drawing him away from the place of her young. Birdsnests display striking and varied indications of contrivance, much resembling the reasoning intellect. The oriole forms its nest of long, flexible grass, which is knit or sewed through and through in a thousand directions, as if done by a needle.* It was this that made a lady, while looking at the curious workmanship, inquire whether the oriole could not be taught to darn stockings.†

The salmon journeys a thousand miles to deposit its

*Jameson's Note to Wilson, I, 215. †Wilson's Ornithology, I, 189.

spawn, surmounts the greatest obstacles, nor stops till it finds a place and conditions suited to its purpose; and then not unfrequently returns to the same place year after year. But the young fish, when hatched, go out uninstructed, following the parent into unknown seas. The nautilus spreads its sail and glides before the wind; the gymnotus, by an electrical discharge, stupefies and then catches its victim.

Some species of the quadruped genus have ever been marked for their intelligence, affection, and other qualities, that ally them to the human mind. The providence which the squirrel, the beaver, and the alpine have, in laying up their stores of food for Winter, shows them to be possessed of a quality in which many of our own race—the lower classes of the Irish, for example—are sadly deficient. The intelligence, docility, and usefulness of the horse and the dog have long been the theme of eulogy.

In fact, surveying the whole ground, we can hardly wonder at the enthusiasm with which a modern writer, quoted by Mr. Brodie, kindles up: "There is," says he, "hardly a mechanical pursuit in which insects do not excel. They are excellent weavers, house-builders, architects; they make diving-bells, bore galleries, raise vaults, construct bridges; they line their houses with tapestry, clean them, ventilate them, and close them with admirably-fitted swing-doors; they build and store warehouses, construct traps in the greatest variety, hunt skillfully, rob and plunder; they poison, saber, and strangle their enemies; they have social laws, a common language, division of labor, and gradations of rank; they maintain armies, go to war, send out scouts, appoint sentinels, carry off prisoners, keep slaves, and tend domestic animals. In short, they are a miniature copy of man rather than of the inferior vertebrata." This description is highly wrought, but not so highly but what its substantial basis, in fact, will be readily recognized.

But what is the solution of all this? How do we know that here is not incompetent reason? Because, first, it acts upon a different principle from reason, as we have already seen. Nor are any of these acts more wonderful than other results of instinct, which, as we shall soon see, must, from the very nature of things, have been performed without forethought and without any previous knowledge. And, indeed, this may obviously be predicated of some of the very acts mentioned. And then, also, whatever this may be, it is unlike reason in the fact that, through all the ages, it has really made not one step of progress; nor has it shown the least additional degree of assimilation to the human intellect. The nightingale sings the same notes now, and with the same melodious cadence it did from the earliest history of the world. Not a new note, not an additional quaver, not the least additional sweetness in cadence has ever been attained in any land or under any circumstances, during the past six thousand years. So of all the song-birds. They warble now just as they ever have done since the first record made concerning them. "The eagle is as incapable of advancement as the sparrow. The common fowl, which is found in all regions and climates of the globe, is in each one exactly alike in its functions, faculties, and habits."* So it is with all the unreasoning animal creation. Their history is the same; they themselves are the same in all ages; not a faculty added, not a faculty improved. All the manifestations of animal ingenuity and skill, instead of being incipient reason, appear more like finished instinct. "They utterly lack the universality, the diversifying capacity, and the self-adapting capability of the human intellect. The bee, with all its wondrous skill, can never be taught to manufacture the coarse paper, nor to construct the rude nest of the wasp

*Turner's Sacred History, I, 269.

and the hornet; the oriole, with all its curious workmanship, could not, by any possibility, be taught to manufacture the ruder structure of the wren or swallow.

And so on through all grades of instinct, and in all the stages of its development, it moves in one definite, determinate line of operation. It is incapable of any other. You may as well attempt to shoot the electrical current along wires of glass as to turn instinct out of its appointed channel; and along that it works with wondrous skill, but with a tenacity which seems either incapable of change or blind to results, however disastrous they may be. From the mass of atoms scattered upon the table the magnet will select the iron filings alone. It picks them out with a facility and an exactness surprising to the beholder. If material agencies, possessing neither intellect nor instinct, can effect results so intricate and wonderful, can we wonder at the skill of instinct even when acting with a blind disregard of results, but impelled along in the line of its function by some blind, unreasoning impulse?

Then, again, was it any more difficult for God to inspire the higher order of instinct—that which seems almost to border upon the realm of the spiritual—than to implant the more common? In fine, was it more difficult for him to implant these acute instincts than it was to originate the peculiar functions of electricity, or to ordain the peculiar processes of vegetable life? It is all the contrivance of the same master Mind—all the work of the same skillful Hand.

But the question of the possible improvability of animal instinct here presents itself. Under certain conditions, and within certain limits, improvement by training seems possible. Many singing birds may be taught a few notes sung by others. The starling and the blackbird learn to whistle a tune; the goldfinch will acquire the song of the canary or the woodlark. A greenfinch may learn to ring bells contrived in a cage; a goldfinch may be trained to draw water in an ivory bucket, and to fire off a pistol; a parrot is taught to say "pretty poll," and a variety of other expressions. The intelligence and affection of the horse have often been the theme of admiration; but perhaps no animal is more in sympathy with man than the dog. The variety of his adaptations, the wide diversity and the instincts of the different species of dogs, the keenness of his perception, the tenacity of his memory, the strength and durability of his affection for his master, and his faithfulness, are subjects that challenge our admiration as well as our study.

But the question before us now is not the keenness or the utility, but the *improvability* of instinct. In all these cases there appears, in some sort, a capability of being taught and of improvement. But it should be noted that in every department of nature there are to be found individual departures from the established type. These are the prodigies, the wonders. One horse, in addition to the ordinary instincts of his race, may possess some peculiar instinct leading him to perform certain actions that seem anomalous; but beyond that he is only a common horse. Among dogs, one is by instinct a shepherd's dog, another a pointer, another a rat-terrier, and so on. In these departments they display wonderful skill and utility; but attempt to convert the pointer into a shepherd's dog, or the rat-terrier into a pointer, and you will soon find that you might as well have undertaken the conversion of a sheep or a calf. There are anomalies, and, indeed, monstrosities, of instinct as well as of bodily form. It is said that dogs have been known to utter human words.* So, on the other hand, instances have occurred—I knew one, the case of a young man—in which, from some strange maternal impres-

* Turner's Sacred History, I, 280.

sion, the individual, in the midst of his human talk, would break out, whenever he became excited, into the sudden, sharp, quick bark of the dog. These facts demonstrate peculiarities—monstrosities, if you please—in congenital organization; but by no means do they imply improvability in the instinct of the animal race, at least not such an improvability as would ally instinct to intellect.

Then, again, it should be borne in mind that it is only the individual bird or beast that acquires new art or skill. There the process ends. Not one of them manifests the capability or the inclination to impart this special acquisition to its fellow. It is not even transmitted to their offspring, either as an improved instinct or by instruction, from the parents. The offspring, instead of beginning where the parents left off, begin precisely where the parents did before them. Or, if these finer qualities of instinct are handed down, it is only as the qualities of the grape or the strawberry, improved by the culture of man, are perpetuated. It is not an intelligence, nor any approximation to an intelligence; but it is as clearly marked with all the distinctive traits of instinct as before.

Nor should it be deemed surprising that there are differences in the quality of instinct in different animals of the same species, just as a finer and more perfect organization in the human species afford finer development of mental power; and so, on the other hand, just as the appreciable qualities of matter, from causes inscrutable, are widely different in the same species. One piece of iron may be more malleable, one more flexible, and one more susceptible of high magnetic power; one kind may be manufactured into the finest steel, and gleam forth in the polished saber, the other is fit only for the huge anchor. All these things demonstrate incidental departure from the original type; they demonstrate a variety of adaptation.

But they no more demonstrate that instinct can grow up into intellect than that the beech may become an oak, the pig an elephant, or the ape a man. The boundary that parts man, in his physical organization, from the brute creation, is not more clearly defined, nor more utterly impassable, than that which separates the human soul from the animal instinct in all its varied forms and supposed improvabilities.

IV. Instinct is without Forethought.

We are here brought to another line of demarkation between the animal instinct and the human soul. Instinct is without forethought on the part of its subject. Mr. Paley makes it the peculiar and distinguishing characteristic of instinct, that it acts "prior to experience and independent of instruction." This was justly criticised by Lord Brougham as leaving out that vital element of distinction between soul and instinct, that in the former there is ever a conscious foresight and intention, which, at least, in many cases in the latter—even in its highest manifestations—are evidently wanting.

The insect, for instance, plies her constructive art when it is certain there can be no *intention* as to results, because there is an absolute ignorance of what results are to follow. Lord Brougham, in his Dialogues on Instinct, says of the bee, "I see her doing certain things which are manifestly to produce an effect she can know nothing about. For example, making a cell, and furnishing it with carpets and with liquid, fit to hold and to cherish safely a tender grub, and knowing nothing, of course, about grubs, or that any grub is to come, or that any such use, perhaps any use at all, is ever to be made of the work she is about. Indeed, I see another insect—the solitary wasp—bring a given number of small grubs and deposit them in a hole which she has made over her egg—just grubs enough to maintain the worm that egg will produce when hatched—and yet this wasp never saw an egg produce a worm, nor ever saw a worm—nay, is to be dead long before the worm can be in existence; and, moreover, she never has in any way tasted or used those grubs, or used the hole she made, except for the benefit of the prospective worm she is never to see. In all these cases, then, the animal works positively without knowledge, and in the dark. She also works without designing any thing, and yet she works to a certain defined and important purpose."

Such is animal instinct, even in its highest efforts, a force, intentionless, and blindly working in the dark. If it works beneficent results, in the main, it is not because the results are foreseen and sought after; but for the same reason that the elective and cohesive forces among particles of matter effect useful combinations; they are guided by laws ordained and carried into force by the Infinite Mind.

V. Instinct controlled by Divine Intelligence.

It will be perceived that we do not question the presence of intelligence. But whose intelligence is it? Not the insect's; for his is obviously a blind instrumentality. To make this more apparent, notice the hexagonal structure of the bee's cell. Here is the utmost possible economy of space, combining the least expenditure of wax. Man has found this out by the most careful and complicated mathematical calculations. Is it not certain, then, that with the bee, it is an unintelligent and controlled agency? This is all the more apparent from the fact that the young bee, uninstructed and without experience, is equally skillful in the perfection of its angles and the finish of its architecture.

The intelligence here manifested, then, is not in the animal. That is merely an unthinking instrument, working under a higher guidance—the guidance of the Divine Mind. Mr. Pope pertinently expresses this idea in his well-known couplet:

> "And reason raise o'er instinct as you can,
> In this 't is God that acts, in that 't is man."—Essay.

Dr. Tulloch states this argument with great force: "We have here a mental process of a very high order; we must find a mental agent. Such an agent we do not find in the animal. It appears, on the contrary, from all evidence, to be a mere blind instrument. We are forced, therefore, to admit a higher agent. This agent can only be the Supreme Intelligence every-where present in creation."*

There is, then, a distinct line of demarkation between the human soul and the animal mind. Till we find the brute creation exhibiting some of these manifestations of an indwelling soul—reason, conscience, intellect; till we find them cherishing and cultivating moral feelings and motives, exercising moral virtues and charities, recognizing and obeying the law of conscience, recognizing the being and moral government of God; and, in fine, cherishing the hopes and expectations of another life—we must be compelled to recognize a radical and eternal distinction between the human soul and the brute instinct.

VI. Concluding Suggestions.

The theme here presented, and the lines of distinction drawn, are pregnant with suggestive lessons concerning the Divine economy, and affecting every line of duty.

1. *If mere instinct had been given, there would have been a wonderful waste of skill and adaptations in the material*

* Theism, p. 232.

world. All those hidden resources and wonderful contrivances of nature which challenge investigation; all those landscape and ocean views which are adapted to call forth emotions of the beautiful, the grand, and the sublime—would have been without their correspondent faculties in the world of mind, and would therefore have failed of their ultimate purpose. The inexhaustible stores of coal and of metals, laid away in the bowels of the earth with such infinite providence, would have been an infinite waste. Indeed, the evident care of nature to provide materials, almost infinitely varied in adaptations and number, to be employed in the various appliances of art, would have been without adequate purpose or aim. Nay, the very capability of culture and production with which our earth has been endowed would have been a useless endowment. Every thing in nature shows that not only the curious workmanship of the body, but this material garniture of the earth and the heavens has direct reference to soul and soul-culture. When the Almighty prepared the heavens and set a compass upon the face of the deep, when he gave to the sea its bounds and to the earth its foundations, still his "*delights were with the sons of men.*" *

2. *We have here also distinct intimations of man's dominant relation to the animal creation.* Had the historian of creation never placed upon record that man was to "have dominion over the fish of the sea, and over the fowl of the air, and over every living thing that moveth upon the earth," still the fact of his appointed dominion would be manifested in his very organization. Not indeed in his physical nature, for that is inferior, in many respects, to that of some of the brute creation. But when he comes forth, a human body, inspired and empowered by an indwelling, living soul, he stands confessed *the lord of creation.*

* Prov. viii, 31.

3. *The endowment of spirit involves the idea of higher duties and responsibilities, as well as of higher powers.* Every thing in nature has its appropriate sphere and function. But with most creatures that sphere is exceedingly circumscribed. Their capacities do not admit of a wider range. All the functions of their being seem bound up in a narrow compass, and they are soon accomplished. How different is the case with man! His intelligence sweeps over the whole range of the material creation; and, above and beyond that, holds mysterious connection with the spiritual universe, unlimited and eternal. The animal needs only to provide for its physical wants, and that for the briefest period. Animal necessities are the smallest of man's wants, and they scarcely begin the wide range of the duties and responsibilities devolved upon him by his organization, no less than by command of his God.

4. *The endowment of a spirit is accompanied with intimations of man's superior destiny.* The consciousness of selfhood in man, connected as it is with a succession of ideas, to which there is no limit, is of itself an intimation of immortality. "Reason," says Dr. Moore, "is dogmatical, and she asserts her nobility, by demanding a life suited to her nature; she discourses with intelligence, and draws an argument for her deathlessness from the fact that to love truth is to love existence for its highest purposes." These purposes are immortal.

> "And can it be? Does this
> Weak, trembling frame conceal within itself
> A soul ethereal and immortal?
> A glorious spark sublime and boundless,
> 'Struck from the burning essence of its God,'
> The great I Am, the dread Eternal?
> O, how tremendous is the awful thought!
> The soul shrinks back alarmed, too weak to gaze
> On its own greatness, or rather, on the greatness
> Of that God who made it!"—Miss M. M. Davidson.

VI.

THE MIND INDESTRUCTIBLE AND IMMORTAL.

"A living soul." GEN. ii, 7.
"Who knoweth the spirit of man that goeth upward." ECCLES. iii, 21.
"Not able to kill the soul." MATT. x, 28.
"Life and immortality are brought to light in the Gospel."

THE indestructibility and immortality of mind are among the sublimest ideas that ever dawned upon the human soul. How it increases the range of its vision! How it multiplies and enhances the objects of its creation! How much grander the destiny it reveals! How it alleviates the dark and gloomy aspect of this world, where changes are incessant and death universal!

"The sun is but a spark of fire,
A transient meteor in the sky,
The soul, immortal as its sire,
Shall never die."

When we assume that the soul in its very nature is indestructible and immortal, we do not mean that it has this nature independent of God, but that the Divine Being has thus endowed it. What God wills it to be that is its nature. If God has made it to be immortal, then is it naturally immortal. The self-existent eternity of matter was a theory of the Epicurean philosophy; and some who have opposed the doctrine of man's immortality represent the Christian philosopher as occupying this old heathen ground. But the distinction is obvious. The one made matter eternally self-existent; the other assumes that neither matter nor soul is self-existent, but that the being, and all the attributes or properties of each, have been derived from the Creator of all; and, further, that each is possessed of such a nature as he has given it.

We assume, then, that immortality is the heritage of the race. On the same grounds that I claim immortality for myself, I claim it for all my kind; for God "hath made of one blood all nations of men to dwell on all the face of the earth." (Acts xvii, 26.) Weakness and darkness, brutality and degradation, do not change this essential characteristic of mind. They may cloud the pathway of the life to come as they do that of the present life, but they have no power to rob the soul of its being.

I. Our first Argument for the Indestructibility of Mind is Drawn from the Acknowledged Indestructibility of Matter.

Matter is incessantly changing its form. The particles of which bodies are composed, though now solid, impervious, may be resolved into their original liquid or gaseous elements—may be dissipated so as to become invisible and impalpable. The process of evaporation may go on till not one drop of water is left in the pool, and yet the existence, nay, even the identity, of those elements is not lost. They may float over continents and oceans; they may be as widely separated as the poles, but not one of them is annihilated. The fire may consume the forest oak till all that is left, distinguishable to sense, is the handful of ashes gathered upon the hearth. All the rest has disappeared—passed away in smoke or been evaporated into air—and yet no single particle of the oak has suffered annihilation.

Thus the process of change is perpetually going on in the forms and relations of matter. The atoms that now pile up the rugged mountain were once, every single one of them, not as they now are. The time will come, away in the ages of the future, when, one by one, each shall have changed again and no longer appear in their present form. But in all this wonderful transformation there is no annihilation. Not a single atom has ceased to be; not one has lost its identity even. That little particle of limestone which nestles so snugly in the bones of the living man is the same particle which once uplifted the mountain's ponderous weight. In regard to the created universe, then, annihilation is no part of the plan of the Creator. The minutest particle to which he has given existence shall never cease to be. It may pass through ten thousand transformations, but its being is untouched.

This indestructibility of matter affords, to say the least, a strong presumption for the indestructibility of soul. Can it enter into the mind of any one that a higher destiny is awarded to the insensate atom than to the "living soul?" Was not the material world created that it might become the training-place of the soul, a handmaid to its early growth and development? To suppose, then, that God has appointed to the former a being that should outlast the latter is to reverse all our ideas of the divine plan of wisdom—of proportionate order and ends—in the universe.

We have not found it necessary to urge the immateriality of mind as a proof of immortality; for matter itself, we have seen, is indestructible; so that had materialists been able to show that the soul of man is a *material substance* it would not have disproved the immortality of the soul. God, for aught we know, could have endowed a material soul with an unending existence. Its heritage would then have been immortality. Nor would this have been more wonderful than the kindred endowment bestowed upon the elementary atoms of material nature. Still, when the fact of the soul's immaterial essence is established, as it is by the most undoubted evidence, the question of immortality rises from mere presumption to the region of demonstrated fact. We can join with the poet in saying of our departed friends—

> "There are no dead.
> 'T is true, many of them are gone;
> Singly they came, singly they departed;
> When their work was done, they lay down to sleep—
> But never one hath *died;*
> Forms may change, but spirit is immortal."

II. Our Second Argument is drawn from the Concurrent Belief of all Ages and all People in a Future State.

There seems ever to have been a remarkable uniformity in the opinions and traditions of the race concerning a future state. Amid all the darkness that has enveloped the human mind, there have never failed to be seen some gleams of light in regard to a future life. "Never," says Dr. Blair, "has any nation been discovered on the face of the earth so rude and barbarous that, in the midst of their wildest superstitions, there was not cherished among them some expectation of a state after death, in which the virtuous were to enjoy happiness." "Man," says Sidney Smith, "in every stage of society, civilized or savage, has universally believed that he is to live hereafter."

If the facts shall be found to justify these broad statements, how are we to account for them? Are they to be traced to an instinctive principle implanted by the Creator? Then must they have some basis in truth, or

> "Nature, there,
> Imposing on her sons, has written fables—
> Man was made a lie."

But let us recur to some of the data which settle the question of fact. The ancient Egyptians represent the soul as being brought at death into the presence of its Judge, and that attendant spirits were present to bear witness for or against it. The ancient Persians represent the wicked as being sent away into "everlasting darkness," and the good as being restored to the bosom of "the universal Father." The poet of Bokhara—Rodski—when speaking of the death of Muradi, embodies this thought in most exquisite and delicate language: "Muradi, alas! is dead! But no, he certainly can not be dead! It is not so easy for death to triumph over such an illustrious man. He has only restored his noble soul to our universal Father; he has only resigned his sordid body to our universal mother."* The Greek and Roman *mythology*—which stood to them in the place of *theology*—represented the soul, when separated from the body at death, as being ferried over the River Styx by Charon, where they were judged according to the deeds done in the body. Those

> "Who suffered wounds
> In fighting for their country's cause; and priests
> Who kept their souls unspotted whilst their lives
> Endured; and pious bards who warbled strains,
> Did honor to Apollo; those who polished
> Life by invented arts, and such as made
> Their memories dear to others by the deeds
> Of goodness,"

were at once admitted to

> "The realms of joy,
> Delighted haunts of never-fading green,
> The blessed seats in groves of happiness,
> Where ether more diffusive robes the fields
> In purple glory."

But the wicked were cast down to hell—a place where hunger, toil, disease, fear, and nameless sorrows reigned supreme.

> "An hundred tongues,
> An hundred mouths, and speech by iron lungs
> Inspired, could not enumerate the names
> Of all their punishments."

*Turner's Sacred History, I, p. 122. Note.

The immortality of the soul was one of the distinguishing doctrines of Socrates, and the assertion of it formed the great charm of the Phædon to Cicero and the most enlightened Romans. It became Plato's most valued work, for this reason, as detailing the last conversation of Socrates with his friends just before he took the poison to which he had been sentenced. His mode of reasoning will be illustrated by a brief extract from the Phædon:

S. "Answer me; what is that which, when in the body, makes it alive?"

Kebes. "The soul."

S. "Will it always be so?"

K. "How can it be otherwise?"

S. "Will the soul, then, always bring life to whatever it occupies?"

K. "Certainly."

S. "Is there any thing contrary to life, or nothing?"

K. "There is."

S. "What?"

K. "Death."

S. "Will the soul receive the contrary to what it introduces?"

K. "By no means."

S. "But what do we call that which does not receive death?"

K. "Immortal."

S. "The soul will not receive death, you say?"

K. "No."

S "Is the soul, then, immortal?"

K. "It is immortal."

S. "When, therefore, death comes upon a man, what is mortal in him perishes, as it is seen to do; but what is immortal withdraws itself from death, safe and uncorrupted?"

K. "This is clear."

S. "We may, then, be sure that, more than all things, O Kebes! the soul is immortal and incorruptible, and that our souls will still be in existence in Hades."*

Seneca, the celebrated philosopher, referring to this universal concurrent belief of the soul's immortality, says: "On the question of the immortality of the soul, it goes very far with me, a general consent to the opinions of a future state of rewards and punishments, the meditation of which raises me to a contempt of this life in hopes of a better." And, after surveying the arguments of the philosophers in favor of the soul's immortality, he exclaims, "I am strangely transported with the thoughts of eternity; nay, with the belief of it."

The eloquent Cicero—one of the greatest orators of antiquity, and one of the most learned and talented men that Rome ever produced—argues as follows: "If I am wrong in believing the souls of men immortal, I please myself in my mistake; nor while I live will I ever choose that this opinion, with which I am so much delighted, should ever be wrested from me." There is a spice of genuine wit, as well as of sublime philosophy, when he adds, "But if at death I am to be annihilated, as some philosophers suppose, I am not afraid lest those wise men, when extinct too, should laugh at my error."

The Roman Emperor, Adrian, in his celebrated address to his soul, clearly indicates, amid the darkness and doubt of heathenism, his apprehension of the fact that the soul in death did not become extinct, but took its flight to some unknown sphere.

"Poor, little, pretty, fluttering thing,
Must we no longer live together?
And dost thou prune thy trembling wing,
To take thy flight, thou know'st not whither?

*Turner's Sacred History, I, p. 102.

Thy pleasing vein, thy humorous folly,
Lies all neglected, all forgot!
And pensive, wavering, melancholy,
Thou hop'st, and fear'st, thou know'st not what."

The ancient Scandinavians taught that the brave were to revel forever in the halls of Valhalla, and drink mead offered them by maidens, from the skulls of their enemies. The future condition of the soul is differently described among different nations; but this one idea—*that death was not the destruction of the living soul*—is apparent in all their traditions and in all their rites. This notion prevailed among the Celts and Druids, the Aztecs and Peruvians, and is found with the inhabitants of the islands of the ocean—the Society Islands, the Friendly Islands, Pelew Islands, and New Zealanders; in Asia, among the Burmans, Samoyedians, the Kalmuc Tartars; in Africa, among the Gallus, Mandingoes, Jaloffs, Feloops, Foulahs, and Moors; and in fine, every-where does it exist, so far as examination has gone. Among the Indians of North America, the doctrine of the soul's immortality was universally recognized. William Penn says of the Indians of that early time: "These poor people are under a dark night, in things pertaining to religion, yet they believe in a God and immortality, without the help of metaphysics." The common idea of the race was that in the future life he would be permitted to enter the great hunting grounds above, where innumerable herds of deer and buffaloes graze upon the verdant hills, and ruminate in the fertile valleys; where the "*pale face* shall *trouble no more.*" Mr. Pope has given a beautiful versification of this sublime conception of the darkened nature of the savage:

"Lo! the poor Indian, whose untutor'd mind
Sees God in clouds, or hears him in the wind;
Whose soul proud science never taught to stray
Far as the solar walk or milky way—
Yet simple nature to his hope has given,
Behind the cloud-topt hill, a humbler heaven;

Some safer world in depth of woods embraced,
Some happier island in the watery waste,
Where slaves once more their native land behold,
No fiends torment, no Christians thirst for gold—
And thinks, admitted to yon equal sky,
His faithful dog shall bear him company."

We might multiply these authorities indefinitely. It may be that a few among the ancient philosophers rejected the doctrine of the soul's immortality, or were in doubt concerning it, just as, in the present day, every Christian doctrine—the most clearly established even—has its skeptics and doubters. But that, by no means, impugns the assertion that all nations and all peoples, on the face of the earth, have, as an aggregate, credited the soul's immortality. In a word, it has been *the sentiment of humanity in all ages.*

In vain do the modern annihilationists, like Storrs, and Hudson, and Dobney, and even Dr. Whately, attempt to deny or throw doubt over the fact of this universal belief. It comes up in all the poetry, the mythology, and the history of antiquity. It is inwrapped as an element of nearly every philosophy. The religious rites and ceremonies of nations and tribes proclaim it. And the deep yearnings of the human heart, in every place and in all ages, give utterance to it.

But what is the lesson to be derived from it? Let the immortal Cicero, representing the highest and noblest thought of any age and any people, unblessed with the light of Revelation, answer—"In every thing the consent of all nations is to be accounted the law of nature; and to resist it, is to resist the voice of God." If it was a local tradition, we might refer it to some local cause. If it had been limited to some one age, we might attribute it to some peculiar development or bias of the mind of that age resulting from a temporary cause.

But what shall we say when we find it bounded by no clime and limited to no age, but one of the deepest and most universal sentiments of humanity? There can be but one answer. The sentiment is inspired with the very consciousness of life, and, therefore, appeals to the great Author of life as its source. It must then be true. A belief thus originated, so universal, can not be without a substantial basis in truth. In a word, it is proof sublime of immortality. It is demonstration that death works only the change, and not the destruction of the soul.

III. A Future Life only can satisfy the Conditions and Capacities of our Mental Being.

Look to the human race as they appear to the mere superficial observer, and what do we see? Merely a succession of evanescent and fading objects! Thousands are coming upon the stage, full of life and hope; and thousands, care-worn and weary, are retiring from it—retiring from it with a deep and anxious consciousness of faculties undeveloped and objects unaccomplished; like bubbles upon the mighty deep, they rise and then disappear. This scene is not only enacting now, but it ever has been since man's first transgression

"Brought death into the world and all our woe."

The multitudes of the dead are more than those of the living. The whole of this vast globe is but an amphitheater, in which are displayed the works, and beneath which repose the bodies of the dead.

But is this all? Are all our interests, is all our being crowded within the narrow compass of the brief span of this life? Are there no fountains within us but what are exhausted in a brief life of sorrow, passed in ignorance and fruitless desire? Take even the most favorable examples of human nature—the mind of Newton, or of Bacon—and inquire, even concerning them, if they were not susceptible of a wider and fuller development! Were their intellects, capacious as they were, susceptible of no further expansion? Had they attained the utmost limit of which their minds were capable? You shall hear the confessions of one of these great men, as they fell from his own lips. Says the immortal Newton, "I do not know what I may appear to the world; but to myself I seem to have been only like a boy playing on the sea-shore, and diverting myself in now and then finding a smoother pebble, or a prettier shell than ordinary, while the great ocean of truth lay undiscovered before me."* If these are the confessions of the greatest intellect that ever lived—if *he* only trod on the *shore* of the boundless ocean of truth, what must be the case with the great mass of men? If even his intellect did not reach its maturity before he was hurried off the stage of being, how can we say, concerning the race of man, that they are susceptible of no greater development; that they have capacities of no higher order than have been brought out and cultivated here? We argue, then, inasmuch as nothing is made without some worthy object and end, that there must be some other allotment to mortals; some other state of being in which these embryo faculties shall expand into full maturity.

Change is indeed one of the allotments of Providence; we see its working every-where. "Few things are in that state now in which they are hereafter to remain. The bird destined for the air sleeps in his shell; the beautiful insect that is to flutter in the sun crawls in the earth till his season of glory is come. The child that requires the hand of a parent to give him food may soon be changed into a saint or a sage. So, also, says the great apostle, is it with the soul of man. This is not its resting-place; it was never

* Brewster's Life of Newton.

intended to remain here, and to be always as it now is; it will be changed as the seed is changed; the corruptible will put on incorruption; the mortal, immortality. The object for which it was created will be made manifest; at the very moment when it seems to perish, it is passing into a higher order of creatures and getting hold of a better life." *

If there be not this allotment, this new and more glorious state, then must be impeached not only the Divine goodness, but also the Divine wisdom. For if man be not immortal; if there be no future state in which these faculties may expand to their full maturity; if the vast ocean of truth is never to be crossed or surveyed, and the unfathomed mines of knowledge to remain forever unexplored, why was he endowed with such capacities and desires—capacities that can never be filled up, and desires that can never be satisfied in this state of existence?

Was the creation of mind an aimless freak of the God of nature? Did he endow it with its transcendent powers, but allot to it no time nor sphere for the development of these powers? Doth he every-where exhibit the most perfect wisdom and goodness in his creation—except in its noblest part? Doth he clothe the fields with verdure, and the lily with beauty; doth he feed the young ravens when they cry; and doth he not provide for him whom he hath created to be in his own likeness and image? In the creation of such a being did his skill forsake him, did his right hand forget its cunning? Reason and religion answer, no! conscience and experience answer, no! all that is elevated in the hopes or dear in the expectations of an immortal being answer, no!

This idea, expressed by Addison in thought and style of such transparent beauty, that, though repeated a thousand

* Sidney Smith.

times, it can never become worn by use. "How can it," says he, "enter into the thoughts of man, that the soul, which is capable of such immense perfections, and of receiving new improvements to all eternity, shall fall into nothing almost as soon as it is created? Are such abilities made for no purpose? A brute arrives at a point of perfection which he can never pass. In a few years he has all the endowments he is capable of; and were he to live ten thousand more, would be the same thing he is at present. Were a human soul thus at a stand in her accomplishment, were her faculties to be full blown, and incapable of further enlargements, I could imagine it might fall away insensibly, and drop at once into a state of annihilation. But can we believe a thinking being, that is in a perpetual progress of improvements, and traveling on from perfection to perfection, after having just looked abroad into the works of the Creator, and made a few discoveries of his infinite goodness, wisdom, and power, must perish in her first setting out, and in the very beginning of her inquiries?

"Man, considered in his present state, seems sent into the world only to propagate his kind. He provides himself with a successor, and immediately quits his post to make room for him.

> 'Heir urges on his predecessor heir,
> Like wave impelling wave.'

He does not seem born to enjoy life, but to deliver it down to others. This is not surprising to consider of animals which are formed for our use, and can finish their business in a short life. The silk-worm, after having spun her task, lays her eggs and dies. But a man can never have taken in his full measure of knowledge, has not time to subdue his passions, establish his soul in virtue, and come up to the perfection of his nature, before he is hurried off the stage. Would an infinitely-wise Being make such glorious creatures for so mean a purpose? Can he delight in the production of such abortive intelligences—such short-lived, reasonable beings? Would he give us talents that are not to be exerted? capacities that are never to be gratified? How can we find that wisdom, that shines through all his works in the formation of man, without looking upon this world as the nursery for the next? and believing that the several generations of rational creatures, which rise up and disappear in such quick successions, are only to receive their first rudiments of existence here, and afterward to be transplanted into a more friendly climate, where they may spread and flourish to all eternity."*

But, again, if there be not a future state—a future life—designed for the fuller development and play of our mental faculties, the endowment of man with an intellect, a "spirit," was not merely useless, but absolutely a curse instead of a blessing to the human race; for what avail to him all the acquisitions of knowledge if he is not immortal? They are scarcely worth a thought or care.

Instinct would have answered every purpose of his present being, just as it does for the brute, and man would have been spared all this feverish solicitude, this anxious and unceasing care for the future. The beast lies down in death with as little thought and as little care as if to a night's repose, but man shrinks back with horror from the chill and misty shadows of the grave. His proud reason stands appalled before "the King of Terrors," and can meet him in peace only when irradiated with the glorious hope of immortality. If, then, this hope is baseless, empty, and vain; if this last stay and support of reason is but a crushed reed; if it is only the precursor of eternal nothingness, then may we deprecate the power

* Spectator.

that gave reason birth; and it would be a fit cause for mourning to the human race that we were born with higher powers than the brute if we are destined to the same common fate. If, as "the frail and feverish beings of an hour," we are

> "Doomed o'er the world's precarious scene to sweep,
> Swift as the tempest travels on the deep,
> To know delight but by her parting smile,
> And toil, and wish, and weep a little while"—

then, rent by all the agonies of despair under this dark and blighting destiny, we may exclaim, with the same poet,

> "Melt, ye elements, that formed in vain,
> This troubled pulse and visionary brain!
> Fade, ye wild flowers, memorials of my doom;
> And sink, ye stars, that light me to the tomb."

Against such a dark and cheerless conclusion all within and all around us utter their solemn and impressive protest. The mortal shall perish, shall return to its native elements; but the spiritual shall live on forever. As the insect flutters from out its chrysalis to soar on wings of beauty and revel amid the glories of nature, so shall this immortal soul, purified by the blood of atonement, go forth from its chrysalis state to contemplate and enjoy the ineffable glories of the spiritual world. Then shall it find scope for all its powers; then shall it reach the consummation of its highest and grandest hopes. Then cheer up, wayworn and sorrowing pilgrim! Sorrow and darkness may surround thee here, but "hereafter thy voice shall be attuned to angel harmonies, and thy home be in that city whose walls are jasper and whose gates are pearl—along whose streets murmurs the crystal river, and in whose midst blooms the tree of life."

> "O, listen, man!
> A voice within us speaks that startling word,
> 'Man, thou shalt never die!' Celestial voices
> Hymn it into our souls; according harps.

By angel fingers touch'd, when the wild stars
Of morning sang together, sound forth still
The song of our great immortality.

Night and the dawn, bright day and thoughtful eve,
All time, all bounds, the limitless expanse,
As one vast mystic instrument, are touched
By an unseen living hand, and conscious chords
Quiver with joy in this great jubilee.
The dying hear it; and, as sounds of earth
Grow dull and distant, wake their passing souls
To mingle in this heavenly harmony."

IV. The Human Conscience is a Prophecy of Immortality.

Conscience is that moral faculty which gives us an instinctive conviction of obligation and duty, and also an instinctive apprehension of a future retribution. Its law is written upon the human heart, and interwoven with the very nature of every moral agent. It is as essential a part of our nature as reason, or judgment, or memory. Its universality is asserted by the apostle Paul, when he says that "when the Gentiles which have not the law, do by nature the things contained in the law, these having not the law, are a law unto themselves; which show the work of the law written in their hearts, their conscience also bearing witness, and their thoughts the meanwhile accusing or else excusing one another." Its existence and authority are also acknowledged, in some form or other, by all the race. While the doctrine of our "great immortality" has demanded recognition among all men, whether savage or civilized, the belief of it has ever been intensified by conscience. It speaks in every chamber of the soul with a voice more potent than any pealing thunder. The heathen offerings of gold, and silver, and precious things to their gods, and all their sacrifices of sheep, and oxen, and even of human beings, for the atonement of sin, are so many sad yet eloquent attestations of the prophecy which conscience makes of our immortality.

Conscience, as well as every other faculty of our moral and intellectual nature, has become impaired by sin; but still, quickened by that Spirit that lighteth every man that cometh into the world, it speaks to the sinner, not in tones of thunder, pealing from Sinai or from thrones of judgment, but in his inmost soul, and in a voice inaudible to the ear of sense, proclaiming the unvailed realities of a retribution as invincible as it is certain. Take away every external source of illumination; blot out every syllable of the written law; extinguish forever the written revelation from God, and still, through the natural conscience, enlightened as it is by the Holy Ghost, man would receive no faint conviction of his obligation to virtue, and no faint impressions of a future judgment and retribution.

The commission of sin, even though no flaming thunderbolt of the Almighty should mark to the eyes of men his displeasure, has its fearful attendants. "A waiting conscience, terrific admonition whispering on his secret ear, prophetic warning pointing him to the dim and vailed shadows of future retribution, and the all-penetrating, all-surrounding idea of an avenging God, are present with him; and the right arm of the felon and the transgressor is lifted up, amidst lightnings of conviction and thunderings of reproach."

"Skeptic, whoe'er thou art, tell, if thou knowest,
Tell why on unknown evil grief attends,
Or joy on secret good? Why conscience acts
With tenfold force when sickness, age, or pain
Stands tottering on the precipice of death?
Or why such horror gnaws the guilty soul
Of dying sinners, while the good man sleeps
Peaceful and calm, and with a smile expires?" GLYNN.

Thus, there is the sacred dread of retribution in another life, running through all the web and woof of our present being. We can not escape it. It enters the halls of mirth, mingles in the gay scenes of dissipation, traverses the dark chamber of wickedness, goes down with us through all the lanes of life leading to the grave, and in a dying hour makes broad and distinct its utterances of immortality.

V. Still another Argument may be Drawn from the Confessions of Infidelity.

These confessions indicate how quenchless is the light of immortality in the human soul. Thomas Paine, after declaring that all "belief of a word of God existing in print, or in writing, or in speech, is inconsistent in itself," nevertheless confesses to the conviction of a future existence. He says: "I content myself with believing, even to positive conviction, that the power which gave me existence is able to continue it in any form and manner he pleases, either with or without this body; and it appears to me more probable that I shall continue to exist hereafter than that I should have had existence, as I now have, before that existence began."

Thus, also, a large portion of that class of infidels who have rejected the written revelation from God, have, nevertheless, been unable to uproot from their souls the instinct of immortality. Men may deny God and scoff at a future life—may decree that "there is no God," and that "death is an eternal sleep"—but, after all, down in the depths of their depraved hearts lingers the consciousness that the soul does not die, and that consciousness, though long clogged by evil passions, and buried up beneath the rubbish of false and damning theories, shall yet come forth and assert its undying nature.

> "E'en at the parting hour, the soul will wake,
> Nor like a senseless brute its unknown journey take." Percival.

Said the dying Altamont, "My soul is full powerful to reason, full mighty to suffer; and that which thus triumphs within the jaws of mortality is, doubtless, immortal." And then he adds: "Remorse for the past throws my thoughts on the future; *worse dread of the future* strikes them back upon the past. I turn and turn, and find no ray. Didst thou feel half the mountain that is on me, thou wouldst struggle with the martyr for his stake, and bless heaven for the flame that is not an everlasting flame, that is not an unquenchable fire." Who can believe that a soul wrought up into such intense agony, with all its powers so terribly quickened, and with its dying confessions and dreadful anticipations still upon its lips, shall suddenly drop into non-existence, and cease its consciousness forever? Nay, these very confessions of infidelity, rising up, as they do, to confront and confound all the professions of a life of unbelief, and to anticipate an impending and eternal doom, are but the soul's assertion of its undying and immortal nature.

VI. It now only remains for us to Verify these Deductions of Reason by the Teachings of Revelation.

We have already seen that a future and eternal life only can satisfy the capacities, aspirations, and wants of the soul, and thus meet the conditions of our being; and now it remains for us to ascertain whether God has given us ground of hope that this future life shall be granted—whether that immortality which only can fill up the capacities and satisfy the longings of the mind shall be given or denied to man. Reason may lead us to *hope*, but revelation produces *faith;* reason affords some glimmering expectations of a future state, but revelation lifts up the impending vail, and brings immortality and eternal life to light. It dissipates the dense mists that hang over the valley of the shadow of death, and enables the soul to revel in the anticipations of a bliss which eye hath not seen nor ear heard, and which it hath not entered into the heart of man to conceive.

Let us commune for a moment with the spirits of the illustrious dead—illustrious, not for feats of valor, nor for conquests achieved upon the blood-stained fields of carnage and death, but illustrious for moral excellence, for exalted piety, for ardent and undying faith. Let us inquire, What was their faith and what were their hopes? Hear the response in the triumphant language of the godly yet afflicted man of Uz: "I know that my Redeemer liveth, and that he shall stand at the latter day upon the earth; and though after my skin worms destroy this body, yet in my flesh shall I see God; whom I shall see for myself, and mine eyes shall behold, and not another, though my reins be consumed within me." (Job xix, 25.) Hear it also in the language of the monarch minstrel: "My flesh and my heart faileth; but God is the strength of my heart and my portion forever." (Ps. lxxiii, 25, 26.) The same faith and the same expectations characterized the language of the great apostle to the Gentiles: "I am now ready to be offered, and the time of my departure is at hand. I have fought a good fight, I have finished my course, I have kept the faith: henceforth there is laid up for me a crown of righteousness, which the Lord, the righteous Judge, shall give me at that day: and not to me only, but unto all them also that love his appearing." (2 Tim. iv, 6–8.) We are ready to exclaim, Can this be the language of dying men? Yes, it is even so! It is the language of men whose bosoms swelled with the hopes and expectations of immortal life. In them the fruits of faith in the blessed Redeemer had ripened into full and glorious maturity.

Whatever may be the change that takes place in death, it is evidently one that does not destroy the identity of the individual. The rich man who lifted up his eyes in hell, being in torment, had not only the remembrance of his luxurious and godless life, but also of his relationship to five brothers, who had probably been the companions of his pleasures and his sins. Our personal identity we carry forward with us into the other life. But, how is this done?

In this life there seems to be a bodily as well as mental identity. In what this bodily identity consists it is not so easy to determine. An unceasing process of change is ever going on in our physical systems. To-day we are not what we were yesterday, nor shall we be to-morrow what we are to-day. Yet, somehow, we think and speak of ourselves as the same. This flux and efflux of the system may go on for half a century, till every particle of it has been changed many times; and yet our identity of person remains. Think of the bodily changes of half a century! rising from infancy to mature life, or going even beyond to the decrepitude of age! And yet the bodily identity is unaffected. But, at death, this body is dropped in the dust. The identity carried forward into another life, then, is not that of the body. It must be identity of soul. And all along in the unfolding of the future life, prior to the resurrection, this identity of the soul, as the very soul that once inhabited the earthly body, is either roundly asserted or distinctly implied.

How clearly is this expressed in that inimitable prayer of our blessed Redeemer for his followers: "Father, I will that they also whom thou hast given me be with me where I am," (John xvii, 24;) not that spirits newly created—however exalted or glorious—but these identical followers and companions in the earthly life! This same identity was proclaimed from the cross of Calvary, and amid the thrilling scenes of the crucifixion—"to-day shalt THOU"—not some other newly-created spirit, but "THOU" crucified, penitent, dying companion in suffering—"be with me in paradise." Our dust returns to the earth, but "the spirit shall return unto God;" when the days of our years are "cut off" we do not become extinct, but "fly away;" the assassin may kill the body, but is "not able to kill the soul;" and as touching those called dead, "God is not the God of the dead, but of the living;" and "we know that if our earthly house of this tabernacle"—the body—"were dissolved," we do not cease to be, but are simply "absent from the body." And then that magnificent apocalyptic vision—"I saw under the altar the souls of them that were slain for the word of God, and for the testimony which they held; and they cried with a loud voice, saying: How long, O Lord! holy and true, dost thou not judge and avenge our blood on them that dwell on the earth?" A more explicit recognition of the conscious existence of the soul after the death of the body it would be difficult to embody in any form. The bodies of these martyrs had been slain; those bodies were still disunited from the soul; and yet there was not only conscious being, but conscious identity of themselves as the sufferers of wrong from wicked men.

It is useless to raise any quibble about the form or speech of disembodied souls. Such objectors only place their own ignorance in opposition to the boundless possibilities of the spiritual realm. We might have enumerated many additional proof-texts, but these are sufficient for full demonstration wherever the authority of the Bible is received.

It is not too much to say, then, that the suggestions and intimations of human reason concerning the indestructibility of mind, are fully authenticated and confirmed by the revelation of God. He who has implanted the instincts of immortality in the human soul has also confirmed its glorious heritage in his Word, and thus given him the double seal of immortality. *He is not the God of the dead, but of the living.*

VII. Objections and Concluding Remark.

With a notice of one or two objections, we close the present discussion.

1. *The objection to the immortality of mind is sometimes made that the mind apparently comes into life with the body, waxes into maturity with it, grows old with it, and dies with it.* The inference the skeptic would draw from this is that the mind also dies with the body. There is something striking—*ad captandum*—in this objection. It appeals to the common observation of life; and, at first view, seems to be sustained by the facts of human history. But, on closer observation, we shall find the facts of history fail to confirm it. The full vigor of body is often, perhaps generally, attained by the age of twenty-five or thirty; while the full vigor of intellect is rarely attained before the age of forty or fifty. Instances almost without number are constantly coming within our observation, in which there is a most vigorous growth of intellect when the body has already begun to decline with age. A single instance of gray hairs, and a debilitated body incasing a soul vigorous in all its mental and moral powers, is sufficient to demonstrate that this assumption is utterly untenable. And who has not seen such instances again and again?

Besides all that, we have already shown, from incontrovertible facts, that the most vigorous intellects are not unfrequently incumbered with weak and sickly bodies; nay, that even amidst the torpor of approaching death, the mind often retains its full vigor up to the very last moment of earthly existence. This analogy of the materialist—by which he would reason from the death of the body to the death of the mind—utterly fails in its essential links; and, therefore, however attractive and imposing in its enunciation, it is, when subjected to the rigid scrutiny of science and fact, found to be without conclusiveness or force.

2. *It is objected, again, that those punitive words, perish, destruction, and death, in the Bible indicate the utter annihilation of the living principle, and, therefore, contradict the doctrine that the mind is immortal.* The objector claims that when it is said, "Except ye repent, ye shall all likewise perish," (Luke xiii, 3,) and that the wicked "shall be punished with everlasting destruction," (2 Thess. i, 9,) and, also, that "the soul that sinneth it shall die," (Ecc. xiii, 20,) the objector claims that these and kindred passages imply that the souls thus condemned will be utterly annihilated, or absolutely cease to exist. This would indeed upset our doctrine of the soul's essential immortality by the will of God. But do the passages teach such a doctrine? do the words contain such a breadth of meaning?

No one will contend that such a meaning is necessarily deduced from any philological analysis of them. We have a short method, then, to take with the objector, and which will show how mistaken are his interpretations, and how groundless his assumptions: "Lord, save us: we perish," (Matt. viii, 25,) said the disciples, when trembling in apprehension, not of annihilation, but of drowning. "It can not be that a prophet perish out of Jerusalem," (Luke xiii, 33,) means nothing more, certainly, than being put to death. The prodigal exclaims, "I perish with hunger." (Luke xv, 17.) Our fastidious objector will hardly make more out of this than that the prodigal was in danger of dying with hunger; annihilation, evidently, did not enter into his thoughts.

So with suffering "destruction." It is not to be annihilated, but to be banished "from the presence of the Lord and the glory of his power." (2 Thess. i, 9.) When God makes complaint against his people, "O, Israel, thou hast destroyed thyself, but in me is thy help," (Hosea xiii, 9,) he can not mean that they had *annihilated themselves;* for what avail would it be to make promises of help to beings that had become utterly annihilated? What mockery to assume to address them even!

Still less reason for supposing the punishment of "death" implies the annihilation of the condemned; for "wherefore as by one man sin entered into the world, and death by sin; and so death passed upon all men, for that all have sinned." (Rom. v, 12.) If the objector chooses to take this in its full force, we do not see how he is to escape the utter annihilation of the race; but if he assumes that there is a "second death," not necessarily included in this, and which does imply annihilation, then let us see what light the Bible sheds upon the nature of this "second death." We are here told that "the fearful and unbelieving, and the abominable, and murderers, and whoremongers, and sorcerers, and idolaters, and all liars, shall have their part in the lake which burneth with fire and brimstone; which is the second death." (Rev. xxi, 8.) This certainly can not be annihilation; for into this lake are to be cast, as partakers of this second death, "the devil," and "the beast, and the false prophet," and "death and hell;" and they "shall be tormented day and night forever and ever." "The same shall drink of the wine of the wrath of God, which is poured out without mixture into the cup of his indignation; and he shall be tormented with fire and brimstone in the presence of the holy angels, and in the presence of the Lamb; and the smoke of their torment ascendeth up forever and ever; and they have no rest, day nor night.'

(Rev. xiv, 10, 11.) Surely this is something far different, and far more appalling, than extinction of being. They teach us that we must live on, and on, and on forever! that if lost no annihilation of being will ever come to relieve the soul of its agony, but that it shall continue to writhe amid the agonies of the second death, while the unending ages roll on.

3. *Finally, if the soul is to endure forever, its condition, in all the ages of the future, should deeply concern us now.* To this end should we seek the revelation of the life of God in the soul. "Everlasting progression and development are involved in our spiritual union by faith with and in him, who is Head over all. Mind answers to mind. Each of us must say, there was a time when I was not; but no man can say the time will ever come when he shall cease to be."

"Immortality o'ersweeps
All pains, all tears, all time, all fears—and peals
Like the eternal thunders of the deep
Into my ears this truth: THOU LIV'ST FOREVER!" BYRON.

Then may we close with the thrilling apostrophe of another to the soul: "Immortal spirit! let thy thoughts travel down the vale of coming ages, and view thyself still enduring, strong in the possession of eternal youth. Thou wilt then look around thee, and from the hights of eternity thou wilt see all the thrones, the kingdoms, the glories, the struggles, and the pains of earth forever vanished and still. Thou wilt seek in vain to behold from afar the wondrous triumphs of art, the renowned cities, the illustrious empires, and the fields of blood, where so much glory was won. The greatness of the mighty dead, and the pomp of the now living, will all have passed away, sunken into one promiscuous and eternal grave. The earth itself may revolve darkly and gloomily in its accustomed orbit; widely-spread solitude and desolation may pervade its once crowded scenes; but thou wilt still remain exempt from mutability and death; still enduring amid so much change, undying amid so much decay. No fearful disaster can quench thy torch of being; no lapse of ages diminish the freshness of thy youth! As lasting as the God who made thee, thou and He alike will outlive the old age and dissolution of the universe itself, and soar above its crumbling ruins, rejoicing in the progression of an endless and deathless duration!"

VII.

DEATH.

"In the day that thou eatest thereof thou shalt surely die." GEN. ii, 17.
"Death by sin." ROM. v, 12.
"It is appointed unto men once to die." HEB. ix, 27.
"The body without the spirit is dead." JAMES ii, 26.

DEATH is a word pregnant with mysteries past conception, and with terrors past repression. It was first uttered in Paradise, conveying to the mind of man an elemental idea terrific in its character as it has become all-pervading in its influence. We discourse largely and loosely of change as one of the laws governing all created things; but this is not merely *change;* it is DEATH. The dread of death is as natural as it is universal. Like an appalling specter, it haunts every pathway of life and dims every vision of joy. O, Death! thou art indeed "the King of Terrors!"

> "The tear,
> The groan, the knell, the pall, the bier,
> And all we know, or dream, or fear
> Of agony, are thine!"

What would have been the physical history of man had he never sinned it is not easy to determine. It is supposed by some that he would have enjoyed the privilege of continued existence and happiness on earth. The tree of life, to which he would have had access, was at once a pledge of permanent being and happiness, and also a means of securing them. The fruit of this tree would, undoubtedly, have healed or averted every evil to which our physical nature might have been subject; it would have restored the natural waste of the animal system, now imperfectly restored by food and sleep, and preserved life through the longest periods of duration.

Or, again, there is nothing inconsistent in the supposition that man might have enjoyed a long life here; and after a long series of years, when the faculties of his body and mind had acquired earthly maturity, by an easy transition, he might have been transferred to a holier clime, to pass through higher scenes of bliss, in his endless progression toward infinite perfection and happiness. How easy might have been the change! how glorious the transition! What unspeakable felicities would have enraptured the soul as every successive change brought it into nearer progression to the exhaustless Fountain of Goodness and Love!

Man was evidently designed to fill a still more exalted sphere in the scale of being than that allotted to him here. Perhaps the race were designed to fill up the vacancy occasioned in heaven by that disastrous rebellion which peopled hell with angels. Can we wonder, then, that beings designed to fill up so glorious a place in the scale of existence should first have their faith and obedience tried, and their habits and characters formed, in a probationary state? But a probation implies a law, inasmuch as there can be no trial, no probation, without a system of discipline and government. A law also implies a prohibition and a penalty. If, then, man was designed to fill up the vacancy in heaven occasioned by the fall of angels, and if he was placed under a law in his probationary state, can we wonder that to a violation of that law was affixed the same penalty which the fallen angels were themselves enduring? Thus it was that when man was created and planted in the garden, which was to be the scene of his probation, the Divine law was given, and the fearful penalty was affixed, "Of the tree of knowledge of good and evil, thou shalt not eat of it; for in the day thou eatest thereof thou shalt surely die." The violation of this command commenced a course of sinning and disobedience that blotted out the glories of our first Eden, and plunged our race from a sphere of exaltation and glory into one of suffering and ruin. Death, then, has become a part of the history of an immortal being.

I. The Sentence of Death.

The sentence of death for sin is expressed in these words: "Thou shalt surely die;" or, more literally, "dying, thou shalt die." This form of expression is peculiar and emphatic, denoting not only the absolute certainty of the punishment denounced, but also the gradual completion of it. "Dying, thou shalt die." In that day thou shalt become incurably mortal; thou shalt gradually but certainly die; all thy days shalt thou be tending to dissolution and death, without the possibility of escape or remedy. This sentence is literally fulfilled upon our race; for "as by one man sin entered into the world, and death by sin; so death passed upon all men, for that all have sinned."

How wide and universal is the dominion death has established! The dark insignia of his power are every-where seen, and wherever living man peoples the earth there are to be found the monuments of his triumphs. No individual can stay his progress or elude his search. From the midst of the populous city and from the lonely glen; from the abode of luxury and from the hovel of poverty; from the bustling scenes of crowded life and from the lounging ranks of ease and idleness, he calls forth his victims to their appointed doom. No one may hope to escape. From the cradle to the grave the monster follows our footsteps with stealthy but steady strides, so that, literally, "dying, we die!"

II. Essential Nature of Death.

We have noticed the sentence of death and the universality of its execution. We have seen man every-where surrounded by the dark and gloomy symbols; we have seen him with the dread sentence, "Thou shalt surely die!" pealing evermore in his ear, and breaking, with its solemn cadences, upon his soul. What, then, is *the essential nature of this physical death?*

It is something more than pain and suffering. We almost daily meet with cases of excruciating bodily distress, when every nerve seems wrought up with intensest agony, but death is not the result. The individual recovers. But, on the other hand, the "silver cord is loosened," sometimes so gently that it is impossible to mark the moment of departure. Indeed, suffering belongs to life; to death, quietude.

It is something more than the exhaustion and emaciation of sickness; for the victim of disease that has pined into the most shadowy form—in which nearly all that is material is wasted and gone—has yet come back to life, and glowed with all the ruddiness of youth and health. Another, in the maturity of his manhood, with the flush of health upon his cheek, the marrow of fatness in his bones, sinks down suddenly without external sign or internal premonition, and is gone.

The arms and the legs have been severed from the body, and the trunk has even suffered mutilation, till almost the very form of humanity was lost; yet life still remained—intellect, affection, and hope survived. So, also, the sight, the hearing, the taste, the smell, and even the sense of feeling, in a large portion of the body, has been lost, and yet neither of these privations constituted death. The whole limbs and body have been paralyzed, even up to the neck, by injury to the spine, and yet something beyond all that must occur before it could be said that the individual was dead. We have already seen that even the brain, the mind's own peculiar organ, may be extensively diseased, and yet life remain. Even respiration, and with it all bodily motion, have, apparently, ceased for days. Few, if any, signs of life remained; yet it was trance, and not death. Death is something beyond all these.

What, then, is death? The answer is so pertinently given by a modern writer that we quote him *in extenso.* He says: "Death is the absolute cessation of all that which makes matter the instrument and dwelling not only of the spirit which is in man, but of the life or animating power which is in brutes, and of the vital operation which is in vegetables, and even of the cohesion which united the particles of the body. A dead body has ceased to have any existence of its own; the merest stone has more; every moment carries off some of its atoms, till all have joined the surrounding elements, so far as the process can be traced by the human eye or by science. The particles of stone adhere to one another till they are forcibly driven asunder or are separated by chemical action; the particles of the human body, after death, fall asunder of themselves, or through the chemistry of nature.

"But the stone has no life, and there is life in the flower or shrub—life from that great vital stream which pervades the universe, but a life simply passive—a similar life to that which carries on the involuntary operations of the human frame, and in death this life, too, is removed. Digestion, absorption, secretion, circulation are, as it were, the vegetable parts of man; the power which gives them action returns at death into the general current of natural operations, from which it has been set apart in his person. The brute has a still higher life. He is conscious of the vital stream; he feels, acts, resists, consents, dimly remembers, almost reasons. His is the same life which in man performs these various operations; so that, in certain states, when they are performed in the least measure, as in infancy, in idiocy, or when the brain has been grievously injured, little more is seen in man than in the inferior animals. In death the senses go out, even the corporeal machinery comes to an utter pause; and this animal life, too, passes from our sight and from its habitation.

"That highest life of all; that which belongs to man alone, among all visible creatures; that life of the spirit which makes him capable of speech, and thus of distinct thought; which makes him a moral being, and therefore responsible to his Maker; that life returns not to the dust, nor to the current of vital power which animates plants or brutes, for it came not from those sources. But it disappears like the rest; this moment it is here, perhaps as clear, as vigorous as ever; the next we gaze upon that which has neither power, nor sensibility, nor expression, and which is as far below the meanest living things as it was lately exalted above them.

"The dissolution of the body, the withdrawal of the vital principle, the departure of the immortal spirit—this is DEATH."

III. Process and Symptoms of Dying.

It is generally admitted by physiologists that different portions of the body die in succession. And this accords with the common observation of the dying process. Prof. Draper says* that the system of animal life dies before that of organic. Of the former, the sensory functions fail first,

*Human Physiology.

voluntary motion next, and that the power of muscular contraction under external stimulus still feebly continues. "The blood, in gradual death, first ceases to reach the extremities, its pulsations becoming less and less energetic, so that, failing to gain the periphery, it passes but a little way from the heart; the feet and the hands become cold as the circulating fluid leaves them, the decline of temperature gradually invading the interior." Some of the organic functions often continue for a time, particularly the secretion and the development of heat.

Hippocrates's description of the appearance and acts of the dying man has rarely been equaled, and never been surpassed, by any descriptions of modern physiologists. It is remarkable for its antiquity, for its descriptive particularity, and also as showing that the heritage of dying man has been the same in all ages. For these reasons we give it entire: "If the patient lies on his back, his arms stretched out, and his legs hanging down, it is a sign of great weakness; when he slides down into the bed it denotes death; if, in a burning fever, he is continually feeling about with his hands and his fingers, and moves them up before his face and eyes, as if he was going to take away something before them, or on his bed-covering, as if he were picking or searching for little straws, or taking away some speck, or drawing out little flocks of wool, all this is a sign that he is delirious, and that he will die. When his lips hang relaxed and cold; when he can not bear the light; when he sheds tears involuntarily; when in dozing some part of the white of the eye is seen, unless he usually sleeps in that manner, these signs prognosticate danger. When his eyes are sparkling, fierce, and fixed, he is delirious, or soon will be so; when they are deadened, as it were, with a mist spread over them, or their brightness lost, it presages death or great weakness. When the patient has his nose sharp, his eyes sunk, his temples hollow, his ears cold and contracted, the skin of his forehead tense and dry, and the color of his face tending to a pale-green or leaden tint, one may give out for certain that death is very near, unless the strength of the patient has been exhausted all at once by long watchings, or by a looseness, or being a long time without eating."

A writer in the London Quarterly gives one or two striking thoughts not expressed above. He says: "Startling likenesses to relations and the self of former days are sometimes revealed when the wasting of the flesh has given prominence to the frame-work of the face. The cold of death seizes upon the extremities, and continues to spread—a sign of common notoriety from time immemorial, which Chaucer has described in verse, and Shakspeare in still more picturesque prose. The very breath strikes chill; the skin is clammy; the voice falters and loses its own familiar tones—grows sharp and thin, or faint and murmuring, or comes with an unearthly, muffled sound. The pulse, sometimes previously deceitful, breaks down—is first feeble, then slower; the beats are fitful and broken by pauses; the intervals increase in frequency and duration, and at length it falls to rise no more. The respiration, whether languid or labored, becomes slow at the close; the death-rattle is heard at every expulsion of air; the lungs, like the pulse, become intermittent in their action; a minute or two may elapse between the effort to breathe, and then one expiration, which has made 'to expire' synonymous with 'to die,' and the conflict with the body is over."

IV. The Terribleness of Death.

Death derives it terribleness not exclusively from causes moral. God has implanted an instinctive love of life in every creature he has made. The counterpart of this is an instinctive dread of death; and this feeling we share in common with the animal creation. Nature instinctively shudders and startles back at the approach of death. This is not a feeling peculiar to our fallen state. It pertains to our humanity. In its first announcement, while yet a simple. elementary, unrealized idea, death was placed as a terror before the minds of our first parents, while yet sin had not subjected them to its dominion; and from that time forth, through all ages, and among all people, death has been the symbol of terror and dread.

Its dread attendants make it terrible—the cold death-sweat, the quivering, failing pulse, the darkened vision, the dying agony, and the utter stillness, helplessness, and rapid decay of the body from which life has departed, never fail to inspire dread. Death is appalling when viewed only as the separation of the soul from the body. This mysterious blending of our physical and spiritual natures, this union of matter and mind, seems here to constitute our very being. All we have enjoyed of life, our intercourse with the world, all the social intimacies, relationships, and endearments of life have come to us through and by virtue of this mysterious union. The separation of these elements, the bursting asunder of this bond of our being, leaving the body a lifeless wreck, a despoiled and wasted ruin, while the spirit departs to regions and to scenes unknown, can not be realized without a pang. No darkness of superstition, no gloom of skepticism, can so cloud the very instincts of our being but that a tremulous anxiety will be awakened by an occasion so momentous; while we behold the one element of our nature a "blackened ruin," stricken down in the dust, the other, a trembling, flying fugitive, seems to be escaping away from us, we know not whither.

But death is appalling, also, when looked upon as sundering the ties of human life, and breaking us off from all the scenes and interests of the present world. To think of bidding an everlasting farewell to earthly friends; to think of mingling no more in the social scenes of life—of closing the eye forever upon the light of day, upon the glory of the earth, the grandeur of the heavens; of listening no more to the sweet accents of affection, or the sweet melodies of nature; nay, to look upon ourselves as the silent, lonely tenants of the grave—the gloom of our habitation cheered by no companionships save such as make the grave terrible; its darkness relieved by no ray of light, its solemn silence broken by no sound; to think of its gloomy solitude, its festering corruption, the rioting of worms in the dark caverns of the dead; to think of its chilling, freezing cold, from which no protection is given, the cold rain dripping down through the loosened earth above us, making damp the dismal bed where we slumber! Alas! these are the things that make death and the grave terrible. The scenes of life will go on in their accustomed course; childhood and youth, joyous and happy, shall sport along the streets and gambol over the fields, treading upon the very dust above us, unconscious of our doom. The festive board shall witness the gathering of friends, but we shall no more be numbered among them; the current of human affairs will roll onward, but we shall be unmoved by the contending emotions, the hopes and fears, joys and sorrows now felt by the living mass. What a gloomy, appalling spectacle does the grave present! It is truly "the land of darkness and the shadow of death; a land of darkness, as darkness itself; and of the shadow of death, without any order, and where the light is as darkness."

But, to one that has no hope in the future, it is armed with tenfold terror; to him that knows only of this life, it is an exile to all that he holds dear forever. It is the withering of all his hopes, it is the blighting and destroying of all his expectations. Darkness is above, and around, and before him, and there is no light! Alas! what can silence the remorse, what can alleviate the pangs of a dying hour! But the dread of impending ruin, the consciousness of being unprepared to stand before the final Judge, fills the soul with anguish and dismay. Do they look back upon the past, its long catalogue of unpardoned sins rises up to haunt their vision and terrify their imagination! Every sin is recorded, and now stands out with fearful distinctness, shaded with the dark hues of moral death. Do they look forward? Ah! the prospect is too appalling for them to contemplate. In the language of the wretched, dying Altamont, they "turn, and turn, and find no ray!" How awfully is realized in the death of the sinner that impressive truth, *The wicked is driven away in his wickedness, and the wrath of God abideth on him!* O, "my soul! come not thou into their secret; and unto their assembly, mine honor, be not thou united."

V. Moral Ends or Uses of these Terrors.

But we are led to inquire again, Why, for what purpose, has death been clothed with such terrors? In this allotment, is there not an unnecessary severity on the part of God? Death may have been a just and righteous sentence, but might not some of its terrors been spared? Nay, if we consider the nature of man and the condition of society, we shall soon discover that these terrors are absolutely necessary, in order to the proper government of the world.

The terrors of death are the great guardians of life. They excite the desire of self-preservation; they prompt us to undergo with alacrity the labors necessary to the support of life; tney restrain from those sinful indulgences and pleasures to which we are prone, and which would break down our health and destroy our lives; they lead us to suffer the ills of life and bear its calamities with patience and fortitude, rather than dare the terrors that are attendant upon the approach of death. How many of the wretched sons of men have been led, like Hamlet, to ponder

> "Whether 'tis nobler in the mind to suffer
> The stings and arrows of outrageous fortune,
> Or to take arms against a sea of troubles
> And, by opposing, end them? . . .
> But that the dread of something after death,
> That undiscovered country, from whose bourne
> No traveler returns, puzzles the will;
> And makes rather bear those ills we have,
> Than fly to others that we know not of."

How often has the hand of the suicide been arrested by those appalling terrors that cluster so thickly around the sad hour of a mortal's departure! how many have been checked from giving up to despondency and gloom, and rushing where their fortunes would be irretrievable, when those fortunes have afterward changed and disclosed a brighter sky!

Again, as a safeguard to society, these terrors have their moral uses. Were death not dreaded as it is, no public order could be preserved in the world. The wicked and desperate would trample upon all law and all government; the sword of authority would be shorn of its power; the gibbet and the scaffold would cease to awaken dread. If society is so often now disturbed, and human and divine laws so often trampled in the dust, what would be the result if the awful penalties with which they are robed were taken away? We are, then, persuaded that death is not unnecessarily armed with terrors; that its dark valley has not been planted so thick with them for no wise or beneficent end. Its first view, perhaps, seemed to arraign and bring into question the goodness of the Deity; but, on closer inspection, we find these terrors as indispensable to the economy of his goodness as to his justice. And till man's moral character is changed, thoroughly, radically changed, there can be no safety in the removal of such a check to vice and the indulgence of unrestrained passion; such removal would be a curse and not a blessing. Nor does this dread, as we shall soon have occasion to show, exist any longer than is necessary to accomplish its benevolent designs.

VI. Philosophy Unable to Remove these Terrors.

But we must notice that philosophy has never been able to remove these terrors. This has been one of the great aims of its discipline, and yet rarely, in the whole range of human experience, has a death-bed scene been exhibited that even philosophy has claimed as being philosophical. Brutal insensibility—nay, even trifling levity—have sometimes marked the dying hour, but it was an unnatural effort, like that of the wretched maniac, whose wild, hollow laugh rings out from some mountain crag, just as the victim plunges down the abyss of ruin and death.

But listen to the voice of reason; hear the arguments of philosophy; tell their sum, consider their amount. She will urge that death is the condition on which you have received life, a debt you must pay; it is the law of your being, an inevitable fate; it is the ordering of that Divine Providence that controls our destinies, therefore we ought cheerfully to submit to our fate. Again, she would urge that every thing else and every individual is mortal and perishing—why should you repine when yours is only a common, a universal doom? The very face of nature is subject to perpetual change; kingdoms and cities pass away; the most durable monuments of art crumble to dust; the great and the good, as well as the low and the vile, all come to one common end. The grave is the home appointed for all the living; nay, at the very moment when your flesh is wasting, your soul departing, thousands all over the wide earth are experiencing the same agony, realizing the same doom. Why, then, do you complain? and why should you seek or desire exemption from that which is universal, which nature has appointed to all?

Again, philosophy would urge that the pain of death is of short duration, and that we often suffer more bodily anguish in attacks from which we recover than is experienced in the process of death; much of the apparent agony of the dying hour is only in appearance, and that, therefore, death is not to be so greatly dreaded. Again, it would urge that the very passions of our nature have triumphed over the fear of death; honor has defied it, shame has sought it as a refuge, and grief has longed for its approach. How much more, then, it would plead, ought reason and philosophy to rise above this pusillanimous, unmanly fear! Again, it would reason, is there not an inconsistency in complaining so much of the evils of life and yet dreading to be released from them? And, again, can it be desirable to protract a life that must be attended with infirmity and pain, with the decay of all the intellectual as well as the sensitive powers, with the loss of friends and of worldly enjoyments? Rather would there not be greater reason to complain if life should be thus protracted? And then, again, it would urge that the fear of death can do us no good; therefore it becomes us, like wise men, to dismiss it, and not let it destroy the comfort of life, nor mar the enjoyments a kind Providence has allotted to our present state. Let us yield to Nature. She knows what is best for us; she will guide us to the fulfillment of our destiny.

Such are the arguments with which reason would assuage the fears of death, prop up the mind, and give it courage in the dying hour. They deserve to be considered well; they are the highest comfort reason can afford, and they are not without their force. But they will do better when we are calmly speculating about Death, as seen in the distance, than when the grim monster, with all his terrors, stands before us with his dread summons to call us away. Alas! in that solemn hour, the agonizing soul cries out for something more, something higher, more substantial, to dissipate its fears and sustain its fluttering spirit as it goes down into the dark valley of the shadow of death. Reason fails, philosophy staggers and reels, unrelieved terrors fill the soul with anguish and horror. Then religion is indispensable; then faith and hope are indispensable; then the soul must hang upon its Creator and Redeemer for support; and only when he feels that the Divine arm is round about him can he exclaim, in holy triumph, "I will fear no evil!"

VII. Higher Agencies in Death.

It is the glory of Christianity that it brings to light higher agencies than earthly philosophy or human reason in death. Though the Christian is enabled to triumph over its fear, his triumph does not by any means result from a disrelish of life or of its blessings. He may have as high an appreciation of the blessings of this life, and as keen a relish for its enjoyments, as the unrenewed man; he may be yet in the bloom of youth and life, with all its inviting scenes spread out before him; he is surrounded by friends, cheered with bright prospects, and ardent in the hope of an honorable and useful career; the strong and tender ties of nature, its high and holy responsibilities, may exert powerful influences upon his mind, and render his longer stay on earth desirable. The dying child might wish to live still longer, to soothe and comfort the declining years of decrepit and afflicted parents. The dying mother may find her very heart yearning in its tenderness over the innocent prattlers around her, so soon to be bereft of care so much needed, so soon to be cast out, perhaps, upon the cold charities of the world. The minister of the Gospel, as, from the spiritual watch-towers of Zion, he looks out over the world, surveys its wickedness and wretchedness, beholds the multitudes that are thronging the road to perdition, may desire longer to live, to proclaim, with the fervor of one raised from the dead, the everlasting Gospel. The Christian's triumph, then, does not result from any disrelish of life—not from any want of attachments to life or objects for which to live. It results not even from any conviction that it is by God's special providence or will that he is called to die *now*. His disease may have been occasioned by some imprudence, some want of care, which, though permitted by God, and, no doubt, overruled by him for good, does not warrant the belief that it is God's will that he should now die. No, the sources of the Christian's triumph lie deeper than any of these.

1. In the first place, this triumph results from the removal of those causes which render death terrible. "The sting of death is sin." Never was truer sentence uttered. Sin pollutes the soul, brings guilt and condemnation, robs us of our faith, and then leaves us a prey to remorse, stricken with the terrors of coming retribution. Restore to us our moral and spiritual purity bring back our lost faith in the Redeemer, and then to lie down in death would be attended with as few terrors as when we lie down

to a night's repose. "Thanks be unto God that giveth us the victory through our Lord Jesus Christ!"

> "This, only this, subdues the fear of death;
> And what is this?—survey the wondrous cure;
> And at each step let higher wonder rise!
> Pardon for infinite offense! . . .
> A pardon bought with blood! with blood divine!"

Said the distinguished Christian philosopher and physician, Mr. Gordon, who was led through many conflicts into the light of Christian experience, "I reasoned, and debated, and investigated, but I found no peace till I came to the Gospel as a little child, till I received it as a babe. Then such a light was shed abroad in my heart that I saw the whole scheme at once. I saw my sinfulness in all its vivid deformity, and found there was no acceptance with God, and no happiness, except through the blessed Redeemer. I stripped off all my own deeds, went to him naked; he received me according to his promise; then I felt joy unspeakable, and *all fear of death at once vanished!*" Well may the Christian say,

> "If sin be pardoned, I'm secure,
> Death has no sting beside;
> The law gives sin its damning power,
> But Christ, my Savior, died."

2. Again: the Christian's triumph results from the conviction that no harm can come to him while passing through the dark valley. He rests upon the promises of his God, and they, firm as the eternal rock, are the unfailing support of his soul. "Fear not; for I have redeemed thee, I have called thee by thy name; thou art mine. When thou passest through the waters, I will be with thee; and through the rivers, they shall not overflow thee." (Isa. xliii, 2.) "The righteous hath hope in his death;" "he is taken away from the evil to come;" his end "is peace." "Precious in the sight of the Lord is the death of his

saints." "Blessed are the dead which die in the Lord from henceforth; yea, saith the Spirit, that they may rest from their labors, and their works do follow them." "There the wicked cease from troubling and the weary are at rest. There the prisoners rest together; they hear not the voice of the oppressor." All these promises to the Christian are ratified and sealed by the death of Christ. Even he has "tasted death," and through death has triumphed over death and the grave.

"The graves of all his saints he blest,
And soften'd every bed;
Where should the dying members rest
But with their dying Head?"

"Thou art with me, thy rod and thy staff, they comfort me." Such was the faith of the Psalmist, as he looked down, through the long lapse of more than a thousand years, to a crucified Redeemer, seen only through the dim types of the law, and the darkly-uttered, distant promise. Yet so clear was his spiritual vision, so strong his faith, that he forgets all intervening time, and, in the fullness of his joy, cries out, *Thou art with me!* No such burden is imposed upon us. We behold a Redeemer, not merely through the type, the shadow, the promise, but through all these fulfilled. How strong, then, in the faith ought we to be! how joyous in confidence, giving glory to God! "Thou art with me." The Christian goes not alone. His Divine Shepherd, with his friendly crook and his spear of defense, goes with him down through the dark valley, and hides from him the fear of evil. I wonder not at his triumph; I wonder not that with his expiring breath he cries out, "I will fear no evil!"

"O would my Lord his servant meet!
My soul would stretch her wings in haste,
Fly fearless through death's iron gate,
Nor feel the terrors as she passed."

3. Again: the Christian triumphs in death, because he looks upon it as the termination of present trials and sorrows, and the gateway that shall conduct him to endless joy. Here ends his weary pilgrimage, and from the summit of Pisgah he looks out over the glorious land of his inheritance. A traveler in the East, speaking of a caravan of great length, traveling from the East to Jerusalem, says that, after climbing over the extended and heavy ranges of hills that bounded their way, often obstructing their passage and making it toilsome and difficult, some of the foremost in the train at length reached the top of the last hill, and when the long-sought object broke upon their vision, throwing up their hands with joyful exclamations, they cried out, "The Holy City! the Holy City!" and fell down and worshiped, while those behind pressed forward to behold the glorious sight. So the dying Christian, when he gets to the last rugged summit of life, and from that hight beholds the glory beyond—the celestial city glittering with the beams of everlasting light—he cries out, with the departing Payson, "I am going to Mount Zion, to the city of the living God, to the heavenly Jerusalem, to an innumerable company of angels, to the general assembly and Church of the first-born, and to God the Judge of all!" or, with Risden Darracott, "I am going from weeping friends to congratulate angels and rejoicing saints in heaven! Blessed be God! all is well! all is well!"

Life is a season of toil, of conflict, and of danger. It is a tempestuous ocean. Thousands have been already stranded upon its shores, while only here and there a wayworn, tempest-tossed, and weather-beaten mariner has gained the everlasting coast, and entered the port of bliss. Such is the day of death to the child of God. Struggling in the midst of life's tempestuous ocean, beset with veering winds and changing tides—with sky perhaps clouded and obscure—thus driven by fierce winds and tossed by raging waves, the desired haven is seen dimly in the distance, and the soul struggles on, sometimes doubtful whether it shall ever reach the port; just then the tempest is hushed, the clouds are parted, the sun beams forth, and a sound like the deep melodies of an angel's song fills the vast expanse:

"Servant of God, well done!
Thy glorious warfare 's past,
The battle 's fought, the race is won,
And thou art crowned at last."

All uncertainty about its destiny now ceases; heaven is sure and God is sure; and while "the everlasting doors are lifted up," the ransomed spirit enters its blissful abode—joins the angelic throng amid the welcomes of glorified spirits, flames in robes of living light, seizes the golden harp and strikes up the eternal anthem, "Unto him that loved us and washed us in his own blood, to him be majesty and dominion, honor and glory, forever and ever!"

Our souls, lonely and sorrowing, sometimes yearn to call back to earth the loved ones that have passed away from us; but is it not our *selfishness* rather than our love that could desire their return? Why should we wish to call them away? why would we expose them again to dangers from which they have so surely escaped to toils and sorrows from which heaven has already granted them release? O, no! we would not call you back. Shine on in your brightness, ye blessed of the Lord! Alone will we willingly bear the burdens and sorrows of life; and when death the mighty day of deliverance draws near, with the light of heaven illuminating the soul, and the smile of triumph brightening every feature, we will welcome its approach and hasten again to enjoy the light of your countenance more heavenly, and to witness again your affection more pure and exalted.

4. Still another and a final reason for the Christian's triumph is, that dying grace is given in a dying hour.

It is the almost universal experience of the righteous, that as death draws near, much as it may have been dreaded before, it loses much of the gloom which makes it terrible to the living. This triumph is no result of natural constitution, of established habit, nor even of strenuous effort; for those who possess least of constitutional courage or philosophical firmness often go down into the dark valley with the most complete triumph over all their past fears and misgivings. I knew a female, naturally timid, distrustful of her Christian experience. For many years she had been a child of affliction, and had often been brought down to the gates of death, and on such occasions her natural timidity often occasioned her the greatest distress. It was with her an almost constant dread and fear that when death came she would be unable to endure the conflict. The dying day at length approached; her friends trembled to break to her the melancholy truth; but, feeling that it must be done, they at length informed her that she was in a dying state, and that it was the opinion of her physician that she could hold out but a few hours longer. In a moment her whole countenance was overspread with a most heavenly expression, her eye beamed with unearthly luster, and her tongue broke forth in the language of triumph and praise. When reminded of her former doubts and fears, she reproached herself most bitterly, exclaiming, "O, that I could ever have distrusted the goodness of God and the power of religion! that I could have ever been so unbelieving as to have questioned the faithfulness of the Divine promises, and the power of Divine grace to sustain me in the dying hour!" Thus triumphing in God, rejoicing in his presence, she continued encouraging and exhorting her friends, till at length casting up her glance, as if to greet some heavenly messenger, her spirit took its flight to join the millions of the redeemed.

It might not be possible, with our spiritual ignorance and darkness, to point out all the Divine agencies employed in bringing about this glorious result of the Christian's triumph. In the first place, the mind is, no doubt, divinely prepared, and the fulfillment of the promise, "as thy day is so shalt thy grace be," is realized. The excellent Sir William Forbes, when dying, said to surrounding friends, "Tell those that are drawing down to the bed of death, from my experience, that it has no terrors; that in the hour when it is most wanted there is mercy with the Most High, and that some change takes place which fits the soul to meet its God." Another of the Divine agencies employed in producing this result may be the more abundant infusion of the Holy Spirit, and a clearer consciousness of the presence and favor of Christ. And, again, who shall deny that ministering spirits are sent down from heaven to watch around the dying couch of the Christian, and to convey his ransomed spirit home to God? When are ministering spirits more needed than when we walk through the dark valley? They gathered around the dying Lazarus, and carried him to rest in Abraham's bosom; and so do they hover around the dying Christian, unseen by mortal eyes, unheard by mortal ears, breathing heavenly influence, shedding holy light upon the scene! A dying infant scholar, of heavenly sweetness and temper, just at the moment of death, looked up, with a joyous expression of countenance, and raising her little hands, as though she would greet the heavenly messengers, cried out, "The angels have come!" and expired. Dr. Bateman, a distinguished physician and philosopher, cried out, "What glory! the angels are waiting for me!"

And here a thought comes in, upon which we may speculate for a moment. Among these "ministering spirits,' who would be more ready to run to our relief, to hover around our dying bed, and to welcome our disinthralled spirit than the dear friends and kindred of earth who have gone before us to God? Is there any thing inconsistent in the idea that they too come down to greet us as we cross the Jordan of death? The mother that watched over us, the sister of our love, the prattling child that passed from our sight, may come down to greet us at the swellings of Jordan, and welcome us to the partnership of their joy. And is it not something more than the mere glow of the imagination which recognizes the presence of the dear departed at the moment of death?

But no one can doubt that to the Christian a clearer insight into spiritual things is given in the hour of death. Heaven was opened to the vision of the dying Stephen, and not to him alone, but to many a saint of God in all ages. Dr. M'Lain, while expiring, said, "I can now contemplate clearly the grand scene to which I am going." The pious Blumhardt cried out, "Light breaks in! Halleluiah!" and expired. Sargent, the biographer of Henry Martyn, with his countenance kindled into a holy fervor, and his eye beaming with unearthly luster, fixed his gaze as upon a definite object, and exclaimed, "That bright light!" and when asked what light, answered, "The light of the Sun of Righteousness!" Dr. Payson, whose spiritual conflicts had been many and severe, writing to his sister, just before his death, said, "I might date this letter from the land of Beulah, of which I have been some weeks a happy inhabitant. The celestial city is full in view. Its glories beam upon me; its breezes fan me; its odors are wafted to me; its sounds strike upon my ears, and its spirit is breathed into my heart. Nothing separates me from it but the river of death, which now appears but an insignificant rill that may be crossed at a single step. The Sun of Righteousness has been gradually drawing nearer and nearer, appearing larger and brighter as he approached, and now he fills the whole hemisphere, pouring forth a flood of glory, in which I seem to float like an insect in the beams of the sun, exulting, yet almost trembling, while I gaze upon this excessive brightness, and wondering with unutterable wonder why God should design thus to shine upon a sinful worm."

> "The chamber where the good man meets his fate
> Is privileged beyond the common walk
> Of virtuous life, quite on the verge of heaven.
> Heaven waits not the last moment, owns its friends
> On this side death, and points them out to men—
> A lecture silent—but of sovereign power—
> To vice confusion, and to virtue peace."

Such is the character and such the resources of the Christian's triumph! Such are the circumstances that clothe with moral sublimity the closing scene of his mortal career! "Let me die the death of the righteous; and let my last end be like his."

How infinitely valuable and desirable is that religion which can give such divine support in a dying hour! It comes here to meet us in our greatest extremity. When the world is fading from our view, when friends weep in vain, when no light of science can illuminate our pathway or direct our steps, it comes and sheds a heavenly radiance over the scene. It gives security while passing through the dark valley of death, and unvails eternal glory to the mortal vision. Through this may we exclaim, "O Death! where is thy sting? O Grave! where is thy victory?" Let disease waste and destroy, let pain rack and dismay, let youth and beauty fade—yea, let the grave open its jaws, let the cold clods fall upon the lifeless dust; but, borne aloft and sustained by Divine power, cherished by the presence of Christ his Redeemer, the Christian may exclaim, "I will fear no evil!" Nay, to the Christian death is gain. From the bed of infirmity and pain he goes to an immortal crown. Can we wonder, then, that he should *have a desire to depart and be with Christ, which is far better?*

"Death is the crown of life!
It wounds to cure; we fall, we rise, we reign!
Spring from our fetters, fasten in the skies,
Where blooming Eden withers in our sight.
Death gives us more than was in Eden lost;
This King of Terrors was the Prince of Peace."

VIII. Last Moments and Dying Words of Distinguished Men.

"The tongues of dying men
Enforce attention like deep harmony;
Where words are scarce, they 're seldom spent in vain,
For they breathe truth, that breathe their words in pain."

So sang Shakspeare, the great poet of human nature. The dying words of men have always attracted attention, and have been treasured by friends as something sacred. The solemn hour of death usually subdues the worldly feelings and passions, and induces men to look soberly upon the circumstances of the present and the prospects of the future.

"A death-bed 's a detecter of the heart;
Here real and apparent are the same."

There are, however, different degrees of mental supremacy in dissolution even among cultivated men, owing, often, to the differences in moral character, and not unfrequently to the nature of the disease or to some peculiarity of circumstance. Let the moralist inquire, if he will, *how a man has lived*, but all feel a curiosity, whether they will confess it or not, to know how a man dies.

Nor is this a mere matter of empty curiosity. These

dying words have for us lessons of deep significance. What a moral grandeur gathers around the death-scene of the great and good of earth when sanctified by a religious faith, and how fearful the contrast when the departing spirit leaves the world all unprepared, unaneled, unblessed, with all the terrible premonitions of a coming judgment!

An eloquent modern writer says: "Life's last hours are grand testing hours. Death tries all our principles and lays bare all our foundation. Vast numbers have been found to act the hypocrite in life who were forced to be honest in the hour of death. What atheists have owned their principles, what worldlings have bewailed their folly, when death approached! Misgivings of the heart, that have been kept secret through life, have come out in death, and many who seemed all right and fair for heaven have had to declare that they had only been self-deceived. It has been said 'man may not dissemble in death,' hence the value of dying testimonies. We gather the last words, the last acts, the last experiences, and we treasure them up as indubitable evidences in favor or against the character of those that wore their value as tests of character, and all have felt their force."

An illustration of the boldness of the man sustained by Christian foresight is found in the last hours of George Buchanan, "the ornament of Scottish literature." When in a dying condition, King James summoned him to appear before the court in twenty days. He sent in reply these words: "Before the days mentioned by your Majesty shall be expired, I shall be in that place where few kings enter."

When the poet Goethe, after more than the usually-allotted term of human existence, was met by the summons, it found him still busy with the pen, the implement at once of his pleasure and his power, and he sank as a child, who, with the glow of the day's activity still on his cheek, looking forward to a morrow of hope and joy, folds himself to sleep. "*Let the light enter!*" were his last words, "echoed, we may suppose," says his biographer, "from a region where all is light."*

Sir Walter Raleigh, being asked by the sheriff which way he chose to place himself upon the block, answered, "So the heart be right, it is no matter which way the head lies."

The last words of Nelson were, "Tell Collingwood to bring the fleet to anchor." Sir Thomas More, mounting the scaffold, said, "I pray you to see me up safe; and for my coming down, let me shift for myself." Frederick V of Denmark said, in his last moments, "It is a great consolation to me in my last hour that there is not a drop of blood on my hands." The Earl of Roscommon, when about to die, uttered, with great energy, these two lines of his *Dies Irae:*

> "My God, my Father, and my friend,
> Do not forsake me in the end."

Tasso died with the words "*In manus tuas Domine*" upon his tongue, having died before he could finish the sentence. Schiller, being asked, when he was dying, how he felt, replied, "Calmer and calmer." Maccail, an eminent and pious Scottish gentleman, exclaimed, "Farewell sun, moon, and stars! farewell kindred and friends! farewell world and time! farewell weak and frail body! Welcome eternity! welcome angels and saints! welcome Savior of the world! and welcome God, the Judge of all!" The poet Keats, when asked, a little before he died, how he was, replied, "Better, my friend. I feel the daisies growing over me." Addison called a dissolute young nobleman, his son-in-law, to his bedside, saying, "I have summoned you that you

*Salad for the Solitary.

may see with what tranquillity a Christian can die." Cardinal Beaufort, who was accused of murdering the Duke of Gloucester, died in indescribable terrors. His last words were, "And must I die? Will not all my riches save me? What! is there no bribing death?" The demise of Beethoven was peculiarly impressive. He had been visibly declining, when suddenly he revived. A bright smile illumined his features as he softly murmured, "I shall hear in heaven," and then sung, in a low but distinct voice, the lines from one of his own beautiful hymns—

"Brüder! über'm Sternenzelt,
Muss ein lieber *Vater* wohnen."

Washington, when dying, said, "It is well;" John Q. Adams, "This is the last of earth;" Madame De Stael, "I have loved God, my father, and liberty;" Commodore Lawrence, "Do n't give up the ship!" Queen Elizabeth, "All my possessions for a moment of time!" Sir J. Stonehouse, "Precious salvation!" John Wesley, "The best of all is, God is with us!" Archbishop Jewell, "This day let me see the Lord Jesus!" General Wolfe, "Who run? the enemy? then I die contented!" Earl of Derby, and also Bishop Broughton, "Let the earth be filled with his glory!" Sir Philip Sidney, "In me behold the end of the world and all its vanities!" Mozart, "Let me hear once more those notes so long my solace and delight!" Hooker, "My days are past as a shadow that returns not!" Cranmer, Hooper, Herbert, and Ferrae, "Lord, receive my spirit!" Archbishop Usher, "O Lord, forgive me; specially my sins of omission!" John Locke, "Cease now!" addressing Lady Marham, who was reading a Psalm; Sir James Mackintosh, "Happy!" Thomas Jefferson, "I resign my soul to God, and my daughter to my country!" John Adams, "Independence forever!" Latimer, "Be of good comfort, brother Ridley, for we shall this day light such a candle in England as, by God's grace, shall never be put out!" the Marquis of Argyle, when advancing to the scaffold, "I would die as a Roman, but I choose rather to die as a Christian!" Lawrence Saunders, kissing the stake to which he was bound, "Welcome cross of Christ! welcome everlasting life!" Melancthon, "Nothing but heaven!" Luther, "Thou hast redeemed me, O Lord God of truth!" John Huss, "I take God to witness, I preached none but His own pure doctrines, and what I taught I am ready to seal with my blood;" the venerable Hilary, A. D. 385, "Soul, thou hast served Christ these seventy years, and art thou afraid to die? Go out, soul! go out!" Grotius, "O, I have consumed my days in labori ous trifling!" Julian, the apostate, "Thou hast conquered me, O Galilean!" Hobbes, "I am taking a fearful leap in the dark!" Cardinal Mazarine, "O, my poor soul! what is to become of thee? whither wilt thou go?" Napoleon, "Head of the army!" Robert Burns, alluding to the Dumfries militia, "Don't let that awkward squad fire over me!" Pope, to a friend who came in just as the physician had gone out, after speaking encouragingly of his symptoms, "I am dying, sir, of a hundred good symptoms!" Erasmus, "Lord, make an end;" Simeon, "Lord, now lettest thou thy servant depart in peace!" St. Stephen, "Lord Jesus, receive my spirit!" St. Paul, "I have fought a good fight;" Bishop Porteus, "O, that glorious sun!"

The closing scene in the life of Mozart is one of the most touching ever recorded. He seems to have suffered all his life, like Johnson, from the fear and dread of death. He had been employed upon his "requiem" several weeks; all the while his soul was filled with the richest melodies. After giving to the requiem its last touch, and breathing into it the soul of undying harmony, which was to consecrate it through all time, as his "cygnean strain," he fell into a gentle slumber. At length the light footsteps of his daughter Emilie awoke him. "Come hither," said he, "my Emilie; my task is done—the Requiem, *my* Requiem, is finished." "Say not so, dear father," said the gentle girl, interrupting him, as tears stood in her eyes; "you must be better; you look better, for even now your cheek has a glow upon it. I am sure we will nurse you well again; let me bring you something refreshing." "Do not deceive yourself, my love," said the dying father; "this wasted form can never be restored by human aid. From Heaven's mercy alone do I look for aid in this my dying hour. You spoke of refreshment, my Emilie; take these, my last notes, sit down by my piano here, sing them with the hymn of thy sainted mother; let me once more hear those dear tones which have been so long my solacement and delight!" His daughter obeyed, and, with a voice enriched with tenderest emotion, sung the following stanzas:

"Spirit, thy labor is o'er;
  Thy earthly probation is run;
Thy steps are now bound for the untrodden shore,
  And the race of immortals begun.

Spirit, look not on the strife,
  Or the pleasures of earth with regret—
Pause not on the threshold of limitless life,
  To mourn for the day that is set.

Spirit, no fetters can bind,
  No wicked have power to molest;
There the weary, like thee—the wretched shall find
  A haven—a mansion of rest.

Spirit, how bright is the road
  For which thou art now on the wing!
Thy home it will be with thy Savior and God,
  Their loud alleluiahs to sing."

As she concluded, she dwelt for a moment upon the low, melancholy notes of the piece, and then, turning from the instrument looked in silence for the approving smile of her father. It was the still, passionless smile which the rapt and joyous spirit had left, with the seal of death upon those features.*

What a contrast to this is afforded in the death of Cardinal Wolsey, for the account of which we are equally indebted to D'Aubigne, and that genial literary purveyor, the author of "Salad for the Solitary." "On Monday morning, tormented by gloomy forebodings, Wolsey asked what was the time of day. 'Past eight o'clock,' replied Cavendish. 'That can not be,' said the Cardinal; 'eight o'clock! No! for by eight o'clock you shall lose your master.' At six o'clock on Tuesday, Kingston, having come to inquire about his health, Wolsey said to him, 'I shall not live long.' 'Be of good cheer,' rejoined the Governor of the Tower.' 'Alas! Master Kingston,' exclaimed the Cardinal, 'if I had served God as diligently as I have served the King, he would not have given me over in my gray hairs!' and then, he added, with downcast head, 'This is my just reward!' What a judgment upon his own life! On the very threshold of eternity—for he had but a few minutes more to live—the Cardinal summoned up all his hatred against the Reformation, and made a last effort. The persecution was too slow to please him. 'Master Kingston,' he said, 'attend to my last request; tell the King that I conjure him, in God's name, to destroy the new pernicious sect of Lutherans;' and then, with astonishing presence of mind in this his last hour, Wolsey described the misfortunes which the Hussites had, in his opinion, brought upon Bohemia; and then, coming to England, he recalled the times of Wickliffe and Sir John Oldcastle! He grew animated; his dying eyes yet shot forth fiery glances! He trembled, lest Henry VIII, unfaithful to the Pope, should hold out his hands to the Reformers. 'Master Kingston,' said he, in conclusion, 'the

*Salad for the Solitary.

King should know that if he tolerates heresy, God will take away his power, and we then shall have mischief upon mischief—barrenness, scarcity, and disorder to the utter destruction of this Realm.' Wolsey was exhausted by the effort. After a momentary silence, he resumed, with a dying voice: 'Master Kingston, farewell! My time draweth on fast. Forget not what I have said and charge you withal; for when I am dead ye shall, peradventure, understand my words better!' It was with difficulty he uttered these words; his tongue began to falter, his eyes became fixed, his sight failed him. He breathed his last at the same minute the clock struck eight, and the attendants standing around his bed looked at each other in affright." He appears to have had a presentiment that he should die at eight o'clock, but had mistaken the day, having fixed it one day too soon.

There is another class of psychological phenomena connected with the dying process, which we must not pass unnoticed. It is a matter of notoriety that those dying from delirium tremens are haunted with the appearance of serpents, horrid forms, black figures, burning flames, and the most appalling spectral forms. Dr. Nelson informs us that in the southern part of the United States, where a friend had often been called to witness the dying scenes of infidels and gamblers, they not unfrequently declared that the evil one was present in the room and visible to them. Similar images often haunt the last hours of men whose dying scene is made terrible by the goadings of a guilty conscience. On the other hand, bright and beautiful scenes seem to kindle the imagination of the holy—snatches of heavenly melody, glimpses of angelic visitants, visions of the celestial city and of the heavenly plains! Surely, there is some significance in all this. Can it be other than a prophecy of the life that is to come?

VIII. Lessons Afforded by the Subject.

Let us, in conclusion, notice a few of the lessons suggested by this discussion:

1. *Death is not the destruction of the living principle in man.* As death approaches, and the body sinks and wastes, the mind often remains in all its strength and luster. This may be said always to be the case, except when disease impedes the functions of the brain, and thus prevents the mental manifestation. Thus, the mind does not even seem to be dynig with the body, but only loosening its hold and preparing to depart from it.

2. *Life is long enough for its purposes.* Long before his threescore years and ten are reached the character is formed—we had almost said stereotyped and sealed for eternity. For the Christian life is long enough. Why should he wish to live longer?

> "The less of this cold world, the more of heaven;
> The briefer life, the earlier immortality."

It is long enough for the sinner. If in the seventy allotted years he has done only evil, what else can we expect from him should his life be prolonged to the greatest period? His evil habits are being constantly strengthened by indulgence; the sphere of his evil influence is ever growing wider and wider. Of what use to him, or the world, or to heaven would be a longer life? In what could it result but greater and more wide-spread evil, deeper guilt, and, in the end, more fearful punishment? In the brevity and uncertainty of human life, then, we find no cause to implead the wisdom or even the goodness of God.

3. *We carry down to death the character we have formed in life.* It is a very common, but at the same time a very mistaken notion, that when we come to death we somehow

take upon us a new character. This idea is not only false in philosophy, but it is pernicious to good morals and religion. We die as we live. We go down to the grave with the characters, the habits, the desires, the feelings we have formed in life. A man may look with horror upon his past life, but that does not change it; a man may, in the terror of approaching death, abhor himself for his worldliness and sensuality, but that does not uproot worldliness and sensuality from his character. Let him be restored to health, and they will sway the same iron rule as before. We fall asleep at night just such beings as we have been through the day, and in the succeeding morning we wake up with characters unchanged. So shall we fall asleep when the night of death comes just such beings as we have been through life's day; and so also shall we awake in the resurrection morning, and such as we have lived we shall remain forever.

4. *Death will come to us all.* None can hope to escape. He is treading even now in our footsteps—when we sleep or when we wake! Noiseless, ceaseless is his advance! Infancy in its purity, youth in its beauty, manhood in its strength, and age in its honor find no exemption. Death is no respecter of persons. Opulence and poverty, power and feebleness, honor and its opposite, are all alike to him. He will come. His footfall shall, erelong, strike upon thine ear! Thou shalt shiver with icy coldness in the chilling atmosphere he breathes around thee! Thou, too, shalt go and join the countless hosts of his victims! thou shalt lie down in the dark and silent home of the dead! What thy hand findeth to do, do it, then, with thy might. Make life a stepping-stone to eternal bliss, the grave a triumphal archway to heaven.

VIII.

THE INTERMEDIATE STATE OF THE DEAD.*

"But man dieth and wasteth away; yea, man giveth up the ghost, and where is he?" JOB xiv, 10.

"Then shall the dust return to the earth as it was; and the spirit shall return unto God who gave it." ECCL. xii, 7.

WE have already seen that death is not an extinction of our being, and also that the soul has been made immortal by its Creator. The condition of the body after death we know to be one of organic decomposition; and when its elements have been dissolved dust and ashes only remain.

But what is the condition of the soul in its separate state? This is a question that profoundly concerns us. Friends of ours, and dear ones strongly and tenderly allied to us, have already entered that state. We ourselves will soon be called to experience its realities. No wonder that the subject has excited universal and earnest attention in all ages. The visible bond that unites our friends to us is severed by death. Our spirit yearns for intercourse with them, but we find them not. We interrogate the grave, but it gives back no response.

This anxiety concerning the departed is an intense and absorbing feeling: hence, in all ages, the efforts to penetrate the vail that conceals their condition from us. Under the influence of this sacred feeling thousands have sought,

* In the revision of the chapters on the Intermediate State, the author has been largely assisted by the excellent work of Mr. Harbaugh on "Heaven, or The Sainted Dead"—a work worthy of *heart-study*.

unwisely and by unholy agencies, to obtain some message from the dead, or to learn something concerning their condition. Necromancers, astrologers, spiritual mediums, and all kinds of impostors, have been consulted. Upon the basis of the same holy feeling Popery has erected the monstrous fraud of purgatory, and made it a source of revenue that once surpassed the revenues of the greatest commercial nations on the face of the globe.

This painful uncertainty about the future also constitutes one of the sources of that terror which death inspires.

> "The dread of something after death—
> That undiscovered country, from whose bourne
> No traveler returns, puzzles the will."

Affrighted at the gloomy prospect, we stand upon the outer edge of our present being and survey the awful scene, the land of darkness and of shadows, just before us.

> "To die; to sleep—
> To sleep? Perchance to dream; ay, there 's the rub;
> For in that sleep of death what dreams may come,
> When we have shuffled off this mortal coil,
> Must give us pause."

And here reason, unillumined by revelation, must ever pause; here it must stand appalled, bewildered, unnerved.

Let us enter the privileged chamber where the saint of God, after a long and glorious warfare, struggles in the last dread conflict. His breathing is short and difficult, his pulse fluttering and failing; cold drops of sweat stand upon his marble brow; receding life leaves the pallor of death upon his countenance; his friends give utterance to their sorrow in the gush of falling tears, or in that anguish that is too deep for tears. Another step, and the transit of the cold Jordan of Death will be complete. Life is fast going out, but the beaming eye speaks of heavenly support. Just then he struggles for utterance, and is heard to exclaim, with faltering speech, "Having a desire to depart and be with Christ!" A moment more, and all is over! The weary wheels of life have ceased to move! all is still! The body is no longer the home of the spirit! it is motionless and dead! *Where has that spirit gone? What is its state now?* What now has become of that hope of passing through the agonies of death to the glorious presence of Christ, and to the blissful vision of heaven? Has it been realized, or has it been blighted forever? What saint of God, who has been sustained in a dying hour, has not fixed his eye upon this one glorious hope—that of dying and *being with Christ?* The body we know shall slumber till the resurrection; but shall the spirit, even in its separate state, fail to reach that heaven where Christ sitteth at the right hand of God?

Let us, then, consider some of the facts, clearly deducible from the Bible, which throw light upon the condition of the soul after death and before the resurrection.

I. There is an Intermediate State of Some Kind.

This is clearly inferable from the fact that man is not represented as being judged, and receiving final adjudication of reward or punishment at the time of death, or even immediately after it. An intermediate period elapses. The resurrection of the body, its reunion with the soul, and the final judgment are events still remote. The Scriptures are clear and conclusive upon these points. Indeed, the subject is so often referred to in the Bible, and placed in such clear and strong light, and reiterated in so many forms, that we wonder how any one could ever have mistaken their import.

At one time we hear "*the resurrection of the last day*" (John xi, 24) spoken of; at another the declaration, falling from the lips of Christ himself, that "the hour is coming, in the which *all that are in the graves shall hear his voice, and shall come forth;* they that have done good, unto the resurrection of life; and they that have done evil, unto the resurrection of damnation." (John v, 28, 29.) Then, again, we hear our Savior saying to those who had made joyful the poor who could not recompense them, "Thou shalt be recompensed *at the resurrection of the just.*" (Luke xiv, 14.) So St. Paul, when defending himself from the malignant charges made against him by the Jews, says, "So worship I the God of my fathers, believing all things which are written in the law and in the prophets; and have hope toward God . . . that *there shall be a resurrection of the dead, both of the just and unjust.*" (Acts xxiv, 15.) So, also, the same great apostle, (2 Tim. iv, 6–8,) when triumphing in the prospect of his speedy and glorious departure, after having fought the good fight, finished his course, kept the faith, still looks forward to "*that day*" when his peculiar and final reward should be received. St. Peter, also, (1 Peter i, 3–7,) though ecstatic in the "lively hope" of "an inheritance incorruptible and undefiled," contemplates it as "*reserved in heaven,*" and "*ready to be revealed in the last time.*" The reader can not fail to perceive that in all these passages there is not only no allusion made to death as being the time when the righteous should receive their final reward, and the wicked their final doom, but that we are pointed directly to *the resurrection* as the period when these great events should take place. The recompense of the righteous, the hope of the apostle, the crown of righteousness, the incorruptible and undefiled inheritance, all are *reserved in heaven, ready to be revealed in the last time.*

To confirm this great truth still further, and to show how wide and comprehensive it is, let us listen again to St. Paul, (Rom. ii, 6–16,) while he declares that God "will render to every man according to his deeds: to them who by patient continuance in well-doing, seek for glory, and honor, and immortality, eternal life; but unto them that are contentious, and do not obey the truth, but obey unrighteousness, indignation and wrath." When, then, is this rendering to *every soul of man* to be made? "*In the day when God shall judge the secrets of man by Jesus Christ*, according to my Gospel," is the distinct and emphatic response. At one time the apostle connects realization of the great end of the holiness of the righteous with "*the coming of our Lord Jesus Christ with all his saints*," (1 Thess. iii, 13, 23;) and, again, the recompensing of tribulation to them who troubled the saints, and vengeance on them that know not God and do not obey the Gospel, to the period "*when the Lord Jesus shall be revealed from heaven with his mighty angels, and in flaming fire;*" and, still again, St. Peter connects "the promise of his coming" not only with the final judgment, but also with the "coming of *the day of God, wherein the heavens, being on fire, shall be dissolved, and the elements shall melt with fervent heat.*" (2 Peter iii, 4–12.) The conclusion to which these passages, and many others of the same import, conduct us is, that the day of final adjudication is not the same as that on which we die, but is at the general resurrection of the dead and the consummation of the present order of things.

Here, then, two errors, somewhat prevalent, find their certain correction. The first is that the righteous are judged at death, which can not be the case, as the Scriptures explicitly declare that both the righteous and the wicked shall be judged in the great and final day. The second is that the saints of God enter upon the full realization of their everlasting felicity immediately at death, and independently of their resurrection bodies; but this can not be the case, for these Scriptures plainly show that the resurrection and the reinvestment of the soul with its body, rendered incorruptible and glorious, must precede the *consummation* of the bliss of the redeemed. Every-where do the Scriptures teach us that it is *in connection with his body* man is to attain his highest destiny. Give place to these two errors, and they will serve but as stepping stones to the denial of both the resurrection and the final judgment; for if the soul is judged at death, and then enters upon its full reward, what can be the advantage of a subsequent resurrection of the body, and what the propriety of a subsequent adjudication of that which has already received judgment?

But says the objector, "Is not the destiny of every individual decided by the character he has formed, and by the relations he has sustained to God in this life, so that no change can be effected in any allotments beyond the grave?" It is true that our character and works in this life fix our destiny in the life to come, and also that there can be no *change of our allotment*—though there may be a fuller development of it—after our brief day of life has ended. Yet the objection, when urged as an objection, overlooks two important facts connected with the final judgment of all men. One of these is that God will judge every man according to his works—the righteous according to his, the wicked according to his. The desert of each individual is to be determined not merely by the motives that gave rise to his actions, but by the influences he has exerted, and by the practical results those influences have brought forth. The influence a man exerts outlives him, and travels on, for good or for evil, to the end of time. The good or the evil actually done in life may be very small compared with that which results from his influence after he is dead. "The prophets who wrote the Old Testament, and the evangelists and apostles who wrote the New, have exerted a wider influence for good since their death than while living. All along down the track of ages, and at the present time, they have been and are now doing untold good. And so every one who writes. Baxter, though dead, yet speaketh. So does Paine; the blighting influence of his Age of Reason travels on, widening as a stream of death in its dark course."* It is fitting, then, that the good should wait for the full realization of their recompense till the full measure of their influence has been reached, which can be done only when the dispensation which circumscribed the sphere of their operations has come to an end. It is fitting, also, that judgment for the wicked should linger till the full measure of their evil has been realized.

But, again, this objection misapprehends the character and design of this final judgment. It is *declaration*—the "*revelation* of God's righteous judgment." It is the day when God shall vindicate his government of the world, as well as his justice and mercy to individual men, to an assembled universe; when he shall draw out the actual characters of men, their good and evil works, and all the influences they have exerted down to the last moment of the now terminated dispensation; and when he shall thus display before the whole moral universe the reasons which have impelled him, as the Supreme Moral Governor, to award eternal death to the wicked and eternal life to the righteous. God might, indeed, in virtue of his foreknowledge, have taken all the consequences that would yet accrue from our actions into the computation, and executed just and final judgment upon us at the very moment of our death; but how, then, should "the revelation" of his righteous judgment be made so that all the universe would say, "It is right," and also even the blighted, scathed, and ruined soul of the wicked with all the hor-

* Attractions of the World to Come, p. 67.

ror of its fearful ruin yawning before it, respond, "It is right?"

Both revelation and reason, then, combine to assure us that the final judgment can take place only at the end of the present dispensation, which will be at one and the same time with the resurrection from the dead. It is, therefore, manifest that between death and the resurrection there must be an *intermediate state.* It is widely different from the present state; for the soul will be disembodied—no longer invested with or clogged by its earthly tabernacle. Its probation, too, will be ended, so far as voluntary action can affect its character, condition, or destiny. It must also be widely different from the glorious resurrection state, in which the soul will be reunited to the body once more; but that body, how changed! This corruptible shall have put on incorruption, and this mortal shall have put on immortality.

The inevitable conclusion to which we are thus brought is, that *there is an intermediate state of some kind;* and the pleasing task of ascertaining, as far as we may, what the state of the soul is, where it is, and what are its character, form, occupations, and prospects, is now left unto us.

II. Errors, Ancient and Modern, concerning the Intermediate State.

Job, speaking of the place of the dead, calls it "a land of darkness, as darkness itself; and of the shadow of death, without any order, and where the light is as darkness." (Job x, 22.) With the lamp of revelation in one hand, let us grope through this region of darkness and death. It is the only light that can guide us in the survey.

We know so little of spirit in its present state that it

should in no wise occasion wonder if we find that we know still less of it in its separate state. Here we find it blended with an organic, material body, and manifesting its being and powers in a thousand ways; and yet it must be confessed that we know very little of its modes of existence even in this world. Such knowledge is in no wise essential to us. How, then, can we expect full and minute knowledge of the modes of its existence in the intermediate state?

1. In the early ages of the world, and even now in some heathen lands, the place of the dead is conceived of as a dark, indistinct, and dreamy region, situated somewhere beneath the earth. This was the first expression of the instinctive longing of the soul after immortality—the first rational or natural denial of the extinction of our being in death. It was natural in the infantile state in which the human mind existed in the early ages of the world, that this childish conception should spring into existence, and exert a controlling influence over the imaginations of men. Their friends died, and their bodies were deposited in subterranean vaults and caves: hence arose the idea of the dark, underground region where they were supposed to live. This region was called among the Hebrews *Sheol*, and among the Greeks *Hades*—terms which mean a place of darkness where nothing is seen, or, specifically, place of the departed spirits. In this land of darkness and silence the dead retained their living personality in the form of mysterious shadows, and, hence, were called *manes*, or shades. This land of shadows was to them desirable, because they expected there to meet again their departed friends, and to enjoy their companionship forever. This was the dawning twilight of the glorious doctrine of the soul's immortality, now so clearly defined and so fully demonstrated.

2. An offshoot of this early conception of the state of the departed spirits has traveled down and been manifested in some instances in our own time. We refer to the idea that the spirits of the dead linger about the places where their bodies were buried. Among many of the ancients the burial of the body was regarded as essential to the repose of the soul. Thus Homer represents the ghost of Patroclus as upbraiding Achilles because he had not secured to him the rites of burial:

> "Let my pale corse the rites of burial know,
> And give me entrance in the realms below;
> Till then the spirit finds no resting-place,
> But here and there th' unbodied spirits chase
> The vagrant dead around the dark abode,
> Forbid to cross th' irremeable flood."

But this idea was not confined to those who had failed of a proper burial. Plato says that "they who only minded the body, and its appetites and pleasures, having something in them ponderous and earthy, shall, after their departure out of this life, be drawn down to earth, and hover about the sepulchers." Dr. Knapp says "that many of the ancients believed that the departed souls remain in or about the graves or dwellings of the dead, either forever or for a long time." He also says that the opinion widely prevailed that departed spirits sometimes return from the kingdom of the dead, and linger around the dead body or the place of burial. These ideas also prevailed, to some extent, among the Jews and early Christians; and thus it was forbidden, in the year 313, to kindle a light near the places of burial, lest the spirits of the saints should be disturbed. A similar feeling still exists among the less intelligent people even in Christian countries. Hence the half-defined, the half-believed idea of the ghost of the murdered man, or of the suicide, haunting the place where the crime was perpetrated. Hence, also, that feeling when we approach the place where the bodies of our departed friends slumber, as though they themselves were there. "Hence it is common for persons, of all grades of cultivation, to seek beneath the willow where they lie a kind of lonely fellowship with their beloved dead. There is a sweet hope, at least, that there they are nearer to them than in all the world besides; and he is regarded as a cold and heartless intruder who would argue away from them the cherished dream. 'She goeth to the grave to weep there.' Sweet mourner! Though we would not rudely drive her away from the spot which has embalmed all she held dear on earth, or forbid her to water the earth with her tears, which she expects will some day yield her back her own again, yet we would whisper softly, 'He is not here. Why seek ye the living among the dead?'"*

It is not necessary to meet this error, any more than that which preceded it, by argument. But while we cherish the spot where the dear departed lie as something sacred and holy in the heart's affections, and though we often go there to commune in our thoughts and feelings with them, yet it is well to dislodge from our minds so gloomy an idea as that their spirits are evermore hovering around the sad, mournful spot. Ah! who could cherish such an idea without a sensible augmentation of sorrow and of deep concern? "The place so cold and lonely. The night winds sigh so dolefully there. How dreadful, in the dead of night, is that dreary and dreamless silence! The snow lies so cold upon the grave; and fiercer than even the cutting anguish of your bereaved heart are the Wintry storms that rave, and drift, and whirl around the monumental marble. Can any one, then, wish the sainted dead to be there? No, no. We would not *wish* them to be there. They are *not* there; it is only inanimate mortality. It feels not its loneliness,

*Heaven, or the Sainted Dead, p. 162.

and is not chilled by the coldness of the place. Banish, then, the thought from your mind; for they are not there. In happier society than that in the city of the dead they live; to sweeter sounds they listen; to the music of angelic choirs they bend an enraptured ear. In genial and stormless climes they have found a home.

"Far from this world of toil and strife,
They 're present with the Lord."*

3. Another error, kindred to each of the former, is that which represents the soul, when it leaves the body at death, as entering into some other body prepared for it. The kind of body into which it then enters is determined by the character of the individual during life. Thus the evil life of the individual was to throw him backward in his gradation to supreme and eternal felicity, or his virtue and piety were to secure to him an advance toward this final consummation of his being. This doctrine was prevalent in the theology of the ancient Egyptians, in the philosophy of Pythagoras and of Plato, and has found advocates in nearly every age. The Egyptians believed that the soul was compelled to pass successively through the bodies of all animals, whether beasts, or birds, or fishes; and when it had completed its circuit, which required three thousand years, it again entered a human body. Pythagoras proposed, by his philosophy, the accomplishment of three things; namely, to lessen the number of transmigrations in order to attain the supreme felicity; to make those passed through favorable in their nature and of short duration; and, finally, to secure for those who should obey all his precepts an entire exemption from any transmigration, and the privilege of going forth at once into ether, and becoming incorruptible and immortal.

*Heaven, or the Sainted Dead, p. 163.

In the darkness of heathensim this doctrine may have sprung up from the analogies of nature—the decaying of the seed which results only in changing the form of organized matter and not in the destruction of its life, and the chrysalis which dies only to resume a new and more glorious life. Connect these facts with the deep and all-pervading feeling that "man has wandered far away from his God, and, in order to approach him again, he must travel with great labor through a long and dreary way," and also the conviction that "nothing which is imperfect or stained with sin can enter into the pure world of blessed spirits, or be forever united with God," and you have the rational origin of this doctrine of the transmigration of the souls, as well as of purgatory, its kindred error. It is, then, the rational conclusion of philosophy, groping in the darkness to which the intellect of man is subject when unillumined by the revelation of God. It is man's method of purification, while yet ignorant of the glorious truth that "the blood of Jesus Christ his Son cleanseth us from all sin."

How dark and gloomy this speculation! how glorious the truth that beams upon us from the revelation of God! *That* presents a faint hope, an uncertain chance of attaining final felicity through many and long gradations of uncertain issue; *this* assures us that the pious dead are present with the Lord.

4. As science advanced and knowledge increased, the old theory of an underworld region where the dead were gathered gave place to the more distinct theory of an *intermediate abode.* The poet thus describes this separate, intermediate abode:

"O see! an awful world is this
Where spirits are detained. 'T is half a heaven
And half a hell! What horrid mixture here!

> I see before me, and along the edge
> Of rayless night, on either side, the sh des
> Of spirits move; as yet unjudged, undo med,
> Or unrewarded. Some do seem to hope;
> Some sit in gloom; some walk in dark suspense;
> Some agonize to change their state. O, say,
> Is all this real, or but a monstrous dream?"

Having received the first indication of this doctrine from heathen philosophy, it was subsequently evolved in Christian light. It first became a part of Christian philosophy, and then a part of Christian faith. The Council of Florence, in 1439, established it as a doctrine of the Papal Church, and it was afterward reaffirmed by the Council of Trent. It is also recognized in the forms of the Episcopal Church. In the Papal Church this intermediate abode is connected with the idea of purgatory and the extension of man's probation to this middle abode. This privilege, however, does not extend to those who have not believed and been baptized into the Church; for all such, they believe, go immediately and without hope to hell. In the Episcopal Church this intermediate abode is regarded as a place where the spirit is detained till the resurrection of the body and its final glorification; and for these events they believe it to be undergoing a preparatory training while in its separate abode.

The special and insurmountable objections to this theory of an intermediate abode will more distinctly appear in our subsequent discussions; but we can not fail here to remark that, so far as it is connected with the idea of probation subsequent to this life, it is palpably opposed to the clearest teachings of Divine Revelation. It would deny the completeness of the healing virtue of a Savior's blood, and derogate from the work of the Holy Spirit as our Sanctifier. What these could not do for the soul in its present state is to be accomplished by the bleachings of purgatory, or by the "sanative influences" of this intermediate abode. O, when will Christians learn to look to Christ, and Christ alone, as the great and all-sufficient source of salvation! He is our life. In him we have wisdom, righteousness, sanctification, and redemption. What more can we need in order to salvation—to fitness for heaven, even—than that which Christ supplies?*

> "Where he displays his healing power,
> Death and the curse are known no more;
> In him the tribes of Adam boast
> More blessings than their father lost."

5. Another error relating to the intermediate state, and one that is more revolting to all the instincts of our nature than any of those we have considered, is that the soul dies with the body. It is strange that such a doctrine should ever have found place with those who believe in the resurrection and in everlasting life after death. Yet such is actually the case. This theory is thus stated by some of its modern advocates: "The whole man, whatever are his component parts, suffers privation of life, in what we call death." And, again, "The period which elapses between the time of death and the resurrection is spent in unconsciousness and inactivity; the soul is either extinct or in a profound and dreamless sleep, forgetful of all that is past, ignorant of all that is around it, and regardless of all that is to come." The philosophical basis of this doctrine is the assumption that the soul is only the result of the physical organization, and, therefore, can have no separate existence. But all reason and all philosophy demonstrate the falseness of this assumption. The premises being taken away, the conclusion is of no force. The Scriptural argument is absurd and unsustained. The assumption that the Bible teaches such a doctrine is a monstrous fraud upon

*Heaven, or the Sainted Dead, p. 122.

all revelation. Quickened and revived, as this doctrine has been repeatedly amid the heresies of the present day, it has so little to give it countenance, either in reason or revelation, and is in itself so repugnant to all the instincts of the soul, that no degree of fanaticism can give to it more than a brief and sickly existence. A sufficient refutation of this assumption will be found in the Scripture doctrines we shall develop in the subsequent discussion of this subject. But we may inquire here, How can this state of unconscious sleep, or of absolute extinction, be consistent with the living union of the believer in Christ? "Because I live, ye shall live also." This is the great pledge of our uninterrupted life. *He that believeth hath eternal life; he that liveth and believeth on Him shall never die; and he that hath the Son hath life.* Christ is the source of our life; and as the source can not become extinct, neither can the life that flows from it. Death has no power here. Instead of locking our faculties up in unconsciousness, and isolating us from our union with Christ, it can only break down some of the obstructions to that intercourse that have heretofore existed.

> "The star that sets
> Beyond the western wave is not extinct;
> It brightens in *another* hemisphere,
> And gilds another evening with its rays.
> O glorious hope of immortality!
> At thought of thee the coffin and the tomb
> Affright no more, and e'en the monster Death
> Loses his fearful form and seems a friend."

III. The Intermediate State of the Dead one of Conscious Existence.

How profound our interest in this question! Many of our dear friends have gone away into this region and shadow of death; our hearts follow after them, and we would fain know where and how they are. We ourselves are trembling, as it were, upon the borders of that dark and dreamy land, and our very instinctive solicitude impels us to the inquiry what our condition will be when we enter there. Never for once has the curtain that hides that invisible land from our sight been thrown aside that we might behold it; no one of its innumerable inhabitants has ever returned to these mortal shores to bring intelligence of our departed friends; no voice nor sound is heard; no sign—signalizing of that dreamy land, and telegraphed across the invisible space that separates us from it—is seen. Philosophy fails us; it has found itself able to solve but few of the subtile mysteries of the soul even in its present state. No wonder, then, that it is still less able to solve the mysteries of its separate state. Here it is blended with an organic, material body, and manifests its being, power, and condition in a thousand ways; and yet it must be confessed that as to the modes of its existence—its peculiar relation to the body, its dependence upon it or control over it—we know comparatively little. How, then, can we expect to unravel all the mysteries of its separate state? Yet we are not left in any necessary darkness in relation to the great facts of that mysterious state. And, perhaps, the most important of all those facts—as it is fundamental to all the rest—is that which we have just announced; namely, *that the intermediate state of the dead is a state of conscious existence.*

"I will hear what God the Lord will speak." And does not God reveal to us this great fact—a fact that constitutes a broad platform upon which rest our most glorious hopes in relation to our intermediate state? If such be not the case, why did St. Paul "desire to depart" that he might "be with Christ?" If the soul sleeps with the body till the resurrection of the dead, he would be no nearer to the accomplishment of his wish in dying than he was while he lived. Indeed, if the doctrine that the intermediate state is one of annihilation or of unconscious existence be true, St. Paul is no nearer heaven than he would be had he lived to the present hour. Neither is he so near the attainment of his desire now as he was during his life; for while he lived he enjoyed communion with Christ, but, being dead, even the communion he did enjoy is cut off, if the spirit sleeps with the body in unconscious repose. All intercourse with the Deity, with heaven, with the saints of God on earth, and even with the glorious truths of the Gospel, is utterly broken off, and in one long oblivious sleep has that intellect so vigorous, those affections so pure and so ardent, and those aspirations so glorious and sustaining, been pent for nearly eighteen centuries; and altogether unconscious of the history of the Church, and of the fate of the Gospel, of the glory of Christ or the bliss of heaven, will he still continue to slumber till the trump of God shall arouse the unconscious dead on the resurrection morning. Call you this "being with Christ?" Alas! then, what is it to be separated from him? If, between death and the resurrection, "the soul is either extinct or in a profound and dreamless sleep, forgetful of all that is past, ignorant of all that is around it, and regardless of all that is to come," how fearfully mistaken was the great apostle when he desired to "depart" in order that he might "be with Christ!" Better, indeed, were it to return to life, for here we may see, even though it be only as through a glass darkly; but there we see it not all! It is, truly, *a land of darkness as darkness itself!*

To the penitent thief upon the cross our Savior said, "To-day shalt thou be with me in paradise." On that very day both our Savior and the penitent thief expired. Did he mean that the penitent thief would with him that day cease from all conscious existence? What mockery to make such a promise as an antidote to the agonies of the dying man!

Upon the Mount of Transfiguration Moses and Elias, though the one had been dead nearly fifteen hundred years, and the other had been translated over a thousand years before, not only appeared in the form of living men, though with bodies glorious—emblematic of the glorious resurrection state—but they also conversed, thus demonstrating that they were not only alive but conscious. And if Moses has a conscious existence in the intermediate state, why may not all others?

While reasoning with the Sadducees, one of whose doctrines was that there is no spirit, no conscious existence independent of the body, our Savior says, "God is not the God of the dead, but of the living." And yet God said to Moses, "I am the God of Abraham, and the God of Isaac, and the God of Jacob," two hundred years after the dust of the last had been consigned to the cave purchased by Abraham in the field of Macpelah. Hence, it must follow, if there be any verity in God, that Abraham, Isaac, and Jacob, though dead, still had a conscious life. The same conclusion will be reached with an equally-invincible force, when we remember our Savior himself declared, "Abraham rejoiced to see my day; and he saw it, and was glad."

The parable of the rich man and Lazarus is also perfectly in point. (Luke xvi, 22, etc.) The beggar died and was carried by angels to Abraham's bosom. The rich man also died, but death was to him no dreamless, unconscious sleep; for in hell he lifted up his eyes, being in torment. From the deep gulf of his misery he beheld Abraham in his blissful abode, and Lazarus in his bosom. From him he besought relief. "But Abraham said, Son, remember that thou in thy *lifetime* receivedst thy good things, and likewise Lazarus evil things; but now he is comforted, and thou art tormented." The objection that this is a parable will not avail to break the force of the great moral truths it teaches. It is either history or a parable. If history, then it is a record of events that have actually taken place; if a parable, then it is a representation of events that may occur. Now, Abraham is here placed before us again as in conscious being—capable of observing, and of receiving and making communications. Here, also, is the poor beggar, delivered from his life-long sorrow and suffering—not by a suspension of conscious being, but by sweet repose in Abraham's bosom. The rich man, too, is here, and, though his "lifetime" was past, is still conscious of his awful state; he remembers the good things of his former life, and would fain have his five brothers warned lest they also become his companions in his awful place of torment.

When St. John, upon the island of Patmos, had heard the wonderful revelations made to him, filled with wonder and astonishment, he fell down to worship the messenger of God; but that messenger said, "See thou do it not; for I am thy fellow-servant, and of thy brethren the prophets, and of them which keep the sayings of this book." (Rev. xxii, 9.) Do we not here obtain a glimpse of not only the conscious being, but the avocations also of those who have died in the faith?

Again, St. John says, "I saw under the altar the souls of them that were slain for the word of God, and they cried with a loud voice, saying, How long, O Lord, holy and true! . . . And white robes were given to every one of them, and it was said unto them that they should rest yet for a little season." (Rev vi, 9, 10.) Those souls not only possessed a conscious existence after they had been "slain" for the cause of Christ, but they were also conscious of the wrong they had suffered, and were looking forward to the period of their vindication with anxious desire. Nor was this all; "they cried with a loud voice," and were afterward robed in white, and told to rest yet a little season. Here, then, they have a conscious existence, power to express their desires, and capability of being comforted by gracious assurances. Though persecution had done its work, and the bodies of the martyrs had been consumed by the fagot, or devoured by wild beasts, or wasted in deep and dark dungeons or dens and caverns of the earth, yet, after it had destroyed the body, there was a conscious life remaining over which it had no power.

Take another case—that of St. Paul when he was "caught up into the third heaven," and enjoyed the rapturous vision of the blessed abode and of God. So rapt was he in the glory of the vision, that "whether in the body or out of the body" he could not tell. Now, whatever this vision may have been, or not have been; sink it, if you please, into the least possible significance; yet it unquestionably develops one thing, and that is that the apostle believed that the soul may have a conscious existence out of the body—an existence in which it may perceive and enjoy—nay, an existence in which it may be filled with the most ecstatic felicity. Else how could he have been in doubt whether his soul was really in the body or not when it enjoyed the glorious vision of God and heaven? Those, then, who assume to know that the soul can have no conscious existence out of the body assume to know more than was known by the great apostle. This passage is all the more important, because it was not with direct reference to this subject that the apostle wrote, and it, therefore, becomes one of those incidental and undesigned passages that corroborate the great and cardinal doctrines of the Gospel.

One more passage upon this point must suffice, though

it would be difficult to exhaust the many Scripture proofs that bear upon it. St. Paul says that Christ Jesus "died for us, that, whether we wake or sleep, we should live together with him." (1 Thess. v, 10.) How emphatic! Whether we wake or sleep, live or die, whether we are in this world or the other, we shall live together with him, shall enjoy his life and the consolation of his spirit here, and, in the eternal world, shall be glorified together with him. These words show that every-where, and in all circumstances, genuine believers, who walk with God, *have life*—and not only life, but also communion with Him who is the source of all life. Indeed, they clearly express that, so far as the great ends of spiritual life and communion are concerned, the living have no advantage over the dead.

What, then, do all these things teach us? Evidently not only the great doctrine of the soul's immortality, but also that its intermediate state, during the time that intervenes between death and the resurrection, is one of conscious being—one of thought, of feeling, and of action. To have attained this position only, to have established only this single truth, brings to us a most glorious deliverance from that cold and cheerless hypothesis, which would crush our hearts as we look down into the grave as a place where all conscious being became extinct, and the soul, as the body, enters upon either utter extinction or upon a long and dreamless sleep, to be broken only at the resurrection.

IV. In the Intermediate State the Righteous Dead are with Christ.

The Scripture authentication of an intermediate state of conscious being is too full and too explicit to leave any room for apprehension on the part of the serious and inquiring mind, or for cavil on the part of the skeptic.

With some, however, not only an intermediate *state* but an intermediate *place* is maintained. It is contended that while *Gehenna* is used in the Bible to denote the *place* of final misery, *Sheol* in the Old Testament, and *Hades* in the New, is used to express the place of departed spirits. With such *Hades* is regarded as a general term, embracing both *Elysium*, or *Paradise*, and *Tartarus*—the separate abodes of the good and the bad. But whence the necessity of supposing them to indicate a *place* distinct from either heaven or hell? The etymology of Sheol and Hades clearly indicates that they are designed to denote general and indefinite ideas. Sheol signifies "the place and state of those who are out of sight, out of the way, and to be sought for." Hades is compounded of two Greek words, which together signify "an indistinct, dark, and invisible region;" and among the Greeks it was used as comprehending the dead without any reference to their moral character here or to their state there. Thus it is evident that these two words are used not to designate a third place, as distinct from heaven or hell, but rather as general terms, comprehending the state, condition, or place of the dead, whatever or wherever they might be.* Just so do we say of the dead, that they have gone to the invisible world, the world to come, the world of spirits, or to eternity. We indicate nothing of their peculiar condition—whether happy or miserable—and least of all do we indicate that they are in any third place, as being distinct from

*Professor Vail, one of the best Hebrew scholars of the age, says: "Our position is, after a careful investigation of every passage in the Old Testament in which the word occurs, and after a careful consideration of opinions advanced by others, besides referring to almost every original source deemed worthy of reference, that *Sheol*, in its generic signification, refers to *the state of the dead, without necessarily specifying that state, whether it be in happiness or in misery*, and hence the kingdom or world of the dead; and, aside from this generic signification, it is applied specifically, (1,) to *the place of torment of the wicked*, and, (2,) to the grave or *sepulcher, as the resting-place of the inanimate body*." (Meth. Quar. Review.)

either hell or heaven. It is really astonishing, when we consider how widely this doctrine of a separate abode has spread, and how long it has prevailed in the Christian Church, that, after all, it is found to have so little authority from Revelation.

It is unquestionably sustained by a feeling to which we have already adverted; namely, that man has wandered very far away from a just and holy God, and that to be restored to him he must travel a great way, and suffer great penance and purgation. Take this sentiment, which is deeply wrought into our nature—take it in connection with a failure to apprehend that it is by the blood of Christ we are "brought nigh," and you have the true basis upon which this pernicious error rests. This sentiment is thus developed by an Episcopal clergyman, in the form of an argument: "The great majority of those who die in the Lord are very far from being eminent saints. They leave the world pardoned and free from sin, indeed, but very imperfect, ignorant, feeble, and unfit for the ineffable blaze of heavenly effulgence, and the society and employments of the ancient and glorious inhabitants of heaven. But paradise is an *intermediate resting-place*, where the soul becomes unfolded, invigorated, and instructed for a superior state and world. The spirit, disinthralled and emancipated from its earthly prison and vehicle, passes into this *place* of abode, perfectly adapted to its disembodied state, and the design of that state. There, under genial and sanative influences, it repairs its losses and injuries, recovers its balance and tone, becomes thoroughly developed, and fully prepared for another and still higher state of being."* The question is well presented and forcibly reasoned; but, after all, it is only one of the superstitious dreams of the world's children, without Scriptural warrant or authority;

*The Dead in Christ, by Rev. J. W. M'Cullough.

nay, further, it wars against the saving provisions of the Gospel as being sufficient to the accomplishment of their great end. It would deny the completeness of the healing virtue of a Savior's blood, and derogate from the work of the Holy Spirit as our sanctifier. What these could not do for the soul in its present state is to be accomplished by the bleachings of purgatory, or by the "sanative influences" of the intermediate abode. O when will Christians learn to look to Christ, and to Christ alone, as the great and all-sufficient source of salvation! He is our life. In him we have wisdom, righteousness, sanctification, and redemption. What more can we need in order to salvation—to fitness for heaven even—than that which Christ supplies?

"Where he displays his healing power,
Death and the curse are known no more;
In him the tribes of Adam boast
More blessings than their fathers lost."

It is generally admitted that the full consummation of bliss is not realized till the resurrection. It is when the soul is clothed upon with its glorious resurrection body, it enters upon the full development of its powers and the full consummation of its bliss! But why is it necessary to suppose that prior to that event it must be put into a separate, independent place, some gradations in advance of earth toward heaven, but yet beneath heaven itself? Why may it not be transplanted at once, not as a fully-developed, but as an embryo being, to expand and mature till its final investiture with an incorruptible body shall gloriously install it among the thrones of heaven?

Such, indeed, seems to be the clear light of Revelation upon the subject. The righteous dead are represented as *being with Christ.* Such seems to have been the views of the first martyr when he cried, "Lord Jesus, receive my spirit." Such also seemed to be the view of St. Paul when he expressed "a desire to depart and be [not in the place of separate spirits, somewhere this side of heaven, but] WITH CHRIST, which is far better." (Phil. i, 23.) And, again, when not only speaking for himself, but for the great body of believers, he says, "Therefore, we are always confident, knowing that, whilst we are at home in the body, we are absent from the Lord; we are confident, I say, and willing rather to be absent from the body, and to *be present with the Lord.*" (2 Cor. v, 6.) The apostle here expresses the strongest conviction that believers, from the moment of death, instead of being in a *separate place*, are "with the Lord." But where is the Lord—where is Christ? Most certainly he has not only ascended on high, but he has entered into heaven itself. "For Christ is not entered into the holy place made with hands, which are but the figures of the true; but INTO HEAVEN ITSELF, now to appear in the presence of God for us." (Heb. ix, 24.) And, again, "Of the things which we have spoken, this is the sum: we have such an high-priest, who is set on the right hand of the throne of the Majesty in the heavens." (Heb. viii, 1.) From these facts it is clearly evident that death ushers the believer into the immediate and glorious presence of Christ.

> "One gentle sigh their fetter breaks;
> We scarce can say, 'They 're gone!'
> Before the willing spirit takes
> Her mansion near the throne."

How consoling such a truth! To know that we shall be with Christ sweetens the bitterness of the dying agony. Death removes us from our kindred here; but it brings us into the presence of that Friend who is dearer than any brother. What enlargement and beatification of the soul's power shall be realized even at the hour of death! and how glorious shall be that transition—even though made through pain and agony—which brings us into the presence of Christ! Feeble nature may drop her tears of sorrow over the departed good;

> "But reason and religion, better taught,
> Congratulate the dead, and crown his tomb
> With wreath triumphant."

V. The Essential Moral Character of the Soul in the Intermediate State will be the same as in the Body.

The Scriptures not only mark the distinction in character between the good and the bad in this life, but also, in tracing their condition and character in the future life, recognize them, each as possessing the same moral characteristics he had in this life. "The wicked is driven away in his wickedness;" that is, he does not leave his wickedness behind him, but he departs in it, and retains it; and for this cause the "wrath of God abideth upon him." The same great truth is set forth in Revelation xxii, 11: "He that is unjust, let him be unjust still; and he which is filthy, let him be filthy still; and he which is righteous, let him be righteous still; and he that is holy, let him be holy still."

Such characters, then, as men form here, such as they possess at the time of death, they will retain after they have crossed the dividing line between time and eternity. "Death, like birth, is the act of passing from one state of existence to another, giving us nothing but a change of situation. Here are two moments of time. Now there is the spirit of a man still tremblingly dwelling within an expiring body. Next moment the spirit lives without the body. The little words *in* and *out* contain the only difference. All that the soul is at death it will be after death; nothing less, nothing more. It varies nothing. It leaves nothing of itself. It only *goes*."

It may be that when we enter the spirit-land we shall be surprised to find so little change has taken place in our moral, and, perhaps, also in our intellectual character—that we are still so much like what we were when we lived on earth. There will, no doubt, be progressive and great changes, especially in the character of the righteous. Notwithstanding their best endeavors, the close of life found them still subjects to many imperfections, still in darkness and error in many respects. But now, how altered their circumstances! how improved their condition! Their probation has ended; the exciting causes of sin are taken away; they breathe an uninfected atmosphere; unholy associations no longer disturb them, for they have Jesus, and angels, and the spirits of the just made perfect for their companions. The angels of God are now their teachers and their guides. Truth, pure from the fountain-head of light, beams with unclouded luster upon them, and chases away the mists of error and the darkness of ignorance. Here, then, amid all these inspiring and genial influences, the soul will expand and mature its moral and intellectual powers—rising higher and still higher in the scale of excellence, and progressing onward in unceasing approximation toward the immaculate fountain of purity and of bliss.

This progression, transcendently glorious as it is, does not imply the assumption of *new* characters, but rather the *development* of those already formed upon earth. Take the vine, placed in some unfavorable spot, where it is excluded from moisture, and light, and air; it has but a sickly life, its leaves fall off, its budding blossoms become parched and dry, and its very stock droops and begins to wither. But change its position; give it light, and air, and moisture; and it revives; it shoots forth new leaves; its buds burst forth into new life, and give promise of a luxurians harvest. It is the same vine, but how gloriously developed! So with the immortal spirit, shining amid the glories of heaven, going forth on angelic wing to survey the vastness and the glory of the Creator's works, and vying with the loftiest archangel in its notes of thanksgiving and praise—that immortal and glorious spirit does now only exhibit the fuller development of a character formed here upon earth, and formed, too, perhaps, amid sighs of sorrow, tears of penitence, and unceasing conflicts with evil.

This truth teaches us the practically-important lesson that in this life, this side of the grave, the essential elements of our future and eternal characters are to be gathered. What our external relations may be will matter but little; but what our feelings, our aims, and habits were will avail every thing. The worldly-minded, the passionate, the selfish, the sensual professor will carry with him all the tarnish and rust his soul has acquired here; and, though he may be saved as by fire, yet he will find himself so much like himself that he will be surprised and ashamed, as the glories of the pure and holy beam upon him and dazzle his vision. How many a sinner—nay, how many a Christian professor—would be ashamed to go forth into eternity, to stand before the scrutinizing eye of God, and in the presence of holy angels and the spirits of holy men, with his present thoughts, passions, and habits! And yet how certain it is that we are not only here what life has made us, but such we shall be in eternity! The waters of death are not waters of ablution to cleanse away sin; nor is there that difference between the living and the dying world that is generally supposed. We shall, no doubt, die very much as we live. And as we die, so are we when we enter upon that intermediate state that leads to consummation of either bliss or woe.

VI. The Soul in the Intermediate State retains its Appropriate Human Form.

The question has, no doubt, often come up to every reflecting and sober mind, What is the form or shape of the soul? how does it exist in its disembodied state? Of the mode of existence, or of the form of the soul, so to speak, when disembodied, our conceptions can not be otherwise than vague and inadequate. Souls, however, in the disembodied state, must still possess qualities that are analogous to form and feature, voice and hearing. Such seems to be the most rational as well as the most Scriptural idea. It is, indeed, the individual soul that gives to the bodily form and features, the voice and hearing, their individual peculiarity and identity even here. Nor do we know that it can be regarded as an absurd hypothesis that every soul has a human form corresponding, in a measure, at least, to that of the body, and that it retains this distinctive form when it enters the spirit-world. A singular physiological fact, mentioned by some writers, may not be unworthy of mention in this connection. If every thing in the human body, except the nerves, were suddenly removed, leaving the tissue of nerves in the same position they occupied when they were connected with the other material elements, there would still be left a perfect human form as addressed to the eye. Take away all except the bones, and you still have a human form. Again, take away all except the veins and arteries, and the same result is obtained. The query raised by these writers is whether this fact may not be suggestive of the soul likewise having a *human form.* This may not be altogether irrelevant to that declaration of an apostle, "There is a natural [physical] body, and there is a spiritual body," (1 Cor. xv, 44;) and, again,

"We know, that, if our earthly house of this tabernacle were dissolved, we have a building of God, a house not made with hands, eternal in the heavens." (2 Cor. v, 1.) The idea of a spiritual body, or of the soul's possessing a bodily form, at least, has the virtue of being a universal, if not instinctive, sentiment of mankind. The heathen poets and philosophers thought and wrote of the manes or shades of their departed friends as still retaining their human form. Their universal teaching, expressed in their philosophy as well as poetry, is that

> "Man, though dead, retains
> Part of himself; th' immortal mind remains;
> The form subsists without the body's aid."

Ulysses, where he is represented in the Odyssey as visiting the regions of the dead, recognizes, by their form, those he had known on earth. Nothing can be more touching than the scene where he discovers the shade of his mother. All the recollections of childhood and of her tenderness and love come back upon him. He rushes to embrace her, but she eludes his grasp, he being yet in the flesh, and vanishes like an empty dream. Finding her eluding his grasp, and escaping away from him, he exclaims, with the most tender affection,

> "Fliest thou, loved shade, while I thus fondly mourn!
> Turn to my arms, to my embraces turn!
> Is it, ye powers, that smile at human harms,
> Too great a bliss to weep within her arms?"

The same general view seemed to be all-pervading among the mass of the people as well as among the philosophers and poets. It was closely connected in their minds with the recognition of each other and their reunion in the spirit-land. Thus they cherished their affection for their departed friends, and death was disrobed of half its terrors by the expectation of greeting again the loved ones already passed away to the regions of the blessed.

The Scriptures most clearly recognize this grand truth; for wherever the dead are spoken of, or represented as making their appearance upon earth, they are uniformly referred to as being in their appropriate human form. Hence it is that recognition and identification take place. This idea has prevailed in all ages. It is the universal conception of human nature. It is an unconscious element of that faith in the heart of the Christian, which exults in the confident expectation of *seeing* the loved ones that have gone into eternity, when he also shall have crossed over the irremeable flood. So does the Bible represent Dives to have seen and recognized Abraham and Lazarus, and them also to have recognized him; so were seen Moses and Elias; and so the great multitude around the throne of God—whose robes had been washed and who had gone up out of great tribulation—so were they seen by St. John. Their form, their words, their actions all marked them as having been once beings of earth, in spite of all the transformations of circumstance, and time, and place. They were disembodied; new scenes enchanted them, new glories blazed upon them; every thing was wondrously new; but through all the human and the personal were visible and distinctly marked.

The mind confidently, almost instinctively, looks forward to a reunion with the departed in another world. "O, how shall I exult," says Cicero, "when I attain the society of my kindred and friends! what intercourse can be more joyous, what meetings and embraces more sweet!" And then, apostrophizing his departed daughter, he exclaims, "Thou, therefore, now separated from me, not deserting me, but sometimes looking back, lead me, where I may yet enjoy the conversation and the sight of thee!" This is not rhetoric, but spontaneous aspiration—the consciousness of immortal life gushing forth in the soul. A crushed heart only can yield an odor that savors so highly of immortality. Eloquent as was this language of Cicero, it was not more sublime than the dying language of an Indian mother. She was the wife of Little Wolf, a chief of the Iowa tribe, and had accompanied her husband to Europe. She had already lost three children, and while in London lost a fourth and only child. The iron truly entered her soul, and she withered and pined away in grief, till she died, soon after reaching Paris. Her husband endeavored to comfort her, and to turn her thoughts again to life, but she only replied, "No! no! my four children recall me; I see them by the side of the Great Spirit; they stretch out their arms to me, and are astonished that I do not join them." There was uttered the true, simple, sublime language of nature. Had you said to that Indian mother that her departed ones had been divested of their human form, and not as children should she know them any more, how would she have exclaimed,

"O, say not so! how shall I know my darling,
If changed her form, and vail'd her shining hair;
If, since her flight, has grown my starling,
How shall I know her there?
On Memory's page, by viewless fingers painted,
I see the features of my angel-child;
She passed away ere vice her life hath tainted,
Passed to the undefiled.

O, say not so! for I could clasp her even
As when below she lay upon my breast;
I would dream of her as a bud in heaven,
Amid the blossoms of the blest.
My little one, she was a folded lily,
Sweeter than any on the azure wave,
But night came down, a starless night and chilly—
Alas! we could not save.

Yes, as a child, serene and noble poet—
O heaven were dark were children wanting there;
I hope to clasp my bud, as when I wore it,
A dimpled baby fair.

Though years have flown toward my blue-eyed daughter,
My heart yearns ofttimes with a mother's love;
Its never-dying tendrils now infold her,
E'en as a child above.

E'en as a babe, my little dove-eyed daughter,
Nestle and coo upon my heart again:
Wait for thy mother by the river water,
It shall not be in vain.
Wait as a child—how shall I know my darling,
If changed her form, and vail'd with shining hair;
If, since her flight, has grown my little starling,
How shall I know her there?"

The demand of this sentiment is met when we come to the recognition of the appropriate human form in the departed. Identity is what we want; nature craves for identity, and Scripture gives back the response that assures us this identity shall remain. All the anticipated glories of a reunion with the departed are enhanced by this prospect. The form may be vastly improved, infinitely more glorious, but it will be the same. Our friends or our children, who have been absent from us a few years, sometimes become so changed that we do not at first recognize them, though their general form and identity are the same. So may it be with our friends in heaven. Our aged parents, who totter with halting step and wasting frame to the grave, may there be rejuvenated and glowing with celestial life. Our children, nipped like the buds of Spring, may be so changed in the transition and by the rapid growth of heaven that it may be necessary for some attendant angel to point them out before we could recognize their beatified forms. It shall gladden our eyes, as we emerge from the gloom of the dark valley, to behold how glorious they have become, and to receive their welcomes to the land of everlasting bliss. "Tell me," says Dr. Berg, "ye who have seen the open tomb receive into its bosom the sacred trust committed to its keeping—ye who have heard the sullen rumblings of the death-clods, as they dropped upon the coffin-lid, and told you that earth had gone back to earth—when the separation from the object of your love was realized in all the desolation of bereavement, next to the thought that you should erelong see Christ as he is, and be like him, was not that consolation the strongest which assured you that the departed one, whom God has put from you into darkness, will run to meet you, when you cross the threshold of immortality, and, with the holy rapture to which the redeemed alone can give utterance, lead you to the exalted Savior, and with you bow down at his feet, and cast the conqueror's crown before him?" How sublime, how glorious these anticipations! Based, as they are, upon the eternal truth of God, and embodied in the elements of a pure and holy Christian faith, they seem almost to rend in twain the curtain that hides the invisible world from us.

"And when glad faith doth catch
Some echo of celestial harmonies,
Archangels' praises, with the high response
Of cherubim and seraphim,"

then, O doubting and fainting child of God, let thy heart revive! Thy dear, departed ones—"the dead in Christ"—are there;

"And ere thou art aware, the day may be
When to those skies they'll welcome thee."

VII. The Transition in Death.

Who has not felt the beauty and power of the following poetic description of the transition in death?

Tread softly! bow the head,
In reverent silence bow!
No passing bell doth toll,
Yet an immortal soul
Is passing now.

O change! O wondrous change!
Burst are the prison bars!

This moment there—so low
In mortal prayer—and now
Beyond the stars!

O change! stupendous change!
Here lies the senseless clod;
The soul from bondage breaks,
The new immortal wakes—
Walks with his God!"

From all that the Bible teaches us, and from all we can learn by a careful scrutiny of the phenomena of death, we are brought to the conviction that the change which occurs is one of evolution and not of transformation. It is, like the event of our birth, a transition. Of this transition we can know by our reason but little more than the unborn infant knows of the transition which is to introduce it into a world of light. "The progress of the departed spirit is imagined with an intense eagerness of conjecture. Does it open its eyes at once, with sudden rapture or alarm, on a scene of unutterable wonders? Does it awake, as we awake from the sleep of night, so gently that the mind is conscious of no struggle, and scarcely of change from activity to slumber, and from slumber to activity again? Does it carry on a continuous thread of perception, and know at once the world which it has left, and the world which it has entered? Does it feel itself alone or among companions? Does the separation from this earth become wider and wider as it advances on the journey beyond the eternal hills? Can we attain to any conception of its sensations, its condition, or its prospects?" These questions are pressed upon us by the very conditions of our being, and by the certainty of that fate which awaits us. Their solution is a natural desire, even if not perfectly attainable here.

Several facts have an important bearing upon the subject, and illustrate in no small degree this transition. It is evidently of short duration, if, indeed, it be any thing more than momentary. Our Savior said to the dying malefactor, "This day shalt thou be with me in paradise;" and yet it was not till just before sunset, at which moment the day ended, that the legs of the malefactor were broken. The Savior had before expired, but the dying agony of the penitent criminal, to whom the promise had been made, crowded hard upon the last moments of the closing day. And yet who shall say that the promise had not a literal fulfillment?

Some have, for a few moments, vibrated, as it were, between earth and heaven, have almost passed the gates of death, and yet have been restored. Others have seemed to die, and yet come back to earth. To such what glimpses of the better land have come—faint adumbrations of glory yet to be realized! So glorious, as in the case of Mr. Tennant, that they were loth to speak of its hidden beauty, but sufficient in its power to wean from earth, and to create "a homesickness for the land which they had but seen from afar." The vision vouchsafed to such was like that of St. Paul when he was caught up into the heavens, and "heard unspeakable words which it is not lawful for man to utter."

Then, too, the experience of the saint of God, when dying in the full triumph of a glorious and unclouded faith, has a touching lesson upon this subject. The idea that to such supernatural manifestations are made must be suggested to all who have witnessed their triumphant departure, and heard them speak of the glories revealed. Heaven itself often seems opened to their vision. Nor, indeed, does there any high degree of improbability attach itself to this idea. The dying linger for a moment on the confines of both worlds; and why may they not, when just leaving the one, catch some glimpse of the other?

"Leaving the old, both worlds at once they view
Who stand upon the threshold of the new."

In death the natural and supernatural meet. The two worlds here bound upon each other. Heaven was opened to the vision of the dying Stephen. Angels gathered around the dying Lazarus, and we may well conceive that their glorious forms broke upon his vision while yet the earth had hardly faded from it. Said a little Sabbath school scholar from my flock, as she threw up her little wasted arms, her eye fixed upon some definite and glorious object, and her whole countenance beaming with unearthly luster, "Mother, the angels have come!" In a moment more she had joined the angel throng. The pious Blumhardt exclaimed, "Light breaks in! alleluiah!" and expired. Dr. M'Lain said, "I can now contemplate clearly the grand scene to which I am going." Dr. Bateman, a distinguished physician and philosopher, died exclaiming, "What glory! The angels are waiting for me!" It is no vain conception that spiritual messengers, as companions and guides, come down to greet the saint of God as he crosses over Jordan.

But what light do these facts shed upon the transition through which we pass? Evidently this: that that transition may be but the work of a moment, and without even the suspension of our consciousness. We shall feel ourselves to be a living continuation of the past. We shall emerge into our new life probably not as by a sudden shock, creating sensations almost of alarm and terror, but as our eyes open to greet the dawning light of some glorious morning. We shall not all sleep, but we shall all be changed. Some may "sleep" for a longer or shorter period, as the soul makes its transit; and from that sleep they may emerge gradually to self-consciousness, and to a perception of their new state and new relations.

The thoughts, the feelings, the wonderments, the amazements of soul with which we shall awaken to the consciousness of another life will form a wonderful chapter in our mental history. Mr. Harbrough touches this theme so beautifully that we quote the passage entire: "When we awake from the swoon or sleep of death, or emerge through the change of death into the realities, circumstances, and affinities of another life, we suppose our first feeling will be that of consciousness of our own identity. We will feel and be conscious that we are ourselves and not another. This we can only do in connection with our past history. It may be the work of an instant; but still it involves a process by which the mind connects itself with what is past, and recollects its previous existence. Thus, for instance, we spend a night in the house of a friend; we wake in the morning suddenly, and scarcely know where we are or who we are. The mind at once enters upon a process of discovery by self-recollection; to do this it goes back and calls up its past history, remembers the way in which it has come, and soon full consciousness of itself and its relations is restored. So in the other world, after the change of death, a consciousness of identity must in some way be preserved. Suppose, however, that in the case of the person just instanced, sleeping in the house of his friend, the room should be furnished in a certain way when he lay down to sleep, and the furniture should be entirely removed and changed while he slept, the difficulty of coming to a consciousness of his identity would be greatly increased. In that case it would become necessary for him to depend upon pure recollection of the past in the way of thought and memory. This must be the case with our souls in passing through the change of death; we will find ourselves in new relations, circumstances, and affinities, and our consciousness of personal identity can continue only as it feels itself the living continuation of the past." This feeling will assuredly come. We may lose it, or be bewildered, for a moment, but our distinct individuality will revive and stand out as the great headland in the sea of our existence.

VIII. Intercourse between the Dead and the Living.

"But tell us, thou bird of the solemn strain,
Can those who have loved forget?
We call—but they answer not again—
Do they love, do they love us yet?
We call them far, through the silent night;
But they speak not from cave nor hill;
We know, we know that their land is bright,
But say, do they love there still?"

We have here an inquiry of touching interest, and one that requires to be treated with great delicacy. We have already shown that the righteous dead are with Christ. To wish that they were constantly with or around us would be as selfish as it would be unkind. We delight in the society of those nearly allied to us on earth—our children—and yet we send them forth from us because we know the great ends of our common being require it. Heaven we know is the home of the angels of God; but we also know that they go forth—nay, even come down to earth as ministering spirits. By this means there is a strange, mysterious intercourse between the ministering angels and living men. They are not always away from heaven, nor would we wish them to be. We would almost fear that something earthly and gross might be contracted by them, and that even their own joy might be marred by their too constant intercourse with sinful and sorrowing beings. We would have them return often to heaven, to bathe in its celestial light, to catch anew its holy joy, and thus to come back to us again, to labor with more ardent zeal for our salvation. So should we feel in relation to the dead in Christ—our own loved dead!

Among those myriads of angelic messengers is it not possible that there should sometimes be found one who was once an inhabitant of earth? Is it not possible that our departed kindred—our parents, our companions, our dear children that passed from us in the bloom of life, a loved brother or sister—may revisit earth, and come to minister to us in that which is holy and good—to breathe around us influences that will draw us heavenward? If it be possible to revisit earth, this, no doubt, is the glorious mission on which they would desire to come.

Is such return to earth possible? One, at least, we may claim on Bible authority, has revisited earth, if the spirit of Samuel appeared to Saul after the incantations of the sorceress of Endor. "Had it been satisfactorily known," says Bishop Burgess, "through any other channel than Divine Revelation, that Saul saw Samuel on the eve of his own fall, and heard his words, 'To-morrow shalt thou and thy sons be with me,' it would still have been a fact in the history of mankind, and would have proved, as truly as now, the possibility of such apparitions. That there was a real appearance of Samuel is the plainest interpretation of the language, was the belief of the ancient Jews, and has been supposed by the best divines. He came, not through any power of the sorceress, it would seem, but to her utter amazement. Once, therefore, a departed spirit has revisited the earth, and has been seen and heard; and it is worthy of remark that he took the form and aspect in which he might be the best recognized." But whatever question or room for doubt there may be in relation to this appearance of Samuel, there can be none in relation to the return of Moses and Elias, many centuries after their removal to the world of spirits. They were seen and heard by Peter, James, and John upon the Mount of Transfiguration.

Dr. Adam Clarke expresses it as his opinion that spirits from the invisible world, including also human spirits which have gone there, may have intercourse with this world, and even become visible to mortals. They are not brought back into mortal life, but only brought within the sphere of visibility. All along through the Bible the thing, at least by implication, is again and again recognized. As when Peter, miraculously delivered from prison, appeared at the gate, the frightened disciples exclaimed, "It is his angel!" or when the Savior appeared walking upon the water, "they supposed it had been a spirit."

We might also cite the universal belief of all ages in not only the possible, but the actual occasional return of the departed from the spirit-world to revisit the earth. There have been numerous accounts of their actual apparition in all ages, but for the most part those apparitions have been made under circumstances that precluded the possibility of proof beyond the testimony of the persons to whom they were made. In other instances a morbid imagination and an excited state of the nerves have furnished the most ready solution. Many other alleged cases, on investigation, have been found wholly wanting in any proper validity from any responsible witnesses. And it must, I think, be conceded that "no single instance of ghostly apparition has been sufficiently authenticated to take its place in history as an acknowledged fact." But, after all, the idea can not be set down as an exploded fancy; for we must yet, with Johnson, regard it, even after so many ages of inquiry and observation, as still an undetermined question. We are still inclined, after setting aside the great number of such alleged events as fictions or as mistaken conceptions, to believe the occurrence of such a thing possible, if not actual. While this view is clearly authorized by the fairest deductions from the Bible, it involves, so far as we can perceive, neither in reason nor in the nature of things, any impossibility.

The form in which the spirits of the departed might be expected most frequently to visit us would be in that of *spiritual communion.* There are seasons when the soul seems to recognize the presence of, and to hold communion with, the departed. They are like angelic visitants; we meet them in our lonely walks, in our deep and solemn meditations, and in our closet communings; we meet them when the lengthening shadows hallow the eventide—mysterious and solemn is their communion; we meet them when sorrows encompass us round about, and hallowed is the influence their presence imparts. Who shall say that at such times there is not a real communion between the living and the dead? Who shall say that there is not, then, a real presence of the dead with the living? Neander speaks of a custom among the early Christians of cherishing the memory of departed friends by celebrating the anniversary of their death in a manner suited to the Christian faith and hope. "It was usual on this day," says he, "to partake of the communion under a sense of the *inseparable fellowship of those who had died in the Lord.* A gift was laid on the altar in their name as if they were still living members of the family." So also, he says, "the whole Church would celebrate the anniversary of those who had died as witnesses of the Lord—the holy martyrs; and the communion was celebrated in the consciousness of continued fellowship with them."

This is a sublime, beautiful idea! How simple, and yet how deep and earnest, the faith of the early and holy people of God! "The communion of the saints," says Dr. Nevin, "regards not merely Christians on earth, but also the sainted dead; according to the true words of the hymn, 'The saints on earth and all the dead but *one communion make.*' There is a pernicious view in the religious world at the present time by which the dead are taken to be so dissociated from the living as to have no part further in the onward movement of Christ's kingdom." It was the impression of Mr. Wesley concerning Emanuel Swedenborg, whom he knew personally, that the strong impression on his mind of the presence of deceased friends, at particular moments, was produced by their actual but invisible presence. Oberlin, also, for many years, claimed to enjoy intimate communion with the dead. And thousands of Christians have had, at times, as clear and overpowering a consciousness of the spiritual presence of departed friends as of their own self-being. And what is peculiarly to be observed is that this communion has been realized only by those most spiritual in their nature, and peculiarly allied by the power of a living faith to Christ.

There is one other fact bearing upon this subject which we can not now forbear. It is the affecting recognition of the presence of the dead in Christ, which is sometimes realized by the dying saint. Parents have recognized departed children as present to welcome them, just at the moment of their own departure; so have children recognized the presence of a sainted father or mother; also brothers and sisters have thus seemed to meet each other on the dividing line between this world and the next. Hannah More, when dying, extended her arms as if to embrace some one, called the name of a beloved sister long before departed, exclaimed, "Joy!" and expired. Most touching is the story of Carnaval, who was long known as a lunatic in Paris. His reason had been unsettled by the early death of the object of his tender and most devoted affection. He could never be made to comprehend that she was dead, but spent his life in the vain search for the long-lost object of his love. She was the absorbing idea of his life. In most affecting terms he would mourn her absence, and chide her long delay. Thus life wore away; and when its ebbing tide was almost exhausted, starting, as from a reverie, the countenance of the dying man was overspread with sudden joy, and, stretching forth his arms, as if he would clasp some object before him, he uttered the name of his long-lost love, and exclaiming, "Ah, there thou art at last!" expired. The eloquent Buckminster, of Boston, died suddenly. The next morning his father, who lived in New Hampshire, and was then in a dying state, suddenly exclaimed, "My son Joseph is dead!" And when those around him attempted to assure him that it was only a dream, he said, with great emphasis, "It is no dream; he is dead!" A moment more and the father had joined his son in the spirit-land.

It was a beautiful conception in Southey's ode on the portrait of Bishop Heber, that many

> "Will gaze
> Upon his effigy
> With reverential love,
> Till they shall grow familiar with its lines,
> And know him when they see his face in heaven!"

This beautiful conception of the poet, as well as the great truth we have been suggesting, seem strikingly confirmed by the following touching incident, which was recorded by an eye-witness of the scene: "A little girl, in a family of my acquaintance, a lovely and precious child, lost her mother at an age too early to fix the loved features in her remembrance. She was beautiful; and as the bud of her heart unfolded, it seemed as if won by that mother's prayers to turn instinctively heavenward. The sweet, conscientious, and prayer-loving child was the idol of the bereaved family. But she faded away early. She would lie upon the lap of the friend who took a mother's kind care of her, and, winding one wasted arm about her neck, would say, 'Now tell me about my mamma!' And when the oft-told tale had been repeated, she would ask softly, 'Take me into the parlor; I want to see my mamma.' The request was never refused; and the affectionate sick child would lie for hours, gazing on her mother's portrait. But

> 'Pale and wan she grew, and weakly—
> Bearing all her pains so meekly,
> That to them she still grew dearer,
> As the trial-hour grew nearer.'

That hour came at last, and the weeping neighbors assembled to see the little child die. The dew of death was already on the flower, as its sun of life was going down. The little chest heaved faintly—spasmodically.

'Do you know me, darling?' sobbed, close in her ear, the voice that was dearest; but it awoke no answer. All at once, a brightness, as if from the upper world, burst over the child's colorless countenance. The eyelids flashed open, and the lips parted; the wan, cuddling hands flew up, in the little one's last impulsive effort, as she looked piercingly into the far above.

"'Mother!' she cried, with surprise and transport in her tone—and passed with that breath to her mother's bosom.

"Said a distinguished divine, who stood by that bed of joyous death, 'If I had never believed in the ministration of departed ones before, I could not doubt it now.'"

And what is there inconsistent in all this? Among the "ministering spirits," who would be more ready to run to our relief, to hover around our dying bed, and to welcome our disinthralled spirit, than the dear friends and kindred of earth who have gone before us to God? Who would be more likely than the mother who watched over us, the sister of our love, or the prattling child that passed from our sight, to come down to greet us at the swelling of

Jordan, and welcome us to the partnership of their joy? The very thought that loved ones, under the conduct of the Captain of their salvation, have already safely crossed the Jordan of death, and now wait on the other side to greet our coming, and to conduct us to the Savior's presence, shall nerve our souls with courage as we step down into the dark domain of death, and hasten to their embrace, and to the glorious vision of our God.

"O blissful scene! when cherished hearts
Renew their ties most cherished;
When naught the mourned and mourner parts;
When grief with life is perished."

IX.

RESURRECTION OF THE HUMAN BODY.

"If a man die, shall he live again?" JOB xiv, 14.

"The trumpet shall sound, and the dead shall be raised." 1 COR. xv, 52.

"The hour is coming, in the which all that are in the graves shall hear his voice, and shall come forth; they that have done good, unto the resurrection of life; and they that have done evil, unto the resurrection of damnation." JOHN v, 28, 29.

IN this world the reign of death is as universal as it is appalling. The young in their beauty and loveliness, and the old in their maturity and wisdom, are borne down and swept away. The dark and gloomy grave becomes the silent home of the living. In one lengthened procession the human race, generation after generation, are marching down to the tomb. How ceaseless the onward movement! What unnumbered multitudes have already gone down into the deep and dark abyss, and appear no more! Low in the silent grave they slumber. Worldly thoughts, and passions, and cares disturb them no more. Their very bones have been turned into ashes, and their dust has become scattered and wasted. The monumental marble once told where they slumbered, and affection once paid its tribute of tears at their tomb. But the marble has crumbled and wasted till that also has ceased to be; and even the friends that wept weep no longer, for they, too, have gone down to join the nations of the dead.

What shall be the fate of these slumbering millions? Shall they slumber on forever—know life no more? or shall the voice of Omnipotence penetrate those dark caverns—

the homes of the dead—and call them forth again to life? "If a man die, shall he live again?"

This is a question of deep and far-reaching importance; it is one of momentous interest to the human race. The inscrutable mysteries that encircle it and the deep interest we have in it, make us almost tremble to raise the question whether these dead shall live again. But we can not refrain from raising it. It constitutes an essential element in the question of man's destiny. It is often forced upon us with a touching tenderness that extorts the inquiry from the very depths of the soul. When our friends die, and we bear their bodies as a sorrowful burden to the tomb, how do we seek to penetrate the dark vail of mystery that shrouds their destiny! Or when we meditate upon our own mortal and dying estate—*what* we shall soon be—*where* we shall be; when all the solemn realities of our coming history rush in upon our minds—how intense and solemn the interest we feel in the question whether "the dead shall be raised," whether they shall be awakened out of the deep and long slumber of the grave!

Let us now bring the question before us with the same earnest thoughtfulness that we will feel when the worn and wasted body begins to give signs of speedy dissolution. Let us now interrogate the holy instincts of reason and listen to their teachings; let us seek to know what Heaven has revealed; and let us do it with the same depth of feeling as when the dust of departed affection lies moldering before us.

We propose to show that the resurrection of the human body is suggested by analogies in nature, is clearly embodied in the teachings of the Old Testament Scriptures, is still more clearly revealed in the New Testament Scriptures, and, finally, that it is demonstrated by individual resurrections.

I. Suggested by the Analogies of Nature.

The resurrection of the human body from death and corruption is peculiarly a doctrine of revelation. Yet it may prepare our minds, in a measure, for a better appreciation of the direct Scripture evidence, if we first glance at some of these analogies of nature which either lessen the force of skeptical objection or directly suggest the resurrection as among the probabilities locked up in that future experience nature has in store for us. They suggest to us, at least, that the mysteriousness or seeming incredibility of the resurrection is possessed of no force when urged as an objection, since results are constantly being produced in nature equally inexplicable and scarcely less wonderful.

1. *Day and night are to us symbols of life and death.* We employ them as such continually. And yet so familiar have we become with the transformations of day and night, that we fail to realize their symbolic power. But in order that we may comprehend how much there really is in this analogy, let us, as some one, we forget whom, has already done, suppose a man to be created, with all the faculties of sense and intellect in full maturity, and placed at midday a solitary intelligence upon the earth, with what astonishment and wonder he gazes upon the glorious creation of God spread out around and above him! With sublime emotions he gazes upon the canopy of the heavens spreading its broad arch above him! He hears the lowing of the flocks and herds, the songs of the birds, and all the varied melodies of nature, with enraptured delight. The glorious landscape spreads out around him; he gazes upon the blooming flowers, the waving grain, the towering forests, and the distant mountains in the dim distance, throwing up

their broad shoulders to the sky. But chief of all, in his wondering gaze, appears the great orb of day tracing its pathway through the heavens. Its brightness dazzles his vision—is too great for a moment's endurance; yet he finds its influence all-pervading; warmth comes from it; the flowers are tinted by it; the life and growth of vegetation, obviously, hold mysterious connection with it, and are dependent upon it; the very music of the birds seems to be an inspiration from it. The newly-created observer, seeking for a cause of all, now begins to inquire whether all that is real in the wondrous scene around him does not proceed from the sun—whether it is not the source of life as well as of warmth and light?

But now the scene changes. The sun declines in the west. Lower and still lower it sinks. It already touches the horizon. Dim shadows creep along the sky and overspread the landscape. The affrighted mortal stretches out his hands to stay its progress, but in vain. He would fain unravel the mysteries of the darkly-approaching future; but no response comes back to his oft-repeated inquiries. The sun at length disappears altogether; dark clouds roll up the sky; the face of nature is robed in utter blackness. Naught is seen; his own person, his hands, his feet have become invisible. The many-voiced music of animals, and birds, and insects has become hushed and still. Affright, terror, despair takes hold of the solitary spectator. The glorious pageant has passed, and, to all appearance, has gone forever. It departed without the slightest intimation—whether from hight above or depth beneath—of any return.

The hours of darkness are worn away in exclamations of affright and in moans of despair; till at last exhausted nature seeks repose, and the man sinks down also and is overspread with that mysterious emblem of death—sleep. Refreshed, he awakes. Lo! a bright streak of light is seen skirting the horizon opposite to that where the sun went down It rises higher, spreads wider, grows brighter, till the whole landscape seems to emerge gradually from the darkness that overspread it. But, more glorious, more wonderful than all! to the astonished apprehension of the beholder, a new sun bursts forth in the horizon and travels up the heavens, in its brightness and glory! A new day has come forth from the womb of night.

Such is the manner in which the shifting scene of day, ending in night, would strike the mind on first beholding the wonder. But does our familiarity with the scene, much as it may blunt our own power of perception, detract aught from its symbolic import? Does not Nature ever symbolize to us that as the darkness of night ends in day, so shall the darkness of death terminate in the light of the resurrection?

2. *The resurrections of Spring also afford striking emblems of the resurrection of man from the dead.* But a few weeks ago it was dead Winter. Standing amidst a wide waste of snow and ice, we realized fully what Thomson so beautifully describes:

"Dread Winter spreads his latest glooms,
And reigns tremendous o'er the conquered year.
How dead the vegetable kingdom lies!
How dumb the tuneful! Horror wide extends
Her desolate domain!"

The trees were leafless and bare; every shrub and flower was belted with ice and covered with snow; the grass, that but a few months before clothed the earth with beauty, was now faded, dead, and buried. The music of no bird was heard among the branches; the hum of no insect came up from the earth around; all was silent. What a picture was this of human life!

"Behold, fond man,
See here thy pictured life; pass some few years,

Thy flow'ring Spring, thy Summer's ardent strength,
Thy sober Autumn fading into age,
And pale, concluding Winter comes at last,
And shuts the scene. Ah! whither now are fled
Those dreams of greatness? those unsolid hopes
Of happiness? those longings after fame?
Those gay-spent, festive nights? those veering thoughts,
Lost between good and ill, that shared thy life?
All now are vanished!"

Should some new visitant to earth, having once glanced at the glories and the life of one Summer, return in the dead of Winter to behold its desolation, would not the scene impress him that vegetable life had departed forever—had become extinct? Its recovery he would deem incredible. And yet what transformations have a few weeks wrought! "Movement, growth, life, joy, appear everywhere, in the place of silence, sadness, and death. Has not a spirit of resurrection, a living soul, entered into nature? Has not the Spirit of God breathed from the four winds upon these dry bones? Do not millions of beings daily break forth into life, in the air, in the earth, and in the waters, even as the elect will 'come forth' on the blissful day of the resurrection of the just? Again, the flowers, which all around are springing out of the earth as from their tomb, fresh as the dew, numerous as the sand, and more beautiful than ever was the mantle of imperial royalty—were not these flowers, a few months ago, either shapeless and coarse roots, or seeds not unlike the vile dust that we tread under our feet? And now, behold! those roots and seeds that were lately buried—even like the human body, which, when in the bosom of the grave, is but an object of disgust—those very roots and seeds, which rot or decompose in our furrows before they spring forth again, are to-day the ornament of the landscape and the charm of our eyes. Observe with admiration how, day after day, these miracles of resurrection, far from any cessa tion, appear in succession and spread every-where with no less rapidity than splendor; how thousands of plants and millions of insects, through an incomprehensible operation of God, issue continually from the earth, to praise, as if in concert, the Almighty Creator, who has redeemed them from death, and brought them to the light of these happy days! See how all creation, released from the grave, seems inspired with life and filled with joy!"*

We do not present these as analogies going to prove the resurrection of man, but as glorious symbolizations of that resurrection elsewhere clearly taught and divinely demonstrated.

"The glorious morn will come! the second birth
Of heaven and earth! awakening Nature hear
The new creating word, and start to life.
The storms of Wint'ry time will quickly pass,
And one unbounded Spring encircle all."

3. *The symbolization of the resurrection in vegetable life is recognized by St. Paul.*—"That which thou sowest is not quickened, except it die." (1 Cor. xv, 36.) When the seed is sown it, to all appearance, dies, becomes corrupted, and out of this corruption, this death, springs the new germ of life. The elemental germen is nourished by the decay of the rest of the kernel; it gathers life from the death and corruption of the rest. "So also is the resurrection of the dead; it is sown in corruption, it is raised in incorruption." (1 Cor. xv, 42.) Whatever link may be wanting to complete the chain of reasoning in the analogy between the resurrected life springing from the seed cast into the earth, and the resurrected life of the human body, there is one point of resemblance that will ever prove most striking. He at whose command the seed germs through death into life, has also given the pledge of our resurrection. And is not that mysterious Power, which is ever displaying the

*Parables of Spring. Gaussen, p. 58.

exuberance of its energy in bringing forth life from death, able to number our poor bodies also among the germs of a coming life? Ages of burial do not extinguish the germ of life in the vegetable seed. Kernels of grain that had been buried for centuries in subterranean deposits, in Europe and Africa, germed into new life when brought forth from their tomb. It is said that the ancient Druid priests in France were accustomed to place a tile under the head of each corpse, and under these tiles, in circular holes, closed with cement a few seeds. A few years since, some of these graves, of two thousand years ago, were opened. The seeds were taken out and planted, and "the heliotrope, the trefoil, and the corn-flower, were seen rising to life again, after being buried twenty centuries." *

If in vegetable resurrections we may trace the process a few steps further, we still seem equally distant from the solution of the mystery, and the act of thus giving life seems equally unapproachable in either case. And does not God set daily before our eyes these wonders of his life-giving power, that we may be more fully impressed with the certainty of that great and wondrous resurrection he will yet work for us?

4. *Animal and insect transformations are also made to symbolize the resurrection.* Of this class the chrysalis state of butterflies, moths, and silkworms furnishes striking examples. Some of these insects exhibit all the phenomena of dying, and for weeks remain in a decomposing and apparently dead state. The dragon-fly is a striking instance. Naturalists tell us that the worm repairs to the margin of a pond in quest of a convenient place of abode during its insensible state. It there attaches itself to a plant or to a piece of dry wood, and then apparently dies. The skin becomes dry and brittle; but the apparently-decayed and

* Gaussen's Parables of Spring, p. 78.

rotten mass within gradually assumes a new form. At length the shell bursts and a winged insect pushes its way forth, expands and flutters its wings, and in a moment more soars away in the air. Now, who, that saw the little hanging coffin which entombed the inanimate insect a few weeks before, could have dreamed of such a result as this? who, from that chrysalis formation, could have predicted a *winged insect* full of life, floating in the air, and possessed of all the functions of animal life? The philosopher will tell us, perhaps, that the elements of this new life were possessed through all these transformations, and that the rudiments of wings were there even while it was living in water. But may it not be also that even in the bodies of men there may be some latent, elemental organization, to be developed at the moment of the resurrection? who shall say that, carefully folded in our God-created forms, may not be the angel wing upon which, when the chrysalis of mortality is cast aside, we shall soar in triumph through the very heaven of heavens? who shall say that what nature unfolds to us in the transformations of the insect and animal creation are not designed to suggest to us the grander, possible transformations we may experience in the putting off of this mortal body, and the putting on of an immortal?

II. Taught in the Old Testament Scriptures.

In opposition to those who assume that there is no distinct recognition of the resurrection of the body in the Old Testament Scriptures, we shall undertake to establish three facts, namely: 1. That it is directly asserted either in relation to individuals or as a general thing; 2. That inspired men expressed the utmost confidence in the resurrection of the body; and, finally, 3. That the doctrine of the resurrection was generally received among the Jews.

1. *The resurrection of the body is directly asserted in the Old Testament, either in relation to individuals, or in a general manner.* One of the texts quoted at the head of this discussion is to the point here. "If a man die, shall he live again?" This is not a question implying doubt, but one of assurance. Hence "will I wait till my change come;" or, as the Septuagint has it, "till I live again." And even the Hebrew word rendered *change*, in the expression "till my change come," implies *renovation*, like the springing of grass after it is once withered—a very expressive emblem of the resurrection. The whole passage, then, implies that Job was so confident that he who died should live again, that in patience would he wait till his final *renovation* came. That the doctrine of the resurrection is clearly imbedded in this passage scarcely admits of a doubt.

Take, again, Hosea xiii, 14: "I will ransom them from the power of the grave; I will redeem them from death; O death, I will be thy plagues; O grave, I will be thy destruction." This passage is highly figurative. The Jews in their captivity are represented as *dead* and *buried*. But their God would ransom them from death and bring them forth from the grave. And thus was symbolized a grander resurrection in the last day, when the Redeemer should be *the destruction of the grave itself.* Kindred to this is the passage in Isaiah xxv, 8: "He will swallow up death in victory." Both these passages were undoubtedly in the mind of the inspired apostle, when, in that sublime discussion of the doctrine of the resurrection, he says, "Then shall be brought to pass the saying that is written, death is swallowed up in victory. O death, where is thy sting? O grave, where is thy victory?" Thus have we the testimony of inspiration itself, that the doctrine of the resurrection from the dead is imbedded in no uncertain or doubtful form in the Scriptures of the Old Testament.

Again, (Isaiah xxvi, 19,) from the dark overspreading of sorrow and gloom breaks forth in the exultant strains of an assured victory over death and the grave: "Thy dead men shall live, together with my dead body shall they arise. Awake and sing, ye that dwell in dust: for thy dew is as the dew of herbs, and the earth shall cast out the dead." Language like this, so specific and involving so many particulars, can hardly be claimed to be merely figurative—referring only to the political resurrection of the Jews and their deliverance from bondage. The figure, as well as the language, is of deeper import. The emblems of a higher resurrection are employed. A power is to come down like that of the dew upon the dried and withered herbs, and the *earth shall cast out the dead.* Dr. Albert Barnes says, "This is language which is derived from the doctrine of the resurrection of the body; and shows also that that doctrine was understood by the Hebrews in the time of Isaiah. The sense is, that as the earth shall cast forth its dead in the resurrection, so the people of God in Babylon should be restored to life, and to their former privileges in their own land."* To deny as much as this to that sublime passage is to rob it of all significance as applied to the case before the prophet.

Take, again, the prophecy of Daniel, (xii, 2.) After referring to the end of time, in which Michael shall stand up, and, amidst calamities and terrors, such as nations had never before experienced, deliver those "that shall be found written in the book;" he says: "And many of them that slept in the dust of the earth," or *as many* as slept in the dust of the earth, "shall awake, some to everlasting life, and some to shame and everlasting contempt." This passage may have had a primary reference to the resurrection of the Jewish nation from their degradation and bondage;

*Notes on Isaiah, vol. ii, p. 177.

but its imagery receives its full significance only when referred to the resurrection at the last day. This becomes still more evident when we compare the imagery employed here with that employed in the Revelation to mirror forth the resurrection. No one, after such a comparison, will question that they refer to the same solemn and momentous scene.

We might also refer to the vision of the valley of "dry bones." It is to be noted here that though this striking imagery is employed to describe the civil and spiritual resurrection of the Jews, it is based upon the idea of a resurrection of the body, a resurrection taking place after the flesh was wasted and the bones had become bleached and dry. Otherwise the imagery has no pertinence, no force of application.

Thus we might show that the whole tenor of the revelation of God to the Jews embodied the essential doctrine of a resurrection from the dead. It beams out with a brightness too obvious for mistake, and is expressed with a distinctness of enunciation that left little ground for cavil or doubt.

2. *Inspired men in the Old Testament day have expressed the utmost confidence in the resurrection.*

The Psalmist says, that "man being in honor abideth not: he is like the beasts that perish." "Like sheep they are laid in the grave; death shall feed on them; . . . . and their beauty shall consume in the grave." (Ps. xlix, 12, 14.) This is a vivid description of the wonderful contrast experienced in death by the rich, the great, and those who have lived luxuriously in this life. Utter decay and rottenness shall waste them away. But to the Psalmist there was a brighter hope: "But God will redeem my soul from the power of the grave." (Ps. xlix, 15.) "That is,' says Dr. Adam Clarke, *in loco*, "by the plainest construction, I shall have a resurrection from the dead, and an entrance into glory. Death shall have no dominion over me." One can not fail to notice the unhesitating confidence with which David asserts that God will redeem him from the grave. There is no doubt, no questioning; but his soul enters into the full conviction of the power and faithfulness of the Divine Word. A striking comment upon this passage is found in Ps. xvii, 15: "I shall be satisfied, when I awake, with thy likeness."

Let us, also, note the force of that memorable declaration of Job, (xix, 25, 27:) "For I know that my Redeemer liveth, and that he shall stand at the latter day upon the earth; and though after my skin worms destroy this body, yet in my flesh shall I see God: whom I shall see for myself, and mine eyes shall behold, and not another; though my reins be consumed within me." We are aware that this is a disputed passage; some making it refer simply to Job's restoration to health and happiness, and others regarding it as an announcement of his faith in a coming Redeemer, and through him of the resurrection from the dead. We think no one will doubt that the impression made upon the common reader will be that Job refers to Christ and to the resurrection from the dead. This first impression is strengthened by the solemn manner in which the passage is introduced. Job was evidently laboring with some momentous thought. What he had uttered before in defense of himself and in refutation of his friends, he is willing should pass away. But now—so momentous is the truth to which he is about to give utterance, that he would not have the least portion of it lost. "O that my words were now written! O that they were printed in a book! that they were graven with an iron pen and lead in the rock forever!" (Job xix, 23, 24.) Nothing could be more apt or appropriate, if by a Divine afflatus *he was about* to announce the sublime doctrine of redemption and the resurrection, that he should desire every word and every syllable to be preserved as a testimony among the generations yet to come. But if he referred simply to his personal temporal deliverance, to desire such a record of it as this particular point for the ages to come, borders closely upon the absurd.

But when we come to examine the terms and figures employed in the passage itself, it is difficult to avoid the conclusion that, in the sweep of his inspired vision, Job comprehended the great Redeemer of men. My Redeemer *liveth*—is alive now. But in the latter day he shall *stand upon the earth;* and through him should be the resurrection from the dead. What though *after my skin worms shall have destroyed this entire body*, yet in my flesh shall I see God. Nay, in this identic body that has been decomposed and devoured by worms, should he behold him! for he was to see Him for or by himself and with his own eyes. We leave it for the skeptic and the infidel to explain how all these events could happen without a resurrection from the dead.

3. *Coincident with the foregoing propositions, and going to show that the doctrine of the resurrection was taught in the Old Testament, we notice the fact that it was generally received by the Jews.*

Gaussen says it was a beautiful custom among the Jews of his acquaintance, on entering the cemetery for the purpose of burial, to bow themselves three times toward the earth, and then taking up some grass from the spot where the grave was to be dug, to throw it behind them, while they together repeated aloud these words of the prophet, "Your bones shall flourish like an herb." (Isaiah lxvi, 14.) Thus was symbolized, that as the herb was resuscitated from the death of Winter, so should the remains of their departed brother, now returned to dust, revive again in the resurrection Spring. This custom had its origin, no doubt, in a faith that had come down to them from the ancient time.

Incidental evidence of the existence of this faith among the Jews is afforded in the exclamation of Herod, when he heard of the wonderful works of Christ: "This is John the Baptist; he is risen from the dead." (Matt. xiv, 2.) Such a thought would hardly have occurred to him, had not the doctrine of the resurrection of the dead been generally received.

Another evidence is found in the fact that the rejection by the Sadducees of the doctrine of the resurrection is so often referred to as a marked peculiarity of that small and ignoble sect. Had not the doctrine been generally received by the Jews, its denial would not have been regarded as the characteristic badge of a peculiar sect—distinguishing it from others.

Again, when our Savior comforts Martha with the promise, "Thy brother shall rise again," she, supposing that he was simply applying to the case the common and comforting doctrine of the resurrection, responds, "I know that he shall rise again in the resurrection at the last day." (John xi, 23, 24.) Here, most clearly, the general resurrection of the dead is referred to as a doctrine known and received. Else, when Jesus spoke of the resurrection of Lazarus, Martha would not have supposed he referred to the "resurrection at the last day."

We know that some endeavor to evade the force of this conclusion by saying that *anastasis*, the word employed here, means merely the future existence of man, without any reference to a resurrection. But Martha speaks of an event that shall take place "at the last day." And our Lord, in the very next verse, makes a distinction between *anastasis* and *the future life:* "I am the resurrection (*anastasis*) and the life," (*καὶ ἡ ζωή*.) But to place the matter beyond all doubt, the sacred writers speak of the *resurrection of Christ* from the dead as an *anastasis*. In Acts i, 22, Peter speaks of the apostles as being "witnesses of his resurrection"—*anastasis*. In Acts ii, 31, it is said of David: "He, seeing this before, spake of the resurrection (*anastasis*) of Christ, that his soul was not left in hell, neither did his flesh see corruption." (See, also, Acts iv, 33.) "And with great power gave the apostles witness of the resurrection (*anastasis*) of the Lord Jesus." The apostle Peter speaks of the "elect" as being "begotten again unto a lively hope, by the resurrection (*anastasis*) of Jesus Christ from the dead." (1 Pet. i, 3.) These passages refer not to the *future life* of Christ in glory, but to *the resurrection of his body* from the grave. They are absolutely conclusive of the subject.

In the eleventh of Hebrews, all through which the apostle portrays the nature of faith, and its triumphs amid persecutions and deaths, he reaches the climax in those who, in the midst of their tortures, would not accept deliverance at the sacrifice of their faith, "that they might obtain a better resurrection." (Heb. xi, 35.) Thus, in the darkness and gloom of that earlier age of type, and shadow, and prophecy, the glorious coronal of the resurrection was the hope and the stay of God's suffering and persecuted ones.

One other fact to show that this doctrine was generally received among the Jews. We refer to the speech of Paul before Felix, in which, referring to the Jews, he says: "They themselves also allow that there shall be a resurrection of the dead, both of the just and unjust." (Acts xxiv, 15.) When we consider the person uttering this declaration—how thoroughly versed he was in all manner of questions among the Jews; and when we consider the occasion upon which it was uttered, and the audience that heard it without denial, we can scarcely conceive of evidence that could be more conclusive, that the doctrine of the resurrection of the dead was generally received among the Jews as a part of their religious faith, taught in their sacred writings.

III. The doctrine of the resurrection is still more clearly asserted in the Scriptures of the New Testament.

In the New Testament we find the references to this doctrine so numerous, that, without classification, we shall fail to present the subject as clearly as we wish. It will be our business, then, to enunciate a few points.

1. *The doctrine of the resurrection had, on various occasions, the tacit assent of Christ.* Had the belief in the resurrection been an error, it would have afforded our Savior an excellent opportunity to correct the error of the people, when the Sadducees came to him caviling at the doctrine. But instead of showing that the Jews had mistaken the Scriptures, and that the doctrine of the resurrection was not revealed in them, he shows simply that the cavils of the Sadducees sprung from their ignorance of the power of God. The doctrine of the resurrection could hardly be asserted with more force than is here done by Christ. The very fact that it is a sort of tacit recognition, and at the same time an uncovering of the folly of an ignorant, pretentious objector, gives to this incident peculiar pertinence.

Again, also, when Martha refers to "the resurrection at the last day," our Savior makes no correction of her faith. He does not blast her hope by saying that the dead rise not, and that there is no resurrection. It is utterly inconsistent with all our ideas of his character to suppose that would have left so dear a friend the dupe of so false a hope. Here, then, is the tacit assent of our Savior to the doctrine. But we stop not here.

2. *The doctrine of the resurrection of the dead is distinctly taught and affirmed by our Lord.* When teaching to his disciples the exercise of humility and charity to the poor who could not recompense them, he told them they should not lose their reward; for, says he, "thou shalt be recompensed at the resurrection of the just." (Luke xiv, 14.) Now, if there is no resurrection at all, and consequently none of the just, the *time* of their recompense could never come. One of two things must be admitted—either that Christ received and taught the doctrine of the resurrection, or that he here presents false motives to his disciples, and inspires groundless hopes in their hearts.

But in John v, 28, 29, our Savior speaks in more emphatic terms, and gives a more comprehensive view of the resurrection. Referring to the spiritual transformation of those who hear the Word of God and believe on him, he says: "Marvel not at this: for the hour is coming, in the which all that are in the graves shall hear his voice, and shall come forth; they that have done good, unto the resurrection of life; and they that have done evil, unto the resurrection of damnation." Here, the resurrection spoken of is that of those who are *in the graves;* and it numbers both classes, the good and the wicked. Nay, the very agency by which the resurrection shall be effected is mentioned; "they," while sleeping in their graves, *shall hear his voice.*

Again, our Savior says that it is the Father's will "that of all which he hath given me, I should lose nothing, but should *raise it up again at the last day.*" (John vi, 39.) He also declares that every one that believeth on the Son hath everlasting life: "And I will raise him up at the last day," (verse 40.) And, again, of each one of those who, drawn by the Father, comes to Him, "I will raise him up at the last day," (verse 44.) And still again, that "whoso eateth my flesh and drinketh my blood, hath eternal life; and I will raise him up at the last day," (verse 54.) This series of passages evidently all refer to the same time and the same event that Martha referred to, when she said, "I know that he shall rise again in the resurrection at the last day."

The establishing of the point before us does not require further Scripture quotation. But we recur again to our Savior's reply to the cavilings of the Sadducees, in which he makes a most striking enunciation of the resurrection. "They which shall be accounted worthy to obtain that world, and *the resurrection from the dead*, neither marry, nor are given in marriage: neither can they die any more; for they are equal unto the angels; and are the children of God, being the children of the resurrection." (Luke xx, 35, 36.)

3. *The doctrine of the resurrection was affirmed in various ways by the apostles.*

(1.) They asserted that God had raised the dead. "Women received their dead raised to life again." (Heb. xi, 35.)

(2.) They declared their own confident expectation of a resurrection from the dead. "I have hope toward God," said Paul, as he reasoned before Felix, "that there shall be a resurrection of the dead, both of the just and the unjust." (Acts xxiv, 15.) And again, he says, "We groan within ourselves, waiting for the adoption, to-wit, the redemption of our body." (Rom. viii, 23.)

(3.) They connected the resurrection of Christ with the resurrection of the believer. "God hath both raised up the Lord, and will also raise up us by his own power." (1 Cor. v, 14.) "Knowing that he which raised up the Lord Jesus shall raise up us also by Jesus." (2 Cor. iv, 14.)

(4.) It is directly asserted that God will raise the dead.

"He that raised up Christ shall also quicken your mortal bodies." (Rom. viii, 11.) "God which raiseth the dead." (2 Cor. i, 9.) In the fifteenth chapter of first Corinthians, the apostle not only asserts the resurrection of the dead, but undertakes its demonstration in one of his most conclusive and masterly arguments. He shows, first, that Christ has risen, and from hence infers that there must be a resurrection of the dead. This thought he elaborates and amplifies, meeting the cavils of the objector, exhibiting the glory of the resurrection body, declaring the Divine agency by which we obtain the victory over death and the grave, and finally applying the practical inferences which flowed so richly from the subject.

(5.) This doctrine was not only asserted by the apostles, but it entered largely into their preaching, and formed an important and distinguishing feature of their doctrine. Hence it is said that the priests, and the captain of the Temple, and the Sadducees, were "grieved that they taught the people and preached, *through Jesus*, the resurrection from the dead." (Acts iv, 2.) St. Paul also refers to this as one of the elementary doctrines of the Christian faith, and speaks of it as "the doctrine of the resurrection of the dead." (Heb. vi, 2.)

(6.) This doctrine was also made a ground of objection to their teaching. "And when they heard of the resurrection of the dead, some mocked." (Acts xvii, 32.)

(7.) They expressed wonder at its rejection by others. "Why should it be thought a thing incredible with you that God should raise the dead?" (Acts xxvi, 8.) "How say some among you that there is no resurrection of the dead?" (1 Cor. xv, 12.)

(8.) They also reasoned with objectors. After introducing an objector as saying, "How are the dead raised up? and with what body do they come?" (1 Cor. xv, 35,) the apostle replies by showing the corresponding analogies in nature, instead of disclaiming the doctrine.

(9.) They also rebuked those who claimed that the resurrection was already passed. "Who concerning the truth have erred, saying, that the resurrection is passed already."

(10.) Finally, the grand scene of the resurrection is graphically portrayed in the Revelation. "And I saw the dead, small and great, stand before God; and the books were opened: and another book was opened, which is the book of life: and the dead were judged out of those things which were written in those books, according to their works. And the sea gave up the dead which were in it; and death and hell gave up the dead which were in them: and they were judged every man according to their works." (Rev. xx, 12, 13.)

We have now shown the following facts in relation to the doctrine of the resurrection; namely, that our Savior tacitly assented to it when casually mentioned before him; that he distinctly affirmed and taught it; that the inspired apostles asserted that God had raised the dead, expressed their own confident expectation of a resurrection, and asserted the doctrine of the resurrection in the most positive manner; that the doctrine entered largely into their preaching—was one of the grounds of objection urged against them by their opponents; that they expressed wonder at its rejection by others, and reasoned with objectors; that they rebuked those who said the resurrection was already passed; and finally, that the rising of the dead from their graves in the earth and in the sea is shadowed forth in graphic outline in the Revelation. With these facts proved before us, whatever may be said about the absurdity or the impossibility of the resurrection, it must be admitted that it is a doctrine of the Bible. We may as well question whether light proceeds from the sun, as whether the revelation of such a doctrine is made in the Bible. He who takes the Bible, must take along with it the doctrine of the resurrection.

IV. Demonstrated by Miraculous Resurrections.

It might have been reasonably anticipated that a doctrine so far removed from the ordinary perceptions of sense; standing also, as it were, without the field peculiarly claimed as lying within the scope of science and reason; suggested only by a few dimly-read and poorly-understood analogies of nature; and yet involving and unfolding the most glorious prospect to redeemed humanity—it might have been reasonably anticipated, we say, that such a doctrine would, in some way, receive special authentication and attestation. This reasonable expectation is fully answered. Not only is the doctrine clearly revealed; not only have inspired men gloried amid worldly sorrows and deaths in this great faith; but the grave has been made to utter her testimony; Death, despoiled in his own dark and dread dominion, has been compelled to make confession that his is not an everlasting—a *sealed dominion*. One single case of real miraculous resurrection from the dead, clearly and satisfactorily established, must demonstrate the possible resurrection of every individual from the grave. Let us, then, see what light may be gleaned from individual miraculous resurrections. Such facts are all the more valuable, because they not only exemplify, in some sort, the Scripture revelation of the subject, but also wear another character, it may be equally significant for purposes of argument; namely, that of *testimony founded on facts*.

1. *The son of the widow of Zarephath.* (1 Kings xvii, 17.) Roll back the tide of time till we reach some nine centuries before the coming of our Lord. Let us stand by the gate of the ancient city "that belongeth to Zidon."

Upon the earth has descended neither dew nor rain for many days. The earth is parched and dry, and the people are famishing for food. An old man approaches; his locks are white; his countenance bespeaks one who is conversant with heaven. He approaches a poor widow gathering sticks without the gate, and asks the boon of a little water and a morsel of bread. But the woman, standing up before him like the gaunt figure of famine, declares that of all her wasted store only "an handful of meal in a barrel and a little oil in a cruse" were all that remained to her; and that she is now gathering a few sticks to cook the last meal for herself and her son before they die. But at the instance of the man of God she consents to share with him this her last morsel. But, lo! the meal wastes not, and the oil does not fail from day to day!

But now a new source of sorrow arises. The son of the widow sickens and dies. The bereaved mother bemoans her loss as a visitation of God. "O, thou man of God! art thou come unto me to call my sin to remembrance, and to slay my son?" Her son is dead: no thought or dream, or presentiment of his restoration to life seems to have entered into her mind. Her sins, her loss, her desolation—cheerless, rayless, hopeless—seem to occupy all her thoughts. Elijah takes the son from her arms, carries him to the "loft" where he slept himself, and laid him on his own bed. Then he cries mightily unto God in prayer; and stretched himself three times upon the corpse of the lad, beseeching that his soul may be restored—*come into him again*. Then breath returned into that dead body—"the soul (*nephesh*) of the child came into him again and he revived." And Elijah took the child again in his arms, brought him down and presented him to his weeping mother, saying, "*See, thy son liveth!*"

Rising even above the majesty of the wonderful faith and

the miraculous power that restored this child to life from the dead, is the simplicity and the purity of all this scene. The simplicity of truth is manifest in every part.

Again, the petition—*let this child's soul come into him again*—regards the soul, not as having died within the body, but as having gone out of it, and as being yet alive somewhere without the body. So, also, when it is said that the child's soul—*nephesh*—came into him, *into the midst of him*, it is implied that a *living thing* came back into the *dead body*, and, by reuniting with it, restored that body to life. This whole transaction clearly shows, that, (1.) There is an immortal spirit existing in man. (2.) This spirit can and does exist in a separate state from the body, and does not die with the body. (3.) God has power to remand that spirit back to the body, to restore the connection that had been dissolved by death, and, as a natural result, to quicken the dead body to life.

2. *Son of the Shunamite.* (2 Kings iv, 32–37.) Turn again to another scene: Elisha the prophet is seated in his tent upon Mount Carmel. It is a solemn, impressive place, a place for meditation, for communion with God. The heavens, in solemn grandeur, arch above him; the rich plains and valleys of Sharon are on the east; the restless waves of the "great sea" dash against the mountain's base upon the west. Here Elijah, fifteen years before, had contended with the false prophets of Baal, and brought down fire from heaven to consume his sacrifice. And it was here, too, upon some elevated solitary crag—the loftiest peak of Carmel—that Elijah was gladdened by the little cloud, no bigger than a man's hand, rising from the sea, the sign of God that the famine should cease.

But wonders connected with this hallowed spot have not yet ceased. Yonder approaches a woman, riding in haste. She is at once recognized as the Shunamite, at whose house the prophet had often been rested and refreshed. How tender the salutation of the man of God: "Is it well with thee? is it well with thy husband? is it well with the child?" Strange must have been the feelings of that struggling heart when she answered, "It is well." Yet she bows herself down, and takes hold upon the feet of the prophet, and there pours out the burden of her agony. Her little son, an only child, given by God, and grown to be a lad, going out to his father among the reapers, had fallen, and as he cried, "My head, my head," one of the young men bore him to his mother, upon whose knee he sat till noon, and then died. The light of the dwelling had now gone out. The bereaved mother bore the precious burden in her own arms up to the room she had made for the prophet in her house, and laid him on the prophet's bed; then she closed the door, and hastened to Carmel to lay her burden before the Lord.

Hardly was the tale of sorrow completed, when the prophet, giving his staff to Gehazi, said, "Go thy way; if thou meet any man salute him not; and if any salute thee answer him not again; and lay thy staff upon the face of the child." At the importunity of the afflicted woman, the prophet also follows after. But Gehazi "laid his staff upon the face of the child; but there was neither voice nor hearing." And when Elisha came to the house, the child was still dead, lying upon the bed, and he entered the room and closed the door. Then he prayed unto the Lord, and stretched himself upon the corpse of the child, till his flesh warmed with life, and he opened his eyes; then he called the mother and committed the child to her arms.

This whole narration is also one of touching simplicity. There are no studied parts acted, no labored disguises; the unsuspecting simplicity of conscious innocence and purity mark every act in the scene and every word in the narration.

3. *The man raised to life by touching the bones of Elisha* Elijah and Elisha are two of the most remarkable characters in sacred history. Of Elijah it is difficult to determine whether he was a man or an angel in a human body. Elisha was his student, his companion, and successor. He was present at the ascension of his master, and saw the chariot of fire, and heard the rushing whirlwind with which he passed into the skies. And to him descended the mantle of the departing Elijah. For sixty-five years he remained the witness of God and the wonder of Israel. He then died. Joash, the king of Israel, coming down to him in his last sickness, and weeping over him, exclaiming in almost precisely the same language uttered by the prophet himself upon the ascension of Elijah, "O my father, my father, the chariot of Israel and the horsemen thereof!" In Ecclesiasticus xlviii, 12–14, after referring to the character and works of Elijah, it is said, "Elisha was filled with his spirit; whilst he lived, he was not moved with the presence of any prince; neither could any bring him into subjection. Nothing could overcome him; and after his death *his body prophesied*." Such was the prophet Elisha.

Not long after his death the following event occurred, as recorded in the sacred narrative, and to which evident allusion is made in the close of the extract from Ecclesiasticus: "And the bands of the Moabites invaded the land at the coming in of the year. And it came to pass, as they were burying a man, that, behold, they spied a band of men; and they cast the man into the sepulcher of Elisha: and when the man was let down, and touched the bones of Elisha, he revived, and stood up on his feet." (2 Kings xiii, 20, 21.) This incident is no less wonderful than suggestive. The funeral procession, finding that they could not in safety carry the corpse to the appointed place of burial on account of the near approach of the marauding bands of their enemies, pause in their course. The grave of Elisha is at hand, and here they hasten to make a temporary deposit of the dead. But, lo, a marvel appears! The man who had so honored God in life is now honored of the Most High. His very bones are endowed with miraculous power. As the corpse is lowered down slowly into the tomb of Elisha, it at length touches the bones of the prophet, when instantly it quivers with new life; and, to the astonishment of all, the dead man rises and stands upon his feet. Thus did God not only give demonstration of the divine mission of Elisha, and in a way well adapted to rivet the impression and also the remembrance of his teachings upon the minds of the people, but he also gave them, in their dark age, a wonderful glimpse of his resurrection power.

It may be urged of these most touching and beautiful examples, that the number of witnesses was small, and the miracles were comparatively private. The skeptic may object that there is room for at least the suspicion of collusion or imposture; or, at any rate, that there is not that degree of certainty in these miracles that there would have been had the transactions taken place openly and in the presence of many witnesses. There may seem to be some force to these suggestions; yet they are offset by the manifest truthfulness of the narrations, and by the fact that the miracles were known, acknowledged, and recorded in the sacred books of the Jews. Yet we will gratify the inquirer by seeking examples of greater publicity. They are not wanting in the sacred record.

4. *Daughter of Jairus, the ruler.* (Luke viii, 49–56; Matt. ix, 18–26; Mark v, 22–43.) Imagine ourselves to be standing amidst the solitary ruins of an ancient city, upon the western coast of the Sea of Galilee. As I look around upon the silent desolation of what was once a place

of opulence and splendor, I remember that our Savior once said, "And thou, Capernaum, which art exalted unto heaven, shalt be brought down to hell." (Matt. xi, 23.)

But now a new scene rises before me. I seem to have gone back to Capernaum, as it was when honored as the abode of our Lord. I seem to behold the Savior; near the sloping banks of the sea he stands and discourses to the multitude around him. Just then a man, with hurried step and anxious countenance, is seen making his way through the crowd. He is recognized as the ruler of the synagogue, and the multitude respectfully open a passage for him, as he hurries along. He approaches Christ, and instead of denouncing his doctrine and commanding him to silence, he bows down to the very earth before him, and while his frame is trembling with emotion and the tears of anguish are rolling down over his cheek, he says, "My little daughter lieth at the point of death; I pray thee, come and lay thy hands on her, that she may be healed." This was his only daughter, and she had now reached the age of twelve years. Disease had fastened upon her. Every means that affection, wealth, or skill could devise had been employed without effect; and at last the sorrow-stricken father beholds the dear object of parental affection struggling in the agonies of death. What shall he do? Every resort has failed. Must she die? Is there no hope? O, where shall he now find help? In his extremity he remembers the strange, mysterious person who has been filling the whole land with the fame of his words and his deeds, and whose abode was in Capernaum. He is not his disciple; he believes not his doctrine; nay, he has, perhaps, often treated him with indignity, when he would have taught the people in the synagogue. But now this is his only hope, every other resource has failed; and there is a possibility that he who has just delivered the dweller among the tombs from the legion of devils that possessed him, may heal his daughter. Thus in his extremity he comes to Christ.

Our Savior pauses in his discourse. He goes with the ruler. The multitude, filled with wonder and admiration, press around him and go along. While they are still in the way, a messenger meets them with the announcement that the "daughter is dead." Hope seems to expire in the breast of the father; but Jesus encourages him to "be not afraid; only believe." Then, with Peter, James, and John, he enters the house; and to those that were weeping and wailing greatly, he said, "Why make ye this ado and weep? the damsel is not dead, but sleepeth." But "they laughed him to scorn." But he, when he had put them all out, except the parents and his three disciples, took the maiden by the hand, and said unto her, "Arise!" And, behold, life came into her, and she "arose, and walked!" We wonder not at the astonishment of those who beheld this miracle of Divine power! It is that same power which shall awake to life our sleeping dust in "the resurrection at the last day."

> "The Savior raised
> Her hand from off her bosom, and spread out
> The snowy fingers in his palm, and said,
> 'Maiden! arise!'—and suddenly a flush
> Shot o'er her forehead, and along her lips,
> And through her cheek, the rallied color ran;
> And the still outline of her graceful form
> Stirr'd in the linen vesture; and she clasp'd
> The Savior's hand, and, fixing her dark eyes
> Full on his beaming countenance, AROSE."

Now, let any one scrutinize the facts of this miracle and see how little ground there is to suspect any fraud or imposture in it. (1.) Neither the parents nor friends were the disciples of Christ. (2.) Our Savior was not present during her sickness, nor at her death. (3.) There is full evidence of her death; first, the father declares her in a dying state; second, the messenger meets them in the way and reports her to be dead; third, the attendants in the house had all witnessed her death and bewailed it; and finally, when our Savior, in order that his enemies might not afterward say that she was only asleep, and that she was only awakened out of sleep by him instead of being raised from the dead, suggests that she is not dead, "they laughed him to scorn." (4.) There were at least *five* personal witnesses of this resurrection. (5.) And last of all, she, that was so evidently dead, walked, and ate, and lived.

5. *Son of the widow of Nain.* (Luke vii, 11–18.) Let us now take another case, and one of still more open and striking character. Behold the gate of the city of Nain is thrown open, and a funeral procession marches forth. The corpse is a noble youth—"the only son of his mother, and she a widow." The respect in which that youth was held, and the deep sympathy felt for that bereaved mother, is attested by the vastness of the procession, for "much people of the city was with her." The corpse had been prepared for the burial, and weeping friends are now bearing it to its long home. Prominent in that moving assemblage is she whose affliction touches every heart.

> "There was one,
> Only one mourner. Close behind the bier,
> Crumpling the pall upon her withered hands,
> Follow'd an aged woman. Her short steps
> Faltered with weakness, and a broken moan
> Fell from her lips, thicken'd convulsively
> As her heart bled afresh. The pitying crowd
> Follow'd apart, but no one spoke to her.
> She had no kinsmen. She had lived alone—
> A widow with one son. He was her all—
> The only tie she had in the wide world—
> And he was dead. They could not comfort her."

Just then, a strange man, followed by an equally-strange assemblage, is seen approaching. The sight of the bereaved widow touches his heart, and he says to her, "Weep not." Then he turns and lays his hand upon the bier. They that bear it stand still. Then with sublime and commanding authority—authority such as dwells only in the heart of Omnipotence—authority such as can wake the dead—he says, "Young man, I say unto thee, Arise." In a moment the chains of death are broken; the icy coldness is succeeded by returning warmth; life and animation return. How astonished the multitude! That body just now dead begins to move; the winding sheet is parted; the young man sits up; he speaks! Who can depict the wonder, the astonishment of the gazing multitude! who can conceive the flutterings of hope, joy, transport, in the breast of that mother, as she beholds her son restored to life! Hardly could she be persuaded it was reality till the mysterious personage who had raised him to life committed him to her arms.

I wonder not that fear fell upon all the people, and that they said with united voice "a great prophet has risen among us, and God has visited his people;" nor yet that the fame of such an event—so clearly and so indubitably the work of miraculous power—spread not only through all Judea, but also through all the surrounding region.

6. *Resurrection of Lazarus.* (John xi, 1–54.) One example more of this class of evidence must suffice. At Bethany, near unto Jerusalem, is a family much beloved by the Savior. Their home was his retreat in the time of sorrow, and his place of rest in the time of weariness. Lazarus is now sick, and drawing nigh unto death; but Jesus, the guest and comforter of the family, is away in Bethabara, a day's journey distant. The sisters of Lazarus dispatch a messenger to Christ, saying, "Lord, he whom thou lovest is sick." Scarcely had the messenger departed when their brother died. The day's journey is performed; the messenger comes to Christ, and delivers his message. But still for two days the Savior lingers in the same place.

Why does he thus linger? has he ceased to love his friend? Does he feel no sympathy for the bereaved sisters who have so often ministered to him? or does he fear to test his miraculous power before the scrutiny of those Jews that have come down from Jerusalem? "Surely," they will say, "if he can raise the dead, let him now come and raise his friend; and if he fail to do this, let him be accounted an impostor and a villain."

But, lo, as the fourth day dawns, our Savior says to his disciples, "Let us go into Judea again." But his disciples sought to dissuade him, because the Jews had, just before, attempted to stone him, and were still seeking his life. However, finding their dissuasions of no avail, Thomas said to his fellow-disciples, "Let us also go, that we may die with him."

Slowly and thoughtfully the little group journey back into Judea, and approach the now desolate home in Bethany. Then Martha, as soon as she heard Jesus was coming, went forth to meet him. How affecting her address, "Lord, if thou hadst been here, my brother had not died." How sublime the discourse of our Lord, as he speaks of the resurrection, and endeavors to prepare her mind for that stupendous miracle of power which was to be the wonder of the world.

In the mean time, the other sister, Mary, is called, and goes forth to meet her Lord, followed by the whole assembly of the Jews, who suppose she is going to the grave, there to weep and bemoan her loss. How affecting the scene, as, amid the weeping and the moans of gathered friends, the disconsolate Mary casts herself at Jesus' feet, and cries out, "'Lord, if thou hadst been here, my brother had not died'---our house would not have been desolate, our hearts would not have been broken with anguish!"

The auspicious moment for the exercise of Divine power

had now arrived. Surrounded by the weeping friends, Jesus "groaned in spirit and was troubled." The sympathies of his soul were awakened, and "Jesus wept." The Jews were struck with the Savior's tenderness, and said, "Behold how he loved him!" and said among themselves, "Could not this man, which opened the eyes of the blind, have caused that even this man should not have died?" Neither they nor the bereaved sisters seemed to dream of his resurrection from the dead. So that when they came to the grave, and Jesus bade them roll away the stone from its mouth, they interposed that he had been dead four days, and the body must therefore have become offensive. But at his command the stone is rolled away—the astonished Jews are looking on with wonder—the weeping sisters hardly know whether to hope or fear. He lifts his eyes to heaven, offering a brief memorial of his faith to the Father, and then, with a voice whose tones of authority penetrated the deep cavern of the dead, he cried, "Lazarus, come forth!" Memorable words! "Martha! Mary! dry thy tears; thy brother lives!" He comes forth, with his grave-clothes around him. Ye wondering, doubting Jews, come, with your own hands, "loose him and let him go," that ye may know that he whose death-agony ye witnessed—he, whose body ye laid in the grave, has been truly restored to life.

> "And instantly, bound hand and foot,
> And borne by unseen angels from the cave,
> He that was dead stood with them. At the word
> Of Jesus, the fear-stricken Jews unloosed
> The bands from off the foldings of his shroud;
> And Mary, with her dark vail thrown aside,
> Ran to him swiftly, and cried, 'LAZARUS!
> MY BROTHER LAZARUS!' and tore away
> The napkin she had bound about his head,
> And touch'd the warm lips with her fearful hand—
> And on his neck fell weeping. And while all
> Lay on their faces prostrate, Lazarus
> Took Mary by the hand, and they knelt down
> And worshiped Him who loved them."

7. *The dead bodies of the saints resurrected at the crucifixion.* The prodigies attendant upon the crucifixion were such as filled the land with consternation and dread. Earthquakes rent the solid rocks and opened the graves of the dead. The sun vailed itself in darkness and the earth wrapped around her the sable robes of mourning. "From the sixth hour there was darkness over all the land until the ninth hour." (Matt. xxvii, 45.) This darkness lasted from noon till three o'clock in the afternoon—a period of *three hours.* It was, therefore, clearly a supernatural event—as a total eclipse of the sun can not last longer than a quarter of an hour; and besides that, this being the time of the Passover, was at the full moon, when an eclipse of the sun is impossible. Mention is made of these prodigies by heathen writers; and Dionysius, the king of Egypt, is recorded to have exclaimed, "Either the God of nature is suffering, or the machine of the world is tumbling into ruin." And even the Roman centurion, and those with him, when they witnessed these wonders, "feared greatly," and exclaimed: "Truly, this was the Son of God!" The multitude who were gathered to witness the spectacle were also filled with wonder at the mysterious displays of the power of God, and "smote their breasts and returned" to their homes.

It was among such prodigies as these that St. Matthew says, "And the graves were opened; and many bodies of the saints which slept arose, and came out of the graves after his resurrection, and went into the holy city, and appeared unto many." (Matt. xxvii, 52, 53.) It is not recorded who these saints were, nor yet what became of them. It seems probable, however, that they were persons known in Jerusalem, and thus their ready identification. Their resurrection was no doubt designed, along with the other marvels of the occasion, to confirm the Divine mission of

Christ, and demonstrate him to be the promised Messiah of the Jews. They seem to have been quickened to life *in*, *through*, or *after*—μετά—his resurrection. They did not rob him of his character as "*the first-fruits;*" but they rose with him, and probably accompanied him to glory.

Now, let us glance at this progressive development of this miraculous power of restoring the dead to life. In the case of the daughter of Jairus, death had just taken place. The body was scarcely cold; the flush of life and youth had hardly faded from her cheek; the corpse was still in her father's house, and they who had witnessed her dying agony were still weeping over it. Hardly had the spirit passed the gates of death, when it was summoned back by the great arbiter of life and death, and bid to tabernacle awhile longer in its tenement of clay. With the young man of Nain, death had occurred some time before. The corpse had lain the appointed time; it was no longer fit for the sight of the eye; it had been prepared for burial, and was now being borne to "the house appointed for all living." No Savior had been invited to the house of mourning; none was expected. The widow had *given up* her son. The whole city, moved by compassion, had gone forth; no other result than that of his burial enters into any of their thoughts. Just then the Savior meets them, as it were by accident, in the open highway. He is moved with compassion, touches the bier, and the dead man lives. The case of Lazarus presents features differing from both of these. He had not only been prepared for burial, but the body had already been laid in the tomb, when the Savior came to their now desolate home. The process of decomposition had already commenced, the rioting of the worms begun, and the body had therefore become offensive to the smell. But though the process had advanced further, it was not beyond the power of Omnipotence to check, and from incipient corruption life comes forth renewed in all its healthfulness and vigor. In the resurrection of the "bodies of the saints" there is still an additional feature of striking import. These "bodies" had been long entombed; the flesh had moldered back to dust; the dry bones and scattered dust only remained. But, behold, under the quickening power of the resurrection of the Son of God, these are restored to life. They come forth the type and the demonstration of a universal resurrection. It was the demonstration that Death was now crushed forever beneath the arm of the Almighty. It was the demonstration "that a power existed that could recover the plundered spoils of Death, could re-embody the parted spirit, could restore it to the fullness of its prerogatives as the quickening principle of an immortal frame."

One more fact—the resurrection of Christ—and our chain of argument will be complete. Even skepticism itself can ask no more. "Why, then, should it be thought a thing incredible with you, that God should raise the dead?"

But this theme—the resurrection of Christ—viewed first as a matter of fact, and secondly as the pledge of ours, is a theme so wide in its range, so full in its details, and so momentous in its bearing upon the general resurrection of the dead, that we must reserve it for a separate theme of discussion. In the mean time, let us be thankful that we have found so firm footing on which to plant our feet, as we have felt our way along in our search after truth. Even now, looking upon the cold form of death, we may say:

'Yet through these rigid limbs once more
A nobler life, erelong, shall pour;
These dead, dry bones again shall feel
New warmth and vigor through them steal;
Re-knit and living they shall soar
On high, where Christ lives evermore."

(*From the Ger. of N. Hermann.*)

X.

RESURRECTION OF CHRIST THE PLEDGE OF OURS.

"This Jesus hath God raised up, whereof we all are witnesses." ACTS ii, 32.
"Now if Christ be preached that he rose from the dead, how say some among you that there is no resurrection of the dead?" 1 COR. xv, 12.

THE resurrection of our Lord Jesus Christ has ever been regarded by the Christian Church as a doctrine of vast importance. It derives its importance not merely from its relation to the scheme of redemption—illustrating the office, character, and triumph of Christ—but also from its important relation to the general doctrine of the resurrection of the dead. The two things are closely allied by the apostle: "If there be no resurrection of the dead, then is Christ not risen;" and, on the other hand, "If Christ be not risen," then is our faith in the resurrection vain, and also they "which have fallen asleep in Christ are perished." In fact, so close is the connection between the resurrection of Christ and the final resurrection of those of whom he has "become the first-fruits," that those who admit the former will find little ground to question the latter.

It was a dark and gloomy hour when the Lord of life and glory—the hope of Israel—lay the victim of death, the tenant of the grave. How could the apostles ever have gone forth to preach salvation through a Savior still held by the bands of death? How could they have preached the resurrection of the dead, while he, through whom was the promise and the hope, was still shrouded in the dark prison-house of the tomb? His resurrection was, therefore, an essential element of their faith, and an essential feature of their ministry. To them the assurance of his resurrection was like the dawning of a new day upon a night of darkness and sorrow. They received it as the final confirmation of the Divinity of his mission—the demonstration of the doctrines he taught. They regarded it as completely annulling all those heresies that denied to man a future state, and placing upon an indestructible basis the doctrine of the resurrection of the dead. And in this light has the resurrection of our blessed Lord been viewed by the Church in all ages.

We shall make two points in this discussion; namely, 1. That the resurrection of Christ is strongly confirmed by circumstantial evidence, extraneous to the testimony of the direct witnesses of the fact; 2. That the fact of his resurrection is fully confirmed by direct, competent, and positive evidence.

I. Circumstantial or Corroborating Evidence of the Resurrection of Christ.

Our position here is, that *the circumstances connected with the case—circumstances assented to by the Jews as well as by the disciples—strongly corroborate the direct testimony, and can be satisfactorily accounted for on no other hypothesis than the actual resurrection of Jesus Christ from the dead.* The establishment of this proposition, it is true, will not demonstrate the certainty of the resurrection; but it will show us that all those coincident facts which might be reasonably looked for in connection with such an event do really exist, and that they are such facts as can not be accounted for on any other supposition. The consideration of them will, therefore, prepare our minds to weigh with cando and to feel the force of the direct testimony by which the resurrection of Christ is established as a fixed fact, in history and in religion.

1. *There was such a man as Jesus Christ.* This proposition lies at the very foundation of our faith. For if no such person ever existed, then all the narrations concerning him are forgeries or fictions. But, on the other hand, if it be shown that he actually lived and died as the Scriptures record of him, then have we a first presumption that all they record of him is true.

Here, setting aside for a moment the sacred narrative, we remark, that the reality of the life and death of Jesus Christ, in the earlier ages of Christianity, was universally conceded by both friend and foe. The only questions at issue related to his character and doctrines. Josephus, a bigoted Jewish historian, who witnessed the siege of Jerusalem, and who wrote within the first century of the Christian era, acknowledges that Christ "did many wonderful works," "won many to his persuasion," and, "at the instigation of the Jews and by Pilate's sentence, was suspended upon the cross," and that to the day in which he wrote "there remained a sect of men, who, from him, have the name of Christians, and who believed in his resurrection from the dead." The account of his death is mentioned by both Tacitus and Lucian. The facts of his trial and execution were communicated by Pilate to the Roman Senate; for both Justin Martyr and Tertullian appeal to the acts of Pilate, then extant, to corroborate their testimony concerning Christ.* Nor do they refer to them in an indefinite

* Modern research has brought to light the following curious relic:

Sentence rendered by Pontius Pilate, acting Governor of Lower Galilee, stating that Jesus of Nazareth shall suffer death on the cross.

In the year seventeen of the Emperor Tiberius Cæsar, and the 24th day of March, in the city of the holy Jerusalem, Annas and Caiaphas being high-priests, sacrificators of the people of God. Pontius Pilate, Governor of Lower Galilee,

and obscure manner, or among those who had not the means of refutation. The former, who lived only about a century after our Savior's death, and who suffered martyr dom at Rome, boldly asserts the fact in a letter to the Emperor Antoninus Pius, and refers him to the acts themselves for confirmation. The latter in his Apology, written about fifty years after Justin Martyr, affirms that Tiberius, the Emperor, was so struck with the accounts received from Palestine concerning Christ, that he would have deified him had the Senate assented, and even challenges the Senate to consult their records—*consulite commentarios vestros!*—for confirmation of the fact. This certainly was very rash on the part of these men, were they not borne out by the facts in the case. But again, Julian the apostate, Celsus, and Porphyry—all violent enemies to Christianity—

sitting in the presidential chair of the Prætory, condemns Jesus of Nazareth to die on the cross between two thieves—the great and notorious evidence of the people saying:

1. Jesus is a seducer.
2. He is seditious.
3. He is an enemy to the law.
4. He calls himself falsely the Son of God.
5. He calls himself falsely the King of Israel.
6. He entered the Temple followed by a multitude bearing palm branches in their hands.

Orders the first Centurion, Quilius Cornelius, to lead him to the place of exe cution.

Forbids any person whomsoever, either poor or rich, to oppose the death of Jesus.

The witnesses who signed the condemnation of Jesus are:

1. Daniel, Rabboni, a Pharisee.
2. Joannes Rorobable.
3. Raphael, Rabboni.
4. Capet, a citizen.

Jesus shall go out of the city of Jerusalem by the gate Struennus.

The above sentence is engraved on a copper plate. On one side are written these words: "A similar plate is sent to each tribe." It was found in an antique vase of white marble while excavating in the ancient city of Aquilla, in the kingdom of Naples, in the year 1850, and was discovered by the Commissioners of the arts of the French armies. At the expedition of Naples it was inclosed in a box of ebony, at the sacristy of the Charlatrem. The French translation was made by the members of the Commissioners of arts. The original is in the Hebrew language.

not only admit the existence of Christ, but, to account for his "wonderful works," are compelled to ascribe them to his wonderful skill as a magician. How kindred in spirit to the unbelieving Jews who were personal witnesses of the mighty works performed by Christ, and, unable to deny the fact of their performance, ascribed them to Beelzebub!

It has been left to modern skepticism to attempt the astounding feat of demolishing Christianity by denying that Christ ever lived. Volney, who called upon God and upon Christ when danger and death were before him, pretended to the astounding discovery, that the Gospels, which purport to be the history of the life and actions of Jesus Christ, were compiled with variations and improvements, from Hindoo tales. But, alas, for this shallow fabrication; so often as Christianity has demanded, "Where are the *originals* from which the compilation was made?" echo has responded, "*Where?*" German infidelity, however, has caught up the idea, and, with indefatigable effort, has sought to prove that the Gospels are *myths*—mere fancy sketches, and not a record of facts. It is contended that while such a man as Jesus *may* have lived, that the history of his life, doctrines, works, sufferings, and death, found in the New Testament, is utterly unworthy of credit, and to be regarded only as a succession of fictitious tales of a moral and allegorical character.

That this modern cavil is to supersede the clear and truthful narration of facts found in the Gospels—the constant belief and asseveration of all cotemporary witnesses, both friends and foes—the concessions of even the infidels of all early ages, as well as the authentic history of all ages, is a presumption too monstrous and absurd to obtain credit for a moment. Christianity, in its origin, as well as its progress, is blended with the history of the Roman Empire. The existence of Dioclesian or of Constantine might as well be qustioned as that of Jesus Christ; and neither can be denied without a direct palpable contravention of all the settled laws of human belief.

2. *The prophets not only foretold his appearance and character, but also his death and resurrection.* It was the joyful exclamation of Philip, when he had become conversant with Christ, "We have found him of whom Moses in the law, and the prophets, did write, Jesus of Nazareth, the son of Joseph." (John i, 45.) The Messiah was symbolized in the types of the Jewish dispensation. The offering of Isaac upon Mount Moriah, the lifting up of the brazen serpent in the wilderness, the entombing of Jonah in the belly of a whale, and, indeed, every sacrifice offered upon Jewish altars—all were typical of the sufferings, the sacrificial death, the entombing, and the resurrection of the Lord Jesus Christ.

But what was dimly shadowed forth in the types is exhibited with greater distinctness and with more significant particularity in the prophets. A messenger was to prepare the way before him. He was to come, the Desire of nations; to come before the scepter departed from Judah, four hundred and ninety years from the building of the second Temple, and before it was destroyed; and also to be born of a virgin. The very tribe, and family, and place of his nativity are foretold.* He was to preach, to

* To show the reader how comprehensive the prophecies were, and yet how minute in their statement of particulars, we give a condensed summary of them: 1. *A messenger or a forerunner was to announce his coming.* "I will send my messenger, and he shall prepare the way before me." (Mal. iii, 1.) "The voice of him that crieth in the wilderness, prepare ye the way of the Lord." (Isa. xl, 3.) "I will send you Elijah the prophet." (Mal. iv, 5.) The predictions were fulfilled in John the Baptist: "In those days came John the Baptist, preaching in the wilderness of Judea, saying, Repent, for the kingdom of heaven is at hand." (Matt. iii, 1; Luke i, 17.) "This is Elias which was to come." (Matt. xi, 14.) "Elias is come already." (Matt. xvii, 12; Mark ix, 13.) 2. *He was to come the Desire of nations.* "The desire of all nations shall come." (Hag. ii, 7.) Ancient writers give evidence of the awakened expectation of Eastern nations about the time of the birth of Christ. 3. *Before the scepter departed from Judah.* "The scepter shall not

work miracles, to purge the Temple, to ride in triumph into Jerusalem. But he was also to suffer, to be despised and

depart from Judah, nor a lawgiver from between his feet, till Shiloh come." (Gen. xlix, 10.) Judea was required to pay taxes, indicative that the scepter had departed to the Roman Emperor; and "this taxing was first made" at the birth of Christ. (Luke ii, 1-7.) 4. *He was to come while the second Temple was yet standing.* "I will fill this house"—that is, the second Temple—"with glory." "The glory of this latter house shall be greater than that of the former house." (Hag. ii, 7, 9.) Christ suffered crucifixion only *forty* years before the destruction of this second Temple. 5. *The time of his birth is distinctly specified.* "*Seventy weeks* are determined upon thy people and upon thy holy city, to finish the transgression, and to make an end of sins, and to make reconciliation for iniquity, and to bring in everlasting righteousness, and to seal up the vision and prophecy, and to anoint the Most Holy. Know therefore and understand, that from the going forth of the commandment to restore and to build Jerusalem, unto the Messiah the Prince, shall be *seven weeks*, and threescore and two weeks: the street shall be built again, and the wall, even in troublous times. And after *threescore and two weeks* shall Messiah be cut off, but not for himself; and the people of the prince that shall come shall destroy the city and the sanctuary; and the end thereof shall be with a flood, and unto the end of the war desolations are determined. And he shall confirm the covenant with many for *one week;* and in the *midst of the week* he shall cause the sacrifice and the oblation to cease, and for the overspreading of abominations he shall make it desolate, even until the consummation, and that determined shall be poured upon the desolate." (Dan. ix, 24–27.) The most reliable chronology shows that from the decree of Artaxerxes to Ezra to rebuild Jerusalem to the death of Christ, was a period of 490 years, corresponding precisely to the prophetic period of "seventy weeks," each "week" comprising *seven years*. On this supposition, let us apply the subdivisions mentioned in verses 25, 26, and 27.

1. From the decree till the city was rebuilt—"7 weeks," each of 7 years = 49 years.
2. From that date till the public appearance of Christ—"62 weeks," each of 7 years .... = 434 years.
3. The period of Christ's ministry in the midst of which he was to be "cut off"—"1 week" .... = 7 years.

490 years.

6. *He was to be born of a virgin.* "Behold a virgin shall conceive and bear a son, and shall call his name Immanuel." (Isa. vii, 14.) Christ was born of the Virgin Mary. (See Matt. i, 18–25; Luke i, 28–35.) 7. *His tribe is declared.* "The scepter shall not depart from Judah," etc. (Gen. xlix, 10.) "It is evident our Lord sprang from Judah." (Heb. vii, 14.) 8. *His family is specified.* And there shall come forth a rod out of the stem of Jesse, and a branch shall grow out of his roots." (Isa. xi, 1.) "Of this man's seed, according to his promise, hath God raised unto Israel a Savior." (Acts xiii, 23.) 9. *The place of his nativity is not forgotten.* "Thou Bethlehem Ephratah, though thou be little among the thousands of Judah, yet out of thee shall he come forth unto me, that is to be Ruler in Israel." (Micah v, 2.) "Jesus was born in Bethlehem of Judea." (Matt. ii, 1.) "Christ cometh of the seed of David, and out of the town of Bethlehem where David was." (John vii, 42.)

rejected of men, to be hated and persecuted, to be betrayed by his professed friend and sold for a specified sum; he was to be forsaken by his friends, mocked and smitten by his enemies; his hands and feet were to be pierced, and he was to be "lifted up," to be "cut off," to be "numbered with transgressors." The parting of his garments, the casting of lots upon his vesture, the gall and vinegar with which he should be insulted upon the cross, and the very language he should utter in his dying agony—all are foretold. Thus was he to die; but when dead, his bones were not to be broken, although it was customary to break the bones of those crucified. Though executed as a malefactor, he was to be buried with the rich, and yet not to be left in the grave, nor his body permitted to see corruption. Having risen from the dead, he was to ascend up on high, to be seated at the right hand of God, there to make intercession for his people, and to carry forward the grand designs of his mediatorial office till he shall come to execute final judgment upon all the nations of the earth. Such was the prophetic delineation of the sufferings, death, and resurrection of our Lord Jesus Christ.

3. *He had predicted his own death and resurrection.* What other meaning can we attach to the following declarations: "I am the resurrection and the life," (John xi, 25;) and, again, "Destroy this temple, and in three days I will raise it up," (John ii, 19;) and this "he spake of the temple of his body," (verse 21?) But to his disciples his language was more distinct and emphatic, and it is a matter of astonishment that they were so slow to comprehend it; for as he drew near the close of his ministry, he "began to show unto his disciples how he must go unto Jerusalem, and suffer many things of the elders, and chief-priests, and scribes, and be killed, and raised again the third day." (Matt. xvi, 21). On another occasion, as he was going up to Jerusalem, he took the disciples

apart, and said to them, "Behold, we go up to Jerusalem; and the Son of man shall be betrayed unto the chief-priests, and unto the scribes, and they shall condemn him to death: and shall deliver him to the Gentiles to mock, and to scourge, and to crucify him; and the third day he shall rise again." (Matt. xx, 17-19.) Whether the disciples comprehended these predictions or not, the Jews evidently understood that Christ had foretold his resurrection from the dead; for, after his execution, they went to Pilate, and said, "Sir, we remember that that deceiver said while he was yet alive, After three days I will rise again." (Matt. xxvii, 63.) Such were the predictions made by our Savior, while he was yet alive, concerning his resurrection; and such was the understanding of those predictions by his enemies, and the alarm they occasioned to them.

4. *He was actually crucified, dead, and buried.* The fact of his crucifixion and death is as fully confirmed by all history, sacred and profane, as is the fact of his existence. Both Jewish and Gentile opposers of Christianity in the early ages admit the fact of his crucifixion and burial. The testimony of his actual death becomes complete when we remember that he was wholly in the power of his enemies, and was crucified by them in the presence of a large multitude who witnessed the solemn scene. No one wrested the suffering Jesus from their grasp; they executed upon him, without let or hinderance, the unrighteous decree of the Roman governor; and when their work was done, reported him dead to Pilate, and asked permission to take the body down and bury it, on account of the approaching Sabbath. To be assured of his actual death, Pilate would not permit the body to be removed till the centurion who had been charged with his execution had been called, and the fact duly authenticated. After this he was taken down from the cross and subsequently buried in the tomb of

Joseph, of Arimathea; the Jews assisting at, and being witnesses of his burial.

5. *The utmost precaution was used to guard the body.* The Jews sought to guard his body because he had predicted his resurrection; therefore, fearing that his disciples, if the body remained unguarded, might steal it away, and then say he had risen, they sought from Pilate a guard. Pilate, nothing loth to gratify the Jews, and, perhaps, as he had condemned Christ, desiring to have it fully proved that he was an impostor, granted their request, and placed a guard of sixty men at their disposal. This guard were to keep constant watch over the tomb till the three days were past, and the hope of the resurrection extinguished. The tomb itself was hewn out of a solid rock, and was new. The body had been carefully deposited there by the Jews. A massive stone, difficult of removal, had been placed upon the entrance. The seal of the governor had been affixed to the door; thus anticipating the question, what is there to prevent the guards from taking him away—"*et quis custodes custodiet ipsos?*"—and who is to guard the guards themselves? The guards were required to deliver up, at the end of three days, the body that had been committed to their charge. It is difficult to conceive how greater precautions could have been taken in the case. The most bitter, unrelenting enemies of Christ strictly executed the direction of Pilate, "Make it as sure as ye can."

6. *On the morning of the third day the body had disappeared.* It had probably been the plan of the Jews to bring forth the dead body of Christ after the three days had expired, and to exhibit it as a final refutation of his pretensions, his doctrines, and his predictions. The body was with them, and they alone were responsible for its safe-keeping; and they were pledged to bring it forth. No stronger evidence that the body was missing can be desired

than the fact that, after all, *they failed to produce it.* Especially when the rumor spread abroad that the Savior had risen, and living witnesses began to assert that they had seen him, and conversed with him, felt of him, walked and eat with him, if the body was still in their possession, why did they not bring it forth? Or fifty days later, when the disciples began publicly to proclaim that Christ had risen from the dead, why is not the decaying body produced, to the confusion of those who asserted his resurrection? Nay, why is there not *some* evidence, that should allay excitement and prevent multitudes from being converted to Christianity, brought forward that the grave of Jesus had not been disturbed, or, at least, that those who had assumed the guardianship of the dead body still knew where it was? But the point is given up. The Jews not only fail to produce the body and to refute the disciples by telling where it is, but they are constrained to the reluctant confession that it has disappeared.

7. *The account given by the Jews of the disappearance of the body of Christ is absolutely incredible.* Having confessed to the disappearance of the body of Christ, they were bound to give some rational and authentic account of the matter, if they could. Their account should have the air of probability, should be sustained by fact.

Only two accounts of the disappearance have come down to us. The first is that given by his disciples, and confirmed by many witnesses, and by miracles, signs, and wonders; namely, that he rose from the dead. The second is the account rendered by the enemies of Christ—reported by the guard through the instigation of the priests—namely, that "his disciples came and stole him while we slept." Whatever conclusion we may come to in relation to the evidence of the resurrection of Christ from the dead, this account of the disappearance of the body is *absolutely incredible.*

(1.) It is incredible that *the whole guard* of sixty men, accustomed to the rigor of military discipline in the Roman army, should have been asleep while upon duty. The punishment of such an offense would have been death. The number of the guard, the responsibility of their charge, and especially the severity of the punishment of such an offense, preclude utterly the idea that they were all asleep. Had they really been asleep, and thus, through neglect of duty, permitted the disciples to steal away the body, they would have been much more likely to have feigned a miracle than to have made confession, had they not been bribed and protected by the Jewish priests and elders.

(2.) If the guards were really asleep, how did they know that the body was stolen at all? How could they, when asleep, recognize the persons who performed the robbery so readily and so clearly? It is a novel affair to bring men to testify to things that occurred while they were asleep! It is well that the fact that they were asleep should go along with and constitute a part of the testimony.

(3.) It is, again, utterly incredible that the guard, posted upon and around the tomb, should have slept so soundly that the tomb could be approached by several men, the seal broken, the great stone at the door rolled away, the tomb entered, and the dead body drawn up through the entrance and borne away—and all this with the trepidation and haste that would be inevitable—without awaking them; nay, without awaking a single one of them, who might have alarmed his companions!

(4.) But what motive had the disciples to steal him away, had it been possible to do so? What good could the dead body do them? What use could they make of it? Its resurrection could not be facilitated by being in their hands. And, indeed, they appear to have had no views or clear, distinct convictions concerning the resurrection at all, but were rather overwhelmed with disappointment, terror, and despair.

(5.) But suppose the disciples had both a motive and a disposition to "steal him away," was it very likely they would dare to undertake it? Would a few weak and timid men, such as they were, confront a band of ruffian soldiers? Or, on the other hand, how should the disciples know that the guard were asleep, and thus venture to approach by stealth? How could they know that *every one* of them was asleep? and how could they be assured of the profoundness of their slumber?

(6.) But suppose, again, that the disciples had actually stolen away the body, why were they not immediately arrested, and made to surrender it up? Why were they not punished for breaking the seal? why not for burglary? They were still at Jerusalem; they do not hide themselves away; they travel the streets, walk abroad, and even visit, with astonishment and wonder, the vacant tomb of their Lord. And, indeed, these very disciples were afterward arrested on other charges. Why not arrested upon this? why not charged with stealing the body of Jesus? Nay, when arrested and brought before the council, why do we hear not a word of accusation upon this point?—the very point of difficulty, and which, if once settled against the disciples, would end forever all their hopes and prospects. It would utterly destroy the very foundation of the doctrines they preached, and present them before the public as vile and perjured men. The very silence of the Jews under such circumstances is convincing evidence in favor of the disciples of Christ.

8. *The resurrection was established as a matter of faith in the age in which it occurred, and has ever since obtained credence.* It was first preached where the event occurred, and among the very cotemporaries of our Lord. The Jews

were possessed of every means for its refutation had it been possible; nor were they wanting either in motive or disposition to refute it. But in their very midst, and in spite of all their efforts to prevent it, thousands were convinced of its truth and converted to Christianity. And from the very spot where the living witnesses of the event were found, and where the monuments to commemorate it were first established, it has gone forth, radiating like a new sun risen upon our earth, and sending forth its beams to bless all lands and all people.

Had the destruction of Jerusalem, the dissolution of the Jewish hierarchy, and the dispersion of the people immediately followed the alleged ascension of Christ, it might have been objected to this grand theme, that in the confusion of revolution and war, while men's hearts were failing them with fear, and earthquake, and pestilence and famine, pillage and flame, sword and bloodshed, were sweeping over and desolating the whole land—that the terrified and excited imaginations of the people would be liable to be led away by every wild delusion that might arise. But it was not so. For nearly forty years after the ascension of our Lord, the current of Jewish affairs continued to roll onward without serious interruption. It was a philosophic age. Every opportunity was given to sift the matter to its very bottom; and that, too, upon the very spot and among the very people where these glorious events transpired. Investigation was provoked—nay, absolutely challenged; for the resurrection of Christ was blended with all the preaching of the apostles, at all times and in every place, from the first moment that their tongues were touched with celestial fire upon the day of Pentecost, till, by martyrdom and death, they gave their final and glorious attestation to its truth. Before Jerusalem had been destroyed, it had been preached not only in the temple and in the places of public resort in the Holy City, but throughout the entire land. It had spread into Asia Minor, into Macedonia and Greece. The assembled wisdom of Athens had listened to its proclamation by the great apostles to the Gentiles, in the midst of the Areopagus; and it had obtained foothold within the gates of the Imperial City, and numbered its converts in the very household of Cæsar. And all this had been achieved without force of authority or arms; nay, often in the face of both. The sage and the philosopher, convinced by the might of reason and the force of truth, had brought their trophies and laid them at the foot of the cross. And down through all ages learning and wisdom have paid unceasing homage to the divine truth—heralded by the flaming messenger of heaven—that Jesus "is risen from the dead."

Let us now, in one broad survey, look over this field of collateral evidence, and sum up the circumstances connected with and going to confirm the direct testimony in the case. It is conceded that there was such a person as Jesus Christ, of whose life and actions the Gospels claim to be the history; that his teachings and works were so wonderful that his enemies could account for them only on the supposition of magic or of Satanic influence; that he predicted his own resurrection from the dead; that he was actually crucified, dead, and buried; that his body was guarded with the utmost care and in the strongest manner by his enemies; that on the third day it was missing from the tomb, and his enemies, who had charge of it, could give no rational account of its loss, but it was shown that the story they invented to account for it is utterly incredible and unsustained. It was further shown that the doctrine of his resurrection began immediately to be preached in the very place where the event transpired, that the evidence of his resurrection was received by thousands as satisfactory, and that the doctrine spread and prevailed in spite of the most active and determined opposition on the part of his enemies, and that it has gained credence in every age of the world.

We think, then, that we have established the proposition, that *there are circumstances connected with the case that can be satisfactorily accounted for on no other hypothesis than the actual resurrection of Jesus Christ from the dead.*

II. Evidence Direct of the Resurrection of Christ.

We have already shown that, beyond all question, Christ was crucified, dead, and buried. Now, if it shall be shown that he was subsequently seen, conversed with, handled, gave and received communications, walked, eat, reproved and instructed, declared himself to be alive, and performed the functions of a living man; and if it shall be shown that the personal witnesses of these facts were competent witnesses, that the number of them was large, that they had opportunity to investigate and know the things whereof they affirmed, that their testimony was given at the time and in the place where the things occurred, and, finally, that it was given under such circumstances as attested, on the part of the witnesses, a full conviction and certainty of the fact; if all these facts shall be shown, then, we say, that, according to all the rules of evidence and the established laws of human belief, we must credit the actual resurrection of the Lord Jesus Christ from the dead.

It is very justly remarked by Dr. Dwight, that "in the nature of the case, it is just as easy to determine, whether a person, once dead, is afterward alive, as to determine whether a man is living who has not been dead. Suppose a person who was an entire stranger to us, should come into the family, eat and drink, sleep and wake, converse and act with them, exactly in the manner in which these things are done by us and the rest of mankind; suppose him, further, to enter into business in the manner of other men; to cultivate a farm; or manage causes at the bar; or practice medicine; or assume the office of a minister, and preach, visit, advise, and comfort, as is usually done in discharging the duties of this function—every one of us who witnessed these things would, beyond a doubt, know this stranger to be a living man, in the same manner, and with the same certainty, with which we know each other to be alive."* Such evidence as the above would be complete; it would be satisfactory; it is the only evidence adapted to the case; and if we reject it, we shall have left to us no satisfactory evidence of the actual existence of any living being besides ourselves.

Should we, after becoming acquainted with our stranger, be informed that he had been crucified, dead, and buried, it would not, in the least, invalidate our faith in the actuality of his now being a living man. We might disbelieve the story of his crucifixion, or question whether he were actually dead; but the fact of his now being alive would rest upon too solid a basis to be shaken. But, if we turn to the question before us, the fact of the crucifixion and death of Christ is conceded; and the only point to be established is, that he was subsequently alive. To this question let us apply the above test; let us inquire whether the witnesses had sufficient evidence that Christ Jesus was alive after his crucifixion, whether their competency and number are sufficient, and whether there is evidence that they themselves were fully convinced of the fact.

To render the question more perspicuous and satisfactory, it may be necessary to mention some of the circumstances connected with the crucifixion, death, and burial of our

*Dwight's Theology, vol. ii, pp. 265, 266.

Lord. When he was led away to be crucified, a great company of his disciples, relatives, and friends followed, bewailing and lamenting him. Some of them stood so near the cross that he could speak to them; others stood afar off. Many of them remained till the mysterious darkness that overwhelmed the land had passed away, and the Lord had given up the ghost. Among those who not only witnessed his crucifixion, but tarried till he was laid in the sepulcher, were "Mary Magdalene and the other Mary;" that is, "Mary," the mother of "James." Several women appear to have agreed to embalm the body of our Lord, and, after leaving the tomb, they "prepared spices and ointments" for that purpose. This being done, they rested on the Sabbath, and came as the day was dawning, on the first day of the week, to execute the design. They appear to have been ignorant that the Jews had sealed the tomb, and placed a guard over it; and the two Marys and Salome, who were in advance of the other women, were perplexed how they might roll away the stone from the door of the sepulcher. About this time—before the women had reached the tomb—an angel descended from heaven, rolled the stone from the sepulcher, and sat upon it. The guard were struck with astonishment, and for a moment were like dead men; but recovering themselves, and finding that the body of Christ was gone, they fled into the city, and reported the fact to the Jews.

As the women approached the tomb, they beheld that the stone was rolled away. This filled them with alarm; and Mary Magdalene, concluding that the body had been taken away, ran back to tell Peter and John. The other Mary and Salome approached the tomb, determined to ascertain whether the body was there; but as they entered the tomb, and saw the angel, but not the body, they were affrighted. The angel sought to calm their fears, told them the Lord had risen, and bade them behold the place where they laid him, and then go and tell his disciples. But the women went out quickly from the sepulcher, and fled trembling with affright, saying not a word, but hasting to report what they had seen to the eleven apostles. They had hardly gone when Peter and John came, running in advance of Mary Magdalene, and went into the sepulcher. They found that the body was not there, but saw the grave-clothes lying folded up; and after that they returned to their own home, wondering at what had occurred.

1. *First appearance of Christ.* Mary Magdalene was left alone at the tomb. She had lingered behind to weep, being in much doubt and perplexity as to what had become of the body of Jesus. While weeping she stooped down and looked again into the sepulcher, if perchance there might have been some mistake about the body having been removed. There she saw two angels, robed in white, one at the head and one at the foot, where the body of Jesus had lain. How touchingly beautiful her reply when they asked her why she wept: "Because they have taken away my Lord, and I know not where they have laid him!" Turning back she saw Jesus standing by her; but, blinded by her tears, and bewildered by her apprehensions, she did not recognize either his personal appearance nor yet his voice, when he tenderly inquired the cause of her grief; but, supposing him to be the gardener who cultivated the garden, and who might have removed the body, she said, "Sir, if thou hast borne him hence, tell me where thou hast laid him, and I will take him away." What an affecting evidence of the strength and purity of her attachment to her Lord—an attachment which death had no power to dissolve! And how overwhelming her astonishment and delight when she heard the well-known voice uttering, as if surprised at her want of recognition, "Mary!" She

could doubt no more—the voice and the bodily appearance are both recognized, and she, uttering an exclamation of surprise and joy, prostrating herself before him, held him by the feet and worshiped him. But he bids her make no delay; the time was short; he was about to ascend to his Father and his God; therefore, to haste and tell his disciples. Then she went and told the disciples, as they were mourning and weeping, that she had seen the Lord, and that he had said these things to her; but they believed it not.

All this narrative has an air of simplicity and naturalness, a harmony of parts, a coincidence with collateral circumstances, a correspondence of feeling and action suited to the occasion, the characters, and circumstances, that strongly confirm its truth, and make Mary Magdalene a credible witness for the resurrection of her Lord.

2. *Second appearance of Christ.* The other Mary and Salome appear to have fled away to some retired place, and, perhaps, were so astounded at what they had witnessed that they could not for some time sufficiently recover their self-possession to carry the tidings to the disciples. While in this state their Lord himself met them, calmed their fears, and bade them go boldly and carry the tidings of his resurrection to the apostles, and tell them to meet him, as he had appointed, in Galilee. Still the apostles were incredulous.

3. *Third appearance of Christ.* After the two Marys, and Salome, and Peter, and John had departed from the grave, Joanna, and a company of women with her, not knowing the events that had taken place, came bringing spices and ointments to assist in the embalming of the body. Finding the tomb open, they went into it, and discovered that the body had been removed. While they were full of amazement and perplexity, two angels appeared

to them, and said, "Why seek ye the living among the dead? He is not here, but is risen." When Joanna returned and reported this to the disciples, Peter appears to have gone again in haste to the sepulcher; and it is probably at this time that the risen Savior "was seen of Cephas," according to the declaration of St. Paul. (1 Cor. xv, 5.)

4. *Fourth appearance of Christ.* That same morning, after the women had returned from the sepulcher, two of the disciples—one of them Cleopas or Alpheus, the father of James, and the other probably St. Luke—had left Jerusalem, and were journeying on foot to Emmaus, a village seven or eight miles west of the city. They had probably been up to Jerusalem to attend the Passover, and were now returning home; they were returning with grieved and aching hearts; their Lord, in whom they had trusted and through whom they had hoped for the redemption of Israel, had been crucified and slain. As they talked over the sad events of the feast a third traveler falls in with them, and joins in their conversation. He expounds to them the prophecies relating to the Messiah, and shows that the very events they lamented were necessary, and also that Christ must rise again, that the prophecies might be fulfilled. All this time they did not recognize him; they saw him, heard his voice, and walked with him, as they would with any other man. But when they reached the village, and were about to sup together, near the close of the day, he took bread, and blessed it, and brake, and gave it to them. This significant action opened their eyes, and they were filled with astonishment and wonder to recognize their Lord in the person of their fellow-traveler. But he vanished from their sight. So joyful were they at what they had seen, that they immediately arose and returned to Jerusalem; and when they reached the city, they found the disciples assembled, and were assured by them that the

report received from the women concerning the resurrection of Christ before they left in the morning had been confirmed; for they said, he "hath appeared to Simon." Then the two disciples rehearsed what they had witnessed in the way, and also at the village whither they went. Thus the evidences of his resurrection were so multiplying that the disciples, who had at first doubted, were constrained to say, "The Lord is risen, indeed."

5. *Fifth appearance of Christ.* It is now the evening of the day of our Lord's resurrection, and he had already appeared to six witnesses. Ten of the apostles and many disciples were now assembled to talk over the events that had occurred, and especially to consider to what the reports of that day concerning the resurrection of the Lord might grow. For fear of the Jews, they had closed the door. Just then the Savior appears in their midst, and said to them, "Peace be unto you." But the suddenness and the unexpectedness of his appearance filled them with terror and affright. He, however, calmed their fears, bade them look upon him and to feel of him, to behold his hands and his feet, to assure themselves that he was flesh and bones; then also he ate before them; and afterward, still further to confirm their faith, he opened to their understanding the Scriptures, and showed them that "thus it is written, and thus it behooved Christ to suffer, and to rise from the dead the third day."

A large number were evidently present on this occasion; how many it is impossible to say. Twelve are distinctly mentioned; namely, ten apostles—for Thomas had gone out before the Savior appeared—and the two disciples who had returned from Emmaus; and it is further intimated that it was a general gathering of all who had been with the apostles during the day, and were conversant with the reports of the resurrection. It is probable that the six to whom our

Lord had appeared prior to this, now, for the second time, witnessed his presence.

6. *Sixth appearance of Christ.* Soon after our Savior had appeared on the previous occasion, Thomas came in, and the disciples told him that they had seen the Lord. He, however, disbelieved, and said, "Except I shall see in his hands the print of the nails, and put my finger into the print of the nails, and thrust my hand into his side, I will not believe." On the return of the newly-instituted Sabbath, the eighth day of the resurrection, the eleven apostles, and probably others of the disciples, were again assembled together, Thomas being present with the rest; and Jesus stood in their midst, and addressed them with his salutation of peace. Then turning to Thomas, he upbraided his unbelief, and said to him, "Reach hither thy finger, and behold my hands; and reach hither thy hand, and thrust it into my side; and be not faithless but believing." It was enough. The skepticism of Thomas could withstand no longer, and he cried out, "My Lord and my God!"

No further conversation is recorded of our Savior on this occasion than that which related to Thomas; but it is probable that more was said and done; for the sacred historian says that many other signs did Jesus in the presence of his disciples, of which he has not thought necessary to make any distinct record. The special object of this appearance of our Savior seems to have been to convince Thomas of the reality of the resurrection, and thus to extinguish the last doubt of the fact from the minds of his apostles.

7. *Seventh appearance of Christ.* The feast of the Passover being now ended, the eleven returned into Galilee, as the Savior had directed them. This was their native place, and here they would be less exposed to the malice of the Jews, and could, therefore, with more calmness receive the instructions of Christ, and prepare themselves for that public

ministry so soon to begin at Jerusalem. While here they probably resorted to their several callings as a means of livelihood. Simon Peter, with Nathanael, James, and John, and two others, engaged in fishing, but toiled all night and caught nothing. In the morning Jesus stood upon the shore; and when his disciples did not recognize him, having first asked them if they had any thing to eat, he bade them cast the net on the right side of the boat, which being done, they inclosed no less than a hundred and fifty-three great fishes, which were drawn to the shore and secured. Then they knew it was the Lord; and coming to him, they saw a fish that had been prepared on a fire of coals, and bread. Jesus said to them, "Come and dine;" and gave them bread and fish, and they did eat. It was on this occasion that he so signally reproved the overweening confidence of Peter and his consequent fall.

8. *Eighth appearance of Christ.* The grand assemblage of the disciples, where our Savior was to give a still more public demonstration that he was alive, was upon a mountain in Galilee. This meeting he had appointed before his crucifixion; the angel that announced his resurrection to the women bade them remind the disciples of the Savior's appointment; the Lord himself, also, when he appeared to Mary and Salome, renewed the same message; and it is probable that on the preceding appearance he gave the disciples more explicit information where he would meet as many as might assemble. The number assembled on this occasion exceeded five hundred. Twenty years after this St. Paul publicly declares that the greater part of this five hundred were then living witnesses of the resurrection of our Lord. Here he gave infallible proofs of his resurrection, and spoke of things pertaining to the kingdom of God. Here also he renewed the promise of the Holy Ghost, and bade them go back to Jerusalem and tarry till it came. And it is probable that on

this occasion he gave to the apostles their grand commission, to go into all the world and preach the Gospel to every creature.

9. *Ninth appearance of Christ.* Our Savior after this seems to have made his appearance to James. This appearance the apostle refers to as an evidence of the resurrection, though he gives no particulars of the case. They were omitted probably because they were well known. The James spoken of was James the Less, bishop of Jerusalem, the only apostle with whom St. Paul was favored with an interview when he came up from Damascus after his conversion. It is to be presumed that he then had the fact from the lips of James himself.

10. *Tenth appearance of Christ.* The apostles having returned to Jerusalem according to the command of their Master, about forty days after the resurrection our Savior again appeared to them. Here, after renewing their commission, he gave them the promise of the speedy descent of the Holy Spirit, and commanded them not to depart from Jerusalem till they should "be baptized with the Holy Ghost." Having completed his instructions, he led them out toward Bethany, upon the Mount of Olives. Here probably upon the sacred spot where he had often instructed his disciples and prayed for them—the spot that had witnessed his awful agony that forced the bloody sweat from every pore—the spot where he had been betrayed by the traitorous kiss of one disciple and forsaken by all the rest; upon this spot he lifted up his hands and blessed his disciples; and as he blessed them, he was parted from them—higher and still higher he ascended in the vaulted heavens, till a cloud received him out of their sight, and he was seen no more.

This closes the direct testimony, so far as the recorded evidence of the apostles is concerned. But then we must remember that through the whole forty days, from the resurrection to the ascension, our Lord was more or less conversant with his disciples. For St. Luke, referring to the "many infallible proofs" of his resurrection given to his disciples, says he was "*seen of them forty days*," and during that time was "speaking of the things pertaining to the kingdom of God." St. John also says that Jesus did many other things in the presence of his disciples which he had not recorded; but that from the many, he had selected and made a record of those that were written, in order that men might believe that Jesus Christ is the Son of God, and, believing, might have life through his name. The truth then seems to be, that, without intending a full detail of all the appearances of our Lord, his disciples have placed these on record as constituting a perfect demonstration of his resurrection from the dead. We invite the fullest and most impartial scrutiny of this evidence. We ask any one to consider the number of times our Savior was seen after his resurrection, the circumstances connected with his appearance, the words that were uttered, the significant actions that were performed, the number of witnesses, amounting to no less than six hundred, the length of time through which he held intercourse with them, and the circumstances of his final departure from them; and let him consider also that the witnesses were men of moral integrity and of at least common capability, that they did not conceal themselves in a corner and tell their story covertly, but proclaimed the resurrection at Jerusalem—upon the very spot where Christ had been crucified, and before the very persons that had crucified him—we ask any one to consider this, and then to say whether the testimony that Christ was seen after his crucifixion and death, was not as full and perfect as it is possible for human testimony ever to be.

III. Collateral Points and Remarks.

Let us survey the ground over which we have passed. In the first place, we clearly demonstrated that there were circumstances connected with the case—circumstances assented to by the Jews as well as by the disciples—which strongly corroborate the direct testimony, and can be satisfactorily accounted for on no other hypothesis than the actual resurrection of Jesus Christ from the dead. These we called circumstantial evidence; they are essential to the argument, and, in connection with the direct evidence, are possessed of the highest force. In the second place, we took up the direct testimony, and showed that after his known and acknowledged death and burial, he was seen by his disciples and friends, talked with them, walked with them, was handled by them, and wrought miracles in their presence, giving infallible evidence that he had risen from the dead. We clearly pointed out no less than ten distinct occasions of his appearance—making the number of persons by whom he was seen not less than six hundred—several of whom saw him repeatedly, and some of them were in almost constant intercourse with him forty days. The record of these facts was made and published while most of these persons were living, and they were appealed to as witnesses; and from not one of them were the Jews ever able to extort a denial of the facts. How could demonstration be more perfect?

In concluding the argument, we have a few collateral points of too much importance to be neglected:

1. *The disciples, who were witnesses, gave the fullest evidence of their entire belief in the resurrection of Christ.* The very manner and place in which they proclaimed the fact, must convince us of their sincerity. The fact, also, that

the Christian Sabbath from that time was joyfully observed in commemoration of the event, and that the worship of this holy day is also blended together with those sacred institutions which derive all their significance from the resurrection no less than the crucifixion of our Lord, are also convincing proofs of the certainty of their conviction. But still further, the fact that they devoted their whole lives, amid want and distress, opposition and persecution, scorn and reproach, strifes and imprisonments, and even amid sufferings and death—without hope or prospect of honor or reward from men or upon the earth—in toilsome effort to preach "Jesus and the resurrection" to dying men, must stand as a perpetual monument of the sincerity of their conviction, the purity of their motives, and the indestructibility of their faith.

2. *The disciples could not have been deceived with reference to the appearance of Christ.* They had been in daily and intimate intercourse with him for more than six years, and, therefore, knew his bodily appearance, his manner, and his voice too well to be deceived. Infidelity says they were "rude, unlettered persons." But may not the rudest, the most unlettered plebeian distinguish a friend? especially if the separation from him has been but for a few days? Certainly, then, men—"unlettered and ignorant," as they might have been—who could produce the chaste, the beautiful, the classic, the immortal compositions of the New Testament, were not so ignorant but that they could determine whether the man before them, who walked and talked, ate and drank with them, whose person they handled, and whose wounds they felt, was their friend or an impostor. Deception was wholly impossible.

Nor will the theory of *illusion*, which has often been urged, answer the turn of infidelity. An individual, it is true, may be the subject of illusion; it is possible for men to be deceived, even in matters where the senses are concerned. Such cases, however, are exceedingly rare, even in single individuals. But that two persons should, at the same time, experience the same illusion concerning the same object, and concerning so many circumstances attending it, is certainly very improbable. Such an instance has never been known. But when you increase the number of witnesses, this theory of illusion becomes still more improbable. Increase the number to *eleven*, and "the improbability becomes incalculable;" but when you have raised it "to five hundred, it transcends all limits." But when you extend the illusion through many days, and combine in it all the circumstances, words, and acts connected with our Savior's appearance, "the improbability ceases, and is changed into an impossibility." The apostles could not have been deceived. They had all the evidence that Christ was living which they had of the life of each other; and they might as well doubt with reference to each other—Peter concerning Thomas, and John concerning James—as to doubt whether it were really Christ or an illusion. Nay, they had the same evidence that Christ was living which we have that these we are daily conversant with are living beings, and not mere phantoms. To suppose deception possible, in such a case, is to unsettle all the principles of human belief. Moral certainty would become impossible. One step further in skepticism, and the man would be prepared to doubt whether his own existence was any thing more than a succession of sensations and ideas.

3. *The Sanhedrim themselves were evidently convinced of his resurrection.* Their conduct can be accounted for on no other supposition. They had heard the report of the guard of sixty men; they had been observant of the subsequent events that had transpired. They had great interest to

vindicate themselves; and if they really believed that the disciples had stolen the body away, they would have demanded an investigation of the affair. But they evidently shrunk from such an investigation, and manifested the greatest solicitude that the evidences of the resurrection of the body should not be discussed publicly, or even brought before the people. Hence, when Peter and John publicly declared in the Temple, that the Prince of life, whom they had killed, God had raised from the dead, and with equal boldness also to the Sanhedrim itself, that Jesus of Nazareth, whom they had crucified, God had raised from the dead, the Sanhedrim do not proceed like men who have to do with a shallow and base fabrication, that needs only to be put to the test of truth and fact in order to demolish it, but evidently like men who are conscious of their wrong, and whose only hope is in smothering investigation of the facts and the truth. Like self-convicted men, they have not a word of argument, not an opposing fact; they are willing to release their prisoners if they will only cease to preach the doctrine of a risen Savior, and, in fact, are compelled to release them without even this poor pledge. And, indeed, we find the same council soon compelled again to arrest the apostles for teaching the same obnoxious truths. What do they do now? confront the heresy of the apostles and demolish its falsity? Nothing like it; but with half-appealing, whining tremulousness, they complain, "Ye have filled Jerusalem with your doctrine, and intend to bring this man's blood upon us." Nor have they any thing except "stripes" with which to reply to the apostles.

In both these instances the Sanhedrim studiously avoided the real question at issue. Every thing was suspended on the fact, whether Christ had really risen from the dead or not. If he was not raised he was an impostor, a blasphemer, and, therefore, worthy of death. The whole question, whether he was the promised Messiah, now turned upon this point. If he was a blasphemer—and the thing could be easily shown by proving that he had not risen—then the Sanhedrim had done only their duty in condemning him; but, on the other hand, if he was actually the promised Messiah, they were guilty of crucifying the Lord of life and glory. The apostles boldly charged this crime upon them; and the only reply the Sanhedrim have to make to this charge, is to command the disciples not to declare the thing publicly any more. How can this be accounted for, except on the supposition of conscious guilt, and the conviction, or, at least, the apprehension, that the declaration of the apostles had underlying it a broad foundation of truth? The fact was, they had duped others with their lie about the disciples having stolen away the body of Christ; but they themselves were not deceived by it. *They knew the report was false.*

4. *The miracles performed by the apostles in the name of a risen Savior, can be accounted for only by admitting the fact of his resurrection.* Not only do they prove his resurrection by convincing witnesses, but corroborate the testimony by displaying the Divine power with which they had been endowed by virtue of his resurrection Not among the least of these miracles, is the miracle of the transformation in their own character. A short time before, they were weak and timid—fearful even to accompany their Lord into Jewry, because the Jews had conspired against him—trembling, affrighted, and forsaking him when arrested by a comparatively contemptible band—the boldest among them frightened into a denial of him, with oaths and profanity, even by a maid-servant, who only whispers her suspicion. Hardly two months have passed. The same band—though their Lord has been crucified and slain—now boldly walk forth among their enemies; they

stand in the public places; they raise their voice in the temple; they cower not before the grand and imposing Sanhedrim—with tongues of fire and lips of burning eloquence, they proclaim Jesus and the resurrection. Stripes and imprisonment, torture and martyrdom in their most appalling forms, have no longer any terrors for them. Their minds, once so bewildered and mystified by the simplest sayings and parables, now grasp the profoundest truths of religion, construct the most convincing and powerful arguments, and pour forth, radiant with light, and beauty, and truth, the most sublime eloquence. Whence this change, but that their hearts have been filled and their tongues have been tipped with celestial fire? Thus prepared they go forth, and every-where tell the story of the resurrection; and in confirmation of its truth, signs and wonders are wrought, the sick are healed, the unclean spirits are cast out, the lame leap and the dumb speak, the living die and the dead rise to life. The vision of assembled thousands is dazzled by the resplendent glory that descends in visible form on the day of Pentecost; and in the mingled accents of no less than seventeen dialects, the multitude hear the glad tidings of salvation through a risen Savior.

Thus, with power more than human, and amid sanctions that attest the divinity of their mission, and the certainty of the resurrection, do the apostles go forth and lay the broad foundations of that great spiritual temple of our God, whose pillars shall rest upon the uttermost parts of the earth, whose lofty arches shall reverberate with the echoes of immortal songs, going up from every land and in every tongue, and whose ascending turrets, unmarred in beauty or in strength by the roll of ages, shall forever glitter in the sunbeams of eternity. Immortal men! divinely appointed and divinely sustained, your work has been well done, and through you shall "Jesus and the resurrection" be preached to all men and through all ages.

5. It now only remains, in the discussion of this subject, to show *the relation which exists between the resurrection of Jesus Christ and the general resurrection of the dead.*

The doctrine of the resurrection of Jesus Christ from the dead forms a vital element of the Gospel. It stands forth preëminent in the faith, the preaching, and the writings of the apostles. It is connected with all that is practical and immortal in Christianity. But for the resurrection, the hope of immortality had perished in the grave; the Gospel itself had proved a failure. With what exulting rapture the mind turns from the dark scenes of the garden, the cross, and the tomb, to behold the splendor of the resurrection triumph! The dying agony of the cross is blended with the rising glory of the resurrection. No fact has come down to us with stronger attestations of its reality; none has come to us gathering around it and centering in it holier or sublimer interests; and none can so assure the aspirings of the soul after immortality as the resurrection of Jesus Christ from the dead.

"In his blest life
I see the path, and in his death the price,
And in his great ascent the proof supreme
Of immortality. And did he rise?
Hear, O ye nations! hear it, O ye dead!
He rose! he rose! he burst the bars of death!
This sum of good to man! whose nature then
Took wing, and mounted with him from the tomb.
Then, then I rose; then first Humanity
Triumphant passed the crystal ports of light,
Stupendous guest! and seized eternal youth,
Seized in our name. E'er since 't is blasphemous
To call man mortal. Man's mortality
Was then transferred to Death; and heaven's duration
Unalienably sealed to this frail frame,
This child of dust. MAN ALL IMMORTAL hail!"

Again: the resurrection of Jesus Christ from the dead meets the infidel objection, that the soul dies with the body, and that, therefore, reanimation to life after death is impossible, and demonstrates its falsity. It sets the seal of living verity upon the great mystery of the resurrection. If Christ be indeed risen, how can any one longer say there is no resurrection of the dead? In this grand event—the resurrection of Christ—center two fundamental facts; the one is, that death is not such an extinction of being as to render resurrection impossible, and the other is, that the Divine power is adequate to rescue the body from the grasp of Death. Only let one fact of reviviscence by the agency of Divine power, through all the long ages of the past, be shown; one instance in which Death has been spoiled of his prey and driven back with everlasting defeat from his temporary triumph; and that one fact forever rebukes the vile skepticism that regards it a thing incredible that God should raise the dead. Such a fact we have in the resurrection of Jesus Christ. Others had been restored to life; it was, however, a brief unvailing of Divine power—a brief respite from the power of death and the grave. But the resurrection of Christ was a full and perfect demonstration of his triumph over death and the grave. One day we see him upon the cross groaning, agonizing, dying; the next we behold him the tenant of the grave; but as the morning of the third day begins to dawn, the signal moment of his power has arrived—the bands of death are broken and the mighty conqueror arises. He comes up girded with strength; he lifts up the broken fetters that had once bound him, in token of everlasting victory, and as he rises, to all his followers he exclaims, "I am the resurrection and the life!" The resurrection of the dead is no longer a sealed problem. Its mystery is solved; its truth demonstrated. That same Power that quickened the body of Jesus shall also quicken our mortal bodies, and shall make us immortal.

We are led, then, to remark again that the resurrection

of Christ is the distinct pledge and assurance of our resurrection. We connect these two things as the Bible connects them; they are blended together as cause and effect. We shall rise and triumph over death because Christ, as the great Captain of our salvation, has achieved for us the victory. By him "came the resurrection of the dead;" "Christ hath abolished death." He has become "the first-fruits of them that slept." "He that raised up Jesus shall raise us up also by Jesus." And hence, also, it is said, we are "begotten again unto a lively hope by the resurrection of Jesus Christ from the dead." We may well say, then, that the hope of rising "from the sleep of the sepulcher"—the glory of our reproduced bodies in the resurrection—is not "the hope of worms," but the well-accredited hope of resurrection, in immortal bodies, beyond the grave and above decay. We died in the first Adam, we live in the second; we sunk with the earthly, we rise with the heavenly. Christ's resurrection is the pledge, the proof, and the pattern of ours.

Viewed in this light, we wonder not that the resurrection of Christ was the first and constant theme of the great apostles, who planted and formed the Christian Church. Nay, we wonder not that they caught up the message heralded by the angel of God, "He is risen from the dead," and that this became the burden of their mission and the inspiration of their song. In all ages the message has found a response from Christian hearts—"he is risen from the dead"—and the mighty acclaim has burst upon every land and clime under the face of the whole heaven; and still does the mighty theme continue to gather strength, ever extending the sphere of its dominion and multiplying its trophies, till "Jesus and the resurrection" shall be known in all the earth.

The resurrection of Christ is only the first-fruits of a universal and glorious harvest. The dead shall rise. Small and great shall stand before the throne. They shall come forth from their resting-place. The sea shall give up its dead; the earth shall surrender its. The reviviscence shall be sudden. The blast of the appointed trump shall penetrate all the abodes of death. The sleeping dust shall start to life. Wonder and amazement shall seize an astonished world, and all men shall stand before their final Judge. The grandeur of that solemn event is past all conception, the throne of judgment descending through the parted heavens, the elements of nature dissolving, the graves opening, and the dead coming forth to judgment!

> "Wherever slept one grain of human dust,
> Essential organ of the human soul,
> Wherever tossed—obedient to the call
> Of God's omnipotence, it hurried on
> To meet its fellow particles, revived,
> Rebuilt, in union indestructible.
> No atom of his spoils remains to Death;
> From his strong arm by stronger arm released,
> Immortal now in soul and body both,
> Beyond his reach stood all the sons of men,
> And saw behind his valley lie unfeared."

Christian! forget not that Death himself shall erelong die. "Christianity knocks at the gate of the grave and asks back her dead. Long, solitary, and undisturbed may be the slumber; but when the trumpet of eternity shall pour its thrilling thunder into the deaf, cold ear of the sepulcher, your God-created forms shall spring to life, immortal and renewed." We shall come up in the image of our living head; "this corruptible shall have put on incorruption, and this mortal shall have put on immortality. Then shall be brought to pass the saying that is written, Death is swallowed up in victory."

XI.

POPULAR OBJECTIONS TO THE RESURRECTION.

"Why should it be thought a thing incredible with you, that God should raise the dead?" ACTS xxvi, 8.

"How are the dead raised up, and with what body do they come?" 1 COR. xv, 35.

WE have already shown that the doctrine of the resurrection of the human body is deeply imbedded in the teachings of both the Old and the New Testament Scriptures. In the Gospel, especially, it becomes a foundation truth, radiating from the very center of the system, and illuminating every part. Whatever, then, of absurdity or of philosophical impossibility skepticism has to urge against the resurrection, is so much, essentially, urged against the Bible itself. It is for this reason, with others, that we now propose a more particular examination of the popular objections urged against the resurrection.

When Paul preached "Jesus and the resurrection" among the Epicureans and Stoics of Athens, they said, "he seemeth to be a setter forth of strange gods!" So to many, in every age, the doctrine of the resurrection of the body seems little less than a misty fable, because it has never yet been encircled within the scope of their rational philosophy. Others give to the subject little reflection or thought, but, with Pliny, the ancient heathen philosopher, affirm that "the calling of the dead back to life is among the impossible things that God neither can nor will do." Others would go still further and, with Celsus. denounce the resurrection as "the hope of worms—an abominable as well as impossible thing." Cæcilius, who personates a heathen in the dialogue of Mincius Felix, says of Christians: "They tell us that they shall be reproduced after death and the ashes of the funeral pile, and believe their own lies, so that you might think that they had already revived. O, twofold madness! to denounce destruction to the heaven and stars, which we leave as we found them, but to promise eternity to themselves, when dead and extinguished." There seems, indeed, to have been arrayed against this doctrine a persistency of opposition, wonderful to contemplate, when we consider how clearly it is revealed, and by how many and striking miracles it is demonstrated; and especially when we take into account how very little, that is really valid, reason, or science, or philosophy can urge against it.

In our own day the objections to the resurrection of the body have been drawn out in precise philosophical forms and statements. They thus assume definite and tangible shape. This is well. We can now gain access to them, and subject them to careful examination and analysis. It is often the case that there is a broad, undefined idea that a doctrine is unsound or a thing incredible. The idea, from its very vagueness, presents no salient points of approach, and seems absolutely insurmountable. But the moment the objection assumes definite form, and is distributed into parts, so that each by itself may be subjected to the critical process of examination, one after another they are dissolved, and disappear before the scrutiny of reason and truth.

Let us apply ourselves to an examination, in their order, of the chief objections urged against the resurrection of the dead. If the main intrenchments of the enemy are carried, we need not concern ourselves much about the rest.

1. In the First Place, it is Asserted that the Doctrine of the Resurrection of the Dead is Unphilosophical and Absurd.

This objection is a mere vague generality, and might be left to itself; but it will help us to a clearer understanding of the nature of this discussion, and of the points at issue, if we clear away somewhat of the rubbish it heaps up before us.

An opinion may be unphilosophical without being absurd. To be unphilosophical, is to be at variance with the principles of sound reason. When this variance attains a high degree, so as willfully to stand in opposition to manifest truth, and to the plain dictates of common-sense, it reaches up to the absurd. An unphilosophical proposition may seem to be true, though in reality contradictory to some of the hidden principles of philosophy. An absurd proposition is contradictory to obvious or known truth. The proposition, then, that "the dead are raised," is not *absurd*, because it is not contradictory to any known truth or obvious principle; for its opposite never has been and never can be established.

To say that it is *unphilosophical*, is only to say that it can not, so far as we can see, be brought about upon philosophical principles. And this, after all, may amount to nothing more than this—*that we have not as yet attained to the knowledge of those high philosophical elements employed in bringing about the resurrection of the dead.* To assume that we know it to be absolutely unphilosophical, is to assume that we have mastered all philosophy; and that we have made the application of its principles to the subject and found them inconsistent. The absurdity of such an assumption is too obvious to require exposure. Philosophy is continually enlarging her domain. Even within the present age she has developed new principles and new applications that would have been to former generations as incredible as raising the dead.

But, then, there is another reply to this whole objection. This is not a doctrine of philosophy, but of revelation. The question, then, is, not whether the dead can be raised upon the principles of human philosophy, but whether God, by his own miraculous power, can and will do it. Whatever God does may be above us, and consequently mysterious. It may be incomprehensible to us. Our philosophy may be too contracted, too feeble to rise to the full comprehension of the Divine ways; but his purposes and his acts will ever be in harmony with the sublime philosophy of the universe. They may seem to contradict both our reason and our sense—just as the doctrine of the diurnal revolution of our earth seems to contradict both the sense and the reason of the untutored mind; but the higher revelation of truth may make apparent that it is inconsistent with neither. The objection, then, is nothing more nor less than the opposition of our ignorance to the wisdom and the power of God.

II. The Second Objection is Drawn from the Fact that the Living Human Body is Undergoing a Perpetual Change.

Stating this objection in full, it is this: *As the human body is undergoing a perpetual change, each individual has many bodies during his life—each one of which the soul has inhabited, and it is, therefore, as much his body as that he possessed at the moment of his death; and therefore it is absurd to claim for this last body—possessed, perhaps, but a very little while—an exclusive resurrection.* It is contended that this change extends to every material particle that enters into the body. The time required for this complete renovation of the human body is, by some, limited to seven years. Others extend it to twenty. The caviler inquires whether all these particles that have ever entered into the composition of the human body, and which consequently as much belonged to it as those it happened to be in possession of at the particular moment of death, are to enter into the composition of the resurrection body? and if not all, what portion of them is to be rejected? Some have pushed this objection so far as to descant in terms of ridicule upon the bulky appearance of that resurrection body, which, after remaining here its fourscore years, and being changed many times, should call back all the particles which ever entered into its composition.

This is the old objection encountered by the apostle: "How are the dead raised up? and with what body do they come?" It is an attempt to apply the little we know, and know imperfectly, too, to the mysteries that lie beyond. It richly merits the reply of the apostle—"Thou fool!" We might content ourselves by replying to the technical form of this objection; that its claim for the body of the ownership of all the particles which ever entered into its composition, is a stretch of fancy that would hardly be thought of in any other connection. Just as well might the individual prefer a claim to all the bits and parcels of property he had ever owned during his life, however long ago he might have parted with them, and however regular the process, or full the equivalent received for them. But it will be more satisfactory to enter upon the subject in detail.

Now, with reference to this entire change of the body, it is rather assumed than proved. Some change is, undoubtedly, constantly going on in our system; but that every particle of the body, in process of time, passes from us, and the entire body is changed so that it is made up of an entirely new class of particles, is a supposition not only unproved, but one that is not susceptible of proof by any process known to human science. Certain it is that the bodily identity is still maintained through all the changes of the longest life. The man feels that the present is the same body—*essentially*—that he possessed in past time, and the same he will possess in the future. All his modes of thought, and all his consciousness of accountability, are based upon this idea. The old man, tottering upon the brink of the grave, still adheres to the thought that the body now worn out with age and enfeebled by disease, is essentially the same body that was fresh and blooming in the day of his youth. He does not say, "The body I then possessed was a lively, active body; but it has been exchanged for one that is decrepit and old." No, he says, "*I* have now exchanged the sprightliness of youth for the decrepitude of age." Thus, the bodily identity—that is, the idea of its being essentially the same body—seems as inseparable from us as life itself.

Great changes may take place in our bodies, within short periods of time, but we never waver in the recognition of their identity through all these changes. Disease may shrink us from the full habit to the skeleton form; we may suffer mutilation; the leg, the arm, may be amputated; the eye may be cut out; the flesh torn from the body; and the very form of humanity be almost obliterated; but we rise from all this suffering with an undoubted and unmistaken bodily identity still remaining.

The conclusion, then, to which we are led, is that much of our bodily nature, the coarser parts of the physical system, are not essential to bodily identity; but that the essence of our physical being is, in a sense, independent of these and manufactured by them. In this view the objection loses all its force. Whatever changes take place in the coarser parts of the bodily system, *the elemental part—the essence*—yet remains. And it is this that shall rise from the grave.

Does this appear mysterious? Take that clump of iron ore just from the quarry. Cast it into the furnace. Behold it there burning and seething in the lambent flames; its form changes; it is consumed; gone. But descend now, and behold the pure metal flowing from the furnace. Here again appears the clump; not, it is true, in its crude state, but freed from its earth; purged from its alloy, and yet preserving its elemental identity. *Its essence is there.* So shall it be with this earthly body as it passes through the furnace of death, and comes forth in the resurrection. "It is sown in corruption, it is raised in incorruption; it is sown a natural body, it is raised a spiritual body;" for "flesh and blood can not inherit the kingdom of God." Therefore "the dead shall be raised incorruptible and we shall be changed."

III. It is Objected to the Resurrection that the Elements of which the Body is Composed are not only Dissolved, but Wasted, Scattered, and even Transformed.

After death the body is soon decomposed. The gaseous and watery elements soon escape away, and the more solid parts soon crumble into dust. "The body of a dead man may be burnt to ashes, and the ashes may be blown about by the wind and scattered far and wide in the air and upon the earth. After it is resolved into its earthy or humid matter, it may be taken up by the vessels which supply plants with nutriment, and at length become constituent parts of the substance of these plants."* By these and similar processes, the particles that constitute a single human body may be dispersed over half the globe, may have passed through innumerable transformations, and be combined with other bodies. How can these widely-scattered elements be gathered together? how is it possible that they should be again so reunited as to re-form the body that once crumbled and wasted?

This is indeed mysterious. But is not the organization of our present bodies also mysterious and inexplicable? May not each individual say, "I am fearfully and wonderfully made?" The earth, the air, the sea have all been laid under contribution. The elements that constitute our bodies have been drawn from remote parts of the earth and from the depths of the sea. Some portions of these elements of our bodies have been drawn from the vegetable and animal productions of our own clime. Other portions are the productions of other climes—the tropical regions and the arctic, India and China, the islands of the sea and the mountains of the continents, the rivers and the oceans—have all brought their contributions to the erection of this mysterious temple. A thousand unappreciated and unseen influences have been working, under the all-controlling eye of God, to its completion. Let us, then, not stumble at the mysteriousness of the resurrection of the body from the dead till we have solved the mystery of its first organization. Let us not be over-perplexed because we can not tell how its scattered and wasted elements shall be gathered till we are able to tell how they were originally gathered and organized into a bodily system. If God has done the latter, may he not also be able to do the former?

"Sure the same Power
That reared the piece at first, and took it down,
Can reassemble the loose, scattered parts,
And put them as they were."

* Gregory's Evidences, p. 424.

But this objection is absolutely deprived of all force, when we contemplate processes of daily occurrence, and especially the apparent impossibilities science may and has achieved. Take that ingot of gold. First tell its exact purity and weight, and then give it into the hands of the chemist. He files it to powder; and as you look upon it you say, "My gold will never be gathered again." The chemist gathers that dust and dissolves it in acids; then you exclaim, "I can not even see it; every particle is gone." Again he takes it, alloys it with other metals; he grinds it again to powder; he throws it into the fire; he mingles it with soot, and ashes, and charcoal; and at length, when it would seem as though its very elements were utterly destroyed, he brings it forth, the same fine gold, brilliant and pure as it was before it was subjected to the ordeal.* And does the skill of the chemist transcend the wonder-working power of Jehovah? Nay, the chemist may mistake; he may fail in his experiment; the precious gold may be lost. But over the garnered dust of his saints, God shall watch with that eye which never sleeps; and at the magic of his word, it shall be gathered together and again start to life.†

*Resurrection of the Dead. By Dr. C. Kingsley, p. 33.

† THE SILVER CUP.—THE RESURRECTION ILLUSTRATED.—Dr. Brown, in his Resurrection of Life, cites from Hallet the following beautiful illustration of the resurrection:

"A gentleman of the country, upon the occasion of some signal service this man had done him, gave him a curious silver cup. David—for that was the man's name—was exceedingly fond of the present, and preserved it with the greatest care. But one day, by accident, his cup fell into a vessel of aquafortis; he, taking it to be no other than common water, thought his cup safe enough; and, therefore, neglected it till he had dispatched an affair of importance, about which his master had employed him, imagining it would be then time enough to take out his cup. At length a fellow-servant came into the same room, when the cup was near dissolved, and looking into the aquafortis, asked David who had thrown any thing into that vessel. David said that his cup accidentally fell into the water. Upon this, his fellow-servant informed him that it was not common water, but aquafortis, and that his cup was almost dissolved in it. When David heard this, and was satisfied of the truth of it with his own eyes, he heartily grieved for the loss of his cup; and at the same time, he was astonished to see the liquor as clear as if nothing at all had been dissolved in it, or

IV. It is Objected again that Some of the Elements which Constituted a Part of the Body of one Man at Death, may also Enter into that of Another Man at the time of his Death, and hence it would be Impossible, in the Resurrection, to Restore the same Particles to both the Bodies claiming them.

Some have grown facetious over this objection, and presented us with the grotesque picture of two souls contending over a lump of materiality, each claiming it as belonging to himself. This may avail something among those who substitute fancy for fact and argument. But our humorist should first learn, in so grave a matter, whether, even upon the hypothesis of a resurrection, such

mixed with it. As, after a little while, he saw the small remains of it vanish, and could not now perceive the least particle of the silver, he utterly despaired of seeing the cup more. Upon this, he bitterly bewailed his loss, with many tears, and refused to be comforted. His fellow-servant, pitying him in this condition of sorrow, told him their master could restore him the same cup again. David disregarded this as utterly impossible. 'What do you talk of?' said he to his fellow-servant. 'Do you not know that the cup is entirely dissolved, and not the least bit of the silver is to be seen? Are not all the little invisible parts of the cup mingled with the aquafortis, and become parts of the same mass? How then can my master, or any man alive, produce the silver anew, and restore my cup? It can never be; I give it over for lost; I am sure I shall never see it again.'

"His fellow-servant still insisted that their master could restore the same cup; and David as earnestly insisted that it was absolutely impossible. While they were debating this point, their master came in, and asked them what they were disputing about. When they had informed him, he says to David, 'What you so positively pronounce to be impossible, you shall see me do with very little trouble. 'Fetch me,' said he to the other servant, 'some salt water, and pour it into the vessel of aquafortis. Now look,' says he; 'the silver will presently fall to the bottom of the vessel in a white powder.'

"When David saw this he began to have good hopes of seeing his cup restored. Next, his master ordered the servant to drain off the liquor and to take up the powdered silver and melt it. Thus it was reduced into a solid silver piece; and then, by the silversmith's hammer, formed into a cup of the same shape as before. Thus David's cup was restored with a very small loss of its weight and value.

"It is no uncommon thing for men like David in this parable, to imagine that to be impossible, which yet persons of greater skill and wisdom than them-a state of things as he has supposed can ever possibly occur.

Others meet the case more gravely. Assuming that the same substance may, at different times, enter into and become essential parts of the bodies of different men, they say that in the resurrection, this substance can not enter into *both* of the bodies that once had it in possession. Hence, it is physically impossible for each to recover his own peculiar body; and therefore there lies this physical impossibility against the doctrine of the resurrection.

We shall be able to weigh more exactly the force of this objection if we first consider the circumstances under which this alleged complication of the elemental parts of human bodies is said to occur. The case has been instanced where grain, raised upon a field enriched by the blood of man slain in battle, is eaten; or where the decaying bodies of men have nourished vegetables, which were afterward eaten by other men; or where the bodies of men drowned in the sea

selves can perform. David was as positive that his master could not restore his cup as unbelievers are that it is incredible God should raise the dead; and he had as much appearance of reason on his side as they. If a human body, dead, crumbles into dust, and mingles with the earth, or with the water of the sea, so as to be discernible no more, so the silver cup was dissolved into parts invisible, and mingled with the mass of aquafortis. It is not then easy to be conceived, that as a man has wisdom and power enough to bring these parts of the silver to be visible again, and to reduce them to a cup as before, so God, the Maker of heaven and earth, must have wisdom and power enough to bring the parts of a dissolved human body together, and to form them into a human body again! What though David could not restore his own cup? Was that a reason that no man could do it? And when his master had promised to restore it, what though David could not possibly conjecture by what method his master would do it? This was no proof that his master was at a loss for a method. So, though men can not raise the dead, yet God, who is infinitely wiser and stronger, can. And though we can not find out the method by which he will do this yet we are sure that he who at first took the dust of the ground, and formed it into the body of man, can, with the same ease, take the dust into which my body shall be dissolved and form it into a human body again. Nay, even if a body be burnt, and consumed by fire, the parts of that body are no more really lost than the invisible particles of the dissolved cup. As David, then, was wrong in thinking that it was impossible for his master to restore his cup, it must be at least equally wrong for us to think it impossible that God should raise the dead."

have been eaten by fishes, and those fishes afterward caught and eaten; or still again, where men have fallen into the hands of cannibals and been devoured by them, and thus their flesh enters directly into the composition of other bodies.

We can not answer this objection more conclusively than is done by Dr. Kingsley, in his little work on the "Resurrection of the Dead;" and, therefore, without adhering closely to the language, we adopt, substantially, his argument.* Let us take up the case where vegetation, raised upon soil enriched by the decomposition of a human body, is used for the nourishment of human beings. Here, at the outset, we are met by the fact that a very small part of the earth at all enters into the composition of vegetable existence. This is easy of demonstration. It has again and again been shown, from actual experiment, that if plants or trees be set in pots or urns, and the dirt to which their roots have access weighed, the tree may increase many pounds, while the dirt, if carefully shaken from the roots and weighed, will be found to be diminished only a few ounces. Based upon this fact, we have a calculation furnished to our hand. "Suppose a human being to have eaten grain—in quantity, say one hundred pounds—that had grown upon soil enriched by a human body. Now, not more than one twenty-fifth part of this grain—that is, four pounds—ever becomes actually a part of the human body. But not more than one twentieth part of the grain at first was converted earth; and thus not more than one-fifth of one pound in the hundred is incorporated into the body of the person who has eaten it. And, again, probably not more than one thousandth part of the earth absorbed by the roots of the grain could ever have been human dust. This must be a large estimate. The result, then, would be

*See pp. 36–39.

that of the one hundred pounds of grain eaten, not more than one five-thousandth, or one three-hundred-and-twelfth part of an ounce of matter, could thus be transferred from one body to another. And strong probabilities exist against the transfer of even this small amount. But suppose it to have been actually transferred, a large portion of this small fraction of an ounce would certainly go to the grosser parts of the system, not at all necessary to the resurrection body; and might not the whole be directed in the same way?" Or, again, why may not this small part of human dust, absorbed by the growing grain, be lodged in the roots, the stalk, or the calyxes, without ever becoming a part of the kernel? Thus the objection, when subjected to severe scrutiny, becomes absolutely void.

But let us take the case which the objector regards as his stronghold—that of cannibalism. With reference to the cannibal himself, this kind of food with him was exceedingly rare, and formed but a very small fraction of his food; and then, again, but a small fraction of this fraction can become a part of his body. This small fraction, it is not at all inconsistent to suppose, may be directed to the coarser parts of the body—those parts that shall not enter into the composition of the resurrection body; or if the inquiry relate to the victim, and it is inquired, "How shall he recover his body which has been devoured by another?" it must be observed, that, in all such cases of cannibalism, there are large portions of the body, such as the skull and bones, that are not thus eaten. And, indeed, if the whole body were eaten, the parts essential to the resurrection body might still, as we have already seen, be guarded by the special workings of Divine Providence, or even by an established, yet undiscovered law of nature, which forbids the commingling of that portion of our body, or that essence of our physical nature essential to our bodily identity, thus preserving through all transformations, as well as through all time, our physical as well as mental individuality. This latter idea is of great force—especially when we remember that the blood as well as some other parts of our system are entirely devoid of any nourishing quality, and can not, therefore, be incorporated by the ordinary process of taking and digesting food into any other system. Viewed, then, simply as a matter of rational inquiry, the objection is obviously specious and groundless. It is unsustained by either fact or science. But when we look at the subject in the light of revelation, and observe that it is a question of God's miraculous power and determination, who shall set limits to his skill or bound his power? If he has decreed that "the dead shall be raised and we be changed," can he not so guard the elements of which our bodies are composed that the grand purpose of his wisdom shall be accomplished? The objection is based upon that essential infidelity that would circumscribe the power of God by the cavils of an unbelieving heart.

V. It is Objected, also, that as the Resurrection of the Body Implies the Raising up the Same Body that Died, there would be a Wide Diversity among the Resurrection Bodies.

Some would be young, others old; some fresh and beautiful, others deformed and repulsive; some healthful and vigorous, others wasted and ghastly. The great proportion die of wasting diseases or of old age, so that the body that goes into the grave is a mere skeleton—shriveled, ghastly, repulsive. As the true *anastasis* implies the *standing-up again*, it must be the resurrection of that which lay down—that is, the very body that went into the grave. And this is commonly the worst, the most unsightly and repulsive body possessed by the individual during all his life. Hence, if a literal resurrection is to take place, it would bring forth the most motley as well as the most repulsive assemblage of human beings that ever met the eye.

To all such cavilers we have one reply: "Ye do err, not knowing the Scriptures, nor yet the power of God." (Matt. xxii, 29.) In that glorious resurrection our bodies shall come forth—not as they now are—not as they went down into the grave—but like unto the glorious body of Jesus Christ. Though all the elements essential to bodily identity rise, yet shall they be changed. The mortal and the corruptible shall be purged away:

> "Those bodies that corrupted fell,
> Shall incorrupt arise,
> And mortal forms shall spring to life,
> Immortal in the skies."

But St. Paul meets this objection and solves this difficulty. He tells us that not as it went down into the grave does the resurrected body of the righteous come up in the resurrection. "It is sown in *corruption*, it is raised in *incorruption;* it is sown in *dishonor*, it is raised in *glory;* it is sown in *weakness*, it is raised in *power;* it is sown a *natural* [*animal*] body, it is raised a *spiritual* body." (1 Cor. xv, 42 44.) It is sown an animal body—*σῶμα ψυχικὸν*—that is, says Dr. Gregory, "a body which previously existed with all the organs, faculties, and propensities requisite to procure, receive, and appropriate nutriment, as well as to perpetuate the species; but it shall be raised a spiritual body, refined from the *dregs* of matter, utterly impermeable by every thing which communicates 'pain,'* freed from the organs and senses required only in its former state, and probably possessing the remaining senses in greater perfec-

*"Neither shall there be any more pain." (Rev. xxi, 4.) The Greek word, πόνος, here translated *pain*, comprehends toil, fatigue, and excessive labor of body, as well as vexation and anguish of spirit.

tion, together with new and more exquisite faculties, fitted for the exalted state of existence and enjoyment to which it is now rising."* It is in accordance with this that it is said, "Who [that is, the Lord Jesus Christ] shall CHANGE our vile body, that it may be fashioned like to his glorious body." (Phil. iii, 21.) Here the identical VILE BODY—that is, this body belonging to our state of abasement, subject to infirmities and sicknesses, and condemned to death and dissolution because of sin—is not to give place to *another body*, but to be CHANGED and fashioned after the glory of the resurrection body of Christ. The saints of God are to come forth "IN THE LIKENESS OF HIS RESURRECTION." (Rom. vi, 5.) And so "when he shall appear we shall be like him." (1 John iii, 2.) The RESURRECTION BODY OF CHRIST, then, is the type and model after which the resurrection bodies of the saints are to be fashioned. The crucifixion occurred when the Savior was yet in the vigor of his early manhood. To this age was conformed the resurrection body with which he ascended into heaven. Some of his saints may be gathered home while the dew of life's early morning is yet upon them:

"Their all of life a rosy ray,
Blushed into dawn and pass'd away."

But they fail not of bliss; "For of such is the kingdom of God." (Mark x, 14.) Others, in the decrepitude of old age, are gathered to their fathers. And all along at every stage of gradation, from one extreme to the other, the saints, "planted in the likeness" of Christ, are passing away. As they come up from the grave in the resurrection, something of the distinctions of age, and sex, and peculiar conformation may remain. For St. John says, "I saw the dead, SMALL AND GREAT, stand before God."

* Evidences of Christianity, p. 429.

(Rev. xx, 12.) "Children," says Olshausen, "will not arise as men, nor aged men retreat to the period of youth; but every glorified body will represent clearly his degree of age, with the exception of all that is perishable; so that, all taken together, may declare the entire human race in its degrees and varieties with the most perfect clearness." But each of those shall wear its type of beauty and glory; each shall *be fashioned like unto his glorious body*, who is the "first-fruits of them that slept," and who has declared, "As I live, ye shall live also." There may be diversity then, variety even, among the resurrected bodies of the saints; for "one star differeth from another star in glory." (1 Cor. xv, 41.) But even this diversity, instead of being a blemish in the heavenly society, shall constitute one of its noblest beauties, and prove one of the richest sources of its ever-varying and unalloyed felicity. And even with regard to individuals, each one shall be more perfectly himself, and consequently better prepared to enjoy the heavenly delights now accessible to him, and those to which he shall rise as the ages of eternity roll on, from the fact that there are diversities—grades above and below him—infinitely varied.

Thus the objector has created his objection by casting the dark shadow of his unbelief over one of the most glorious truths revealed concerning the resurrection state.

But there is another thought that presses itself upon our consideration before we leave this point. We have spoken only of the resurrection body of the saints. The Bible assures us that *there shall be a resurrection both of the just and the unjust.* It is a remarkable fact that little light is shed in Revelation upon the resurrection body of the wicked. As it is said in relation to the saints that "flesh and blood can not inherit the kingdom of God," it seems to be implied that those bodies will be fleshly, and not spiritual. Certain it is that they shall be food for the "worm that dieth not," and fuel for the "fire that is not quenched.' Whatever may be the nature of that body, we know it shall die no more. Immortalized in his evil passions, his carnal lusts, his unholy appetites—his resurrection body shall bear the stamp of all that was evil in his nature upon the earth. The burning thirst of the drunkard shall prey upon him forever, without the possibility of quietude or quenching. The miser will still stretch out his thin, bony fingers and peer out of his sunken eyes, imagining that he may yet clutch and count his coveted gold. The thief, the robber, the murderer, the gambler, the debauchee—each with the marks of his vice written indelibly upon every feature of his resurrected body; each still goaded with remorseless energy into unceasing though vain endeavor to gratify its all-controlling and all-consuming passion. Thus is fulfilled the Divine law, "Whatsoever a man soweth, THAT SHALL HE ALSO REAP." (Gal. vi, 7.) This universal and unbending law of Divine retribution comprehends, in the wide amplitude of its range, the broadest and latest results in the lifetime of an immortal nature. But let us draw a vail over that dark picture upon which Heaven has seen fit to shed so little light; but not till we have uttered the prayer, "My soul, come not thou into their secret; unto their assembly, mine honor, be not thou united." (Gen. xlix, 6.)

VI. It is Objected Again that the Body is Composed of Unintelligent, Earthy Particles, and is therefore Unworthy of Resurrection.

This objection would possess some force were there no higher and eternal ends to be accomplished by the reanimation of the body. In this life the body forms an essential part of our being. It is our complex nature—soul and body united—that now lives, holds its distinct individuality, and forms its connections with the physical, intellectual, and moral world without us. It is this complex nature that participates in all that is moral or immoral in life. And to this complex nature all the provisions of the Gospel are applied. And, in fine, the Divine Redeemer took not upon him the nature of angels, BUT OF MAN. He embodied himself in humanity, and thus ennobled our very dust. He poured into the weak elements of human nature all the fullness of the Godhead, and thus showed that even our material bodies are possessed of a higher element of life, and are formed to a higher destiny than is here realized. May not the resurrection of the body be indispensable to the realization of even the soul's destiny? As much as this is certainly intimated in the cry, "How long, O Lord, holy and true?" uttered from "under the altar" by "the souls of them that were slain for the Word of God and for the testimony which they held." (Rev. vi, 9, 10.) Is there not also special significance in the fact that the great apostle to the Gentiles earnestly desired to "attain unto the resurrection of the dead?" Was it not that he might reach that higher perfection which is attained only when the sanctified soul shall be reunited with the body—purged from all that is gross and corruptible, and resurrected from the grave?

VII. Finally, it is Objected that a Material Body would be a Clog to our Spiritual Nature in Another Life.

The grossness of our nature, here, we are ever inclined to attribute to the body rather than to the soul. The body is regarded a as burden upon the soul; it curbs its movements and confines it in space; it is assumed to be the seat of base propensities and gross appetites. Its material grossness darkens the perceptions of the soul, weakens its power and checks its higher activities. It weighs down the soul's aspirations and checks its efforts in the pursuit of knowledge and virtue. The body's demand for sleep consumes almost half the period of our earthly existence; and then its demand for food drives both soul and body like an unceasing taskmaster all the rest. Then, too, is it the seat of infirmities, diseases, and aches without number. It obscures the spiritual vision. Freed from it the soul might "see God," might be blessed with the vision of angels and of the spirits of just men made perfect. Instead, then, of being a companion and a helpmeet to the soul, in this life, the body is claimed to be its bane. And instead of being its tabernacle, its delightful dwelling-place, it is regarded as its prison-house. That is looked upon as a happy day for the soul in which the material tabernacle shall be broken down and the soul released from its prison-house. What need has the ransomed spirit of such a body? And would it not prove, in heaven, not only an unsightly appendage, but a lasting incumbrance and burden to the soul?

So reasons the objector. And there might be force in his argument, if this doctrine of the resurrection implied that the soul was to possess just *such* a body in the future state as it possesses in this. But let us not forget that both soul and body are not to be the same as here. While this vile body is to be fashioned like unto the glorious body of Christ, the soul also is to be transformed by the renewing of the Holy Ghost. So that

> "Soul and body shall his glorious image wear."

That matter may be so transformed as to meet these conditions of our resurrection state, who can doubt after he has seen the wonderful transformations of which it is capable; and how glorious the vilest earth may become! Even from the hand of nature, what new touches of beauty and what varied and glorious forms are given to the same elements. The same substance that begrims the laborer in the charcoal pit, when changed a little, shines with resplendent brightness in the crown of royalty. The dirt, trodden beneath our feet, and which is so offensive to our person, or in our food, after all, changed a little, becomes inviting to the taste; and changed still a little more, behold, it glows upon the cheek of beauty and sparkles in the eye of intelligence. The steam, that with resistless and tireless energy propels the leviathan of the deep in the very face of the winds and waves, or with still mightier energy, upheaves the mountains from their beds; what is it but awakened energies that were just now lying dormant in the sleeping, sluggish waters of the deep? The lightning, which in its destructive course rends oaks and rocks to pieces, in its passage from cloud to earth, or from earth to cloud, is the same element that was just now sleeping gently as the baby in its cradle. At whose bidding do these dormant energies start to life? Who fashions the shapeless dust into forms of beauty? Who gives such exquisite coloring—such dazzling brightness to the sightless lump? And can not the same power cause that "this mortal shall put on immortality?" He who has marked the transformation of the rude clay into forms of life and beauty; he who has seen the rough lump of charcoal made, by a simple change in the arrangement of its particles, to flame forth in the radiant hues of the priceless diamond; he who has marked the speed of electricity, and the impenetration of heat; he who has noticed the expansibility of light and the velocity with which it travels through unbounded space—he can no longer wonder at any transformations the body may experience, or any glories with which it may be invested, or any spiritual adaptations it may attain in the resurrection and heavenly state. Here the material body may prove an element of weakness and of dishonor; but there it shall possess "power" and "glory." Here it may be *animal*, gross and evil; but there it shall be "a spiritual body." Refined from the grossness of that which is merely animal, it shall be endowed with an elasticity of action, a rapidity and a boundless capacity of movement, and also with an imperishable nature, which will make it a fit companion of the glorified spirit. It will undoubtedly be invested with new forms; fitted with new organs; endowed with new and wondrous powers, and thus be adapted to its celestial state. Vitalized anew, beatified with its highest perfection, it shall forever shine forth with undecaying brightness in the kingdom of God.

Thus we have gone through the popular objections to the doctrine of the resurrection. Not one of them, we think we have shown, has any substantial basis or affords any solid objection to the doctrine.

We have already stated that the doctrine is purely a doctrine of revelation—though confirmed by analogies in nature and miracles in religion. God has not seen fit to reveal its processes; science has not been able as yet to discover them. Hence the deep mystery in which they lie hidden. But let no one object on the ground of this mystery. The mysteries that every-where encircle us in the natural world; the striking revelations of human science; and above all, the consideration that we are connected with an inconceivably-glorious system—which is expansive, limitless as God himself—and a very little of which we shall ever know in our present state, should check our presumption, should moderate our confidence, and lead us to distrust our own reason when brought into conflict with the Word of God. Let us beware how we array philosophy against the Author of all philosophy; our short-sighted and imperfect knowledge against the boundless possibilities of infinite wisdom and power. Nay, if we will not reverence because it is God who speaks, let us at least remember that as often as man has arrayed his speculations against the Word of God, so often has he suffered defeat. The terms reason, science, philosophy, are indeed high-sounding words; but they have often been used to cloak the ignorance or pamper the vanity of man. We may, then, bow to the supreme majesty and truth of the Bible, and say with the immortal Newton, "The Scriptures of God are the sublimest of all philosophy."

And, then again, this doctrine only brings to us the assured hope of a future and better life, in which our humanity shall realize the grand consummation of its being. To doubt the resurrection is to cast the shadow of unbelief over our future destiny. It is this blighting skepticism that, in the Hermit of Beattie, utters its sad lament:

"Nor yet for the ravage of Winter I mourn:
Kind Nature the embryo blossom will save.
But when shall Spring visit the moldering urn?
O when shall it dawn on the night of the grave?"

But when the wanderer has been brought back to the light of true reason, he will resume the minstrel's strain.

"'Twas thus, by the glare of false science betrayed,
That leads to bewilder, and dazzles to blind;
My thoughts wont to roam, from shade onward to shade,
Destruction before me, and sorrow behind.
'O pity, great Father of light,' then I cried,
'Thy creature who fain would not wander from Thee;
Lo, humbled in dust, I relinquish my pride;
From doubts and from darkness thou only canst free.
And darkness and doubt are now flying away;
No longer I roam in conjecture forlorn;
So breaks on the traveler, faint and astray,
The bright and the balmy effulgence of morn:
See Truth, Love, and Mercy in triumph descending,
And Nature all glowing in Eden's first bloom;
On the cold cheek of Death smiles and roses are blending,
And Beauty immortal awakes from the tomb."

Finally, the resurrection of the dead consummates the triumph of the Gospel. "The wages of sin is death." "Death by sin." The wasted bodies of the dead generations of the past are so many monuments of the blighting power of sin and of the universal reign of death. The triumph of Christianity over death will not be complete till those monuments are destroyed. "The death by sin" is twofold—the death of the soul and the death of the body. There is a resurrection of the soul—a quickening of it to spiritual life. It is manifested in every sinner brought to Christ; for "even when we were dead in sins, he hath quickened us together with Christ," (Eph. ii, 5;) "It is the Spirit that quickeneth," (John vi, 62;) and "that which is born of the Spirit is spirit." (Gal. iii, 6.) And still again, he that believeth, "shall not come into condemnation, but is passed from death unto life." (John v, 24.) This is the triumph of Christ over the spiritual death produced by sin. It transforms a spirit of darkness into an angel of light; a condemned sinner it makes an heir of God. It plucks an immortal spirit from the clutches of Satan, robes it in transcendent light, and sets it forever as a gem in the crown of the Redeemer.

But Christianity will not stop here. She claims back the dust of the sainted dead. Without this her triumph is incomplete. Death shall be dethroned. It shall be driven from its usurped and dark dominion, and no vestige of its triumph shall remain. Then and then only shall the triumph of the Cross be complete. "THE LAST ENEMY THAT SHALL BE DESTROYED IS DEATH." 1 Cor. xv, 56.

O how wonderful to see
  Death and Life in conflict meet!
Life hath won the victory,
  Trodden Death beneath his feet.
Even as the Scripture shows,
He hath conquered all our foes;
Death was slain, but Jesus rose."

MARTIN LUTHER.

XII.

RECOGNITION OF FRIENDS IN HEAVEN.

"Father, I will that they also, whom thou hast given me, be with me where I am; that they may behold my glory, which thou hast given me." JOHN xvii, 24.

"And behold, there appeared unto them Moses and Elias, talking with him." MATT. xvii, 4.

"In hell he lifted up his eyes, being in torments; and seeth Abraham afar off, and Lazarus in his bosom." LUKE xvi, 23.

"The warmest love on earth is still
Imperfect when 't is given;
But there 's a purer clime above,
Where perfect hearts in perfect love
Unite; and this—is heaven."

FEW themes connected with the great hereafter so deeply concern *the heart* as the question of personal recognition among the redeemed. Dear ones of earth—linked to our hearts by the most tender ties—have departed from us and gone away into the unknown realm. We have carefully and tearfully laid their bodies in the grave to slumber till the great awakening morning. We shall see them no more in the land of the living. And if we are never to know them in the future state, this separation—sad as may be the thought—is eternal. The hour that carries them down to the grave is the hour of final separation. If there is no personal recognition in heaven; if we shall neither see nor know our friends there, so far as we are concerned they are annihilated, and heaven has no genuine antidote for the soul's agony in the hour of bereavement.

By and by we shall go and lie down by the side of those

severed from us by death, and sleep with them the long, unbroken slumber of the grave. In the great awakening morning we shall, side by side, come forth. Will there then be no recognition between us? If not, what will they be to us more than those redeemed in other ages and from other climes? All the precious memories of toil and trial, of conflict and victory, of gracious manifestation and of holy joy, shared with them in the time of our pilgrimage, will have perished forever! or be remembered, perchance, as vague and unreal fancies. We enter heaven as *strangers*, and such we shall remain forever.

The anxiety of the soul with regard to the personal recognitions of the future state is natural. It springs from the holiest sympathies of the human heart. And any inquiry that may solve our doubts or relieve our anxiety is equally rational and commendable.

We shall proceed, then, to argue the fact of personal recognition among the redeemed in heaven, and shall, we think, present considerations which, in their aggregate force, are absolutely conclusive of the subject.

I. Reason Affords Grounds for Expecting this Recognition.

What we mean to assert here is, that the doctrine of personal recognition in the future state has a basis in nature and in reason.

1. *The yearning of the heart for the departed must remain forever unsatisfied without it.* Our loved dead are still linked to us, not only by the cords of memory, but the ties of affection. The monuments carved to their memory, the flowers that blossom above their sleeping dust, and the tears that bedew their graves, are so many living testimonials of our undying affection for them, and the yearning

of the heart for a reunion with them. "She goeth unto the grave to weep there," is the record not merely of Mary, but of the heart-yearning of humanity in all ages. This human feeling finds its consummation only in a recognized personal reunion in heaven. The soul craves the assurance of this reunion, and in response to that craving our funeral hymns take up the blessed strain and whisper it to our hope in sweetest melody. In the faith of it the farewells of the dying chamber are touched with a deeper pathos, and made expressive of a sublimer joy. "Good-by, papa, good-by! Mamma has come for me to-night—do n't cry, papa! we 'll all meet again in the morning!" Such was the language of a dying child as the night-shade of death closed around him. Yes, thanks be to God, *we 'll all meet again in the morning!* How the thought thrills the heart! Have our brethren in Christ, with whom we have taken sweet counsel in the day of our pilgrimage, left us to finish the journey weary and alone? It cheers us by the way to know that "we 'll all meet again in the morning." Bereaved parent, how often is thy yearning heart filled with a holy calmness as angelic whisperings, wafted from the far-off land, come unto thee, saying, "*We 'll all meet again in the morning!*"

"O, wild is the tempest and dark is the night,
But soon will the day-break be dawning;
Then the friendships of yore
Shall blossom once more,
'And we 'll all meet again in the morning!'"

2. *The communion of the saints in heaven is impossible without personal recognition.* The communion of the saints of God on earth is one of the richest sources of comfort, as well as one of the most effective means of spiritual nurture in the Church militant. And we are led to look forward to it as one of the grand consummations of the heavenly state. "If the mere conception," says Robert Hall,

"of the reunion of good men in a future state, infused a momentary rapture into the mind of Tully; if an airy speculation—for there is reason to fear it had little hold on his convictions—could inspire him with such delight, what may we be expected to feel, who are assured of such an event by the true sayings of God! How should we rejoice in the prospect, the certainty rather, of spending a blissful eternity with those whom we loved on earth; of seeing them emerge from the tomb, and the deeper ruins of the fall, not only uninjured, but refined and perfected, with every tear wiped from their eyes, standing before the throne of God and the Lamb in white robes, and palms in their hands, crying with a loud voice, 'Salvation to God who sitteth upon the throne, and to the Lamb, forever and ever!' What delight will it afford to renew the sweet counsel we have taken together, to recount the toils of combat, and to approach not the house, but to the throne of God, in company, in order to join in the symphonies of heavenly voices, and lose ourselves among the splendors and fruitions of the beatific vision!"

But how would it dampen the ardor of our faith, with what a chilliness would it overspread the otherwise delightful prospect of the communion of saints in heaven, if there we are not to recognize them as fellow-pilgrims redeemed from earth! Communion implies personal knowledge of each other. If the glorified spirit shall have communion with the angels of God, it will be with them as beings who have not only a personal existence, but also a personal history that may be remembered and rehearsed. Thus each angel in heaven may run back through all the ages of his personal history—never, at any time, losing, even for one moment, the distinct individuality of his consciousness or his experience. And so must it also be with the saints of God. If their earthly history is lost, how shall we know that there ever was to them any such history? How shall we know that they ever were of the Church militant—redeemed and saved by the blood of Christ? But if their past history is known, how can it be separated from the individual person? If such separation can not take place, then to know the earthly history of the saint passed into heaven is to obtain personal knowledge of him; so that there must be recognition between him and us. If he has an earthly history, and we have an earthly history, and each is capable of communicating his own history, or of receiving the history of the other, so certain is it that personal recognitions must take place. The Christian can never lose his identity, either on earth or in heaven.

3. *Much of the knowledge acquired in this life would be either lost or useless without personal recognition in the life to come.* We can readily conceive how great a blank would be made in the knowledge we possess in this life, if, suddenly, there should be struck from it all that is connected with the recognition of the persons with whom we have been associated or have been brought in contact with. Take away all our knowledge connected with and dependent upon the recognition of father and mother, brothers and sisters, teachers and ministers, children and neighbors, and how little would be left to us! Life, and thought, and intellect would become almost a blank; and what little remained of each would lose half its value. How, then, can it enter into our thoughts that the failure of spiritual recognition can possibly be less disastrous to us in the future world? But this shall not be; for not only will the knowledge acquired in this life be retained in its full measure, and distinctness, and particularity, but it shall be indefinitely enlarged. "Now I know in part; but then shall I know even as also I am known." (1 Cor. xiii, 12.) Whatever else may be implied in this passage, no one can doubt but that it looks

to an increase of knowledge in the future state; and also that this increase has special relation to our knowledge of each other. "Now we see through a glass darkly; but then face to face."

4. *Personal recognition in the future life is essential to the unraveling of the mysteries of this.* In the history of the purest and best men that have ever lived upon the earth there are events, conflicts of mind, and even providential dealings that were dark and mysterious, and in many instances the individuals have gone down to the grave with the darkness unrelieved and the mystery unsolved. Our Savior said to his disciples, "What I do thou knowest not now; but thou shalt know hereafter." (John xiii, 7.) Thus, in the heavenly state, there is to be an unvailing of the mysteries of this. We shall know why the good man was afflicted and his life clouded with sorrow, and why the wicked were permitted to prosper in his wickedness. The knowledge acquired there will be such as to assure us that the Judge of all the earth has done right.

5. *Heart-friendships here have no proper consummation without personal recognition and continued affection in another life.* Friendship is not confined to earth. Abraham is no less "the friend of God" in heaven now, than he was when dwelling in tents and walking by faith in the land of Canaan nearly four thousand years ago. So every other spiritual affection survives the ravages of the tomb. "Go where you will," says Dr. Berg, "we find the sentiment that friendship is perpetuated beyond the grave. It is enshrined in the heart of our common humanity. The pure, unsophisticated belief of the vast majority of the followers of Christ is in unison with the yearnings of natural affection, which follows its objects through the portals of the grave into the eternal world. What but this causes the Christian parent in the dying hour to charge his beloved

children to prepare for a reunion before the throne of the Lamb? He desires to meet them there, and to rejoice with them in the victory over sin and death. The widow bending in bitter bereavement over the grave of him whom God has taken, meekly puts the cup of sorrow to her lips with the assured confidence that the separation wrought by death is transient, and that they who sleep in Jesus shall together inherit the rest that remaineth for the people of God. Thus the wormwood and the gall are tempered by the sweet balm of hope, and heaven wins the attractions earth has lost. Tell me, ye who have seen the open tomb receive into its bosom the sacred trust committed to its keeping, in hope of the *first resurrection*—ye who have heard the sullen rumbling of the death-clods as they dropped upon the coffin-lid, and told you that earth had gone back to earth—when the separation from the object of your love was realized in all the desolation of your bereavement, next to the thought that you should erelong see Christ as he is and be like him, was not that consolation the strongest which assured you that the departed one, whom God has put from you into darkness, will run to meet you when you cross the threshold of immortality, and, with the holy rapture to which the redeemed alone can give utterance, lead you to the exalted Savior, and with you bow at his feet and cast the conqueror's crown before him?" And is this hope vain? Shall we not even know those dear ones in the spirit-world? Was this light of hope that gilded so beautifully the sad, dark hour of human woe, only a mocking *ignis fatuus*, so soon to go out in everlasting darkness? Is this affection—so deep, so holy—yearning over its object with undying love—to be nipped in the very bud of its being? Nay, it can not be. There must have been some higher purpose; God could not delight in the bestowal of affections that were to be blighted in their very beginning, and of hopes that were to end only in the mockery of eternal disappoint ment.

> "If fate unite the faithful but to part,
> Why is their memory sacred to the heart?"
> "Say, can the world one joyous thought bestow
> To friendship, weeping at the couch of Woe?
> No! but a brighter soothes the last adieu—
> Souls of impassioned mold, she speaks to you—
> Weep not, she says, at Nature's transient pain,
> Congenial spirits part to meet again."

II. Teachings of Revelation in Regard to Future Recognition.

In affirming that the Bible fully warrants the naturai and reasonable hope of a recognition of friends in heaven, we do not mean that it is any where put into the precise formula of a proposition. Some of the most elementary truths of religion are passed by without any such formal statement; but they are constantly recognized in its general teachings, and, by obvious implication at least taught in many of its most striking recorded transactions. So it is with the doctrine of spiritual recognition. It is interwoven in the very texture of revelation and runs through the whole scope of its teachings.

1. *The mental basis of recognition, namely, personal identity, consciousness, perception, and memory, are recognized as being retained in the future state.* All this is implied in the song heard by St. John sung in heaven, "Thou wast slain, and hast redeemed us to God by thy blood out of every kindred, and tongue, and people, and nation." (Rev. v, 9.) No one could sing this song for himself without a remembrance of the redeeming love of the Savior, as it found him a lost and ruined sinner upon the earth, and made him a king and a priest unto God; and all this too from among a certain nation, people, tongue, and kindred. Nor could any one join with *others* in saying, "Thou hast redeemed *us*,"

without some recognition of each one of the great company as having been once, like themselves, possessed of definite place, and language, and kindred upon the earth.

Then, again, in the narration of his sublime vision St. John tells us, "I saw under the altar the souls of them that were slain for the Word of God, and for the testimony which they held. And they cried with a loud voice, saying, How long, O Lord, holy and true, dost thou not judge and avenge our blood on them that dwell on the earth?" (Rev. vi, 9, 10.) Here certainly were identity, and consciousness, and memory in strong and earnest exercise. There was not only a memory of blood that had been shed upon the earth, but a recognition of themselves as the identical persons whose blood had been shed, and superadded to all was a consciousness of unavenged wrong which they had suffered upon the earth.

The same is also implied in that declaration of our Lord, "That every idle word that men shall speak, they shall give account thereof at the day of judgment." (Matt. xii, 36.) For unless these deeds be remembered, and remembered too in their connection with our personal identity, how shall we render the account? Or, take, again, the language of St. Paul, "Every one of us shall give account of himself to God." (Rom. xiv, 12.) Here, too, it is implied that there is a memory, or at least a knowledge of the items of this account as being connected with our past history.

But still more emphatic and impressive is that picture of the rich man and Lazarus. "The rich man also died, and was buried; and in hell he lifted up his eyes, being in torments, and SEETH ABRAHAM afar off, AND LAZARUS in his bosom." (Luke xvi, 22, 23.) Here, by some means, he *perceived* two individuals, and one he *recognizes* as the old patriarch—"the father of the faithful"—and the other the poor beggar who was once "laid at his gate." And then when he would fain importune for one drop of water, Abraham replies, "Son, remember." What a world of meaning in that word REMEMBER!

It is not necessary to argue this question further. These points are not only conclusive as an argument, but they are also impressive for the moral lessons they teach.

2. *Passages almost without number imply the personal recognition of friends in the future life.* Among the passages of this kind may be reckoned that which describes the patriarchs, and Moses and Aaron, and others, as being, in death, *gathered unto their people.* These expressions do not relate to their burial but to their dying; for the people of Abraham were buried in Ur of the Chaldees, while he was interred in a new burying-place. The union, then, was one of *souls* and not of *bodies.* So of Isaac; his burial by Esau and Jacob is described as taking place *after* he had been "gathered unto his people." And Jacob "was gathered unto his people" in Egypt, but *afterward* his body was carried up to Canaan and laid in the burying-ground of his fathers. Aaron was *gathered unto his people* "in Mount Hor, by the coast of the land of Edom," though it was far away from the place where any of his ancestors had been buried. And Moses upon Mount Nebo, after beholding the promised land, was *gathered unto his people,* though his body was buried amid the solitude of an unknown valley, and "no man knoweth of his sepulcher unto this day." (Deut. xxxiv, 6.) Nothing further can be needed to show that this being "gathered" does not refer to the *place* of burial, nor yet to the general *fact* of burial, but to being gathered among their people in the spirit-land. It finds its counterpart in that prayer of the Psalmist, "Gather not my soul with sinners; nor my life with bloody men." (Psa. xxvi, 9.)

That is, according to Adam Clarke, "let not my eternal lot be cast with them! may I never be doomed to spend an eternity with them!" Deliver me from their companionship and from their doom.

David, when his child was dead, but the body, unburied, was still with him, said, "I shall go to him, but he shall not return to me." (2 Sam. xii, 23.) That is, our separation will be brief; though he may not come back from the spirit-land to me, I shall soon rejoin him there—rejoin him, too, as my son who went before! This is a common feeling and sentiment of Christian faith. It is evidently based upon the expectation of a recognition of the departed, as well as of a union with them.

In one of his discourses (Matt. xii) our Savior rebukes the unbelief and wickedness of the generation to whom he preached, declaring that the men of Nineveh who repented at the preaching of Jonah, and the Queen of the South who came to hear the wisdom of Solomon, should *rise up in the judgment and condemn it.* Here it is clearly implied that the inhabitants of ancient Nineveh who were alive and heard the preaching of Jonah, and the Queen of the South who came to Solomon, and also the Jews who listened to the preaching of Christ yet repented not, will all be *recognized* in their individual characters, and their connection with the events brought in review be fully known.

The case of the rich man and Lazarus (Luke xvi) is also to the point. And the fact that it is possibly a parable, does not militate against the force of its testimony, for even a parable can not teach any lesson or doctrine contrary to truth. Here is an unvailing of the future world, and at the same moment we catch a glimpse of heaven and of hell; but in both personal recognition is discovered and distinctly announced. Nor is it a personal recognition that is confined to those in its own sphere. Dives, looking across the great gulf of separation, recognized the beatified and favored person now reclining upon Abraham's bosom, as the poor beggar that was once fed with the crumbs that fell from his luxury-laden table. And Lazarus, looking forth from the midst of his unbounded joy, likewise recognized him with the parched tongue in the midst of the tormenting flame, as the rich man who once was clothed in purple and fared sumptuously every day. There is something intensely thrilling in this interview and recognition between parties separated by the great gulf fixed by eternal justice! It intimates something in the possibilities of eternity from which we would fain turn away our eye.

In the parable of the talents and of the pounds, and also in that of the householder hiring men to work in his vineyard, the reckoning is made with each individual, connecting each with what he has done; and not only this, but also showing throughout a distinct recognition of each other and the relative claims of each.

The transfiguration scene, in which Moses and Elias appeared talking with Christ, to the wonder and admiration of the three disciples, evidently implies that Moses and Elias fully recognized each other, and that both recognized Christ and were also recognized by him. Here, though it may not have been the original design of the transaction to teach or illustrate the spiritual recognition, yet that recognition is most certainly implied.

We need not dwell longer upon the incidental allusions that imply the future recognition. They stand out in almost every chapter of the Bible, are interwoven into all its teachings in reference to the future state, and are strikingly illustrated in the pious expressions and the dying hopes of the saints of God. The value and entire conclusiveness of this incidental testimony can not be overestimated. The Bible, if it no where asserts nor attempts to prove in terms this recognition, takes it for granted, just as it does the existence of God, and grounds its teachings upon the presumption of it, so that the declaration of it in the most formal manner could not render the Scripture testimony more complete.

3. *The doctrine of the resurrection, as taught in the Bible, implies both a preserved and a recognized individuality.*

"Faith sees the bright, eternal doors
  Unfold to make his children way;
They shall be clothed with endless life
  And shine in everlasting day.

The trump shall sound, the dead shall wake,
  From the cold tomb the slumb'rers spring;
Through heaven with joy their myriads rise,
  And hail their Savior and their King." DWIGHT.

We do not undertake now to argue the fact of the resurrection of our bodies from the dead. That has already been done. But we now present a single point; namely, that this resurrection implies both a *preserved and recognized individuality* in the persons so resurrected.

Job says, "For I know that my Redeemer liveth, and that he shall stand at the latter day upon the earth; and though after my skin worms destroy this body, yet in my flesh shall I see God: whom I shall see for myself, and mine eyes shall behold, and not another." (Chapter xix, 25-27.) In this early foreshadowing of the resurrection it is only stated that Job should in his resurrection body see "God;" not that God should see him, or that any body else should see him; but it is manifestly implied not only that he should see, but also that he should *be seen*.

Isaiah is still more explicit: "Thy dead men shall live, together with my dead body shall they rise." (Chapter xxvi, 19.) It is inconceivable that he should have employed such language if these dead were to rise unknowing each other What avails rising *together*, and how can the promise bring cheer or comfort if we shall neither know nor be known in the rising?

When Jesus said unto Martha, "Thy brother shall rise again," (John xi, 23,) her reply was, "I know that he shall rise again in the resurrection at the last day." (Chapter xi, 24.) Both the Comforter and the comforted in this interview must have had more in mind than an abstract assurance of a mere resurrection. There was implied *restoration*. The yearning heart of the sister grasped the idea that her loved brother should not only be raised from the dead, but should be restored to her arms.

But notice the particularity with which the resurrection is described; how distinct the different classes and the different individuals stand out. "Marvel not at this: for the hour is coming, in the which all that are in the graves shall hear his voice, and shall come forth; they that have done good, unto the resurrection of life; and they that have done evil, unto the resurrection of damnation." (John v, 28, 29.) "And this is the will of him that sent me, that every one which seeth the Son, and believeth on him, may have everlasting life: and I will raise him up at the last day." (John vi, 40.) It is not implied that they shall come up from the grave with characters different from those with which they went down into it, but with the same. For "many of them that sleep in the dust of the earth shall awake, some to everlasting life, and some to shame and everlasting contempt." (Daniel xii, 2.) If it should be announced that those sleeping in the night should awake in the morning, the announcement would imply that they should awake the same persons, recognizable and recognizing, as when at nightfall they lay down to sleep. So in the resurrection morning. The announcement that we shall "awake," that we shall "come forth," "rise again," and "the dead, small and great, stand before God," can not by any possibility allow of so great a detraction from our personality as to render recognition impossible.

But to settle this question and place it beyond all doubt and all controversy, let us also be reminded of the resurrection of the body of Christ and its recognition by the disciples. This has something more than a formal and technical application to us and to our race. He arose the "first-fruits," and the model after which the resurrection bodies of his saints shall be formed, for he "shall change our vile body, that it may be fashioned like unto his glorious body." (Phil. iii, 21.) Or again it is said, "For if we have been planted together in the likeness of his death, we shall be also in the likeness of his resurrection," (Romans vi, 5,) and "when he shall appear we shall be like him." (John iii, 2.) And yet the body raised was identified and recognized by the disciples as "that same Jesus" whom the Jews had taken and crucified with wicked hands. They knew his form, they recognized his voice, they saw the nail prints in his hands and his feet, the scar of the wound in his side; they felt him and found him flesh and bones; they walked with him, and from the summit of Olivet saw him ascend into heaven. The recognition was perfect. The apostles and the early converts had undoubting faith of it—"so we preached and so ye believed," (1 Cor. xv, 11,) was the testimony of Paul. If, then, Christ's resurrection body was clearly distinguished and recognized, and if his resurrection body was the type and pattern of ours, surely we shall recognize each other in the resurrection state.

4. *The descriptions of the judgment scene in the Bible represent each as standing out in his individual person and character among those to be judged.*

"And must I be to judgment brought,
And answer in that day
For every vain and idle thought,
And every word I say?

> Yes, every secret of my heart
> Shall shortly be made known,
> And I receive my just desert
> For all that I have done."

These solemn lines by our grandest lyric poet, Charles Wesley, do but sum up the universally-received idea of the Church with regard to the teaching of the Bible in relation to the future judgment.

In that judgment each individual is represented as standing out in his own distinctive character. "We must all appear before the judgment-seat of Christ, that every one may receive the things done in his body according to that he hath done, whether it be good or bad." (2 Cor. v, 10.) "Behold, the Lord cometh with ten thousand of his saints to execute judgment upon all, and to convince all that are ungodly among them of all their ungodly deeds which they have ungodly committed." (Jude 14.) "And I saw the dead, small and great, stand before God; and the books were opened; and another book was opened which is the book of life; and the dead were judged out of those things which were written in the books, according to their works." (Rev. xx, 12.) "Who shall give account to him that is ready to judge the quick and the dead." (1 Peter iv, 5.) "For God will bring every work into judgment with every secret thing, whether it be good or whether it be evil." (Eccl. xii, 14.) "I say unto you that every idle word men shall speak they shall give account thereof in the day of judgment." (Matt. xii, 36.) "So then every one of us shall give account of himself to God." (Rom. xiv, 12.) In all these descriptions of the judgment there stand out before us an aggre gate of individuals, each one of whom is to be subjected to the forms of trial. The deeds of their life are to be rehearsed, and that, too, in the presence of neighbors, and friends, and associates. It seems utterly incredible that all this could be gone through without any personal recognitions among them. Why, to these very idle words and these deeds of which I shall give account, my neighbor was perhaps a party. How, then, when he stands by my side and hears the account rendered in the judgment shall he not know me? Nothing can be more obvious than that these general descriptions imply a recognition of persons among the parties assembled in the judgment.

But there are other passages of more specific import upon this point. In showing the decisions of the final judgment and the grounds of those decisions, St. Paul draws the line of distinction—"to the Jew first and also to the Gentile," (Rom. ii, 10)—showing that the Jew will be known as a Jew, and the Gentile as a Gentile, in the judgment day.

Again, our Savior representing the judgment scene describes the Judge as separating the righteous from the wicked as a shepherd divideth his sheep from the goats, and placing the one on his right hand, the other on his left. The very manner of the transaction indicates it to be one in which the parties are recognized. But when we hear the Judge saying to the righteous, "Inasmuch as ye have done it unto *one* of the least of *these my brethren*, ye have done it unto me," (Matt. xxv, 40,) we can hardly avoid the impression that the commended disciple must have looked around upon the assembled multitude, assuring himself by observing one after another of the suffering and sorrowing ones of earth to whom he had ministered "in the name of a disciple." And so, also, when we hear the Judge replying to those on his left, "Inasmuch as ye did it not to one of the *least of these* ye did it not to me," (Matthew xxv, 45,) we can not but feel that personal witnesses rose up before them for their condemnation. Certain it is that the recognition of individuals as well as of parties is implied all through this striking description of the judgment scene.

But we have a more sure word of prophecy. Our Savior said to his apostles, "Ye which have followed me, in the regeneration, when the Son of man shall sit in the throne of his glory, ye also shall sit upon twelve thrones, judging the twelve tribes of Israel." (Matt. xix, 28.) And St. Paul, speaking by the same Divine authority, addressing the Corinthians, says: "Do ye not know that the saints shall judge the world?" (1 Cor. vi, 2.) It must be apparent that if the saints are to take part in the judgment, they must be able to distinguish the individuals brought before them, and also to connect the earthly history of each—"the deeds done in the body"—with the individual himself. Without such knowledge they would be utterly incompetent to exercise the functions of judgment. But how is it to be obtained? By personal acquaintance with them in life; by the recorded books in heaven; by the testimony of angels who waited upon them as ministering spirits; by the testimony of those who knew them in life, and by their own confessions. Such are the conceivable modes of evidence employed in reaching the decisions of the great day; and yet each one of them involves the necessity of personal identification, and consequently of the recognition of individuals in the future state.

5. *The revelations given us concerning the heavenly state clearly imply personal recognition among the saints in heaven.*

The gathering of the saints home to heaven is thus described by our Lord: "Then shall he send his angels, and shall gather together his elect from the four winds, from the uttermost part of the earth to the uttermost part of heaven." (Mark xiii, 27.) And they "shall come from the east and west, and shall sit down with Abraham, and Isaac, and Jacob in the kingdom of heaven." (Matt. viii, 11.) "And I will appoint unto you a kingdom as my Father hath appointed unto me, that ye may eat and drink at my table in my kingdom." (Luke xxii, 29, 30.) Is there not here recognition of individuals? St. Luke adds that the wicked thrust out from this scene "shall see Abraham, and Isaac, and Jacob, and all the prophets in the kingdom of God." (Luke xiii, 28.) Surely higher privileges of recognition will not be given to the wicked thrust out of the kingdom of God than to the elect gathered into it.

St. Paul teaches us the joy the faithful pastor shall feel in the salvation of those to whom he has preached and for whom he has labored. He addressed them as his "joy and crown," exhorting them to steadfastness, that he might "rejoice in the day of Christ," for "ye also are our rejoicing in the day of the Lord Jesus." (2 Cor. i, 14.) And then he adds, "For what is our hope, or joy, or crown of rejoicing? Are not even ye in the presence of our Lord Jesus Christ at his coming?" (1 Thess. ii, 19.) But how is this consummation to be reached? The apostle tells them, "He which raised up the Lord Jesus shall raise up us also by Jesus, and shall PRESENT US WITH YOU." (2 Cor. iv, 14.) How sadly deluded was the apostle if those saved through his ministry were to be personally unknown to him in the heavenly state! To "present US with YOU" means something more than gathering up a bundle of abstractions, however holy they may be.

But in the delineations of the heavenly state this knowledge is still further implied. Witness the language of the Savior to his disciples: "In my Father's house are many mansions; I go to prepare a place for you. And if I go and prepare a place for you I will come again and receive you unto myself, that where I am there ye may be also." (John xiv, 2, 3.) Witness, also, that comprehensive prayer of the Redeemer for all them that should believe on him—"that they all may be one, as thou, Father, art in me and I in thee, that they also may be one in us. . . . Father, I will that they also whom thou hast given me be with me where I am, that they may behold my glory which thou hast given me." (John xvii, 21, 24.) All these expressions imply mutual and endearing intercourse. It is the communion of the *heavenly family*, especially among those members of that great family who have been redeemed from earth, and to whom the bliss of heaven is hightened by the remembrance of that redemption. How, then, can it be supposed that they know less of each other than when in the pilgrimage state? Rather, is it not certain that in them has been realized that, though once they *saw through a glass darkly, now they see face to face, knowing even as they also are known?* This only can fulfill the conditions of a *heavenly family* mingling in social fellowship, beholding each other, sitting, and eating, and drinking at the table of their common Lord, and joining with united heart and voice in celebrating the amazing love that sought them out while sinners and aliens, redeemed them to Christ, made them often sit together in heavenly places in the time of their pilgrimage, and now has exalted them to be kings and priests to God and the Lamb forever and forever. And such a family are they who are now gathered into one in Christ Jesus.

III. Spiritual Recognition a Universal Faith.

To vindicate the claim of a faith to universality, it is not necessary to prove that every individual of the race has received it; but only that it has generally been received by the race in all ages and among all classes. We have purposely said "the universal faith," without the limiting word "Christian," because we find it occupying a field wider than that of Christianity itself.

1. *Let us then glance at the testimony of ancient philosophers and poets.* There is scarcely one of these philosophers and poets of any note, even though they lived in the early twilight of time, who has not left on record noble sentiments in regard to the companionships of the future life. We refer to them for two especial reasons. First, they may be regarded as representing the sentiments of the most enlightened minds of their age; and, second, as giving utterance to the voice of that humanity whose very instincts claim the fellowships of another life.

Socrates was one of the purest and best of the Grecian philosophers. Of him the infidel Rousseau made the declaration, "If the life and death of Socrates were those of a philosopher, the life and death of Jesus Christ were those of a God." Socrates was condemned to suffer death by poison, through the blinded fury of an ignorant and superstitious populace. He calmly submitted to his fate, discoursing to his friends almost to the last moment upon the immortality of the soul. In his speech made to his judges, after his sentence, he said: "If death is a removal to another place, and what is said to be true—that all the dead are there—what greater blessing can there be than this, my judges? For if, on arriving at hades, [the place of departed spirits,] released from those who pretend to be judges, one shall find those that are true judges, and who are said to be there—Minos and Radamanthus, Æacus and Triptolemus, and such others of the demi-gods as were just during their own lives—would this be a sad removal? At what price would you not estimate a conference with Musæus, Hesiod, and Homer? I, indeed, should be willing to die often, if this be true. For to me, the sojourn there would be admirable, when I should meet with Palamedes, and Ajax the son of Telamon, and any other of the ancients who has died by an unjust sentence. The comparing my sufferings with theirs would, I think, be no unpleasing occupation. But the greatest pleasure would be to spend my time in questioning and examining the people there as I have done those here, and discovering who among them is wise, and who fancies himself to be so and is not. At what price, my judges, would not any one estimate the opportunity of questioning him who led that mighty army against Troy, or Ulysses, or Sisyphus, or ten thousand others whom one might mention, both men and women? with whom to converse and associate, and to question them, would be an inconceivable happiness. Surely, for that the judges there do not condemn to death."*

The expressions "if" and "what is said," were evidently uttered in accordance with his cautious way of speaking. That there was no doubt in his own mind is evident from his whole style and manner. That this personal recognition and intercourse were confidently expected by him, is clearly shown in his conversations with his friends just before his death, as recorded by Plato in his Phædon. In one part of this conversation he exclaims: "For my part, if I thought I should not find in the other world gods as good and as wise, and men infinitely better, than we are, it would be a piece of injustice in us not to be troubled at death."† But following on, and speaking of what is reserved for the dead after this life, he adds: "Therefore it is that death is no trouble to me." Thus it becomes evident that the darkness and gloom of the dying hour were cheered by the confident expectation of meeting with the great and the good in another life.

Cicero, the unrivaled orator of Rome, whose deep spiritual nature often glowed with the sublimest hopes, speaks in raptures upon his expectation of a reunion with the

*Bohn's Classical Library—works of Plato, vol. i, p. 28.

†Plato's Phædon; translated by Madam Dacier; New York: W. Gowan, 1833; p. 55.

noble dead. "For my own part, I feel myself transported with the most ardent impatience to join the society of my two departed friends, your illustrious fathers, whose characters I greatly respected, and whose persons I sincerely loved. Nor is this my earnest desire confined to these excellent persons alone, with whom I was formerly connected. I ardently wish to visit also those celebrated worthies, of whose honorable conduct I have heard and read much, or whose virtues I have myself commemorated in some of my writings. To this glorious assembly I am speedily advancing; and I would not be turned back in my journey, even on the assured condition that my youth, like that of Pelias, should be again restored.

"O glorious day! when I shall retire from this low and sordid scene, to associate with the divine assembly of departed spirits; and not with those only whom I have just mentioned, but with my dear Cato, that best of sons and most valuable of men! It was my sad fate to lay his body on the funeral pile, when by the course of nature I had reason to hope he would perform the same last sad office for mine. His soul, however, did not desert me, but still looked back on me in its flight to those happy mansions, to which he was assured I should one day follow him. If I seemed to bear his death with fortitude, it was, by no means, that I did not most sensibly feel the loss I had sustained; it was because I supported myself with the consoling reflection that we could not long be separated." *

There is a touching pathos in this passage, showing how deeply the heart of the great orator was moved by the prospect of a reunion with his friends in another life. The wonder is that a soul unenlightened by Revelation could ever be possessed of such exalted views or give utterance to such noble sentiments.

* De Senectute.

We have taken Socrates and Cicero as the representatives of the ancient philosophers. Of the ancient poets there are no more fitting representatives than Homer and Virgil. The former preceded Socrates more than five hundred years; but from the depths of that remote antiquity, his voice has come ringing down through the ages, giving utterances that tell how deeply this sentiment is interwoven in the very texture of the human soul.

In the Odyssey, B. IX, Ulysses is represented as visiting the regions of the dead. Among the persons whom he beheld there was his mother:

"There as the wondrous vision I survey'd,
All pale ascends my royal mother's shade:
A queen, to Troy she saw our legions pass;
Now a thin form was all Anticlea was!
Struck at the sight, I melt with filial woe,
And down my cheek the pious waters flow."*

As was natural, the long-wandering, affectionate son rushes to clasp that mother in his arms:

"Thrice in my arms I strove the shade to bind;
Thrice through my arms she slipped like empty wind."

Wild with despair, he exclaims:

"Fly'st thou, loved shade, while thus I fondly moan?
Turn to my arms! to my embraces turn!
Is it, ye powers that smile at human harms,
Too great a bliss to weep within her arms?"

His mother then explains to him that when life leaves the body, all are such as he finds her.

"No more the substance of the man remains,
Nor bounds the blood along the purple veins;
Those the funeral flames in atoms bear,
To wander with the wind in empty air,
While the impassive soul reluctant flies,
Like a vain dream, to these infernal skies."

She then tells him how she had died from grief at his protracted absence; how his aged father still lives; describes

*Pope's Translation. London: G. Routledge.

the princely state and character of his son; and extols the unfaltering faithfulness of his wife through so many years of absence. Tiresias recognizes Ulysses and holds a long conversation with him, foretelling the various fates he is yet to encounter. The shades of the ancient heroines gather around him, each appearing in her appropriate character. Then appear, among others, Agamemnon, Achilles, Ajax, Tityus, Sisyphus, Tantalus, and Hercules. Agamemnon holds a long conversation; Hercules also deigns a few words. But throughout the various shades do not appear as strangers, but are represented as holding intercourse with each other as well as with their anomalous visitor. They are also represented as occupying positions corresponding to those occupied in life. The characters and results of life were also manifested in them.

Another description of these regions is found in B. XXIV, where the ghosts of the suitors of Penelope, slain by the hand of Ulysses, descend to the land of souls. They, too—*these disembodied souls*—are represented as also recognizing the heroes and heroines of Greece, and being recognized by them. And, what is worthy of attention, all through these descriptions kindred characters are grouped together, and those united in life are found also united in the spirit-land. Then, too, each one manifests a deep concern for the friends and companions of earth, and are anxiously looking for their coming.

No one can doubt that this is a full unvailing of the popular as well as philosophic sentiment of the age in regard to the recognitions and the intercourse of souls in the future state.

Virgil, who wrote over eight hundred years after Homer, and only about fifty before Christ, makes frequent allusion to the state of the dead. He represents the shades as recognizing each other at first sight; and this recognition as not being confined to heaven, but taking place even in the lowest hell. In the Æniad, B. VI, the poet represents his hero as visiting the place of departed souls. There he is not only *recognized, but welcomed.*

"The gladsome ghosts in circling troops attend,
And with unwearied eyes behold their friend,
Delight to hover near, and long to know
What business brought him to the realms below."

His father, the venerable Anchises, discovers him as he approaches, and

"Meets him with open arm and falling tears.
'Welcome,' he said, 'the god's undoubted race!
O long-expected to my dear embrace!
'T is true, computing time, I now believed
The day approached—nor are my hopes deceived.'"

The affectionate son responds to the ardor of parental love:

"'Reach forth your hand, O parent shade, nor shun
The dear embraces of your loving son!'
He said; and falling tears his face bedew;
Then thrice around his neck his arms he threw."

As the Sibyl guides him through the different departments of the regions of the dead, he discovers almost everywhere some he knew on earth. The recognition is mutual; and these spirits, in various forms, show the interest they still take in the affairs of the world they have left behind, and in the friends whom they are expecting to join them in the spirit-land. The ties of love that bound them to kindred and friends while living, were not sundered by the separations and the changes wrought by death. There was a beautiful tradition among the heathen that from the spirit-land a "messenger-bird" came back to convey tokens of affection to the living. Upon this Mrs. Hemans constructs that beautiful poem:

"But tell us, thou bird of the solemn strain,
Do those that have loved forget?
We know, we know that their land is bright;
But do they love, do they love us yet?"

The instinctive sentiment of humanity waited not for the dawning light of written revelation from God, but boldly asserted an undying fellowship among kindred spirits in the land of souls, and a certain reunion with those who had gone before.

We might multiply our citations from the philosophers and poets of antiquity to almost any extent; but with the testimony of Socrates and Cicero, of Homer and Virgil, so distinctly uttered, what need we more? Their utterances may be taken as reflecting the sentiments of the purest and best minds, not only of their own age, but of that which preceded them; and as to the ages that succeeded, these utterances may be said to have formed as well as represented their prevailing ideas of the condition of disembodied souls.

2. *It is recognized even in the teachings, rites, and faith of all systems of heathen religion.* We have heard of the Vale of Tempe, the Hesperian Gardens, the Elysian Fields, and the Islands of the Blest. All these were so many forms in which the pagan faith expressed the great expectation of reunion and recognition in another life. We have read of the immolation of widows upon the funeral-pyre; of the killing of slaves, subjects, and friends that they might accompany the souls of the departed, and sustain to them relations kindred to those sustained in this life. These cruel practices have been almost coextensive with heathenism itself; they now exist, or formerly existed, in nearly all the vast heathen empires of Asia, in the benighted regions of Africa, among the Indians of both North and South America, and upon nearly all the vast and populous islands of the Pacific and Southern Oceans. In nearly all the vast empire of ancient India the widow was accustomed to throw herself upon the funeral-pile and be burned to death in the fire which consumed the body of her

deceased husband, so that she might rejoin him in the spirit land. The King of Dahomy perhaps even yet slaughters his thousands who are to be the companions of his predecessor in the other world. Many of the petty kings and princes in that blighted division of the world, if they wish to send a message to the shade of some friend, or companion, or ancestor, simply summon a messenger, give him the message he is to deliver, and then cleave his head from his shoulders to send him forth upon his mission. These revolting practices have their bright as well as a dark side. It is the darkened soul's brutalized expression of the conviction of another life; and that the friendships formed here are to be perpetuated there. This idea is the silver lining of a cloud which else had been one of unmitigated blackness.

A beautiful story is told of the wife of Little Wolf, one of the chiefs of the Iowa Indians. She had accompanied her husband on a mission to Europe. They had already lost three children, and in London a fourth died. The grief of the bereaved mother was so intense that, soon after their arrival in Paris, it brought on an affection of the lungs of a most alarming character. Her husband sought to console her and win her back to life; but her constant reply was, "No, no; my four children recall me. I see them by the side of the Great Spirit. They stretch out their arms to me, and are astonished that I do not join them." She soon after died, rejoicing in the prospect of rejoining her little ones by the side of the Great Spirit. This touching incident has found expression in verse:

"My beautiful, my blest!
I see them there, by the Great Spirit's throne;
With winning words and fond beseeching tone
They woo me to my rest.

They chide my long delay,
And wonder that I linger from their home;
They stretch their loving arms to bid me come—
Now would ye have me stay?"

Thus do we find this sentiment of humanity interwoven into the workings of human thought, and conscience, and affection.

> "Who reads his bosom reads immortal life,
> Or Nature there, imposing on her sons,
> Has written fables—man was made a lie."

3. *The early Church and the Christian fathers received and taught it.* The doctrine of recognition has ever lived in the Church. Not only has it ever been embodied in those brief formularies of faith called "creeds," but it has been a living principle, received and proclaimed by the witnesses of the Lord Jesus Christ. The Christian fathers received it from the apostles, and not only cherished it as an element of living faith, but placed on record their unutterable joy at the prospect of meeting the great and the good, "the loved and lost," in heaven, and enjoying their communion forever.

Cyprian says, "We ought not to mourn for those who are delivered from the world by the call of the Lord, since we know they are not lost, but sent before us—that they have taken their leave of us in order to precede us." In another place, speaking of heaven as the home of the saints, he exclaims: "A great host of beloved friends awaits us there! a numerous and various crowd—parents, brethren, children—who are secure in a blessed immortality, and, only still concerned for us, are looking with desire for our arrival! To see and embrace these—what a mutual joy will this be to us and them! . . . To these, dearly-beloved brethren, let us hasten with strong desire, and ardently wish soon to be with them and with Christ."

St. Ambrose, of the third century, in his funeral oration upon the death of the Emperor Valentinian, speaks of him as "being conjoined with his brother, Gratian, and with him enjoying the pleasures of everlasting life."

The communion of the saints was a theme very prominent

in the primitive Church. In that communion all the saints of God—the whole family of the redeemed—whether on earth or in heaven—were believed to be *actual partakers.* "Hence," says Neander, "was derived the Christian custom which required that the memory of departed friends should be celebrated by their relations on the anniversary of their death. It was usual on this day to partake of the sacrament under a sense of inseparable fellowship with those who had died in the Lord." "So," he adds, "whole communities celebrated the memory of those who had died as witnesses for the Lord. On every returning anniversary the people gathered around their graves, and there the story of their confession and sufferings was rehearsed, and the communion was celebrated in the consciousness of a continued fellowship with them." Thus "the dead in Christ" were recognized as being yet alive, and expression given to the abiding faith of a reunion with them. This faith was also illustrated in the modified forms of the lamentations for the dead. He further says, "From the first, Christianity condemned the wild and at the same time hypocritical expressions of grief with which the funeral procession was accompanied—those wailings of the women who had been hired for the occasion; yet it required no stoic resignation and apathy, but mitigated and refined the anguish of sorrow by the spirit of faith and hope, and of childlike resignation to that eternal love which takes in order to restore what it has taken under a more glorious form; which separates for the moment, in order to *reunite the separated in a glorified state through eternity.*"

Such are the views of this subject that have come down to us from the very age of the apostles. This is suggestive not only of their origin, but also of the millions in all ages of the Church, that have felt the inspiration of this faith and rejoiced in hope of a reunion with the sainted dead.

4. *The testimony of theologians and divines.* Allow us to group, in brief, the sentiments of various theologians, whose names are honored in the Church of God.

Dr. Paley says: "If this (Col. i, 28) be rightly interpreted, then it affords the manifest and necessary inference, that the saints in the future life will meet and be known again to one another; for how, without knowing again his converts, in their new and glorious state, could St. Paul desire or expect to present them at the last day?"

Dr. Edwards.—"It is reasonable to believe that the saints shall know that they had such and such a relation to one another when they were on earth. The father shall know that such a one was his child; the husband shall remember that such a one was his wife; the spiritual guide shall know that such a one belonged to his flock; and so all other relations of persons shall be renewed and known in heaven. The ground of this assertion is this, that the soul of man is of that nature that it depends not on the body and sense, and, therefore, being separated, knows all that it knew in the body. And for this reason it is not to be doubted that it arrives in the other world with the same desires and inclinations it had here. So that the delights of conversation are continued in heaven. Friends and relations are familiar and free with one another, and call to mind their former circumstances and concerns in the world, so far as they may be serviceable to advance their happiness."

Dr. Nevin.—"That the saints in glory shall continue to know those whom they have known and loved on earth, seems to me to flow necessarily from the idea of immortality itself; for this can not be real except as it includes personal identity or a continuation of the same consciouness."

Archbishop Tillotson.—"When we come to heaven we shall

meet with all those excellent persons, those brave minds, those innocent and charitable souls, whom we have seen, and heard, and read of in the world. Then we shall meet many of our dear relations and intimate friends, and, perhaps, with many of our enemies, to whom we shall then be perfectly reconciled, notwithstanding all the warm contests and peevish differences which we had with them in this world, even about matters of religion."

Baxter.—"I must confess as the experience of my own soul that the expectation of loving my friends in heaven, principally kindles my love to them on earth."

Fenelon.—"Very soon they who are separated will be reunited, and there will appear no trace of the separation."

Zuinglius.—"There you may hope to see the society, the assembly, and the dwelling together of all the holy, wise, faithful, heroic, and virtuous, who have lived since the beginning of the world. There you shall see the two Adams, the saved and the Savior. There you shall see Abel, Enoch, Noah, Abraham, Isaac, Jacob, Moses, Joshua, Gideon, Samuel, Elijah, Isaiah, and the mother of God, of whom he has prophesied. There you will see David, Hezekiah, Josiah, John the Baptist, Peter, Paul, etc. There you will see yours who have gone before you, and all your forefathers who have departed this life in the faith. In a word, no virtuous person, no holy mind, no believing soul, has lived from the beginning of the world, or shall yet live, that you may not then meet with God."

Dr. Knapp.—"The enjoyment of the saints in the future world will doubtless be very much hightened by friendship, and by their confiding intercourse with each other. That we shall then recognize our former friends and shall be again associated with them, was uniformly believed by all antiquity. This idea was admitted as altogether rational, and as a consoling thought, by the most distinguished ancient philosophers. Even reason regards this as in a high degree probable; but to one who believes the Holy Scriptures, it can not be a matter of doubt and conjecture."

Dr. John Dick.—"It has been asked whether in this blessed abode the saints will know one another? One should think that the question was unnecessary, as the answer presents itself to every man's mind; and it could have occurred only to some dreaming theologian, who, in his airy speculations, has soared far beyond the sphere of reason and common-sense. Who can doubt whether the saints will know one another? What reason can be given why they should not? Would it be any part of their perfection to have all their former ideas obliterated, and to meet as strangers in the other world? Would it give us a more favorable notion of the assembly in heaven, to suppose it to consist of a multitude of unknown individuals, who never hold communication with each other; or by some inexplicable restraint are prevented, amidst an intimate intercourse, from mutual discoveries? Or have they forgotten what they themselves were, so that they can not reveal it to their associates? What would be gained by this ignorance no man can tell; but we can tell what would be lost by it. They would lose all the happiness of meeting again on the peaceful shore, those from whom they were separated by the storms of life; of seeing among the trophies of Divine grace many of whom they had despaired, and for whose sakes they had gone down with sorrow to the grave; of knowing the good which they had been honored to do, and being surrounded with the individuals who had been saved by means of their prayers, and instructions, and labors. How could those whom he had been the instrument of converting and building up in the holy faith, be to the minister of the Gospel a crown of joy and rejoicing in the day of the Lord, if he did not recognize them when standing at his side? The saints will be free from the turbulence of passion, but innocent affections will remain; and could they spend eternal ages without asking, Are our children here? Are our still dearer relatives here? Have our friends, with whom we took sweet counsel together, found their way to this country, to which we traveled in company till death parted us?"

Dr. William Dodd.—"This is the joy, this is the grand source of consolation under the loss of friends—we shall meet again! They are delivered from their trial, while we are left behind a few weary years longer; and behold, the time of our departure also cometh, when we shall follow our friends, and be forever with them and with the Lord! There shall the enraptured parents receive again their much-loved child; there shall the child, with transport, meet again those parents in joy, over whose graves, with filial duty, he dropped the affectionate tear; there shall the disconsolate widow cease her complaints; and her orphans—orphans now no more—shall tell the sad tale of their distress to the husband, the father—distress even pleasing to recollect, now that happiness is its result and heaven its end! There shall the soft sympathies of endearing friendship be renewed; affectionate sisters shall congratulate each other, and faithful friends again shall mingle converse, interests, amities, and walk high in bliss with God himself."

Dr. Mellvill.—"It is yet but a little while, and we shall be delivered from the burden and the conflict, and, with all those who have preceded us in the righteous struggle, enjoy the deep raptures of a Mediator's presence. Then, reunited to the friends with whom we took sweet counsel upon earth, we shall recount our toil only to highten our ecstasy, and call to mind the tug and the din of war only that, with a more bounding throb and a richer song, we may feel and celebrate the wonders of redemption."

These are only a few of the many, the almost innumerable testimonies that might be gleaned upon the subject from every department of Christian theology. Nor have we collated these so much for the purpose of argument, or proof, as to show how the purest and best writers have expressed themselves upon the subject. But these selections, brief as they are, show us that the doctrine is deeply imbedded in the faith and the experience of the saints of God in all ages. And it is, at least, comforting to know that we have this faith in common with the great body of saints that, in all ages, have loved our Lord Jesus Christ, and looked for his appearing.

5. *The Christian poets have been enraptured by the prospect of it.* After alluding to the fable that Orpheus, by the power of song, won back his beloved wife from the land of shades, Mr. Harbaugh says: "Though it will not bring our loved ones back, as did the notes of Orpheus, it may teach us whither they have gone, and encourage us to look for them again—and this it will do, not in cold, abstract logic, but in the sweet, persuasive language of the heart. It may be to our hearts what the warm breath of the South is to flower-buds—it can cause them to open in love and hope toward those whose warm affections seem for a time to have retired from us into the silent mysteries of the tomb. It can soothe us, as with a soft, friendly voice, while we continue to weep along life's checkered way. Who has not felt its power? The wisest and the best have crowned their wisdom with its garlands, and have sat, like children, at its feet in the quiet hours of life. Even the Bible is not ashamed of it. It hangs its heavenly colorings around the visions of the prophets, and mingles its strains with the public and private devotions of the saints.'

It is with this view that we would gather up a few of the utterances of the Christian poets upon the prospect of a reunion with and a recognition of the sainted dead.

Perhaps none could sing with stronger assurance than John Wesley:

"For me my elder brethren stay,
And angels beckon me away,
And Jesus bids me come."

There is also something touching in the allusions of Charles Wesley to the same subject:

"Awhile in flesh disjoined,
Our friends that went before
We soon in paradise shall find,
And meet to part no more;
In yon thrice-happy seat,
Waiting for us they are;
And thou shalt there a husband meet,
And I a parent there!"

Or, again, in his "Communion with the Saints," with what rapture does Charles Wesley look forward to a reunion with the blessed! In this sacred song he soars to the loftiest altitude, and attunes his lyre to melodies rarely sung this side of heaven:

"Come, let us join our friends above
That have obtained the prize;
And on the eagle wings of love
To joys celestial rise.

Let all the saints terrestrial sing,
With those to glory gone;
For all the servants of our King,
In earth and heaven are one.

One family we dwell in Him,
One Church above, beneath,
Though now divided by the stream,
The narrow stream of death.

One army of the living God,
To his command we bow;
Part of his host have cross'd the flood,
And part are crossing now.

Ten thousand to their endless home
  This solemn moment fly;
And we are to the margin come,
  And we expect to die.

His militant embodied host,
  With wishful looks we stand,
And long to see that happy coast,
  And reach the heavenly land.

Our old companions in distress
  We haste again to see,
And eager long for our release
  And full felicity.

E'en now, by faith, we join our hands
  With those that went before;
And greet the blood-besprinkled bands
  On the eternal shore.

Our spirits, too, shall quickly join,
  Like theirs with glory crown'd,
And shout to see our Captain's sign,
  To hear his trumpet sound.

Lord Jesus, be our constant guide:
  And, when the word is given,
Bid death's cold flood its waves divide,
  And land us safe in heaven."

Montgomery's "Not Lost, but Gone Before," has touched many a heart with its exquisite beauty. But the hidden source of its power—that which makes the heart love to linger upon it—is found in its delicate apprehension of the reunion of kindred souls:

"Friend after friend departs;
  Who hath not lost a friend?
There is no union here of hearts,
  That finds not here an end:
Were this frail world our final rest,
Living or dying none were blest.

Beyond the flight of time,
  Beyond the reign of death,
There surely is some blessed clime,
  Where life is not a breath;
Nor life's affections transient fire,
Whose sparks fly upward and expire.

There is a world above,
  Where parting is unknown;
A long eternity of love,
  Formed for the good alone;
And faith beholds the dying here,
Translated to that glorious sphere.

Thus star by star declines,
  Till all are passed away,
As morning high, and higher shines,
  To pure and perfect day;
Nor sink those stars in empty night,
But hide themselves in heaven's own light."

Bishop Ken beautifully describes the intercourse of the saints in heaven:

"The saints on earth, when sweetly they converse,
And the dear favors of kind Heaven rehearse,
Each feels the other's joys, both doubly share
The blessings which devoutly they compare.
If saints such mutual joy feel here below,
When they each other's heavenly foretastes know,
What joys transport them at each other's sight,
When they shall meet in empyreal hight!
Friends, even in heaven, one happiness would miss,
Should they not know each other when in bliss."

Bishop Mant also says in relation to our knowledge of each other in heaven:

"I count the hope no day-dream of the mind,
  No vision fair of transitory hue,
  The souls of those whom once on earth we knew,
And lov'd, and walk'd with in communion kind,
Departed hence, again in heaven to find.
  Such hope to nature's sympathies is true;
  And such, we deem, the holy word to view
Unfolds; an antidote for grief designed,
One drop from comfort's well. 'T is true we read
  The Book of Life: but if we read amiss,
By God prepared fresh treasures shall succeed
  To kinsmen, fellows, friends, a vast abyss
Of joy; nor aught the longing spirit need
  To fill its measure of enormous bliss."

In his prose poetry Mr. Tupper also sings this great expectation of our Christian faith:

"I look to recognize again, through the beautiful mask of their perfection,
The dear familiar faces I have somewhile loved on earth;

I long to talk with grateful tongue of storms and perils past,
And praise the mighty Pilot that has steered us through the rapids."

Passages, almost without number, and rich in all the grand conceptions inspired by the sublime foreshadowings of the coming life, might be quoted; but these are sufficient to show how the Christian poet has entered into it, and the place it occupies among the themes that lend inspiration to his muse. We must, however, add one more—the believer's parting song—one that will never fail, when sung with the full measure of its power, to inspire the loftiest fervor in the soul:

"When shall we meet again—
  Meet ne'er to sever?
When will Peace wreathe her chain
  Round us forever?
Our hearts will ne'er repose
Safe from each blast that blows
In this dark vale of woes—
  Never—no, never!

When shall love freely flow,
  Pure as life's river?
When shall sweet friendship glow,
  Changeless forever?
Where joys celestial thrill,
Where bliss each heart shall fill,
And fears of parting chill—
  Never—no, never!

Up to that world of light,
  Take us, dear Savior;
May we all there unite,
  Happy, forever:
Where kindred spirits dwell,
There may our music swell,
And time our joys dispel—
  Never—no, never!

Soon shall we meet again—
  Meet ne'er to sever;
Soon will Peace wreathe her chain
  Round us forever:
Our hearts will then repose
Secure from worldly woes:
Our songs of praise shall close—
  Never—no, never!

6. *It has ever been a comfort and a watchword to the dying Christian.* In no other place does this expectation of a reunion, on terms of knowledge, intimacy, and love, so brighten and glow as in the closing scene of the Christian's earthly pilgrimage. Bishop Burgess says: "The inexpressibly-affectionate looks of the dying fix sometimes a recollection more precious than any treasures. But this dying love for friends reveals itself peculiarly in the desire, the hope, and the assurance of a reunion. It reaches to the dead as well as the surviving, and exults with a peculiar rapture in the approaching meeting with such as stand already on the everlasting shore. A few hours before the death of Luther, he rejoiced in this prospect. "We shall, I think," said he, "be renewed in the other life through Christ, and shall much more perfectly recognize our parents, wives, and children." Melancthon, a few days before his death, told Camerarius that he trusted their friendship should be cultivated and perpetuated in another world. Cruciger, another of the school of the reformers, spoke, in his last hours, of meeting and recognition. Casper Olevianus, a divine of Heidelberg, when his son had been summoned to see him before he should die, sent to him also the message that "he need not hurry, they should see one another in eternal life." So Joseph Scaliger spoke of "soon meeting and embracing no longer the subjects of age and infirmity." "What pleasure there is," said the pious Mrs. East, "in the thought that we shall together adore the Savior; and that, if permitted, I shall gladly welcome you on your admittance into heaven." Recollections of dear departed friends come often with such a vividness that, looking on, we are almost persuaded to deem them near. The aged Hannah More, in her last distress, stretched out her arms as if catching at some object, uttered the name of her deceased sister, cried "Joy!" and sank into death.

The prospect of meeting with the great and the good of all ages, and of being reunited with the loved companions of our pilgrimage who have gone before, often fills the mind of the departing saint with the most ecstatic joy. Risden Davacott said: "I am going from weeping friends to congratulate angels and rejoicing saints in heaven."

Then, too, a gleam of light seems reflected in what is by no means an uncommon experience in the dying hour—the presence of angel-messengers and even of departed kindred to cheer the pilgrim in his passage across the dark valley.

This faith in the recognitions of another life, so cheering to the dying Christian, remains to comfort the living. In full conviction of its truth, the minister employs it in all his funeral discourses. It is carved upon the monuments of the dead in all Christian lands. Thus life and death combine in testimony to the firm and abiding foundation of this sublime faith of the Christian life.

XIII.

RECOGNITION OF FRIENDS IN HEAVEN—CONTINUED.

"Father, I will that they also, whom thou hast given me, be with me where I am; that they may behold my glory, which thou hast given me." JOHN xvii, 24.

"And behold, there appeared unto them Moses and Elias, talking with him." MATT. xvii, 4.

"In hell he lifted up his eyes, being in torments; and seeth Abraham afar off, and Lazarus in his bosom." LUKE xvi, 23.

WE resume the discussion of this theme. There are two points of too much importance to be omitted. We refer to the objections urged against the doctrine of the recognition of friends in heaven, and to the moral influence the expectation of a reunion with the friends of earth, in heaven, should have upon us.

IV. OBJECTIONS TO SPIRITUAL RECOGNITION CONSIDERED.

The mere fact that objections are sometimes urged against a doctrine is of no force, since that is an event that has happened to every doctrine of Christianity, no matter how clearly established or how generally believed. The facts and arguments presented in proof of personal recognition in another life are so explicit and so conclusive that we at first thought to omit, as being wholly unnecessary, any review of the objections to it. But we finally concluded to so far change our purpose as to pass in review those which seem most forcible, or which have been most frequently a source of disquietude to the heart of the believer.

1. *The bodily changes undergone at death and in the resurrection are so great that personal recognition will be highly improbable, not to say impossible.* We would not underrate the greatness of this change; it would, perhaps, be impossible for us to overrate it. But do we not know that the greatest bodily changes here work no loss of recognizable identity? The plumpness and ruddiness of health may be succeeded by the ghastliness of extreme emaciation, by sickness, or may be disfigured by accident, till no single feature of the individual's former self is recognizable; yet a smile upon the lip, an expression of the eye, the tone of the voice, or a gush of affection, will reveal the former friend—alas, how changed; yet the same! This suggests that identity is as much of the soul as of the body—nay, more.

Then, again, we must remember that the change in the resurrection is not an investing of the soul with a new body, but it is the complete development, the perfection of the old. The changes wrought in the body from infancy to fifty years are very great; yet the man is the same, recognized and recognizing all along. This does not seem wonderful, the change is so gradual, extending through so many years. But suppose it were possible for this transformation to take place in a single night, so that the individual that laid down at evening an infant should rise in the morning a man of fifty years, having undergone the transformation of half a century in a single night. It would be a wonderful transformation! And yet he would be the same individual: identity would be untouched. It is not another individual different from the infant we had seen, but it is the same person *developed.* So shall it be in the resurrection—a wondrous change, sudden, resistless, transforming every part, and infusing new power into every faculty; but still it is the same identical person as before.

But we are not left to the force of reason alone in removing this objection. Revelation sheds no doubtful light upon the resurrection body, glorious as it is, possessing and displaying marks that shall identify it with its earthly being. What an illustration of this was given in the transfiguration! The Redeemer was recognized by his disciples even through the dazzling brightness that radiated from his beatific body. Moses and Elias, too, who had come back from the spirit-land to commune with the blessed Messiah, were not without marks of recognition. Then, also, after the Savior's resurrection, the disciples readily recognized the person of their blessed Lord. His resurrection body was the type and pattern of our own—only inconceivably more glorious. If his was recognizable, so must also be ours. The change, great and glorious as it may be, is not such as will change our essential character, or obliterate the elements of identification.

Indeed, we can not help thinking that our knowledge of each other in the future state will be vastly more perfect than in this. "For now we see through a glass, darkly; but then face to face." The communion of individuals here, and their knowledge of one another, is necessarily imperfect. We stand "face to face," it is true; but we can behold each other only through the dim and soiled "glass" of humanity, and hence but imperfectly—"darkly." But when this vail is taken away, "then shall we know even as also we are known."

2. *It is objected, again, that the contemplation and glory of Christ will so entirely occupy us in the future state, that we will never think or desire to make search for friends or kindred.* That Christ will be the chief object of attraction in heaven, and the perpetual theme of adoring wonder and praise, we have not the shadow of a doubt. But that the soul is to be so absorbed, as to know nothing

else, to look at nothing else, and to feel the thrill of joy flowing from no other source, the Scriptures no where intimate. Their general tone and teaching, as well as all the analogies of the Divine government, and all the constitutional elements of the human character, indicate exactly the reverse. Christ is best loved and served on earth—not by perpetual inactive adoration, however tender and true—but by active sympathy and coöperation in all his works, and by active obedience to all his commands. The cup of cold water ministered to the least of Christ's children is as spontaneous an outflow of the true Christian heart as the loftiest hymn of praise; and infinitely more precious must it ever be in the eyes of the blessed Redeemer, than the most complacent admiration of his character and person. And will it be different in heaven? Christ and Christianity are the same whether in earth or in heaven. The person who here loves Christ so intently that he can neither know any other object, nor feel any other emotion, nor perform any other act, may be a very *sentimental*, but not a very *Scriptural* Christian. The love of Christians is at once the evidence and the manifestation of our love to Christ. "If we *love* ONE ANOTHER, God dwelleth in us, and HIS LOVE is perfected in us." (1 John iv, 12.) Nor is it a passive, inoperative love; but one that manifests itself in act as well as in word. Then, too, if we love Christ, we shall love his children for his sake, and because they bear his image. This heavenly abstraction, then, is rather a weakness of earth than a mirror of the heavenly glory. The saints in glory are represented, not as gazing upon God, but as *serving him day and night*. "Then also Christ is to be glorified *in* his saints, and to be admired *in* all them that believe." (2 Thess. i, 10.) That is, they are the representatives of Christ; show forth his wonderful work, and mirror his glory. Suppose we should enter the studio of some celebrated painter, and instead of looking upon and studying the wonderful creations of his art, hung all around upon the walls, should appear entirely inattentive to them, while we fixed our gaze upon the person of the artist. Such anomalous action might spring from great admiration of the artist and great love for his person; but it would savor more of a weak and sickly sentimentalism than of any just appreciation of his character and work. And to him, it could be only distasteful and offensive. We can hardly imagine such sentimentalism will find place in heaven. The character of Christ and his relations to his redeemed children forbid it. The very nature of a soul, invigorated, ennobled, and purified in the process of being saved and fitted for heaven, forbids it.

3. *It is objected, again, that the declaration of the Savior that "in the resurrection they neither marry nor are given in marriage," implies the abnegation of the relations peculiar to this life, and, consequently, personal recognition as the individuals to whom we once sustained such relations must cease.* The Sadducees, caviling at the doctrine of the resurrection, had suggested the case of a woman who had seven husbands, and inquired which of the seven should have her as his wife in the resurrection. Our Savior replies that "in the resurrection they neither marry nor are given in marriage, but are as the angels of God." (Matt. xxii, 30.) He here simply asserts that the *marriage relation* will not be continued in another life, not that we shall be unacquainted with each other. So far from asserting this, the very reverse is implied in the declaration that they *are as the angels of God;* for, certainly, it will not be denied that the angels of God are acquainted with each other.

But let us be understood. It is not the *remembrance* of this relation that is to be obliterated, but simply that the relation is not to be continued. As this relation constituted a part of our life in this world, so it must survive in the recollections of that life. Then, too, the moral and spiritual affections fostered and matured in and by this relation shall survive—nay, shall be quickened, exalted, and purified. So essential a part of our humanity, one connected with all that is great and good in our lives, can not be lost.

4. *Still another objection urged against the recognition of friends in the future life, is the pain that would be experienced from missing in the heavenly company some who had been tenderly allied to us on earth, and in whose salvation we had taken a deep interest.* It seems natural that the tender mother, who had long prayed and labored for the salvation of some loved though wayward boy, who at length died away from home and unknown, will feel the old agony experienced on earth coming back upon her soul with even tenfold force, when in heaven she discovers that the wayward son is not there. And the question often arises, Will not the pain of missing those who are lost more than offset all the pleasure that could arise from merely knowing one another in heaven? Having established so clearly the fact of recognition, we might safely leave this perplexing question with the assurance that God would solve it in some way consistent with the Divine administration and the good of his children. But the heart craves some immediate solution, and such solution we believe is practicable.

At the outset it will be well to observe that the denial of all recognition of friends in the future life will not relieve the case; for then we shall be in everlasting uncertainty about *all* our friends: the problem would not be fully solved, in our minds, about any of them. This uncertainty would mar the very bliss of heaven. Better *know* that the great proportion of them are really saved, even if it be accompanied with that other and dreaded knowledge—

the knowledge of the loss of some—than to be in an eteı nal uncertainty about all.

It was an ingenious suggestion of the late Archbishop Whately, that the saints in heaven would free themselves from all disquietude in relation to their lost friends, by *wholly withdrawing their minds from all thoughts of the matter.* He says: "As for the grief which a man may be supposed to feel for the loss—the total and final loss—of some who may have been dear to him on earth, I have only this to remark, that a wise and good man in this life, in cases when it is clear that no good can be done to him, strives, as far as possible, to withdraw his thoughts from evil which he can not lessen, but which still, in spite of his efforts, will often cloud his mind. We can not, at pleasure, draw off our thoughts entirely from painful subjects which it is in vain to think of. The power to do this completely, when we will, would be a great increase of happiness; and this power, therefore, it is reasonable to suppose, the blest will possess in the world to come, and will be able by an effort of the will, completely to banish and exclude every idea that might alloy their happiness." *

These suggestions have great force, and yet they do not fully cover the case. This power to *withdraw* the thoughts is only a temporary expedient, bringing temporary relief. It does not and can not strike the great evil—the source of our sorrow—from our knowledge. It is a momentary obliviousness to it, like when a man momentarily forgets his pain in sleep. On waking the pain is there, and the anguish is all the keener because of the momentary obliviousness. Then, again, this explanation assumes that the Prince and Lord of the redeemed has performed an act, which they, though in heaven and before the Throne, can not look upon without pain, and must, therefore, choose to

* View of the Scripture Revelations concerning the Future State.

forget it so as not to mar the felicity of heaven. This explanation fails us, is unsatisfactory. The question must be solved not upon exceptional incidents, but upon deep and broad principles imbedded in the Divine government.

It may be a step toward its solution to note the fact that even in this life a deep and broad gulf often opens between one pursuing a sinful and profligate career and the virtuous and holy, however nearly connected they may be in the relations of life. The very presence of the dissolute, depraved wretch becomes offensive and abhorrent, even when the heart has not yet ceased to sigh over his fall and ruin, and to pray for his deliverance. Indeed, while the very heart bleeds at the sight of his wretchedness, there is in the soul a sentiment of justice which approves of the judgment, and would not mitigate it except with the renovation of the character and habits of the criminal. The relation to them has been a source of affliction; their presence and society have become undesirable; nay, often intolerable, even in this life. It can hardly be supposed, then, that we should wish to renew it—knowing their characters to be still unchanged—amidst the pure and peaceful associations in heaven.

That the sufferings of the lost are distinctly known by the Savior and by the angels, is declared in terms unmistakable. For "the same shall drink of the wine of the wrath of God, which is poured out without mixture into the cup of his indignation; and he shall be tormented with fire and brimstone *in the presence of the holy angels and in the presence of the Lamb.*" (Rev. xiv, 10.) Who has loved these lost souls more deeply than the Savior? Who has suffered so much for their redemption, or waited so long that he might be gracious unto them? And yet, now that the harvest is past, the Summer ended, and the justice of God overtaken them, even their suffering can not mar the felicity of the Son of God. These angels, in whose presence they suffer and before whom the smoke of their torment ascendeth forever, once went forth as willing messengers to win them to Christ. And yet their own felicity is unclouded and will be forever. And, if the punishment of the wicked is not a matter of pain to the Savior, nor yet to the angels in his presence, have we not reason to believe it will be so also with those "redeemed from among men?"

Indeed, to go a step further, the punishment of the wicked is a source of praise and thanksgiving in heaven. Thus when "the third angel poured out his vial upon the rivers and fountains of waters, and they became blood," (Rev. xvi, 4,) then, says St. John, "I heard the angel of the waters say, Thou art righteous, O Lord, which art, and wast, and shalt be, because thou hast judged thus. For they have shed the blood of saints and prophets and thou hast given them blood to drink; for they are worthy. And I heard another out of the altar say, Even so, Lord God Almighty, true and righteous are thy judgments." (Rev. xvi, 5–7.) In the eighteenth chapter of Revelation we have a prophetic description of the utter and terrible destruction of the wicked, under the figure of Babylon, in which "was found the blood of prophets and of saints, and of all that were slain upon the earth," and whose "sins have reached unto heaven." The destruction is complete. "In one hour is she made desolate." And while all the earth, the "kings," and the "merchants," and "every ship-master," and all that had profited by her commerce or been partakers of her iniquities, stand afar off and bewail her destruction, the righteous are called upon to rejoice: "Rejoice over her, thou heaven, and ye holy prophets and apostles; for God hath avenged you upon her." (Rev. xviii, 20.) And then we have an unvailing of what took place in heaven over so great a destruction of wickedness, and such fearful and just judgments upon the ungodly. "And after these things I heard a great voice of much people in heaven, saying, Alleluia: Salvation, and glory, and honor, and power, unto the Lord our God: for true and righteous are his judgments: for he hath judged the great whore which did corrupt the earth with her fornications, and hath avenged the blood of his servants at her hands. And again they said, Alleluia. And her smoke rose up forever and ever." (Rev. xix, 1–3.) "Alleluia"—*praise Jehovah*—is a word of pious joy and exultation. The ground of that joy here is the vindication of the righteous judgments of God upon the wicked, and the glorious salvation of the righteous.

The exegesis of these passages brings us to the conclusion that the redeemed in heaven find deliverance from the pain occasioned by the knowledge of friends suffering the wrath of God in perdition—not, as Dr. Whately suggests, by choosing to *forget* them and their agony—but from causes more in harmony with the principles of the Divine government, and more honorable to the Divine ruler.

A sense of the justice of the doom of the wicked, however nearly the individual may be allied to us, will greatly mitigate our anguish at his suffering; so that we may join in the heavenly acclamation, "Great and marvelous are thy works, Lord God Almighty; just and true are thy ways, thou King of saints!" (Rev. xv, 3.) Then, again, there will be that perfect acquiescence in the will of God, that harmony with God, that union with God, which will exclude forever any possibility of feeling otherwise than in harmony with all the Divine purposes and acts. There is force of truth as well as depth of sympathy in those lines of Bishop Mant:

"Fear not the prospect of the realms of woe
Shall mar thy bliss, or thence sad thoughts arise

To blunt thy sense of heavenly ecstasies.
There, if thy heart with warm devotion glow
Meet for thy place, 't will solace thee to know
No friend of thine, 'mid those keen agonies,
In that dark prison-house of torment lies;
For none is there but is of God the foe,
An alien thus from thee. The ties of blood,
And earth's most sacred bonds, are but a twine
Of gossamer, compared with what is owed
To Him, the Lord of all! On Him recline;
He shall thy heart of every care unload,
He bid thy day with cloudless luster shine."

And, still again, those from whom we are eternally separated may in the end be actually forgotten. Unpleasant and repugnant even, as this thought may be, it has its basis in the laws of our being, and can not, therefore, be regarded as impossible, or even improbable. Mr. Harbaugh, in his excellent work on the Heavenly Recognition, says: "It is, moreover, not difficult to believe, that even without any miraculous interposition on the part of God, but just in the regular process of things, the remembrance of the lost may gradually fade from our memories. We see traces of this in this life. Those feelings of grief over the death of wicked friends, which were so pungent and almost intolerable at first, have gradually settled down into quiet resignation. Time flows on, and the wound is healed and forgotten. What even remains of this kind of sorrow in the heart, in this world of infirmity and imperfection, may entirely disappear in heaven, as the worm drops its groveling attachments as soon as he rises into the nobler capacity of a light-winged inhabitant of the upper air. . . . We will venture the remark that it is proved by experience that in this world the cords of affection which bind pious persons to impious relations, are gradually weakened till at length they have scarcely any power except what remains of instinctive feeling, and the mechanical power of habit. . . This process of inward alienation will be greatly accelerated by the disorganization which the rupture of death produces; and, as in heaven the saints will have more intolerance to sin than they can possibly have here, what remains at death of this instinctive and habitual affection, will be cast back to forgetfulness with a kind of abrupt and holy violence. Or, if even the remembrance of sinful friends should be, for a time, compatible with heavenly felicity, the unpleasantness—we have no better word—of such remembrance would gradually lead to entire forgetfulness." *

In accordance with these views, the same writer proceeds to say, and with his remark we will leave this point: "We find that in this world events which afford us no pleasure are not revolved in our minds, and thus by degrees fade from our recollection, while such as are pleasant fill their place and become prominent in our memories, though they may not have been so when they transpired. It is upon this principle, and by this process, that many of the sins of a Christian's past life are graciously made to fade back into dim forgetfulness, and finally into entire oblivion. Thus, the past life of the saints, so far as it is marked by any thing that is not meet to enter the heavenly world with them, is followed by the shades of dark annihilation, while before them in a hopeful and cloudless heaven the sweet stars arise as an eternal protest against the darkness of earth, and an ever-recurring promise of brighter and purer realms on high." †

5. *Still another objection is that which regards special personal affections as incompatible with heaven, but still must ever be inseparable from personal recognition.* That special or partial affections are likely to spring into being wherever individuals are gathered into society, is quite obvious. We need not deny that. But do these affections imply any thing wrong? Are they incompatible with the heavenly society?

* Pp. 263, 264. † P. 265.

We think not. And here is our answer to the objection We believe that special friendships for individual, pious friends will not only be carried forward into the coming life, but that new special friendships will be formed even in heaven.

These particular friendships on earth are at once the bond and the beauty of human society. Show me an individual whose love of humanity, in the general, is so great and so all-comprehending as not to admit of its descending to individual preferences or special friendships, and I will show you a man who is destitute of the first requisites of a true humanity.

Even our blessed Lord had his special friendships. Love for the whole race brought him from heaven to earth; yet this did not prevent special affection for and interest in his chosen disciples. And even among these, Peter, and James, and John seem to have had special preference. They witnessed the glory of his transfiguration upon the Mount, and were with him in his mortal agony in Gethsemane. Still, again, it occasioned no envy among them that John was called "the disciple whom Jesus loved." (John xx, 2.) Then, also, the special affection of the Savior for the family at Bethany is manifest; for it is said, by way of distinction or eminence, "Now, Jesus loved Martha, and her sister, and Lazarus." (John xi, 5.) Thus do we find, in the very life and character of our blessed Lord, demonstration that particular friendships are compatible with the purest sanctity and the sublimest benevolence.

The remarks of the late Archbishop Whately upon this point are so comprehensive and conclusive that we favor the reader with an extract. "It is supposed," he says, "that particular friendships will be swallowed up in universal charity, and that any partial regard toward one good man more than another is too narrow a feeling, and unworthy of a 'saint made perfect.' Do we, then, find any approach toward this supposed perfection in the best Christians on earth? Do we find that, in proportion as they improve in charity toward all mankind, they become less and less capable of friendship—less affectionate to their relations and connections, and to the intimate companions whom they have selected from among their Christian brethren? Far from it. It is generally observed, on the contrary, that the best Christians, and the fullest, both of brotherly love toward all who are of the household of faith, and of universal tenderness and benevolence toward all their fellow-creatures, are also the warmest and steadiest in their friendships. Why, then, should it be otherwise hereafter? Why should private friendship interfere with universal benevolence in heaven more than it does on earth?

"I am convinced, on the contrary, that the extension and perfection of friendship will constitute a great part of the happiness of the blessed. Many have lived, in various and distant countries, who have been in their character—I mean not merely in their being generally estimable, but in the agreement of their tastes and suitableness of dispositions—perfectly adapted for friendship with each other, but who, of course, could never meet in this world. Many a one selects, when he is reading history, a truly-pious Christian—more especially, in reading sacred history—some one or two favorite characters with whom he feels that a personal acquaintance would have been peculiarly delightful to him. Why should not such a desire be realized in a future state?

"In this world, again, our friendships are limited, not only to those who live in the same age and country, but to a small portion of even them—to a small portion even of those who are not unknown to us, and whom we know to be estimable and amiable, and who, we feel, might have been among our dearest friends. Our command of time and leisure to cultivate friendships imposes a limit to their extent—they are bounded, rather, by the occupation of our thoughts than of our affections; and the removal of such impediments in a better world seems to me a most desirable and a most probable change. I see no reason, again, why those who have been dearest friends on earth should not, when admitted to that happy state, continue to be so, with full knowledge and recollection of their former friendship." *

Thus do we find that special Christian friendships, instead of being the bane of heaven, shall prove one of the sources of its most exalted joy; and, instead of rendering us unfit for its sacred associations, shall be revived in the blessed world; new ones, also, shall be formed there, and they shall be cultivated and improved as the unending ages of eternity roll on.

V. The Influence of the Doctrine of Spiritual Recognition is Salutary and Precious.

We have now fairly passed through the question whether friends will meet again and know each other in heaven. From the various sources of reason and revelation we have shown how conclusive are the evidences of this future recognition. And we have also met the objector in his strong positions, and shown how little those positions can avail against the careful scrutiny of truth under the illumination of God's altar. But after we have thus canvassed the ground, we should still feel that our discussion was incomplete did we not pause to notice some of the practical and salutary effects this doctrine should produce.

1. *It suggests principles that should control us in forming*

* Scripture Revelations concerning a Future State.

the social relationships of life. Not only are we creatures of imitation, but we are so constituted as to be the subjects of unconscious influence from those with whom we associate. Hence, it is said, "Whoso walketh with wise men shall be wise; but a companion of fools shall be destroyed." (Prov. xiii, 20.) This insensible but all-powerful influence is one of the strong motives for the selection of virtuous companions in life, and for the avoidance of those who are wicked. "Blessed is the man that walketh not in the counsel of the ungodly, nor standeth in the way of sinners, nor sitteth in the seat of the scornful. . . . He shall be like the tree planted by the rivers of water, that bringeth forth his fruit in his season. . . . The ungodly are not so; but are like the chaff which the wind driveth away." (Psa. i, 1, 3, 4.)

But here is brought to view another motive for the selection of virtuous companions, that can not fail to appeal strongly to the heart. We naturally desire our friendships perpetuated. How, then, must we feel to have for our most intimate companions those from whom we are liable to be separated forever by death? If we desire the companionships of time to be renewed and perpetuated in eternity, we must select those for our companions in whose moral and religious character there is a foundation for this hope. If this applies to the ordinary friendships of life, how much more to that most intimate of all mere earthly associations—the marriage relation? For a pious person to be wedded to and to love one who is irreligious, and to bear about them the consciousness that death will work an eternal separation between them, it appears to us must prove a life-long agony. Hence, the nervous language of inspiration, "Be ye not unequally yoked together with unbelievers." (2 Cor. vi, 14.) We might refer to the self-deception employed in the delusive plea of becoming instruments of salvation to the objects of their regard; how it begins with a compromise of Christian principle, and ends usually in a sad disappointment in regard to that particular result. We might recur to the embarrassments of the household where religion and irreligion intermingle in often very unequal parts; and how often, instead of a profligate reclaimed, the result is a Christian backslidden, and perhaps lost. We might refer to the sad disappointments even in the worldly advantages expected; to the impossibility of the proper religious training of children—their nurture in the admonition of the Lord. We might also refer to the frequency, the many forms, and the solemnity of manner in which the Bible gives line upon line and precept upon precept in relation to the matter; but we come to the one point—*the ever-present, painful consciousness which the Christian must ever have, unless his Christian consciousness become blunted and seared—that this union must end in everlasting separation.* Before this one thought, reaching down to the very depths of the heart, the believer must ever feel that a life-long shadow falls upon his path and darkens all his way. We repeat, then, with all the emphasis superadded by our theme, "Be ye not," either in the social or the domestic relation, "unequally yoked with unbelievers."

2. *Such a doctrine and such a hope should elevate and ennoble our Christian friendships here.* Mere worldly affections are short-lived; they spring into being as the offspring of passing events or of temporary interests, and then pass away with the incidents that gave them birth. But Christian friendship rests upon a broader foundation; its principles are vital, spiritual, eternal—"charity never faileth"—it reaches forward into the future life. Said the heavenly-minded Baxter: "I must confess, as the experience of my own soul, that the expectation of loving my friends in heaven principally kindles my love to them on

earth. If I thought I should never know them, and consequently never love them, after this life is ended, I should, in reason, number them with temporal things, and love them as such, at the same time allowing for the excellent nature of grace; and I now delightfully converse with my pious friends in a firm persuasion that I shall converse with them forever; and I take comfort in those of them who are dead or absent, as believing I shall shortly meet them in heaven; and love them with a heavenly love, as the heirs of heaven, even with a love that shall there be perfected and forever exercised." The blessed hour of the saint's reunion shall erelong come.

"Blest hour, when righteous souls shall meet,
  Shall meet to part no more;
And with celestial welcome greet
  On an immortal shore!
Each tender tie, dissolved with pain,
  With endless bliss is crowned;
All that was dead revives again,
  All that was lost is found."

We can not forbear adding a paragraph from Mr. Harbaugh: "How elevating to our affections is the thought that friendships are eternal if pure; that the ties we form on earth, on virtuous and holy principles, will continue through death, and be made perfect and permanent in heaven! This makes the cultivation of friendship a high aim. Even the pursuit of knowledge, so far as it has merely this world in view, and is unsanctified by religion, is low compared with this; for 'charity never faileth; but whether there be prophecies, they shall fail; whether there be tongues, they shall cease; whether there be knowledge, it shall vanish away.' All our intercourse with our friends will be more holy and heavenly if we regard them as those who shall be ours in heaven as well as upon earth. "The addition of a good friend or relative will be the addition of one who will share with us the joys of im mortality, who will enter with us into the city of the living God, and be our everlasting companion in glory."

3. *A belief in this doctrine should induce tenderness, for bearance, and justice.* In this world we are all encompassed with infirmities, and liable to err in thought, in feeling, and in action. Sometimes our censoriousness rises above our charity; mistaken prejudice or enmity nips the buds of tenderness; and selfishness beclouds and overmasters our sense of justice. Slight causes, seen through distorted mediums, often alienate hearts most tenderly allied, and the "roots of bitterness" spring up where only the flowers of paradise ought to grow. Now, the thought that these friends, whom we can not unchristianize even in our alienation, are to be our companions in eternity; that there, with all the mists of earth and sense cleared away, we shall recall these events, and reëxamine our motives, our feelings, and our acts—can not but exert a salutary influence upon us here. We will want those friends, when they go away from us into the heavenly world, to carry with them feelings of confidence and affection; we will want them to possess that state of feeling toward us that would give us a rich welcome to the partnership of their immortal joys. The lesson from the unjust steward, as drawn by the Savior, was, "Make to yourselves friends of the mammon of unrighteousness; that, when ye fail, they may receive you into everlasting habitations." (Luke xvi, 9.) Are our friends emigrating to a new country, and are we expecting soon to follow and to become their life-long neighbors? What carefulness will we employ that we may secure a welcome greeting from them when we arrive? All causes of discord or of distrust will be removed; all differences will be adjusted; firm and friendly relations will be established. So should it be with those pilgrims and strangers

of earth who seek a better country—a heavenly—who are expecting to become denizens, fellow-citizens of that country, and to be affected and influenced by each other forever. What can be a stronger incentive to "be kindly-affectioned one to another with brotherly love, in honor preferring one another?" (Rom. xii, 10.) How strong the bond of attachment in time is this expectation of renewing and perpetuating our friendships in eternity! They who are looking forward to eternal companionship will never allow their hearts to be alienated by the jars of time, however harsh and rugged they may be. None but those in whose hearts are no roots of bitterness and no alienation of feeling can truly sing—

> "When shall we all meet again—
> Meet ne'er to sever?
> When shall Peace wreathe her chain
> Round us forever?"

4. *A belief in this doctrine must be a source of great comfort in the hour of bereavement.* A Moravian missionary, who had buried two of his little ones upon the Labrador coast, said: "I was once standing by the grave of my departed children, under a brilliant and cloudless sky, when suddenly a shadow passed over the green turf. Looking up for the cause, I beheld a snow-white gull winging her lofty flight through the air. The thought immediately struck me—thus it is with the dear objects of my mournful remembrance. Here lies the shadow, but above is the living principle. Nor was the reflection without comfort to my wounded spirit, since of such is the kingdom of heaven." The thought which proved a source of comfort to the poor Moravian missionary in his distant field of labor, comes laden with comfort to every bereaved heart.

The grave hides the dear objects of our affection from our sight, but we know that the separation is only for a time. They are "not lost, but gone before." And with David we can say, "I shall go to him, but he shall not return to me." (2 Sam. xii, 23.) We shall see them again; talk with them; enjoy their society; behold their unfold ing intellectual and spiritual beauty; and dwell with them forever. The separation will be brief; the reunion glorious. Fellowship is suspended but for a moment—nay, hardly suspended at all; but when, after a brief relapse, it is renewed, it shall be unbroken and even unclouded forever:

> "A few short years of evil past,
> We'll reach the happy shore,
> Where death-divided friends at last
> Shall meet to part no more."

This coupling of our bereavements with the day of our own departure, is happily presented by Mr. Harbaugh. He says: "The thought that many of our friends have gone before us, and that we shall shortly rejoin them in heaven, must be peculiarly animating and consoling to us, at that trying hour when we ourselves shall be called to die. Death will be but going away from friends on earth to join a greater number in heaven; and, in addition to this, we have also the assurance that even those we leave behind will soon follow us. Death, in that case, will be like going home. It will be but a short farewell to those we leave behind, and an eternal reunion with those who have gone before. Dying will be as when one taketh rest in sleep—and, O, what a blissful waking!

"The same reasons which induce us to believe in a final reunion with our sainted friends, encourage and warrant us also in the belief that they now remember us and feel interested in us. This idea, too, is full of consolation! It is sweet to be remembered by friends on earth, but how much more so to be assured that we live in the memory of those who are now saints in light! Being raised higher, their interest in us must increase in proportion as they become acquainted with those heavenly joys which await us also, and which they already possess. As they approach toward their perfection, their benevolence and love must increase; and, when we consider that we think most about our friends when we ourselves are most blessed, we can not but believe that they regard us with special concern. To have friends in heaven, then, is to have an inheritance in which we may well delight, and after which we are sweetly constrained to long. We, who are heirs of such celestial treasures, may enter fully into the spirit of the poet's holy boasting:

> 'My boast is not, that I deduce my birth
> From loins enthroned, and rulers of the earth;
> But higher far my proud pretensions rise—
> The son of parents passed into the skies,' "*

5. *The doctrine of reunion and recognition in heaven also presents strong motives to elevated piety.* After referring to the expectation of beholding Christ, and being with him and enjoying the heavenly society, St. John adds: "And every man that hath this hope in him purifieth himself, even as he is pure." (1 John iii, 3.) We make preparation to meet our friends in the social circles of life; we make preparation to go up with them to the house of God to mingle in the assembly of the saints. We would not appear in an unseemly garb, nor in an uncongenial state of mind. How much more should we seek fitness for the social circles of the heavenly state, and for the higher and nobler worship of the great assembly in heaven!

The pure only are there. And none but the pure in heart can relish their joys or become partakers of their bliss. Then, too, in this life we find social and intellectual gradations. One class rises above another. And each in-

*The Heavenly Recognition, p. 287.

dividual, by a sort of social affinity, eventually gravitates to his natural level. He may desire to rise higher, to enter into social circles of a more elevated type—of purer affection and of broader intellectual view; but he feels that he must have fitness. *He must rise himself.* So shall it be in heaven. There are gradations there. "One star differeth from another star in glory." (1 Cor. xv, 41.) Is it not, then, a noble aim to rise high in the social intimacies of heaven? The toil of years is cheerfully undergone to gain admission into the learned professions and to prepare one's self for professional life. Its associations and compensations repay the toil. Should not a higher ardor fire the heart of the Christian? For what noble associations and for what blessed occupations in the heavenly world may he not prepare! No place so near the throne but what he may reach it. No Wesley, or Whitefield, or Paul, or John, so radiant with heavenly brightness, but what the poorest pilgrim of earth, who has walked with God, may feel the glow of that heavenly brightness, and stand in the very midst of that heavenly halo, while he holds converse with the mighty men of faith and of action in the cause of Christ. This thought should inspire the faith and fire the heart of the believer. It should elevate his aims; it should be a perpetual stimulus to Christian growth. To such a one the goal will not be reached—"Till we all come in the unity of the faith, and of the knowledge of the Son of God, unto a perfect man, unto the measure of the stature of the fullness of Christ." (Eph. iv, 13.)

"O, what are all my suff'rings here,
If, Lord, thou count me meet,
With that enraptured host to appear,
And worship at thy feet!
Give joy or grief, give ease or pain,
Take life or friends away,
But let me find them all again
In that eternal day."

C. Wesley.

"Heaven," says Robert Hall, "is attracting to itself whatever is congenial to its nature, is enriching itself by the spoils of earth, and collecting within its capacious bosom whatever is pure, permanent, and divine; leaving nothing for the last fire to consume but the objects and slaves of concupiscence; while every thing which grace has prepared and beautified shall be gathered and selected from the ruins of the world, to adorn that eternal city, 'which hath no need of the sun, neither of the moon, to shine in it; for the glory of God doth enlighten it, and the Lamb is the light thereof.'" O, who would not desire to be brought within the sphere of that attractive influence, and thus move onward toward that "General Assembly and Church of the first-born, which are written in heaven?" Who would not desire to become one of that congregation that is "without fault before the throne of God?"

6. *This reunion and recognition opens the most glorious prospect of social communion in heaven.* "We but depart," said the Roman lyrist, "to meet our Æneas, and our Tully, and our Ancus." So may the Christian say, We but depart to form a reunion with our loved dead; we but go to behold the blessed Savior in all the glory of his resurrection state, and of his princely reign; we but go—the mother to clasp the lovely infant that passed away like the morning flower, to her arms once more; the father to greet the son whose life failed in the early dawn of a noble manhood; the child to bask once more in the sunshine of a mother's love, and to catch as of old the inspiration of her holy teaching. We go—the poet, to mingle in the society of those noble bards who have thrilled the ages with their song; the student, to converse with the philosophers and men of science of all ages; the child of faith and of love, to enjoy the communion of the confessors and martyrs who have endured persecutions and deaths; the minister of the

Cross, to catch higher inspiration as he gazes upon the noble form and listens to the heavenly words of a Huss, a Luther, a Melancthon, a Wesley, a Whitefield, an Edwards, a Payson, and a host of others—men of might and power, whose all on earth was consecrated to Christ, and whose glorying was in the cross.

Says a modern author, "Every shining witness, the bright rays of whose holy example have shone down to us through the living history of the Church since time began to be, will be our well-known companions there. Also the noble army of confessors and martyrs—those glorious men and women whose lives, for their deep and unquenchable love to Jesus and his truth, were worn-out in horrid dungeons, or devoured by wild beasts, or who, by racking, consuming tortures, rode in chariots of fire to heaven. Nor these alone: ministers of the Gospel of every age and country will be there—God's delegated servants who were admired while on earth and whose memories are still fragrant as Lebanon. What transport will it be to see these peers of the celestial world—to go in and out with the *elite* of heavenly society—to confederate with 'thrones, dominions, principalities, and powers'—those glorious beings 'who excel in strength,' and are 'ministering spirits, sent forth to minister for them who shall be heirs of salvation'—and to spend a blissful eternity in their fellowship, without shrinking from or being the least embarrassed in their presence! If the heart of Socrates, when near his death, bounded for very joy at the thought of meeting and communing with the spirits of Homer, and Orpheus, and others who had loved and maintained the cause of truth and virtue, how much more profound and rapturous should be our joy at the thought of meeting and communing with Adam and Abel, Enoch and Noah, Abraham and Moses, David and Isaiah, Paul and John, Polycarp and Cyprian, Luther and Calvin, Wesley and Whitefield, Watts and Cowper—in a word, with all those who shine as a galaxy of brighter stars in the firmament of glory! O, what a spectacle will the one Church of Jesus then exhibit to the intelligent universe!—one congregation, gathered in one temple—the temple of the Divine Presence, with one service, one psalmody, one Sabbath—and that eternal! Then will the ancient prophecy be fulfilled: 'There shall be one fold, and one Shepherd.' The sects who have divided its fellowship, and the schisms which have rent its bosom; the din of controversy which, alas! has mingled with, and often drowned, its sweet messages of salvation, and the petty jealousies which have kindled 'strange fire' on its altars of love, will never cause separation and sorrow more. Paul and Barnabas, Luther and Zwingle, Toplady and Wesley, will contend for no difference of theological or ecclesiastical opinion. All will be 'made perfect' in knowledge and love, and therefore 'see eye to eye.' A childlike simplicity, a harmony of sentiment, a community of interest in Christ Jesus, will constitute the mighty millions of glory *one* in spirit, and *one* in endeavor. And from the friendship of 'the whole family in heaven,' thus knit in perfect sympathy and love, will spring a pleasure and a joy which the harps of glory will scarce have chords to express." *

*Our Heavenly Home, p. 200.

XIV.

DURATION OF MEMORY AND ITS RELATION TO THE FUTURE LIFE.

"Every one of us shall give account of himself to God." ROM. xiv, 12.

"Every idle word which men shall speak, they shall give account thereof in the day of judgment." MATT. xii, 36.

"And the dead were judged out of those things which were written in the books, according to their works." REV. xx, 12.

THERE are few faculties of the intellect of more practical importance in the intercourse and conduct of life, or more essential to the actual education of the soul, than the power of recollection, or memory. It is the mysterious and hidden link that connects the present with the past. Sunder that link, and our past existence, as well as the vast eternity that stretches away in immeasurable extent behind us, would be to us as if it had never been. The bright, the sunny days and scenes of childhood and youth would have perished under an impenetrable cloud of forgetfulness. Those acts of friendship, of generosity, of high and devoted philanthropy, that do honor to human nature—acts that cast their warm and genial influences over the soul and kindle its nobler sensibilities, too often frozen and paralyzed by the cold selfishness of the world, would fall from the bright firmament of intellect and quench their light in the darkness of oblivion. The light of experience would cease to throw its radiance upon the pathway of life; and all that is honorable and dignified in human nature, all that is lovely in morals, pure and elevated in virtue, and all in human experience that can touch the chords of sympathy and fill the heart with aspirations after that which is great and good, would be blotted from that cluster of virtuous incentives which now burn, like so many lamps, all along the pathway of human experience.

In ancient mythology the dead are represented as inhabiting a sort of *nether-world*, the dark and boundless dominion of Pluto. Through those vast, infernal regions rolled five rivers—the Styx, or *Dread*, whose waters were piercing cold; Acheron, or *Grief*, the stream over which the dead were ferried; Cocytus, or *Lamentation;* Phlegethon, or *Flaming*, whose waves rolled in perpetual billows of flame; and Lethe, or *Oblivion*, which flowed sluggishly through the fragrant and beautiful valleys of Elysium. Of the waters of this last river those only were permitted to drink who were about to return to earthly bodies; and by that draught all memory of the past was forever washed away. These creations of mythology were only conceptions borrowed from the soul-experiences of this life: the waters of Dread, of Grief, of Lamentation, all are tasted here. So, also, the burning pangs of remorse remind us of the horrible Phlegethon, so frightful for its billows of flame; while the treacherous memory seems evermore to be hovering along the banks of the dread river of Oblivion, now sprinkled with its spray, and now plunged beneath its flood. In the ordinary experience of life no one can have failed to observe that as length of time intervenes, our recollection of an object or event becomes less distinct. Most of the events of the past day, though many of them may be of trifling importance, are remembered with but little effort. The memory grasps them, even in their minutiæ, with a distinctness and perspicuity characteristic of its nature. We remember where we have been, the individuals we have met, what we have said, and what we have done;

but in the lapse of a few days nearly all these things will be forgotten. The entire day, so far as our recollection of any incident or event that transpired in it is concerned, will have become a blank in our past being. The petty annoyances we experience, the little vexations and trials of daily life—nay, our very sufferings and sorrows, however distinctly they now stand out in our painful recollection, will, after the lapse of a few weeks or months, become indistinct in the memory, and, at length, be forgotten. Increase the lapse of time to years, and the dark cloud of oblivion will so completely cover them that no effort at recollection will be able to recall them. I appeal to the experience of every individual—how few of the events of his past history he is able to call up by an effort of memory. Fragments of sculptured stone and disjointed ruins, scattered in the midst of solitude and desolation, now mark the places where the great cities of the world once stood, and are the only monuments that remain of their former opulence and power; so, amid the shadowy past, only here and there a solitary and disjointed monument remains of all we thought, or did, or experienced. Such is the experience of man; the Lethean stream flows around and behind him, and the past is buried beneath its dark and turbid waters.

A modern writer has not inaptly compared the lighter events of life to the traces drawn by the truant schoolboy upon the bank of sand, and which are soon filled up by the drifting element and disappear; events of higher moment, and which have made a deep impression upon the soul, to letters engraved on monumental marble, which for a long time resist the corrosive action of the elements; but, at length, they, too, become obscure and illegible.

As the mariner holds on his course out into the boundless ocean, the forms of objects upon the shore which he is leaving behind him become indistinct and confused. His straining eyes can no longer descry the rude cottage by the beach, where dwell the buds of affection and the flowers of promise—all have become a dim and shadowy mass. The lofty mountain, the towering Alp, may still present its broad outline and seem to mock the tardy progress of the laboring bark, and to defy the effect of distance; but that, too, shall disappear. Even while the mariner strains his vision to catch the last view of his native hills, their dim and fading outlines become enveloped in the misty haze, so that what is mountain and what is shadow can no longer be ascertained. But shall not that mariner, when the voyage is completed, return and gaze upon that scene once more? The same bald mountain shall again be seen lifting up its broad shoulders to the sky, and the same objects of interest scattered all along the shore shall break once more upon his sight, and cause his heart to thrill with sorrow or with joy.

Shall it not also be thus with the voyager upon the sea of life? Shall not memory come back to survey, not merely the headlands of the voyage, but the very indentations all along the shore?

We read of a process by which the old manuscripts that had been entombed in cloistered cells for ages, and had become charred and defaced by the lapse of time and the action of the elements, are unrolled and their letters made to appear. Thus, treasures of thought, which seemed to be irrecoverably lost, are brought up, as it were, from the grave in which they had been buried for ages, and enter anew into the currents of human thought and experience. So with the thoughts and experiences of the past life, which appear to have faded away from memory. May it not be that, by the hidden and mysterious sources of intellectual power within us, they are still retained, each in its own distinct moral and intellectual characteristic; so that even after the lapse of years or ages, the soul, touched in its hidden springs of action, or vitalized anew and intensified in its power and capacity, shall call forth, with all the freshness of present reality, all the thoughts, and acts, and experiences of the past life, and hold them up in array before us? The book of memory is a book of many pages, but each one of them is stereotyped in the foundery of eternity. "The everlasting future grows upon the past; remembrance is the basis of eternal knowledge. Memory has its office in the present life, but it also runs forward into the future. It seems intended to treasure impressions, and thoughts, and feelings in all worlds, and to carry forward the recollection of them into the illimitable future."

Lord Bacon makes the supposition that no thoughts are absolutely lost from the human mind; and Mr. Coleridge suggests, from the known facts of human pathology, that all thoughts are in themselves imperishable. "In the very nature," says he, "of a living spirit, it may be more possible that heaven and earth should pass away, than that a single thought should be loosened or lost from that living" storehouse of human knowledge—the memory. The position assumed is that *nothing is absolutely lost from the memory; the ideas that seem to be forgotten are virtually retained, and it requires only a new order of things in our physical economy, or a quickening of our mental action, to bring them back to our recollection.*

I. The Imperishability of Memory is Inferable from the Tenacity, Grasp, and Particularity often Exhibited by it in this Life.

Memory, like all other mental faculties, varies in different individuals. We need not speculate about the causes of this diversity. While with some it is weak, with others it is possessed of rare and wonderful power—indicating what the mind is capable of under circumstances favorable to the development of its power.

We can not place this point more distinctly before our readers, than by instancing some of the surprising feats of memory that have come to us well authenticated. An instance of remarkable power of memory in an Indian orator, is given in Smith's History of the Colony of New York. In 1689 commissioners from Boston, Plymouth, and Connecticut had a conference with the Five Indian Nations, at Albany; when a Mohawk sachem, in a speech of great length, answered the message of the commissioners, and repeated all that had been said the preceding day. The art they had for assisting their memories was this: The sachem who presided had a bundle of sticks prepared for the purpose, and at the close of each principal article of the message delivered to them he gave a stick to another sachem, charging him with the remembrance of that particular article. By this means the orator, after a previous conference with the sachems who severally had the sticks, was prepared to repeat every part of the message, and to give to it its proper reply. This custom, as the historian remarks, was invariably pursued in all their public treaties.

Seneca says of himself, "I do not deny that I myself possessed powers of memory in a very considerable degree. It was not only sufficient for the ordinary business of life, but appeared to some to be almost miraculous. When single verses were prescribed to each individual who came to attend our preceptor, on hearing them prescribed, I recited them in order, beginning with the last and ending with the first." Pliny mentions similar instances. Cyrus knew the names of all the soldiers in his army. Lucius Scipio knew the names of the Roman people. Mithridates, who ruled over twenty-two kingdoms, delivered laws to them in as many languages, and publicly addressed the natives of each kingdom in their own tongue, without an interpreter. Charmidas, or rather Carneades, could name all the books in a great library as they stood in order. Bonaparte is said to have had, in many respects, a wonderfully-retentive memory.

It is related of Moderata Fonte, an Italian lady and an authoress of note, that she could repeat, *verbatim*, a sermon or discourse which she had heard but once. The same is related of Thomas Fuller, author of the "Worthies of England." Sir Walter Scott possessed a remarkable memory. Hogg, the Ettrick Shepherd, records a striking evidence of this. On a fishing excursion in the Tweed, the party sat down upon the bank. "Scott," says the Ettrick Shepherd, "desired me to sing them my ballad of Gilman's Cleuch. Now, be it remembered that this ballad had never been printed; I had merely composed it by rote, and, on finishing it three years before, had sung it once over to Sir Walter. I began it, at his request, but at the eighth or ninth stanza I stuck in it, and could not get on with another verse; on which he began it again, and recited it every word from beginning to end. It being a very long ballad, consisting of eighty-eight stanzas, I testified my astonishment, knowing that he had never heard it but once, and even then did not appear to be paying particular attention." Sydney Smith had an extraordinary memory, always ready. He could repeat pages of poetry, English, Latin, and French—when, where, or how he learned them no one of his family pretended to know; but they were always ready and appropriate in company, when conversation turned that way. The memory of Grotius was so retentive that he remembered almost every thing he read.

Professor Porson possessed a prodigious memory. When a boy at Eton school, he discovered the most astonishing powers of memory. In going up to a lesson one day, he was accosted by a boy in the same form—"Porson, what have you got there?" "Horace." "Let me look at it." Porson handed the book to the boy, who, pretending to return it, dextrously substituted another in its place, with which Porson proceeded. Being called on by the master, he read and construed Carm., 1, x, very regularly. Observing the class to laugh, the master said, "Porson, you seem to me to be reading on one side of the page, while I am looking at the other; pray whose edition have you?" Porson hesitated. "Let me see it," rejoined the master; who, to his great surprise, found it to be an English Ovid. Porson was ordered to go on; which he did easily, correctly, and promptly, to the end of the ode. It is said that Dr. Leyden had so strong a memory that he could repeat correctly a long Act of Parliament, or any similar document, after a single perusal. Woodfall's extraordinary power of reporting the debates in the House of Commons without the aid of written memoranda, is well known. During a debate he used to close his eyes and lean with both hands upon his stick, resolutely excluding all extraneous associations. The accuracy and precision of his reports brought his newspaper into great repute. He would retain a full recollection of a particular debate a fortnight after it had occurred, and during the intervention of other debates. He used to say that it was put by in a corner of his mind for future reference. It seems sometimes more easy to exert the memory than to suppress it. "We may remember," says Fulton, "what we are intent upon; but with all the art we can use, we can not, knowingly, forget what we would. Nor is there an Etna in the soul of man but what the memory makes."

These are only examples drawn from a vast number on record. They reveal the surprising power of memory—how tenacious its grasp, how definite its particularity, and how wide its range! And is it not an intimation of still higher power, and still grander comprehension, when it shall act free from the incumbrances and obstructions with which it is hedged around in this life?

II. The next Argument we shall employ for the Confirmation of this truth is drawn from the simple Fact that Memory, in its ordinary Action, or when stimulated by extraordinary Circumstances, often calls back to Mind Things which seemed entirely forgotten.

How often does the mind, startled by some sudden excitement, leap over the intervening space of years and call up the buried memories of incidents and friends! The sight of a face resembling that of some early companion will often call up the recollection of him in a manner surprising to ourselves—perhaps, when we may not have thought of him for years. The bare mention of a name, the melody of some old familiar tune, the sight of a cottage, landscape, or water-fall, the peals of a church bell, will often come to the soul laden with the precious memories of the past. They awake the memory from its slumber, and the vivid picture of former scenes flashes upon the vision. "At such a moment, who has not been astonished at the recollections called forth—the resurrection of withered hopes, of perished joys and sorrows, of scenes and companionships that seemed to be utterly forgotten and lost!"

"Lulled in the countless chambers of the brain,
Our thoughts are linked by many a hidden chain,
Awake but one, and lo, what myriads rise!
Each stamps its image as the other flies."

The most touching instances of memory quickened by objects of sight are scattered all along the pages of history. Need I mention the case of little Montague? He was decoyed away by a chimney-sweep in Paris. His gay clothes were exchanged for a garb that completely disguised the features of the child, and his visage was begrimed, and his active limbs trained to his sooty work. If any recollections of home remained, they were dim and misty. But after a while, the child was employed in cleaning the chimney of a mansion; and descending into a chamber, he uttered an exclamation of joy, and, rushing forward, cast his wearied limbs, in his sooty clothes, upon a cot. That room proved to be the nursery of the little child; and it had been left by his grieving parents just as it was when its walls reëchoed to the joyous sports of their only son. The sight of it kindled the vivid recollections of infantile hours, and restored him to parents who had already begun to despair of his recovery. Thus, in very infancy, does the memory begin to treasure up impressions, which may be carried forward through all the periods of the soul's existence.

Mrs. Hemans, in one of her poems, describes a palm-tree, which had originally been transplanted from India, but was now towering up magnificently in the midst of trees of European growth. A lonely youth, who had been brought from India, and who, amid new scenes and amusements, had seemed to lose the recollections of home and kindred, wanders through the grove. Suddenly he comes upon that tree of his native isle. Quick as lightning the recollections of home and kindred rush back upon his soul.

"To him, to him, its rustling spoke;
The silence of the soul it broke!
It whispered of his own bright isle,
That lit the ocean with a smile;
Ay, to his ear that native tone
Had something of the sea-wave's moan!

His mother's cabin-home that lay
Where feathery cocoas fringed the bay;
The dashing of his brethren's oar;
The conch-note heard along the shore—
All through his wakening bosom swept;
He clasped his country's tree, and wept.'

Equally potent are sounds addressed to the ear to stir up the memories of the soul. The following is an illustration of touching beauty: "In the Cathedral of Limerick there hung a peal of bells which, it was said, were brought from a convent in Italy, for which it had been manufactured by an enthusiastic Italian, with great labor and skill. The artist, having afterward acquired a competency, fixed his home near the convent cliff, and for many years enjoyed the daily chime of his beloved bells. In some political convulsion that ensued, the monks were driven from their monastery, the Italian from his home, and the bells were carried away to another land. After a long interval, the course of his wanderings brought him to Ireland. On a calm and beautiful evening, as the vessel which bore him floated along the broad stream of the Shannon, he suddenly heard a peal from the Cathedral tower. They were the bells—the long-lost treasures of his memory, of home, happiness, and friends—all of his early recollections were in their sound. Crossing his arms upon his breast, he laid himself back in the boat, and gazed and listened. When the rowers looked around, they saw his face still turned toward the Cathedral, but his eyes had closed forever on the world. Such a tide of memories had swept over the sympathetic chords of his heart, that they had snapped under the vibration."

Dr. Moore, in his admirable treatise on the "Power of the Soul over the Body," relates that "a gentleman engaged in a banking establishment made an error in his accounts, and, through an interval of several months, spent days and nights in vain endeavors to discover the source of the error. At length, worn out by fatigue, he went to bed, and in a dream called to mind all the circumstances that gave rise to the error. He remembered that on a certain day several persons were waiting in the bank, when one individual, who was a most annoying stammerer, became so excessively impatient and noisy that, to get rid of him, his money was paid before his turn, and the entry of the sum neglected." The man awoke from his sleep, and the next day verified the fact as the memory had so mysteriously called it up. In this latter case, the memory borrowed no aids, either from sight or sound; it seems to have been a pure effort of the soul, escaping away from the benumbing influence of sleep, and deciphering inscriptions upon her tablet, which the strongest light of day had failed to reveal to the outward eye.

These facts clearly prove that ideas may, for a long time, and through a great variety of circumstances, remain in a latent or imperceptible state in the mind, and yet not be stricken from the tablet of memory. Thus, they afford the ground-work for the presumption that *no idea*—however minute or trifling—is absolutely obliterated from the memory; that *no idea* can escape away from it so far, but what it may be called back and made, even after the lapse of years—it may be, of ages—to stand forth with the same distinctness as if it were an event of the present moment.

III. Another Class of Facts here Challenges our Attention—in the Peculiar Phenomena exhibited in the Memory of Old People.

In old age memory becomes weak and wavering; it fails in the distinctness of its perception and the tenacity of its grasp. The current events of life are forgotten by them almost as soon as past. The period of middle life has also become a blank in their recollections. They forget even their own children, their own business in former years, and not unfrequently their own names. But away back, over the long interval that separates between youth and extreme old age, there is a land still radiant with sunshine and fragrant with flowers. The very incidents of childhood now come thronging upon the memory with all the distinctness and freshness of present life.

But it should be borne in mind that in middle life, when the man was immersed in business and loaded with cares, when his bosom was swayed by the desire of power, and the love of praise fastened upon his heart—these events, now so distinctly remembered in old age, had been forgotten and seemingly lost from the recollection. Fasten your thoughts upon this one fact, that, though the scenes of childhood and youth are forgotten in middle life, yet they live again in the recollections of old age. They slumbered in the memory, perchance for half a century; but they perished not.

A beautiful illustration of this occurred in the life of Niebuhr, the celebrated Danish traveler. When he had become old, blind, and his mind almost oblivious to things occurring around him, "he used to describe to his friends the scenes which he had visited in his early days, with wonderful minuteness and vivacity. When they expressed their astonishment, he told them that every thing else seemed to be shut out of his mind, and the pictures he had seen in the East floated before his mind's eye, so that it seemed as though he had seen them but yesterday."

Oliver Goldsmith's picture of the old soldier, who

> "Sat by the fire, and talked the night away,
> Wept o'er his wounds, or, tales of sorrow done,
> Shoulder'd his crutch, and showed how fields were won,"

reminds one of Revolutionary tales, listened to with thrilling interest in his youth, as they were told by scarred veterans, baptized by suffering and blood to the cause of freedom in times that tried the souls of men. How many hours have I listened to just such a veteran in the time of childhood! His head was crowned with the glory of nearly eighty years well spent. Yet the thrilling adventures of early life in new and wild settlements, and the incidents of our Revolutionary struggle, through the whole of which he had passed, were told with a historical exactness equaled only by the vividness of the description. And yet, the memory of present things had become so entirely paralyzed, that he had forgotten his own son with whom he lived. His memory seemed like the ruffled water which sinks to repose, and leaves no trace of the impression made upon it.

Let me also instance the case of an old lady who had passed beyond her fourscore years and ten. Her eye had become sightless, and her mind, cut off from all sympathy with the living, was left to its own communings. Her power of present recollection seemed almost extinct. Her children's children, like ministering angels, hovered around her; but she knew them not. The use of the cup from which she drank, and the knife and fork with which she eat at a former meal she would lose the recollection of before the next. . . . But the intellect, whose expiring embers emitted no light, still had a flame—a flame that burned deep in the mind's recollections. The mind that was cut off from the world of present reality still possessed a world—a world for the exercise of its thought—a world for the flow of its affections. The companions of her youth, though the rude blasts of scores of Winters had swept over their moldering dust, were the only companions of her soul; the circles of youth were the only circles in which her imagination moved; and names that had long been engraved on monumental marble were the only names that dwelt upon her tongue. The young friend that called to see her would be greeted with expressions of joy; and yet, how affecting to find herself mistaken for one who, perhaps, had been the tenant of the tomb for half a century!

These are lessons of human frailty; but they teach us something more: they are pregnant with great and momentous truths. As the breaking of the casket reveals the diamond within, so the crumbling and wasting of our clayey tabernacle reveal the resources of intellectual power within us. They tell us that our ideas, though forgotten, are not lost—that they still live; and the memory, by virtue of its own mysterious power, can call them forth. Now, if ideas may thus slumber in the mind for half a century, and then be restored, why not still longer? Why may they not slumber even till the judgment day, and then be called forth by the inherent powers of the soul, and arrayed in the broad field of its contemplation?

IV. A Fourth Class of Mental Phenomena Bearing upon the Subject is found in the Surprisingly-Quickened Action of the Memory in the Case of Drowning Persons.

In many instances of this kind the memory seems to have been so astonishingly quickened, that the whole past life—even its long-forgotten incidents—rushed back upon the soul, so as to appear in clear and distinct view upon the broad field of its vision.

An individual of my personal acquaintance was nearly drowned some years since. He stated that when first precipitated into the foaming deep, he fully realized the hopelessness of his condition; but almost at the very moment the recollection of former events and of former years came rushing upon the memory. Its action was intense and rapid. Every thing was remembered with all the distinctness of present life. Incidents, events, acts, words—all started up in rapid succession, till his whole past life seemed to be reflected as from a mirror. His memory seemed to have grasped every event from very childhood to middle life, and hung them up, as though painted on canvas, before the broad glance of the drowning man. Almost by a miracle he was plucked from the very jaws of death; but ever after was he accustomed to dwell with astonishment and wonder upon the singular developments of his memory while the floods compassed him about, and to declare that he believed it possible for the mind to recollect every thing that had ever come within the range of thought and feeling.

Admiral Beaufort, of the British Navy, gives a like account of the action of his mind when placed in circumstances precisely similar. After a momentary sense of suffocation his mind subsided into a state of most perfect tranquillity, so far as any sensation was concerned; but its powers of recollection were invigorated with an activity and an intensity which defied all description. Thought after thought came back upon the memory with a rapidity of succession which was not only indescribable, but probably inconceivable to any one who has never been placed in similar circumstances. "Every incident of my life," said he, "seemed to glance across my recollection—not in mere outline, but the whole picture filled up with every minute and collateral feature. The whole period of my existence seemed to be placed before me in a kind of panoramic review, and each act of it seemed to be accompanied by a consciousness of right and wrong."*

* This whole account is so striking that we give it entire. It is taken from the Life of Sir John Barrow, published in London, and is contained in a letter from Admiral Beaufort, addressed to Dr. Wollaston. It is as follows:

"Many years ago, when I was a youngster on board one of his Majesty's ships in Portsmouth harbor, after sculling about in a very small boat, I was endeavoring

We cite still another incident to the same point. A gentleman residing near James River, in Virginia, while bathing in that river one day, was discovered to be drowning. He had already sunk to the bottom several times and

to fasten her along side the ship to one of the scuttle-rings; in foolish eagerness I stepped upon the gunwale, the boat of course upset, and I fell into the water; and not knowing how to swim, all my efforts to lay hold either of the boat or of the floating sculls were fruitless. The transaction had not been observed by the sentinel on the gangway, and therefore it was not till the tide had drifted me some distance astern of the ship that a man in the foretop saw me splashing in the water, and gave the alarm. The first lieutenant instantly and gallantly jumped overboard, the carpenter followed his example, and the gunner hastened into a boat and pulled after them.

"So far these facts were either partially remembered after my recovery, or supplied by those who had latterly witnessed the scene; for during an interval of such agitation a drowning person is too much occupied in catching at every passing straw, or too much absorbed by alternate hope and despair, to mark the succession of events very accurately. Not so, however, with the facts which immediately ensued; my mind had then undergone the sudden revolution which appeared to you so remarkable, and all the circumstances of which are now as vividly fresh in my memory as if they had occurred but yesterday.

"With the violent but vain attempts to make myself heard I had swallowed much water; I was soon exhausted by my struggles, and before my relief reached me I had sunk below the surface; all hope had fled, all exertion ceased, and I felt that I was drowning.

"From the moment that all exertion had ceased—which I imagine was the immediate consequence of complete suffocation—a calm feeling of the most perfect tranquillity superseded the previous tumultuous sensations—it might be called apathy, certainly not resignation; for drowning no longer appeared to be an evil, I no longer thought of being rescued, nor was I in any bodily pain. On the contrary, my sensations were now of rather a pleasurable cast, partaking of that dull but contented sort of feeling which precedes the sleep produced by fatigue. Though the senses were thus deadened, not so the mind; its activity seemed to be invigorated in a ratio which defies all description—for thought rose after thought with a rapidity of succession that is not only indescribable, but probably inconceivable, by any one who has not himself been in a similar situation. The course of those thoughts I can even now in a great measure retrace—the event which had just taken place; the awkwardness that had produced it; the bustle it must have occasioned—for I had observed two persons jump from the chains—the effect it would have on a most affectionate father; the manner in which he would disclose it to the rest of the family, and a thousand other circumstances minutely associated with home, were the first series of reflections that occurred.

"They took then a wider range—our last cruise—a former voyage, and shipwreck—my school—the progress I had made there, and the time I had misspent—and even all my boyish pursuits and adventures. Thus traveling backward, every past incident of my life seemed to glance across my recollection in retrograde succession; not, however, in mere outline, as here stated, but the picture filled up with every minute and collateral feature; in short, the whole period of my exist-

was floating away under the water, when his companions succeeded in rescuing him. With great difficulty he was restored to consciousness, and afterward remained in a state of complete exhaustion for several days. Prior to this event he had had a serious difficulty with a neighbor. He

ence seemed to be placed before me in a kind of panoramic review, and each act of it seemed to be accompanied by a consciousness of right or wrong, or by some reflection on its cause or its consequences; indeed, many trifling events which had been long forgotten then crowded into my imagination, and with the character of recent familiarity.

"May not this be some indication of the almost infinite power of memory with which we may awaken in another world, and thus be compelled to contemplate our past lives? Or might it not in some degree warrant the inference that death is only a change or modification of our existence, in which there is no real pause or interruption? But, however that may be, one circumstance was highly remarkable—that the innumerable ideas which flashed into my mind were all retrospective; yet I had been religiously brought up; my hopes and fears of the next world had lost nothing of their early strength, and at any other period intense interest and awful anxiety would have been excited by the probability that I was floating on the threshold of eternity; yet at that inexplicable moment, when I had a full conviction that I had already crossed that threshold, not a single thought wandered into the future—I was wrapped entirely in the past.

"The length of time that was occupied by this deluge of ideas, or rather the shortness of time into which they were condensed, I can not now state with precision; yet certainly two minutes could not have elapsed from the moment of suffocation to that of my being hauled up.

"The strength of the flood-tide made it expedient to pull the boat at once to another ship, where I underwent the usual vulgar process of emptying the water by letting my head hang downward, then bleeding, chafing, and even administering gin; but my submersion had been really so brief, that, according to the account of the lookers-on, I was very quickly restored to animation.

"My feelings while life was returning were the reverse, in every point, of those which have been described above. One single but confused idea—a miserable belief that I was drowning—dwelt upon my mind, instead of the multitude of clear and definite ideas which had recently rushed through it—a helpless anxiety, a kind of continuous nightmare seemed to prevent any one distinct thought, and it was with difficulty that I became convinced that I was really alive. Again, instead of being absolutely free from all bodily pain, as in my drowning state, I was now tortured by pain all over me; and though I have been since wounded in several places, and have often submitted to severe surgical discipline, yet my sufferings were at that time far greater, at least in general distress. On one occasion I was shot in the lungs, and after lying on the deck at night for some hours bleeding from other wounds, I at length fainted. Now, as I felt sure that the wound in the lungs was mortal, it will appear obvious that the overwhelming sensation which accompanies fainting must have produced a perfect conviction that I was then in the act of dying; yet nothing in the least resembling the operation of my mind when drowning then took place; and when I began to recover, I returned to a clear conception of my real state."

had settled a claim against that neighbor and taken his note for several hundred dollars, having some time to run. At its maturity he found he had put the note away so carefully that he was unable to find it. Every search was fruitless. He knew that the note had not been taken up, and also that it had not been traded away. In this dilemma he called upon the maker of the note, and stated the facts. To his surprise the man utterly denied the debt, or that he had ever given such a note. Under these circumstances there was no redress, as there were no witnesses of the transaction, and several years had now transpired up to the period when the gentleman came so near drowning. The first thing he did, when he was able to leave his bed, was to go to the bookcase and take down a book. From that book he took the long-lost note and handed it to a friend who was present. He then stated that when sinking down in the water to rise, as he supposed, no more, there stood out before his mind, as in a picture, every act of his life, from the hour of childhood to that moment, and among these acts was that of putting the note in question into the identical book where it was found, and of soon after placing the book in the case.*

These are not only curious, but they are highly-suggestive facts. They are the faint indications of an appalling power, hidden in the soul of man. They strangely suggest the almost infinite power of memory with which we shall awaken in another life. They give no faint indication that in that future world memory shall run back over the history of our past probationary being and call up all its events, however much we may desire to bury the past in utter oblivion. If such be the developments of the memory, when the mind is acted upon by extraordinary circum stances, what may we not expect when this *terrestrial* body

*Cist's Advertiser.

shall be exchanged, and the soul be clothed upon with its celestial body? The mind, no longer cramped and straitened by its clogs of materiality, shall display the full grandeur of its mysterious and eternal power. The keen vision of its eye, undimmed by distance, unobscured by mist or cloud, shall sweep along the entire range of our past being.

V. A fifth Class of Facts illustrating the Extraordinary Powers of Recollection possessed by the Human Mind, may be found in the Mental Phenomena Resulting from Injury to the Brain.

In such instances the action of the memory has been of a most remarkable character. Sir Astley Cooper relates the case of a sailor, who was received into St. Thomas's Hospital in a state of stupor from an injury upon the head. By a surgical operation he was suddenly restored to consciousness, and was able to talk, but no one could understand him. Soon after, a Welsh nurse entering the ward at once comprehended his language, for he spoke Welsh, which was his native tongue. On inquiry, however, it was found that he had been thirty years absent from Wales, and previous to the accident had so entirely forgotten the language that he could not speak a single word in it. Now, he conversed fluently in Welsh, but could not remember a word of any other tongue. What is still further remarkable, upon the perfect recovery of his health he lost again his Welsh, so as to be utterly unable to speak it, and spoke only the English. . . . Dr. Abernethy mentions a similar instance of a Frenchman, who had for many years entirely lost the knowledge of his native tongue, but while under medical treatment for an injury upon the head, he spoke only the French.

Dr. Pritchard mentions a man who had been employed with a beetle and wedges splitting wood. "At night he put those implements in the hollow of an old tree, and directed his sons to accompany him next morning in making the fence. In the night, however, he became insane. After several years his reason suddenly returned, and the first question he asked was whether his sons had brought home the beetle and wedges. They, being afraid to enter into an explanation, said they could not find them; on which he arose, went to the field where he had worked so many years before, and found, in the place where he had left them, the wedges and the iron rings of the beetle, the wooden part having moldered away." . . . Another instance of still more striking character is thus given: "A British captain, at the battle of the Nile, was giving an order from the quarter-deck of his vessel, when a shot struck him in the head, depriving him instantaneously of sense and speech. Living, however, he was taken home, and remained in the Greenwich Hospital fifteen months. At the end of that period, during which he had exhibited no signs of intelligence, an operation was performed upon him by a skillful surgeon that in a moment restored him to his faculties. He immediately rose in his bed and completed the order." Instances of a similar character might be multiplied to almost any extent. But these clearly show the astonishing power of reminiscence in the human soul.

VI. But we must pass to another Class of Facts of still more frequent Occurrence, and still more striking Import; namely, The Quickened Action of Memory occasioned by Disease.

As a general thing, disease affects the mental as well as the bodily powers, and in the same way. It engenders weakness, lack of vital action. But there are special instances in which the reverse has been the case. The nicely-adjusted blinds upon a house in a dark night may conceal from the outer world the brilliant illumination within; but let one of those shutters become misadjusted or fractured and the light within will beam out. So disease often makes rents and crevices in this outer bodily tenement of the soul, through which the mysterious light within beams out with dazzling brightness.

Mr. Flint, in his Recollections of the Valley of the Mississippi, referring to a period of partial derangement from a severe attack of bilious fever, says: "I repeated whole passages with entire accuracy, in the different languages which I had read. I recited, without losing or misplacing a word, passages of poetry, which I could not so repeat when I had recovered my health."

The late Professor Fisher, of New Haven, has recorded facts concerning himself very similar in character, though not resulting from the same physical cause. He says that, while in this half-delirious state, "ideas crowded upon me. My thoughts flowed with a rapidity that was prodigious, and the faculties of association and memory were gifted with wonderful power. I could render different languages into English, and English into Hebrew, with a fluency which I was never before nor since master of."

Dr. Abercrombie relates the case of a child, who, at four years of age, underwent the operation of trepanning while in a state of stupor from a fracture of the skull. After his recovery, he retained no recollection of either the operation or the accident. But at the age of fifteen, during the delirium of a fever, he gave his mother an exact description of the operation, of the persons present, their dress, and many other minute particulars. A lady mentioned by Dr. Pritchard, when in a state of delirium, spoke a language which nobody about her understood, but which was discovered to be Welsh. None of her friends could form any conception of the manner in which she could have become acquainted with that language; but after much inquiry it was discovered that in her childhood she had a nurse, a native of a district on the coast of Brittany, the dialect of which is closely analogous to the Welsh. The lady at that time learned a good deal of this dialect, but had entirely forgotten it for many years before this attack of fever. How striking that these half-acquired ideas of childhood, after slumbering in forgetfulness for years, and when the very circumstances which gave them origin had also been forgotten, should be so mysteriously revived in later years! Dr. Mackintosh, of Edinborough, gives a similar case of a woman under his care. She was a native of the Highlands, but accustomed to speak English. When she was recovered from her stupor to intelligence and speech, no one could understand the language she spoke, nor could they make her comprehend what they said to her. At length some one addressed her in Gaelic, when she replied with ease and fluency. It was then discovered that she had lost her English and recovered the forgotten speech of her childhood.

One more instance, narrated by Mr. Coleridge, must suffice: In a Catholic town in Germany, a young woman of four or five and twenty, who could neither read nor write, was seized with a nervous fever, during which she was incessantly talking Greek, Latin, and Hebrew. Ignorant, and simple, and harmless, as this girl was known to be, no one suspected any deception, and the case attracted much attention. Some began to think it a supernatural inspiration, and the poor, ignorant girl came very near being manufactured into a saint. Others, viewing the case as one calling for philosophical investigation, at length ascertained that the girl, at nine years of age, had been taken to reside in the house of a Protestant minister, and that it was long the habit of this minister to walk in his hall, reading aloud from the Greek and Latin fathers; and that the girl, attracted by curiosity, sometimes opened the kitchen door to listen. Some of the coherent passages uttered by the young woman, were written down by a German scholar as they fell from her lips, and, on comparison, were found to be favorite passages with the old minister. One mystery was now solved; but another was called up. It was no longer a mystery as to the origin of these passages. The question of supernatural inspiration was disposed of, and the poor girl lost her chance of being placed upon the calendar of the Romish saints. But a fact of deep philosophical moment, revealing something of the mysterious power of the human intellect, was established. It is not probable that this young woman reduced a single one of these passages to memory, so as to be able to repeat it at the time. But now—years after all traces of the impressions they had made seemed to be utterly obliterated—they are called forth, while the memory is quickened into extraordinary action, with a clearness and a precision that almost transcends belief.

These facts give unmistakable indication that the history of the past—including all its events, however minute or apparently unimportant—is stereotyped upon the soul in characters never to be effaced; and that it only requires a quickening of our intellectual powers to cause all that past to be unfolded, like a written roll, till every thing it contains shall be spread out before the broad and piercing gaze of the soul.

VII. But we can not Close this Discussion without Glancing at the Mental Phenomena sometimes exhibited on the Approach of Death, as shedding Additional Light upon the Indestructible Character of the Memory.

It has been seen in the case of Admiral Beaufort and others, that in this quickened action of the soul, the memory seems to *retrace* its past history in the inverse order of the actual occurrence of its events. Taking the present as the point of its departure, it goes back through all the gradations of life to childhood and infancy.

The celebrated Dr. Rush mentions the case of an Italian gentleman, who died of yellow fever in the city of New York. At first, he spoke English; as his disease progressed, he spoke only French; but on the day of his death, the attendants were compelled to converse with him in Italian—the language of his childhood. The same gentleman also states in one of his medical works, that a Lutheran clergyman of Philadelphia informed him that Germans and Swedes, of whom he had considerable numbers in his congregàtion, when near death, always prayed in their native languages, though some of them, he was confident, had not spoken these languages for fifty or sixty years.

With another class of persons, dying moments are not unfrequently the occasion for the resurrection of abused privileges and perverted blessings. To the guilty conscience

> "It is the busy, meddling fiend
> That will not let it rest."

From the burial-places of memory, these recollections stalk forth to foreshadow his doom, and to strike deep into the soul the conviction that it is just.

Others, again, calmly dying, have spoken of the incidents of their lives as being all simultaneously presented before them as in a magic mirror—every line as if fixed upon a tablet by the light, with all the exactitude and distinctness of present reality.

These manifestations of intellectual and spiritual perception in the hour of death, seem to be but the first movement of that mighty expanding of intellectual power which shall characterize our transition from time to eternity. These facts, therefore, make it highly probable that thought is absolutely imperishable; and that *whatever is written once upon the memory lives there forever.* The conclusion that absolute forgetfulness, or obliteration from the memory is impossible, is warranted, then, by the sound induction of philosophy and the plain teachings of Revelation.

The events of our past history are written upon our living spirits, and will remain there forever. The facts, then, seem to justify the declaration of Mr. Coleridge, that in the very nature of a living spirit, it may be more possible that heaven and earth should pass away than that a single thought should be loosened or lost from the great chain of our mental operations. A thousand incidents may spread a vail between our present consciousness and the record on the soul; but there the record remains—not an inscription obscured or effaced—waiting the judgment of God. "The portrait of the soul is the perfect reflection of itself; and every man must see his own character thus forever visible to the eye of God, and, probably, hereafter, to angels and to men."

The power of reminiscence slumbers, but does not die. At the judgment-day—we are entirely at liberty to suppose, from what we know of the powers of the mind, and what we learn from the Revelation of God—it will awake!

It will summon up thought and feeling from its hidden recesses, and present before us the perfect form and representation of the past:

> "Each fainter trace that memory holds,
> So darkly of departed years,
> In one broad glance the soul beholds,
> And all that was at once appears!"

This is, undoubtedly, that "book of remembrance" that shall be opened in that great and terrible day of the Lord. By its records we shall be judged, and by its testimony will our doom be fixed.

A rich landlord in England once performed an act of tyrannical injustice to a tenant who was a widow. The widow's son was a witness of it, and afterward becoming a painter, he transferred that scene to canvas. Years afterward the rich man saw it. As his eye fell upon the picture, he turned pale and trembled; he sought to purchase it, and offered any sum that might be named as its price, that he might be able to destroy a picture that so harrowed his guilty conscience. If every scene of wickedness through which a man passes should be painted, and the paintings hung up around him, so that he would always see the portrait of himself, with the evil passions expressed on his countenance, and himself in the very act of wickedness, with nothing to mitigate the dark coloring of the picture, he would be appalled at the spectacle. Yet such a picture-gallery there is; its walls, all around, are hung with life-pictures of the soul! The deed of darkness and of sin may have been the work of a moment; but the colors that now enshrine it are fadeless and eternal! Why should not those walls be hung with pictures of taste and beauty—portraying scenes of love, and purity, and beneficence—scenes that may feast the intellect and ravish the soul—seeing it is to be its dwelling-place forever?

With what interest does the antiquarian dig up from the sands of Egypt or of Assyria some fragment of ancient art, on which he finds graven the portraits, the attitudes, the dresses, and the pursuits of men who lived and died three thousand years ago!—every lineament, every shade, every expression, just as the artist left it ages long gone by! Such life-pictures are we now inscribing upon tablets more enduring than the polished stone or the molten brass. Those pictures now pass from our view; but not to perish! And who can describe or comprehend the interest we shall feel, when from the silence of eternity shall be brought up the sculptured history of the soul, faithfully preserved, not a line broken, not a shade dimmed—hung up as a spectacle for men and angels—hung up to be gazed upon forever!

We are not only living a life, but we are writing a biography. The philosophy of Bacon may perish, the science of Newton be forgotten, the sublimest inventions in art may fail of record and of remembrance; but the simple volume of life, the autobiography each individual is now writing out of himself, can be neither lost nor forgotten; for it is written upon the very texture of the soul. And as the soul moves forward through all the ages of coming eternity, it shall carry along with it this marvelous record of its former life. The grand catastrophe of the world's destruction shall strike no passage from this book. Other books may become dim and dingy with age; but no lapse of time or of eternity can obscure a single page in this. From other books offensive passages may be stricken out—whole pages and chapters may be recast; but from this book nothing can be stricken, no part of it can be annulled, no part of it changed. O, then, let passages, and pages, and chapters of beauty, and love, and purity be written upon the memory, that, in the ages to come, when the thrones and empires of earth have crumbled away and been forgotten, and the globe itself been dissolved—they may be read and re-read with ever-increasing delight! Thus, the memories of the past shall furnish one of the sublimest sources of felicity to the soul, as it journeys onward in its unending progress to the consummation of its destiny.

XV.

CONSCIENCE THE MINISTER OF JUDGMENT.

'I am tormented in this flame." LUKE xvi, 24.

"God shall bring every work into judgment, with every secret thing, whether it be good or evil." ECCL. xii, 14.

"There is no peace, saith my God, to the wicked." ISA. lvii, 21.

"Then shall ye return and discern between the righteous and the wicked, between him that serveth God and him that serveth him not." MAL. iii, 18.

"A wounded spirit who can bear?" PROV. xviii, 14.

THE doctrine of a future and general judgment is a doctrine of Revelation; and as such, must be judged of by the written Word. By "the law and by the testimony" it must stand or fall.

It is no part of our present object to enter into a set defense of this doctrine by collating or comparing it with the Scripture testimony. This has been so often and so ably done; indeed, the doctrine itself holds so prominent a place in the teachings of Revelation that but few who reverence the Bible, and receive its teachings, without change or detraction, as Divine, will dare say aught against the Scripture *fact*. But there are thousands who are full of the *philosophical doubt*, on the question of a future judgment. To such persons there is something inexplicably intricate connected with the *facts* and the *modus operandi* of a judgment-day. They see not how, or by what process, God shall bring every work into judgment, with every secret thing, whether it be good or whether it be evil. They limit not the power of God, but question the exercise of that power for the registration of things, many of them so insignificant and so contemptible. Again, to them it seems inexplicable that every tongue in that day shall confess, and all men give an account of every idle and sinful thought, word, and act. And the objection is often raised, that the condemned soul can never realize the justice of the verdict that seals its everlasting doom, without a full and clear knowledge of the facts on which that decision is based; and such knowledge they deem impossible. We will not stop to expose the fallacy of these objections. They manifestly originate in imperfect views of the economy of the Divine government, and of the vast resources of intellectual and moral power with which the human mind has been endowed.

We again repeat, that we are not proposing to establish the doctrine, that we now argue not the Scripture fact, but the philosophic doubt upon the doctrine of a final judgment. Its Scripture authority must be regarded as settled. The doctrine is so fully enunciated, so explicitly declared, and so frequently reiterated and urged, and men are so constantly warned of its approach, that, though human reason should tower like a bulwark against it, it were worse than idle to attempt to evade its Scripture authority.*

*"It is appointed unto men once to die, but after this the judgment." (Heb. ix, 27.)

"And I saw the dead, small and great, stand before God; and the books were opened; and another book was opened, which is the book of life; and the dead were judged out of those things which were written in the books, according to their works." (Rev. xx, 12.)

"For God shall bring every work into judgment, with every secret thing, whether it be good or evil." (Eccl. xii, 14.)

"As I live, saith the Lord, every knee shall bow to me, and every tongue shall confess to God. So, then, every one of us shall give account of himself to God." (Rom. xiv, 11, 12.)

"But I say unto you, That every idle word that men shall speak they shall give account thereof in the day of judgment." (Matt. xii, 36.)

"Woe unto the wicked! it shall be ill with him; for the reward of his hands shall be given him." (Isa. iii, 11.)

"There is no peace, saith my God, to the wicked." (Isa. lvii, 21.) "Who among us shall dwell with the devouring fire? Who among us shall dwell with everlasting burnings?" (Isa. xxxviii, 14.)

What we now propose, is to look into our own nature, to examine the susceptibilities of our own minds, to see if we may not there find corresponding powers and capacities.

If we recur to the general experience of mankind, we shall see enough in the operation of moral causes to convince us that memory and conscience, connected as they are with a knowledge of the moral character and consequences of our sins, have an important agency in the great system of moral government, with which we are indissolubly connected. And, if we find them thus empowered and performing these high functions here, is there not every reason to infer that they are destined to fill the same office and perform the same functions hereafter? If so, then man contains within himself all the elements of that process that shall determine his future destiny.

The general doctrine we proposed to establish is this: *That in memory, with its mysterious power and its inalienable laws, is to be found the "book of remembrance" in which our sins are recorded; and that in conscience is to be found a principle that will respond to the inexorable decree of the final Judge, and that will execute the mandate of Heaven upon us—that it is the undying worm and the unquenchable fire.*

We have already seen how memory responds to the functions of this high office. It now only remains to inquire whether, in the conscience, may be found a corresponding capacity and power.

Without aiming at scientific precision, we would define conscience to be *a power of moral judgment or discrimination, combined with a susceptibility of moral emotion.* This definition, which is at once concise and comprehensive, presents conscience under a twofold point of view.

I. A Moral Judgment or a Discrimination of the Moral Quality of our Actions, by which Conscience determines that they are Right or Wrong.

This judgment passes its decisions upon the moral quality of our acts, not only before, but also after their performance. The perceptions of this moral judgment are more or less distinct, as circumstances and habits are favorable or unfavorable. The sinner who yields to the impulses of passion, and refuses to obey the monitions of conscience, gradually, but surely, impairs its discriminating power. With him, "the dividing line between right and wrong seems gradually to become obliterated." And yet the fearful distinctness with which conscience sometimes reveals his guilt to the sinner—notwithstanding the force of habit, and prejudice, and passion, and interest—gives us at least a faint indication of the keen, piercing power of discrimination that it still possesses.

But, again, this discriminating power of the conscience may be improved as well as impaired. Reflection upon the past—especially when aided by a vivid recollection of our acts—will often arouse the discriminating power of conscience to an intense and astonishing degree. It would seem as though it were our very judge, bringing out every shade of darkness and holding it up to our view. May we not, then, infer that in a future state of being—when this cumbersome vehicle of clay shall have been thrown off, and the soul shall revive its crippled powers, and call back its energies at present straitened and enfeebled—the conscience shall possess a keenness of moral discrimination, of which, at present, we are able to form very inadequate conceptions?

We will not pause longer upon the discriminating power

of conscience. Every individual is conscious of its existence. Every individual recognizes a right and a wrong in his own action. And, indeed, this power of moral discrimination forms one of the broad lines of separation between man and the brute. It can never become extinct without disrobing the soul of some of its essential characteristics. Death, then, has no power over it. Eternity shall not dim its eye; but from the inconceivably-distant recesses of futurity shall it throw back its piercing glance upon time, whose record is eternal.*

II. A Susceptibility of Moral Emotion.

This moral emotion is also of a twofold character. It is both prospective and retrospective. That is, it is experienced before as well as after a deed has been committed. And if the deed be one that the moral judgment decides to be right, the moral emotion prompts us to do it; and on the other hand restrains us from the commission of that which the moral judgment disapproves.

This power of moral emotion is seen in the clear and strong notes of *remonstrance* which conscience whispers in the sinner's ear. Shakspeare, a close observer and critical delineator of human nature, in a masterly manner portrays the workings and the power of this moral emotion, even in the bosoms of abandoned men. One of the murderers of the Duke of Clarence, while struggling to suppress his moral emotions, preparatory to the act of assassination, is represented as thus speaking of his conscience: "I'll not meddle with it; it is a dangerous thing; it makes a man a coward; a man can not steal, but it accuseth him; a man can not swear, but it checks him. 'T is a blushing, shamefaced spirit, that mutinies in a man's bosom; it fills one full

*See Wayland's Moral Phil. for a fuller discussion of this topic.

of obstacles. It made me once restore a purse of gold, that, by chance, I found. It beggars any man that keeps it."

It is the power of this moral emotion that so often makes the sinner pause between the conception and the execution of his crime. It is this that occasions the feverish excitement, the tumultuous war of contending emotions within, before the sinner can acquire hardness of heart and strength of nerve to execute the deed of darkness. There is a voice within that protests against the commission of wrong; it rallies all the elements of moral power in the soul to the defense; it brings up in fearful array all the Divine judgments of Heaven against iniquity. Nay, the very commission of sin has its dread attendants—"terrific admonition whispering on his secret ear; prophetic warning pointing him to the shadows of future retribution;" and thus, in the very moment of transgression, lightnings of conviction flash in his eye, and the thunderings of reproach peal their solemn tones in his ear. This is conscience forestalling and resisting the commission of sin.

On the other hand, after the act has been committed, there is not only a moral judgment—a clear perception of the moral quality of the action, but apart from and beyond this, there is a distinct emotion of approval or disapproval. There is not only *perception*, but also *feeling*. And there can be no question that, as our remembrance is clear and distinct with regard to the transactions of our past lives, conscience is prompt to lisp approving whispers, audible only to the soul addressed; or to rend the soul with anguish—according as the act has been good or bad.

"Guiltiness will speak, though tongues were out of use."

The working of a guilty conscience within the soul beams out through the eye, and is expressed by every action. Remorse, or shame, or fear, is ever written upon the very countenance of the guilty man. "The spirit of a man will sustain his infirmity, but a wounded spirit who can bear?" "A man before the commission of crime can foresee no reason why he may not commit it with the certainty of escaping detection. He can perceive no reason why he should be even suspected; and can imagine a thousand methods in which suspicion awakened, might with perfect ease be allayed." But the moment he becomes guilty, his relations to his fellow-men have become changed, and a correspondent change has also taken place in his own feelings. "The boldness of innocence and the timidity of guilt" have long been observed. "The wicked flee when no man pursueth, but the righteous are as bold as a lion."

> "Suspicion always haunts the guilty mind;
> The thief doth fear each bush an officer."

So, also, the vile Macbeth, after the murder of Duncan, exclaims:

> "How is it with me, when every noise appalls me?"

Whence results this fear, this timidity, this insurmountable apprehension of undefined and unspeakable evil? It is the voice of conscience speaking within, and will not be silenced. Thus, too, "often the wicked is snared in the work of his own hand."

How many are the criminals who have acknowledged their guilt—who have fled to the gibbet and to the halter to escape the more fearful punishment of a guilty conscience! To them, even the halter has no terrors that can equal the deep goadings of remorse. Not many years since, a foul murder was committed in the vicinity of one of our large cities, upon an aged and defenseless couple. Suspicion fastened upon a young German. He was arrested, tried and convicted. The evidence, though strong, was circumstantial. The jury recommended the criminal to mercy. With regard to his guilt there were many doubts in the public mind. He was also a stranger in a strange land—ignorant of the language and usages of the country, and equally destitute of friends. Public sympathy was awakened in his behalf; a strong petition went up to the Executive for his entire pardon—or at least a commutation of his sentence; Christian benevolence ministered to his comfort. But, alas! what could ease a troubled conscience, or stifle the goadings of remorse? His countenance became haggard, his frame emaciated, and his averted expression bordered upon despair! The very offices of kindness and love seemed only to augment his misery. Scarcely had he endured his mental agony for six weeks, when he sent for a Catholic priest, confessed to him his guilt, and declared that the gallows was nothing compared to the pangs of remorse that drank up his spirit, and gnawed like a consuming fire upon his soul. From the sad hour of the murder— to which he had been tempted by the hope of gain—the shriek of despair and the groan of death uttered by his victims had not died away upon his ear; their specters had not ceased to haunt his vision. His spirit found no rest; the mark of Cain was upon his forehead; the consuming vengeance of the Almighty preyed upon his soul.

Dr. Beecher mentions the case of a man at East Hampton, Long Island, who, smitten down by the power of conscience, for three days suffered indescribable anguish and then died, without bodily disease or bodily pain. . . A son of Dr. Rush, having killed a man in a duel, was afterward so troubled by remorse that his reason became unsettled, and he was consigned as a maniac to the asylum in Philadelphia. Here he would for a long time stand in profound reverie, immovable as a statue. Then he would arouse to consciousness, pace off the distance, give the word, "Fire!" then cry out, "He is dead! he is dead!" Al Montasa, having assassinated his father, was some time after strongly reminded of his crime. From that moment a deathly paleness came over his countenance; sleep departed from his eyes, or visited him only to excite new horrors; the sentence of death was written upon his soul, and diseased only in his conscience, he expired at the early age of twenty-five.*

Just while these pages are passing through the press, a new illustration of the power of conscience is added to the thousands that had gone before. The fearful murder of a young man in the bank of Malden, Massachusetts, in open day, and the robbery of the bank, in December, 1863, created much excitement. But, for some two months, no clew to the perpetrator of the deed was obtained. The public

*Some of our readers will remember the story of "A Night with a Duelist." It is pertinent to our subject, and is, in brief, as follows: A duel was fought near the city of Washington, under circumstances of peculiar atrocity. A distinguished individual challenged his relative, who was once his friend. The challenged party having the choice of weapons, named muskets, to be loaded with buckshot and slugs, and the distance ten paces; avowing, at the same time, his intention and desire that both parties should be destroyed. They fought. The challenger was killed on the spot; the murderer escaped unhurt! Years afterward, a gentleman was spending the Winter in Charleston, South Carolina, and lodged at the same house with this unhappy man. He was requested, by the duelist, one evening, to sleep in the same room with him, but he declined, as he was very well accommodated in his own. On his persisting in declining, the duelist confessed to him that HE WAS AFRAID TO SLEEP ALONE; and as a friend who usually occupied the room was absent, he would esteem it a great favor if the gentleman would pass the night with him. His kindness being thus demanded, he consented, and retired to rest in the room of this man of fashion and honor, who some years before had stained his hands in the blood of a kinsman. After long tossing on his unquiet pillow, and repeated half-stifled groans, that revealed the inward pangs of the murderer, he sank into slumber, and as he rolled from side to side, the name of his victim was often uttered, with broken words that discovered the keen remorse that preyed like fire on his conscience. Suddenly he would start up in his bed with the terrible impression that the avenger of blood was pursuing him; or hide himself under the covering as if he would escape the burning eye of an angry God, that gleamed in the darkness over him, like lightning from a thunder-cloud! For him there was "no rest, night nor day." Conscience, armed with terrors, lashed him unceasingly, and who could sleep? And this was not the restlessness of disease, the raving of a disordered intellect, nor the anguish of a maniac struggling in chains! It was a man of

had already begun to settle down in the conviction that this was one of the murders that will not out, when it was again startled by the announcement that the murderer had been discovered, and had confessed the deed. The criminal was a Mr. Green, the postmaster of the village, a young man of twenty-seven years, married within a year, respectably connected, and hitherto of a fair local reputation. Suspicions were excited against him from various circumstances, till at length he was taken to the house of a neighbor, confronted with half a dozen of his fellow-citizens, and coolly confessed the crime. The description of the sad affair will be best given in the language written at the time: "He says that he bought a revolver ten days before the murder, for the sole purpose of doing this deed; he kept it in his office till two days before, then loaded it, and carried it about his person. Satan had now got complete possession of him, and drove him headlong to his fate. The morning

intelligence, education, health, and influence, given up to himself, not delivered over to the avenger of blood, to be tormented before his time; but left to the power of his own CONSCIENCE, suffering only what every one may suffer who is abandoned of God!

Not many years since, Professor Davis, of the Virginia University, was shot by a Southern student by the name of Semmes—whether a relative of the pirate Semmes, we know not. The young man escaped the judgment of the law of his country, but not that of his conscience. This followed him, with all its horrors, till he brought his life to an end with his own hand. The final tragedy was enacted at the house of his brother, in Washington, Georgia. He shot himself with a pistol, the ball entering the left eye and penetrating the brain, and lingered in a state of total insensibility from about seven o'clock, A. M., till half-past one, P. M., of the same day, when the family was called to his room by the report of a pistol. When his room was entered he was found in a chair, placed at a table. A pistol was lying across his lap, and on the table was an open razor. On the table was found, also, a note, stating, in the form of a certificate, dated July 9th, 1847, that his death was occasioned by himself, and was brought about either by pistol or razor.

Our readers will remember the name and political character of George C. Dromgoole. While the brightest prospects of honor and eminence were opening before him, he was betrayed by that code of Satan, falsely called "honor," and killed his antagonist upon the spot. From that moment, he knew no peace. He sought to stifle the voice of conscience by inebriation, and at an early age sunk down to the grave a ruined man. His entire property he left to the children whose father and protector he had destroyed.

of the murder he entered the bank three times to effect his purpose. Being on familiar terms with Converse, he went behind the counter, once to get a bill changed to a greenback, the second time to get a torn bill changed. Somebody entering each of these times prevented the consummation of the crime. The third, the coast was clear. He glided beside and behind his victim, put his revolver within a foot of his head, and fired. The poor lad looked at him, he says, as he was falling. What a look! How it must freeze his soul! What a horror it casts over his night visions! How can he sleep with those dying eyes fixed upon him?

> 'And when they meet at compt,
> That look of his will cast his soul from heaven.'

He kept his secret for six long weeks, suffering, as he says, 'what God only knows.' He has done little but weep and talk of his crime, not his fate, since his confession and confinement." The first step to this crime was thieving from the mails; and thus, step by step was he led on, till the guilt of one of the foulest murders blackens his soul, and harrows his conscience with unbearable remorse.

Conscience—mysterious, solemn power! What can equal the pangs of shame, of self-reproach, and of remorse it can inflict upon the guilty soul! Could the sinner fly from himself—could he bury the past in forgetfulness—could he forget what he is, and where he is going—his troubled soul might find momentary ease. But, alas! no lethean waters can wash out the memory of the past—no opiate of earth can ease the pangs of a guilty conscience! The language of the conscience-smitten wretch is:

> "*Me* miserable! which way shall I fly,
> Infinite wrath and infinite despair?
> Which way I fly is hell; *myself* am hell!"

Conscience may, indeed, seem to slumber for a time; but the day of its resurrection will arrive. Joseph's brethren for over twenty years concealed their guilt within their own breasts; and, perhaps, rarely did they permit themselves to think of their betrayed and lost brother, or to meditate upon his probable fate. But no sooner do they find themselves arrested, and their lives endangered in Egypt, than the past is forced upon their recollection. Conscience speaks within them; the lips of confession are unsealed—"And they said one to another, We are verily guilty concerning our brother, in that we saw the anguish of his soul, when he besought us and we would not hear; therefore is this distress come upon us." Solemn is the hour of the visitation of conscience to a guilty man! There is no anguish to be compared to that which preys upon his soul! His mind is distracted; his whole soul is overspread with darkness and horror; it is tossed to and fro like a troubled sea when it can not rest, *whose waters cast up mire and dirt.* "The arrows of the Almighty are within him, the poison whereof drinketh up his spirits; the terrors of God set themselves in array against him."

You may have read of the individual who murdered his master, and then robbed him of his treasures. With the price of blood in his hands, he fled to a distant part of the country, engaged in business, and by degrees rose till he became a judge in one of the superior courts. Thirty years of prosperity, of affluence, and of honor had almost erased from his recollection the foul crime that had stained his soul with guilt. One day, however, a prisoner was brought before him, charged with the murder of his master, under circumstances strongly calculated to remind the judge of the dark period in his own history. The crime was clearly proved; the jury rendered their verdict, and nothing remained but for the judge to pass the sentence of death. Silence pervaded the court. The judge moved not. A deathly paleness overspread his countenance—relieved only by vivid flashes of shame and horror; his whole body shook with convulsive agitation. Conscience—so long smothered—so long stifled—had now burst forth from every inthrallment! It thundered in his ear; it touched the chords of memory, and the past flashed up in his recollection; it plunged its scorpion fangs into his heart, and his soul writhed in unutterable anguish; it wound its serpent folds around him, and there was no escape. He descended from the bench and placed himself by the side of the criminal, confessed his guilt, and asked that he might expiate his offense by suffering the extreme penalties of the law. This is *conscience*; this is the unfolding of its requisitions—the revealing of its power!

There have been instances of human suffering, of intense bodily anguish, which the stoutest heart was unable to contemplate without feelings of horror; and yet the individuals themselves, though on the verge of eternity, have declared that their bodily anguish was nothing compared to the horrors of a guilty conscience which they then suffered. Dugdale, upon whose perjured testimony the Earl of Stafford had been executed, was ever after pursued by the furies of an evil conscience; and, upon his dying-bed, with loud, unearthly shrieks, he besought his friends to take away the specter of his victim. Witness the death-bed scene of the profligate and licentious Altamont, as pathetically described by Dr. Young. Hear him addressing a friend who had been poisoned by his skepticism and ruined by his licentiousness: "No, no! Let me speak on; I have not long to speak. My much-injured friend! My soul, as my body, lies in ruins, in scattered fragments of broken thought. Remorse for the past throws my thoughts upon the future; worse dread of the future strikes them back upon the past. I turn, and turn, and find no ray. Didst thou feel half the mountain that is on me, thou wouldst struggle with the martyr for his stake, and bless Heaven for the flame that is not an everlasting flame, that is not an unquenchable fire! And is there another hell? O thou blasphemed, yet indulgent Lord God! Hell itself is a refuge if it hide me from thy frown!" He who has stood by the dying couch of the ungodly—he who has witnessed the pangs of remorse and the awful forebodings of damnation that haunt the dying moments of the infidel, may form some faint conception of the terrific power of conscience when the unfolding of its power and the day of visitation have arrived. O, these are but the faint and feeble precursors of the unuttered and unutterable woe of the "worm that never dies!"

A young man who had been religiously educated, but had subsequently become skeptical, very nearly succeeded in winning over his father to the cold, bleak, barren system of infidelity. His father, however, barely escaped; for being suddenly taken sick with a mortal disease, he earnestly returned to Christ, and died in the triumphs of a glorious faith. The son was now overwhelmed with anguish, his infidelity vanished, and deep and mighty torrents of remorse overwhelmed his soul. His agony for three months was indescribable, and seemed to be insupportable. While in this state he visited a friend who was superintending a furnace. After looking for some time upon the workmen as they were pouring out the melted ore, seething and burning like liquid fire, he turned and said to his friend, with his lip trembling, his face pale as death, and his whole frame quivering with emotion—"Were that lava to be poured out upon my flesh, the pain it would inflict would be less than the agony, and anguish, and horror of mind which I experience almost incessantly. There is no need that hell should be composed of elemental fire, as a means of punishing the ungodly. *Sir, God has let my con-*

science loose upon me, and that is more painful to me than if I were bathed, as to my body, in that liquid element. The fire that burns within fastens upon the soul; the agony which it occasions is the agony of an immortal nature." No need, then, of a literal "lake of fire and brimstone" in order to inflict retribution upon the soul. God has chosen these elements to convey to our minds, as far as the nature of the case will admit, some appropriate idea of the inconceivable intensity of that anguish the soul will feel when God shall unfetter the guilty conscience and let it loose upon the individual accursed. Nor do we mean to say that God may not employ the most terrible material agencies in effecting the retributions of eternity. All we affirm is, that here, in the very laws of our intellectual and moral being, there is the revelation of powers that should make us tremble. Men may scoff at the idea of an elemental hell or material suffering, a fire that is not quenched, a worm that never dies, a lake that burneth with fire and brimstone; but it is quite another thing to break away from the control of the Almighty, "who knows how to reserve the unjust unto the day of judgment to be punished"—quite another thing to suppose God may not *let the sinner's conscience loose upon him!*

III. Lessons Afforded by Memory and Conscience.

In conclusion, let us sum up the views we have endeavored to establish in this discussion:

1. And first, if the views we have presented in relation to the duration of memory be true—and who can doubt but what they are, in view of the facts by which they have been considered?—then does it become obvious that our ideas are absolutely imperishable. The soul is the tablet upon which they are engraved, and the inscription is as inde-

structible as the soul itself. "Reason and Revelation agree, then, in asserting that absolute forgetfulness, or obliteration, is impossible; and that all the events of our history are written in our living spirits, and, whether seen or unseen, will there remain forever, unless removed by the act of a merciful Omnipotence! It is true that a thousand incidents will spread a vail between our present consciousness and the record on the soul; but there the record rests, waiting the judgment of God." The power of reminiscence slumbers, but does not die. At the judgment-day memory will awake; it will summon up thought and feeling from its hidden recesses, till, as upon a sheeted canvas, the whole history of the past shall be hung up for the inspection of the soul.

2. That God has instituted conscience not only to enable us to perceive duty, and prompt us to its performance, but also as an instrument of punishment, is abundantly evident, even without any light of Revelation.

"Go where you will, turn over the pages of this world's history, and the natural dread of an accusing conscience will be found to have been the rod of terror in all ages of the world. No man will or *can* long abide the action of self-reproach."* Remorse is a fearful word; when written upon the soul it is the precursor of despair. What will not a man do, and to what will not he flee, to escape from the inner pangs of remorse? Its sting is like that of the scorpion; it makes the soul a desolation. "Think not," says Cicero, "that the guilty require the burning torches of the Furies to agitate and torment them; their own frauds, their remembrance of the past, their terrors of the future—these are the despotic furies that are ever present to the mind of the impious." "Could the sinner fly from himself, could he obliterate the memory of the past, could

* Dr. Hibbard's sermon in the Methodist Episcopal Pulpit.

he forget for a moment what he is, his case would not be altogether destitute of relief. But this can never be;

'He bears his own tormentor in his breast;'

and *that worm dieth not.* The remembrance of what he was, and what he should have been—what he now is, and must forever be, haunts him like specters of the injured dead. The hours of misspent time now repeat their solemn knell; the neglected mercies, the unheeded admonitions, the tender sympathy and counsel of pious friends, the opportunities of repentance, the half-formed purpose of reformation—all that he has done, and all that he has left undone, now glance before the mind, and awaken the bitter lament—'How have I hated instruction, and my heart despised reproof!'"

"So do the dark in soul expire,
Or live like scorpion girt with fire;
So writhes the mind remorse hath riven,
Unfit for earth, undoom'd for heaven;
Darkness above, despair beneath,
Around it flame, within it *death!*"

3. And now, from these dark scenes of wretchedness and guilt, of horror and of despair, exhibited in this life, let us cast our glance into the future; let us boldly lift up the curtain, and, from our eminence of mercy and of grace, look down upon that abyss of darkness and of death, whose victims "have no rest day nor night." We have marked the horrors of conscience for sin in this life; but if such be the compunctions of the conscience for one sin, if such be the agony of one hour, how must the sinner be overwhelmed when the recollection, not of one sin, but of a *life of iniquity*, shall press upon his soul, and press upon it forever! If such be the agony of a moment, what shall be the agony of that age, that ceaseless age of horror, that shall succeed a life of folly and of sin? Conscience, crushed, weighed down under the rubbish of human folly

and the leaden weight of human crime, in the dread day of eternity undergoes a fearful resurrection in its tremendous energies. Its thousand stings pierce with consuming, ceaseless, remediless remorse. Turn, writhe, and flee as may the damned soul, the Gorgon terrors of conscience, more frightful than the flames of hell, still stare him in the face, still hold up the mirror of his follies and his sins, still upbraid his rejection of a Father's mercy and a Redeemer's blood. This, *this* is the burning of the fire that is not quenched, the gnawing of the worm that dieth not! Beyond this we need not look to inquire in what the misery of the lost shall consist.

But is there no remedy? Shall the miserable soul thus loathe existence, and pant for annihilation forever? Shall the frightful action of a ruined and disordered intellect never become stagnant in the pool of death? Shall memory, thus running back to past sins and follies, never wear out by lapse of time? Shall the eye of conscience never become dim with age, its voice never become silent through plenitude of years? Sinner, canst thou turn back the river to its source? Canst thou remove from their foundations the granite bulwarks of the everlasting hills—those pyramids of the Almighty's power? This mayest thou do sooner than abrogate the laws of mind; for they are immutable and eternal. Thou mayest break the bands of adamant, thou mayest hold the elements of nature harmless at thy feet—the willing ministers to do thy bidding; but thou mayest not enter into the secret chambers of the soul to annul its laws or to change the conditions of its being! Are these the results of sin—these the retributions of eternity? Then let each one of us pray, "*Gather not my soul with sinners, nor my life with ungodly men. My soul, come not thou into their secret, and unto their assembly, mine honor, be not thou united!*"

XVI.

HEAVEN: OR, THE HOME AND AVOCATIONS OF THE BLESSED.

"We, according to his promise, look for new heavens and a new earth, wherein dwelleth righteousness." 2 PET. iii, 13.

"A city which hath foundations, whose builder and maker is God." HEB. xi, 10.

"Ye have in heaven a better and an enduring substance." HEB. x, 34.

"I go to prepare a place for you." JOHN xiv, 3.

"We have a building of God, a house not made with hands, eternal in the heavens." 2 COR. iv, 18.

"And there shall be no night there." REV. xxii, 5.

HEAVEN is a theme of profound interest to the Christian believer. Dimly seen in the visions of his faith, yet is it looked forward to as his eternal home. A pilgrim and a stranger, he desires "a better country, that is, a heavenly." Amid the crumbling ruins of earthly hopes, he looks forward to "a city which hath foundations, whose builder and maker is God." The more perfect his knowledge is of that "better country," and of that "foundation-city," the more vital and realizing will be his faith.

The attempt to gather up and to place in clear view the facts revealed concerning the heavenly state, embodies a holier purpose than the mere gratification of human fancy. Vague and unreal views have ever been the bane of the Christian life. If we can but realize that *heaven is real*, as earth is real; that it is not a strange land, but one clothed with scenery like our own—only a thousand times more beautiful; that the dwellers there are not strangers, but our kindred and friends—still human—*glorified hu-*

manity—we shall catch inspiration from so sublime a view; the gloom of the dark valley will disappear; and we shall realize that *faith is the substance of things hoped for.* For practical ends, then, should the Christian seek to penetrate this great mystery of the unseen and eternal.

In regard to our future being—its conditions, associations, and avocations—our only certain knowledge is derived from the Revelation of God. Science may unvail the hidden elements of nature which seem to have reference to another and a higher state of being. Philosophy may suggest its analogies and build up our hopes. The instinctive intimations of immortality may be strong in the human soul. But the true interpreter of all these is God's own Revelation. And when thus interpreted, their teaching is sublime. They give the response of nature and reason to the oracles of the living God, showing the true harmony that exists between the two.

There is a somewhat general impression that all revelation concerning heaven and the condition and avocations of the redeemed, is vague, and of doubtful import. Nothing can be more opposed to fact, more pernicious in effect, or more unjust to God. With our limited faculties, blunted by sense and sin, we poorly comprehend what is revealed. But a careful analysis will assure us that the light shed upon the subject in the Bible is not doubtful in its character, nor does it lack either comprehension or minuteness. If heaven is not unvailed to the full vision of sense, neither is it concealed from spiritual, nor even intellectual apprehension. We may comprehend enough of it to constitute a sure foundation for our faith, to inspire ardent longings, and to call forth earnest endeavor in the Christian life. Even if we can not learn all we desire, the study of what is revealed and the acquirement of what may be known will prove a source of unmeasured comfort.

I. Types of Heaven.

The employment of types for the unvailing of spiritual truths, or of truths lying beyond the range of ordinary human knowledge, has always been a characteristic of inspiration. It was thus that the character and coming of the Messiah were revealed through the long ages that preceded his advent. And perhaps in no other form is heaven, the future home of the believer, so distinctively unvailed as by the types employed by inspiration to represent it to us. As the calm lake mirrors back to our view the overarching sky, so these types seem to mirror the very image of heaven to our faith.

1. *Eden was a type of heaven.* It would transcend human power to describe the loveliness of man's early and earthly paradise. Eden means pleasure or delight; and the garden planted in its midst must have combined the richer beauties of the country. "And the Lord God planted a garden eastward in Eden; and there he put the man whom he had formed. And out of the ground made the Lord God to grow every tree that is pleasant to the sight, and good for food; the tree of life also in the midst of the garden, and the tree of knowledge of good and evil. And a river went out of Eden to water the garden; and from thence it was parted, and became into four heads." (Gen. ii, 8–10.) Simple is the description of this glorious earthly paradise; but it must have been a spot surpassing all others in its ethereal delights. As such it even now floats in the imagination like a vision of purity and love—after the lapse of nearly six thousand years of forfeiture and banishment.

This "paradise" lost dimly shadows the "paradise" we may gain. Our Savior says to the penitent thief, "To-day shalt thou be with me in paradise." (Luke xxiii, 43.) And when St. Paul would convey an idea of that heaven, the glory of which he had beheld, he speaks of himself as having been "caught up into paradise." (2 Cor. xii, 4.) St. John, also, in his apocalyptic vision, received from the Spirit this message, and conveyed it to the Churches: "To him that overcometh will I give to eat of the tree of life, which is in the midst of the paradise of God." (Rev. ii, 7.) And not only does the "tree of life" reappear in the heavenly paradise, of which the earthly was the type, but the river that watered the earthly Eden finds its antitype in that "pure river of water of life, clear as crystal, proceeding out of the throne of God and of the Lamb." (Rev. xxii, 1.) To the Jew this imagery and the promise it embodied awakened the most tender and joyous feelings. The paradise they had lost on earth was still guarded by the cherubim and the flaming sword, so that they could enter it no more. But this, though lost, now mirrored to them another paradise—richer in its transcendent glory and perennial in its duration—into which they might enter through the great Messiah. So, also, the Christian finds in Eden the type of that paradise in which the consummation of his hopes shall be reached. In sacred song he anticipates the day when,

> "Of our paradise possess'd,"

we shall

> "With God in Eden live."

But what are the lessons suggested by this type? What light does it shed upon our future home and destiny? Let us see: If the paradise of Eden was the most lovely spot of the primeval earth as it came, unblighted by sin, from the hand of the Creator, may we not infer that the heavenly paradise shall be, above all other places, the spot of most transcendent beauty in all the universe of God? Was Eden a place of social intercourse, sweet and unalloyed; of love pure, undefiled, and lasting; of holiness unmarred and glorious? In all these endearments it shall be infinitely surpassed by its heavenly antitype. The rivers that watered the earthly Eden were but the type of that "pure river of water of life, clear as crystal," that gushes forth from beneath "the throne," and rolls onward through the heavenly plains; and both symbolize the purity and fullness of the joy of the redeemed. So the trees of the earthly Eden find their counterpart in that unfailing "tree of life" growing abundantly upon the banks of either side of the river of life, and in the very streets of the city, and bearing all "manner of fruits," and yielding them month by month, so that supply might never fail; and both symbolize the exhaustless resources of the Divine beneficence treasured up in heaven. But last of all, and above all, as God held personal intercourse with the dwellers in the earthly Eden, so much more shall he unvail his presence and his favor to those who have gained the heavenly Eden.

Such are some of the characteristics of our heavenly home, as shadowed forth by the earthly Eden. Surely it will be joyful to dwell in the Eden of God, to behold its celestial beauties, to be regaled by its fruits, to share in its blissful associations, and, above all, to be crowned by the Divine and glorious Presence.

"Fair land! could mortal eyes
But half its charms explore,
How would our spirits long to rise,
And dwell on earth no more!"

2. *Canaan was also a type of heaven.* For two thousand years the people of God knew no type of heaven more glorious than the Eden of our first parents. Then a new picture was presented to their view. "While Paradise lay in

the past, and was receding silently to a still more indistinct distance, there grew up in the horizon of the hopeful future an image of, perhaps, still greater attraction, and one which had this advantage, that it was drawing ever nearer to them. This was the land of Canaan, the land of promised inheritance. This, accordingly, was also made a type of heaven; and they gazed at the land of their hopes, beyond the skies, through its lovely images. This was the picture, yonder was the reality; this was the shadow, yonder was the substance; this was the eartnly, yonder was the heavenly Canaan, the true inheritance." *

This earthly Canaan was a place of habitation, a home for the people of God. It was a land flowing with milk and honey; of corn and of wine; of balmy air and genial skies. To the ancient Jews earth could not furnish a fairer type of heaven. How gloriously it contrasted with their present condition! Now they were a wandering, homeless people; that was to be their abiding home. Now they tread the sands of a waste and burning desert; that was a land of abundance and beauty. Now they are in want, in peril, and in sorrow; but in the promised Canaan abundance, safety, and joy shall be theirs forever. Jordan only separated them from their longed-for, goodly land. Thus is prefigured the heavenly Canaan. In this dim foreshadowing the Christian catches glimpes of his eternal inheritance. Bright in their living reality, they convey no uncertain indications of the nature of our heavenly home.

"Sweet fields beyond the swelling flood
Stand dress'd in living green;
So to the Jews old Canaan stood,
While Jordan roll'd between."

3. *Jerusalem is also presented as a distinctive type of heaven.* It was a glorious city, beautiful for situation; a

* Heavenly Home. By Rev. H. Harbaugh, p. 60.

great city, and goodly palaces were in the midst of her; and God was worshiped in her sanctuaries, and Jerusalem was the chief place in Israel. "The Lord loveth the gates of Zion more than all the dwellings of Jacob. Glorious things are spoken of thee, O city of God." (Psa. lxxxvii, 2, 3.) God is also spoken of as *dwelling* in Mount Zion, (Isa. viii, 18; xviii, 7; Joel iii, 17,) and as putting his name (2 Kings xxi, 4) and making his abode in Jerusalem. (Ezra vii, 15.) In all these respects is Jerusalem the type of heaven.

Do God's ancient people come up to Jerusalem to worship? It is only a type of that grander scene when the redeemed of the Lord shall return, and come with singing unto Zion; "and everlasting joy shall be upon their head; they shall obtain joy and gladness, and sorrow and mourning shall flee away." (Isa. li, 11.) Does the Revelator, inspired by Heaven, attempt to unvail to mortal view the glory of the invisible heaven? The vision of the "New Jerusalem coming down from God out of heaven" (Rev. xxi, 2) breaks upon our wondering gaze. The earthly Jerusalem may be subjected to bondage; "but Jerusalem which is above is free, which is the mother of us all." (Gal. iv, 26.) The earthly Jerusalem may be destroyed and become desolate; but of the heavenly it is declared, "Violence shall no more be heard in thy land, wasting nor destruction within thy borders; but thou shalt call thy walls salvation and thy gates praise." (Isa. lx, 18.) The darkness of night may brood over the earthly Jerusalem through long ages; but of the heavenly it is said, "There shall be no night there." (Rev. xxi, 25.) "The sun shall be no more thy light by day, neither for brightness shall the moon give light unto thee; but the Lord shall be unto thee an everlasting light, and thy God thy glory. Thy sun shall no more go down, neither shall thy moon withdraw itself; for the Lord shall be thine everlasting light, and the days of thy mourning shall be ended." (Isa. lxi, 19, 20.) This was the true Jerusalem seen in the faith of even God's ancient children; for we are told that the spiritual vision of even the patriarch to whom the promise was made, stretching far beyond the earthly Jerusalem, "looked for a city which hath foundations, whose builder and maker is God." (Heb. xi, 10.) So the heirs of faith with him, recognizing the grandeur and beauty of the type—the earthly Jerusalem—they are led to "desire a better country, that is, an heavenly: whereupon God is not ashamed to be called their God; for he hath prepared for them a city." (Heb. xi, 16.) So it is in the faith of the Christian. Jerusalem stands forth as the type of that blessed city toward which all his longings aspire, and in which all his hopes center. Like the patriarchs of old, the burden of their song is—

"Strangers and pilgrims here below,
This earth, we know, is not our place;
But hasten through the vale of woe,
And, restless to behold thy face,
Swift to our heavenly country move,
Our everlasting home above.

We've no abiding city here,
But seek a city out of sight;
Thither our steady course we steer,
Aspiring to the plains of light—
Jerusalem, the saints' abode,
Whose founder is the living God."

4. *Heaven is typically represented by the Temple and the Church.* A temple is a building erected and set apart for the worship of God. The Church of the blessed Redeemer constitutes the assemblage of true worshipers who serve him. It is said of those who had entered heaven through great tribulation, that, "therefore, they are before the throne of God, and serve him day and night in his temple."

(Rev. vii, 15.) "Him that overcometh will I make a pillar in the temple of my God, and he shall go out no more." (Rev. iii, 12.) One has beautifully said that "the great universe is the temple of God's presence; the Church is the temple of his grace; and heaven is the temple of his glory"

5. *In an especial sense was the Holy of Holies the type of heaven.* It is said that "Christ is not entered into the holy places made with hands, which are the figures of the true; but into heaven itself, now to appear in the presence of God for us." (Heb. ix, 24.) In the *sanctum sanctorum* of the Temple dwelt the shekinah, the mysterious and supernatural emblem of the Divine Presence. Here, from the mercy-seat, he condescended to commune with his people. As this was the *Holy of Holies* in the Temple, so heaven is *the Holy of Holies in creation.* There God revealed himself in mysterious symbols; in heaven shadow and symbol are thrown aside, and he is seen with unclouded vision.

"The holy to the holiest leads."

Thus have we "boldness to enter into the *holiest* by the blood of Jesus, by a new and living way which he hath consecrated for us, through the vail, that is to say, his flesh." (Heb. x, 19, 20.) The very idea that heaven is a *holy place* is dear to the heart of the Christian. He delights to contemplate it as mirrored to his spiritual vision on earth, through the *Holy of Holies* in the Temple of God! "Who shall ascend into the hill of the Lord, and who shall stand in his holy place? He that hath clean hands and a pure heart; who hath not lifted up his soul unto vanity, nor sworn deceitfully." (Psa. xxiv, 3, 4.)

6. *The home and the family are also used as types of the heavenly place and relations.* Among all the gorgeous images that mirror heaven to the view of mortals, none

comes more touchingly to the heart than that of *home*. Even the blessed Redeemer, when he would present heaven in its most endearing aspects to his fainting disciples, so as to lift up their hearts with faith and joy, employs this very type. "In my Father's house are many mansions; if it were not so I would have told you. I go to prepare a place for you." (John xiv, 2.) In all this wide earth there are few things more delightful than home. There is magic in the word. It awakens irrepressible and longing desire. "To be home," says an eloquent divine, "is the wish of the seaman on stormy seas and lonely watch. Home is the wish of the soldier, and tender visions mingle with the troubled dreams of trench and tented field. Where the palm-tree waves its graceful plumes, and birds of jeweled luster flash and flicker among gorgeous flowers, the exile sits staring upon vacancy; a far-away home lies on his heart; and, borne on the wings of fancy over intervening seas and lands, he has swept away home, and hears the lark singing above his father's fields, and sees his fair-haired boy-brother, with light foot and childhood's glee, chasing the butterfly by his native stream. And, in his best hours, home—his own sinless home—a home with his Father above that starry sky—will be the wish of every Christian man. He looks around him—the world is full of suffering; he is distressed by its sorrows, and vexed with its sins. He looks within him; he finds much in his own corruptions to grieve for. In the language of a heart repelled, grieved, vexed, he often turns his eye upward, saying, 'I would not live here alway. No: not for all the gold of the world's mines—not for all the pearls of its seas—not for all the pleasures of its flashing, frothy cup—not for all its crowns and kingdoms, would I live here alway!'"

But heaven is not an empty home—a deserted habitation. A large part of the family are already there. The rest will be gathered by and by. The redeemed are not only "fellow-citizens with the saints," but are also members "of the household of God." (Eph. ii, 19.) "Of whom the whole family in heaven and earth is named." (Eph. iii, 15.) The angels of God, created through all the ages of eternity, are members of that family; and the saints, redeemed from earth, of every clime and age, entering there, shall send forth the joyful acclaim, "Home at last!"

7. *The Sabbath is also made to symbolize heaven.* The idea of the Sabbath is *rest.* God rested on the seventh day and sanctified it. So the Jews ceased from all their labors on the Sabbath; and the very soil of the ground was permitted to *rest* in the Sabbatic year. Thus was typed to the believer the eternal Sabbath of God. Ever as he journeyed along in his pilgrimage, the cheering promise was luminous before him—"There remaineth, therefore, a rest for the people of God." (Heb. iv, 9.) Cheered by the glorious prospect, he gives vent to his joy in sacred song:

"Thine earthly Sabbaths, Lord, we love,
But there's a nobler rest above;
To that our lab'ring souls aspire,
With ardent hope and strong desire."

Mr. Harbaugh beautifully says of the Sabbath: "It is the repose of God himself; for the first and deepest reason given for its existence is, that on it *God rested!* Whatever be that repose which can properly be predicated of God, it must include the returning into himself of creative energies. No wonder that on the Sabbath all nature, in a sense more than merely poetic, ebbs back into a position of profound repose. No wonder that man—man in unison with God—should feel, with a sympathy deeper than his reason, the sweet serenity of Sabbatic hours! No wonder that weary man should feel an influence from out the infinite, laving his spirit, reminding him that beyond the changings and heavings of time and space there remains a full rest for the soul, toward which the Sabbath, as a type, strongly allures him. It did so among the Jews. Every Sabbath was to them a prophet, proclaiming a coming rest, more undisturbed and holy than any they had yet enjoyed—a rest of which this was but the shadow cast over into time. To the Jews and first Christians, exposed as they were, in their eventful times, to many changes of fortune, and to much painful uneasiness, this view of heaven must have been very consoling. No less does each individual believer, in his own wearisome pilgrimage, find it delightful to refer his harassed and perplexed spirit to this promise of a final rest to all the weary. To many—very many—toil-worn and heavy-laden Christians, heaven presents a prominent feature of its attractions when it promises to those that die in the Lord, that they shall 'rest from their labors.' The cessation from toil and care, together with the delights of worship which the day of holy rest affords, presents a picture of blessedness worthy of heaven."

These several types are not mere repetitions. They comprise a wide range of significance. And not one of them but reveals particulars concerning heaven, which is not expressed by any of the others. Eden was a revelation of beauty; Canaan, of distinct locality and exhaustless abundance; Jerusalem, of compactness, wealth, and power; the Temple, of sublime and ennobling worship; the Holy of Holies, of that holiness which shall mark both the place and the inhabitants; the home and the family, of those social endearments, those deep and abiding affections, that shall blend the hosts of heaven into one family and kindred; and, finally, the Sabbath comes in to shed the glow of its mellow light over the long and unbroken *rest* of the redeemed. Thus every symbol has its place and its significance. And in the combined light of all these types, how much of heaven is revealed! It begins already to open up to our vision as something more than mist and shadow. We already behold the limnings of Divine and glorious reality.

II. Figures Employed to Represent Heaven.

Passing from the more permanent and distinctly-recognized types of heaven, we find a large number of figures employed to represent it. These all have their use—each unvailing, to some degree, distinctive and peculiar characteristics of our heavenly home.

1. *Heaven is a place.* "I go to prepare a PLACE for you." (John xiv, 2.) Glorious in itself, it is to be the home of not only ransomed spirits, but of glorified bodies forever.

2. *Heaven is a house, a building.* "We have a BUILDING of God, an HOUSE not made with hands, eternal in the heavens." (2 Cor. v, 1.) Built by the great Architect of the universe, this house is inconceivably beautiful and glorious. There perpetual homage shall be rendered "unto the Father of our Lord Jesus Christ, of whom the whole family in heaven and earth is named." (Eph. iii, 14, 15.)

3. *Heaven is a city.* "Here we have no abiding city, but we seek one to come." (Heb. xiii, 14.) "For he looked for a city which hath foundations, whose builder and maker is God." (Heb. xi, 10.) "God is not ashamed to be called their God, for he hath prepared for them a city." (Heb xi, 16.) Here, like Abraham of old, our dwelling is in tents, and we never continue in one stay; or, like Israel, we wander "in the wilderness in a solitary way." But God leads forth his saints "by the right way, that they might go to the city of habitation." (Psa. cvii, 7.)

"That is the city of the living God. It was built by him; it is governed by him; and it is placed under his immediate protection. Other cities perish; but that is eternal; in other cities death reigns; but the cities of heaven are immortal." A great city is a place of concourse. Multitudes are gathered into it from all parts of the earth. But even this is a feeble expression of the great multitude that shall be gathered from the north and the south, from the east and the west, to people that great city "whose builder and maker is God."

4. *Heaven is a kingdom.* In the great day of judgment, the Son of man is represented as saying to them on his right hand, "Come, ye blessed of my Father, inherit the *kingdom* prepared for you from the foundation of the world." (Matt. xxv, 34.) "I appoint unto you a kingdom." (Luke xxii, 29.) "It is your Father's good pleasure to give you the kingdom." (Luke xii, 32.) "For so an entrance shall be ministered unto you abundantly into the everlasting kingdom of our Lord and Savior Jesus Christ." (2 Pet. i, 11.) In that kingdom "the Lord God Omnipotent reigneth." There is none to dispute his power nor to resist his sway. He reigns in equity and justice; "just and true are thy ways, thou King of saints." (Rev. xv, 3.) His dominion is eternal. Other dynasties shall fail; other kingdoms shall come to an end; and other thrones crumble to dust. But here is a kingdom and a throne that shall never fail. Other kingdoms may be clouded, but there shall be no night in this; others may be desolated by war, but this is the kingdom of "peace." The righteous shall inhabit it; and from it every thing unholy shall be excluded. O what a kingdom is this!

"O'er all those wide-extended plains
Shines one eternal day;
There God the Son forever reigns,
And scatters night away."

5. *Heaven is also a country.* Even in the land of promise the people of God sojourned "as in a strange country." And all they who follow the example of faith set by the patriarchs, still "declare plainly that they seek a country." The Ur of the Chaldeans from which Abraham went forth, or the Canaan of promise toward which he directed his steps, were crowned with genial skies and a balmy atmosphere. They were rich in all the productions of the most genial climes. But as compared even with those garden spots of earth, this is "a better country, that is, an heavenly." The glories of that better country are but partially unvailed. There is the goodly city; the river of the water of life; the tree of life, growing every-where and bearing bounteous fruit. There is the unclouded sky; night is unknown; and there is no more sea, to separate nations and peoples or to be lashed by storms. And there, too, are the assembled hosts of God's elect, gathered from every country on the face of the whole earth.

"O the transporting, rapturous scene,
  That rises to my sight!
Sweet fields array'd in living green,
  And rivers of delight.

There generous fruits that never fail,
  On trees immortal grow;
There rock, and hill, and brook, and vale,
  With milk and honey flow.

O'er all those wide-extended plains
  Shines one eternal day;
There God the Son forever reigns,
  And scatters night away.

No chilling winds, or pois'nous breath
  Can reach that healthful shore;
Sickness and sorrow, pain and death,
  Are felt and fear'd no more.

When shall I reach that happy place,
  And be forever blest?
When shall I see my Father's face,
  And in his bosom rest?"

6. *Heaven is an inheritance.* St. Peter speaks of the children of God as having been begotten again "to an inheritance incorruptible, and undefiled, and that fadeth not away, reserved in heaven." (1 Pet. i, 4.) This inheritance, once lost by the fall, is assured to be ours again "by the resurrection of Jesus Christ from the dead." To the converted Jew this promise was full of meaning. His earthly inheritance had been corrupted; to many of them it was absolutely lost, and they were exiles from the land of their fathers. But here was an inheritance that was incorruptible. The brand of destruction might sweep away his earthly inheritance, but it could not reach up to the unfading inheritance in heaven.

Again, an *inheritance* is endeared to the heart by precious memories. It comes from another. It was gathered by his toil and sacrifice; preserved by his care and watchfulness. And now it comes to us as an expression of his kindness and love. Because of all this it is more precious. The gratitude and the love that spring up in the heart toward a benefactor so kind, a parent so loving, or a brother so self-sacrificing, shed additional brightness upon the rich inheritance bestowed. With such emotions will the child of God contemplate his inheritance in the prospect; and when he enters upon the glorious possession, we can hardly wonder that he loses himself in acclamations of thanksgiving and songs of praise.

III. Heaven a Local Habitation.

As we have passed along through the types and figures employed by Inspiration to bring heaven within our human conception, we have found it impossible to resist the idea of a definite locality as pertaining to the heavenly world. Much of the force and expressiveness of every type and figure depends upon this. They all point not merely to a certain state of mind *in* man, but also to places, things, persons, and relations *without* himself—the denial of which would seem to rob heaven of all reality.

But it will be desirable to make a more direct examination of the question of the locality of heaven. This involves the twofold question, Does heaven occupy a definite locality in space? Where is that locality? For purposes of demonstration these questions are not dependent upon each other. We may be in possession of sufficient evidence to determine the fact of its locality, while its place in space may be wholly conjectural, or, at best, only suggested by what little is known of the grand organization of the universe.

1. *The very terms employed to designate heaven imply locality.* It is localized in the types and figures that are employed to represent it to us. "Eden," and "Canaan," and "the Temple," and "Jerusalem," "the home and family," "the Holy of Holies," "the Sabbath," and especially those other figures—"a place," "a house," "a city," "a kingdom," "a country," and "an inheritance"—all of them, with more or less definiteness, imply a distinct locality. Take, again, those forms of expression—"in heaven," "to heaven," "high as heaven," "from heaven," "into heaven," "out of heaven"—they indicate that heaven is a place to which we may go and from which we may depart, as is a city or a country. The very adverbial designations, "where" and "there," as applied to heaven, are the designation of a place, occupying a definite space, distinct in its locality from every other.

2. *Heaven, as the home of the resurrected bodies of the saints, must be a place.* Enoch and Elijah were translated soul and body to heaven. Thither, also, ascended the resurrected body of our blessed Lord; and to his followers he

evermore proclaims, "WHERE I am, THERE ye may be also." (John xiv, 3.) That is the blessed land,

> "Where rivers of pleasure flow bright o'er the plains,
> And the noontide of glory eternally reigns."

It is objected that, in the resurrection state, the bodies of the saints will be "spiritual," and therefore not subjected to the conditions of place and local habitation. St. Paul says, "It is sown a natural body, it is raised a spiritual body." And again, "Now, this I say, brethren, that flesh and blood can not inherit the kingdom of God." (1 Cor. xv, 44, 50.) This objection is fully met and canceled when we remember that it is not a mere *spirit* that is possessed by the saints, but a *spiritual* BODY. It is obvious, then, that *bodies* are not excluded from heaven. They shall not, indeed, be bodies organized and sustained as ours now are, subject to like infirmities, and possessed of the same tendencies to corruption and death. This is what we understand to be meant by "*flesh and blood.*" Knapp says: "According to the New Testament, man will possess a *body*, even in the future life, and continue to be as he now is, a being composed of both sense and reason.' Such a body demands a local habitation. Nor can we doubt that the scenery of heaven may bear some resemblance to that of earth. Holiness and materiality have no antagonism to each other. Adam and Eve, when created, though pure as the angels of God, were not only placed in the garden of Eden, but were instructed "*to dress it and to keep it.*" Even the beauties of creation are material as well as spiritual. Who, then, will say that flowers shall not bloom in the paradise of God—that landscapes surpassing the loveliness of Eden shall not greet the eye?

> "We speak of the realms of the bless'd,
> Of that country so bright and so fair,
> And oft are its glories confess'd,
> But what must it be to be there?"

3. *The obvious impression made by the Bible is that heaven is a fixed and definite locality.* It is from this cause that the great body of Christians have, in all ages, received the idea of a material heaven. They may be scarcely conscious that such is their faith; they may be equally unconscious of the time and the mode in which they were led to the reception of the idea; and yet they find it in their hearts and minds, nor can they fail to discover that it has flowed along with the receptive influences of their Bible reading. So deeply rooted is this conviction that it is rarely removed.

The fact that the great body of the learned and wise men, who have made the Bible a subject of profound study, have embraced and taught this doctrine, must strengthen the faith of men in the popular sentiment. Then, again, so far as we are aware, not a single passage in the whole Bible can be made, by any fair interpretation, to stand in opposition to this view.

4. *The soul holds an intimate relation to the material world in this life, and it is therefore a fair presumption that it will be the same in the life to come.* It is linked to matter by its affiliation with the body, and its connection through the senses with the external world. Its joys and its sorrows, its works and its plays, its progressions in knowledge and holiness, and its lapses from virtue, and indeed its very being all through its earthly lifetime, are constantly more or less intimately allied with and dependent upon materiality. The soul has had all its experience and all its nurture for heaven in connection with a material body and in a material world. Thus it seems to us that unless great violence is done to its nature—a violence that will rob it almost of its identity—it must have something of the same surroundings in the future life.

Isaac Taylor, in his "Physical Theory of Another Life,"

endeavors to meet this obvious demand of the conditions of our being for a future material abode, by the ingenious suggestion that within the material universe cognizable by the senses, is another material universe interpenetrating it every-where—an *imperium in imperio*—or rather *a world within a world*, and *a universe within a universe.* "Our planets," he says, "in their sweep do not perforate the structure of this invisible creation; our suns do not scorch its plains; for the two collateral systems are not connected by any active affinities." He further suggests that the dwellers in those unseen material spheres may be as unconscious of our existence as we are of theirs. Death is simply passing from our material sphere into that other which is all around us; and therefore it is simply "a change of affinities."

The author is as ingenious in his arguments for the support of his theory as he is in the presentation of the theory itself. Some have become so bewildered by these arguments that they have been led to inquire whether that which appeared to be only an airy speculation is not a reality. His Scripture argument only reaches up to the conclusion that the theory is not in conflict with the Bible. To this it may be replied that the same is true of a great many other absurdities, simply because the Bible makes no recognition of them whatever. His physical argument, at best, could only prove that an unseen material creation is possible. But they are so ingenious that we indulge in a momentary survey of them. He claims that the possibility of an "unseen world" is suggested by the fact that there are material elements, like electricity, light, and the atmosphere, which, to a great extent, are not cognizable to the senses. It is further suggested by the fact that one material substance may penetrate another and occupy the same space without enlarging the latter or disturbing any of its properties—as, for instance, the penetration of transparent bodies by light. Then, again, the suggestion is made that there may be elements in nature altogether unknown to us in our present state; and, further, that the soul in the future life may be endowed with new bodily senses, capable of appreciating elements altogether new. And still again, science has revealed animalculæ in the water, in the air, in the earth, and even in the solid rock. Thus creation swarms, life within life. Upon these vague analogies, and these speculative guesses, he has built up, or rather suggested that there might be built up, a theory of *a world within a world* and *a universe within a universe.*

A serious refutation of a theory so visionary need not be attempted. Its bare statement is sufficient to show that it has its origin in the imagination of *what may be*, rather than in the knowledge of *what is.* Then, too, there is the same reason for supposing the existence of a *third* as a second world. For if heaven is here—a present material world—without our knowing it, why is not hell also? It will certainly be a "new creation" when we are endowed with bodies that can pass through the mountains and the earth, and dwell in the solid rock! But there do not appear to be in all this many gleams of the heavenly paradise.

Equally unsubstantial is the theory of "progressive ascensions," which represents the saints of God as being transferred, in successive lives, or rather successive stages of life, from planet to planet, from star to star, and from system to system, perpetually approaching the presence of the Eternal. These successive worlds, it is claimed, are indicated by the "many mansions" of the Savior; for "our Father's house is the whole universe." According to this theory, the saint is to be a pilgrim and a stranger through all eternity. Very unlike this is that permanent home revealed to our faith in the mercy of God. It is not a succession of temporary homes; not a series of transportations from world to world; but "an abiding city"—"a house not made with hands, eternal in the heavens."

5. *Where is heaven?* To this question numerous answers have been given, each sustained with more or less force of argument. Among these may be classed the *world in world* theory of Mr. Taylor, and also the theory of "progressive ascensions," both of which have been already noticed. There still remain, however, three answers in addition to those already noticed, that have been given, each of which is worthy of notice.

The first is that which suggests *the creation of a new world* which is to be the home of the blessed. We are not certain that we are not indebted to the fertile mind of the author of the "Physical Theory of Another Life" for the suggestion of this theory also. It assumes that God created the present world *from nothing*, ordained it for a specific purpose, and appointed to it a certain limit of existence. When that limit is reached, and God withdraws the force of his ordaining and upholding will, the globe will fall back into its primeval nonentity. Then shall the "new heavens" and the "new earth" spring to life, created by the Almighty Word. "The visible universe, replete everywhere with various forms of animal life, is to fill one period only in the great history of the moral system, and it is destined, in a moment, in the twinkling of an eye, to disappear and to return to its nihility, giving place to new elements and to new and higher expressions of omnipotence and intelligence." This beautiful frost-work of theory suddenly dissolves beneath the warm rays of the light of Revelation. Here we are assured that the kingdom inherited by the righteous was *prepared before the foundation of the world*, (Matt. xxv, 34,) that our Father's *house is already built, and that the many mansions are already there*, (John xiv, 2,) and that the inheritance of the saints is already prepared, and is now simply *reserved in heaven* for them. (1 Pet. i, 4.)

Another answer is that which suggests that *our earth, purified and refurnished, is to be the heaven of the saints.* This idea seems to have its origin in certain passages that speak of a "new heaven and a new earth" that shall succeed the old. It has received the sanction of many learned and pious men. Dr. Griffin says: "A grand destiny awaits this world of sins and sorrows. This earth, purified by judgment fires, shall be the home of the blessed. Under laws accommodated to the new economy, the wide world shall become one Eden, where, exempt from physical as from moral evils, none shall shiver amid arctic frosts, nor wither under tropic heat: these fields of snow and arid sands shall blossom all with roses. From the convulsions of expiring, or rather the birth-pangs of parturient nature, a new-born world shall come, a home worthy of immortals, a palace befitting its King." We must confess that we have never been able to feel the force of the reasonings employed to sustain this idea; nor can we perceive the conclusiveness of the Scripture proof adduced for its support. It is in many respects a grand idea, and it is countenanced by some beautiful analogies; but, after all, it is *unproved.*

Nor is this all. Objections of insuperable moment lie against it. The surface of the earth would be insufficient for the habitation of so great a number. Then, too, heaven is represented as the home of not only the saints, but also of the angels of God, and of Christ, and God himself. Then, again, it is referred to as a building, a city, a kingdom, a country—*already prepared.* Beautiful, then, as are the visions of our regenerated earth, we are taught still to look beyond and higher for our true inheritance—our heav enly home.

The third idea, and the one that appears by far the most rational and probable, is that which makes heaven the *astronomic center of the material universe.* That there is such an actual material heaven, into which the glorified body of Christ has already entered, and where the souls of many of the saints are also waiting for the resurrection, to make perfect their immortal nature, no one can doubt after a careful examination of the overwhelming force of argument upon the subject. But the *exact locality* of heaven, in relation to the earth, the Scriptures do not fix; but they do refer to it as occupying a place in the universe. It is placed in contrast with the earth, spoken of as *away from* the earth. Take such passages as these:

"Heaven is my throne, and the earth is my footstool;" "The Lord hath prepared his throne in the heavens." "There is," says Dr. Dick, "an astronomical idea which may help us to some conception of this 'glorious high throne,' which is the peculiar residence of the Eternal. It is now considered by astronomers as highly probable, if not certain, from late observations, from the nature of gravitation, and other circumstances, that all the systems of the universe revolve around one common center, and that this center may bear as great a proportion, in point of magnitude, to the universal assemblage of systems, as the sun does to his surrounding planets. And since our sun is five hundred times larger than the earth and all the other planets and their satellites taken together, on the same scale, such a central body would be five hundred times larger than all the systems and worlds in the universe. Here, then, may be a vast universe of itself—an example of material creation, exceeding all the rest in magnitude and splendor, and in which are BLENDED THE GLORIES OF

EVERY OTHER SYSTEM. If this is in reality the case, it may with the most emphatic propriety be termed, 'The Throne of God.'

"This is the most sublime and magnificent idea that can possibly enter into the mind of man. We feel oppressed and overwhelmed in endeavoring to form even a faint representation of it. But however much it may overpower our feeble conceptions, we ought not to revolt at the idea of so glorious an extension of the works of God, since nothing less magnificent seems suitable to a being of infinite perfections. This grand central body may be considered as the capital of the universe. From this glorious center embassies may occasionally be dispatched to all surrounding worlds, in every region of space. Here, too, deputations from all the different provinces of creation may occasionally assemble, and the inhabitants of different worlds mingle with each other, and learn the grand outlines of those physical operations and moral transactions which have taken place in their respective spheres. Here may be exhibited to the view of unnumbered multitudes objects of sublimity and glory, which are no where else to be found within the wide extent of creation. Here, intelligences of the highest order, who have attained the most sublime hights of knowledge and virtue, may form the principal part of the population of this magnificent region. Here the glorified body of the Redeemer may have taken its principal station, as 'the head of all principalities and powers;' and here, likewise, Enoch and Elijah may reside, in the mean time, in order to learn the history of the magnificent plans of the Deity, that they may be enabled to communicate intelligence respecting them to their brethren of the race of Adam, when they shall again mingle with them in the world allotted for their abode, after the general resurrection. Here, the grandeur of the Deity, the glory of his physical and moral perfections, and the immensity of his empire, may strike the mind with more bright effulgence, and excite more elevated emotions of admiration and rapture, than in any other province of universal nature. In fine, this vast and splendid central universe may constitute that august mansion mentioned in Scripture, under the designation of THE THIRD HEAVENS—THE THRONE OF THE ETERNAL—THE HEAVEN OF HEAVENS—THE HIGH AND HOLY PLACE—AND THAT LIGHT THAT IS INACCESSIBLE AND FULL OF GLORY."*

This theory of a grand central world in the universe, which Dr. Dick speaks of as a "highly probable" truth, may now be considered as one of the grandest demonstrations of astronomy. Nor are the suggestive discoveries of this sublime science, in this direction, limited to this one theme. Herschel has demonstrated that while our system is far removed from other systems, and our sun from other suns, in the distant regions of heaven the stars and systems are more closely clustered. Advancing into this region thickly studded with "star-clusters," the brightness must constantly increase, till at length we reach ETERNAL SUNSHINE! Sublime commentary upon that revelation of heaven which declares "there shall be no night there!" As we stand, and in thoughtful wonder gaze upon this sublime picture, we seem almost, with John of Patmos, to catch a glimpse of "the Holy City, the New Jerusalem, coming down from God out of heaven!" and there seems to be opening up before us a vista growing brighter and brighter as an ascending pathway to the throne of God.

No wonder that such astronomers and philosophers as Herschel, and Sir David Brewster, and Schubert, and Dr. Dick, and Dr. W. Pfaff, and others, have kindled with rapture at this sublime conception. Prof. Lange, after sur-

*Philosophy of the Future State, p. 224.

veying the bearings of astronomy in this direction, says: "The idea of the existence of such a high and central throne in the universe, such an illuminated summit in the creation of God, must at once commend itself to thoughtful minds in the full power of its glorious truth. God manifests himself every-where in his works; but his works ever present themselves to us in a regular and discernible and upward gradation. Every-where there are degrees in creation; there are, as it were, winding steps in every department of life, which tend ever upward, and point us to a grand summit, an eternal Mount Zion. In the stone formations of earth we behold already the image of a divine thought reflecting its light upon us. The same thought is imaged forth in a way still more intelligent, more tender, and more lovely, in the rose; more wonderful and moving still in the tones of the nightingale's song; but most glorious and spiritual of all, in the human eye. Thus, from the stone to man there is a gradual ascent of many steps; but from the smallest, or even from the most excellent of men, up to Him who is the fairest among the children of men—in whom dwells the fullness of the Godhead—what a path from an abyss up to a blessed hight! But Christ himself, in his human nature, had an ascent to make. This is seen in his transfiguration upon the Mount, which at first only broke forth as an adumbration from his servant-form, but which was afterward to manifest itself in completeness in his ascension to heaven! Thus does a beautiful thought first dawn in the soul in the form of a lovely feeling, and afterward gradually grow to perfection. So it is in reference to whole regions. Not over the whole earth is dispersed the same life, light, and beauty. There are solitudes in the earth which none can or will inhabit. There are barren and dreary regions which men assign to evil spirits as their habitations. There are, moreover, rough regions only beloved by a few whose 'sweet homes are there, or by poets to whom the hidden beauties of the world are known, and who look upon the dark wastes of earth as suitable shades in the background of that wonderful picture which they construct out of the world as a whole. Then appear, also, the lovely and the lovelier regions of the earth, and from among them the eye that has the keenest perception of the beautiful selects yet the loveliest, those in which the richest fullness of thought, of love, of life, and of harmony are exhibited. But now the same train of reflections will lead our thoughts upward through the realms of heavenly space. Thus, there must be—this mode of thinking leads us to conclude—above all these fields of light a grand and glorious throne-summit, where the Divine glory is unfolded in its highest conception; where we shall be enabled, in the most perfect manner, to view the works and the ways of God's wisdom, omnipotence, love, all-sufficiency, and omnipresence; and where his unseen essence shines forth with the most transparent and glorified forms and organizations of creative power.

"This conclusion, to which we are led by following those Zion-like ascents which are manifest in the world around us, receives, also, confirmation from the Holy Scriptures. They teach us to worship God as dwelling in the heavens, notwithstanding they also teach his omnipresence, by which he dwells also on earth. They tell us that the Lord's throne is in the heavens, and that the earth is his footstool. The prophet Isaiah saw God in a vision. He sat upon a throne, high and lifted up; his train filled the temple, and the seraphim covered their faces before him with their wings. In this way does the prophet distinguish this high and holy place, where God appears as the highest king, from the temple which is only filled with his train—the outer edges and folds of his royal robe. In his immediate presence, moreover, the blaze of his divine majesty is so transcendent, that the highest spirits give evidence of its presence, in that they vail their faces as a token that even they are not able to endure the sight of such excellent glory with open face! Hence, also, says St. Paul: 'God dwells in light which no man can approach unto; whom no man hath seen or can see.' This expression, however, he qualifies and completes when he says: 'Now we see through a glass, darkly; then face to face: now I know in part; but then shall I know even as also I am known.' *Here* we gain our knowledge by mere transient flashes, as the spiritual is reflected upon us from the cloudy mirror of the coarse, material world—we learn by signs and symbols; but *there* shall we have direct and glorious visions of blessedness, a view of God in his highest revelations, such as the Savior refers to when he says, 'Blessed are the pure in heart, for they shall see God.' As there was 'the Holy of Holies' in the Jewish Temple, so this is the holy of holies of the Divine Presence in the great temple of the universe."

These visions of beauty and glory, now ideal, are yet to become actual to the Christian. He can look up and say, This is MY FATHER'S HOUSE! "And if children, then heirs, heirs of God and joint-heirs with Jesus Christ."

"Far out of sight, while yet the flesh infolds us,
Lies the fair country where our hearts abide,
And of its bliss is naught more wondrous told us,
Than these few words, 'I shall be satisfied.'"

V. THE SAINTS IN HEAVEN.

We have patiently and earnestly interrogated nature, and science, and man, and Revelation, to gather what light we may concerning heaven, its locality, its characteristics, and especially its fitness to become the home of the glorified.

If we have not gained all the insight we desired, yet, nevertheless, every step has been fraught with interest, and the conclusions such as must ravish the soul with delightful anticipations and longing desires for "the better country." But our interest goes beyond the *country*—it extends to the inhabitants as well. We would know what they are, how they live, and what they do. A brief survey of the field here opened must close our discussion of the delightful and deeply-interesting themes of this volume.

1. *The individual in heaven.* Whatever may be the transformations wrought in our nature in the resurrection and in our transmission to heaven, man, admitted there, will still be composed of SOUL AND BODY. The resurrection body will retain its materiality; purged of all that is gross and evil, refined and made spiritual, it shall be the partner of the soul forever. They together shall constitute *glorified humanity* in heaven. Whether its organs of sense shall be precisely what they are in this life, it is unnecessary to inquire; but we do know that, in the future life, we shall possess an insight into, and an appreciation of, the beauties of even material nature infinitely transcending all the possibilities of the present life. There the intellectual powers shall be immensely enlarged and quickened, and the emotional nature shall glow with a fervor and a delight unknown to earth. There, also, the moral nature, purified from every taint of sin, filled with all "the fullness of God," shall be the center of the holiest affections and the purest joy.

2. *Society in heaven.* We shall not find heaven a solitary country. St. Paul says: "Ye are come unto Mount Zion, and unto the city of the living God, the heavenly Jerusalem, *and to an innumerable company of angels.*" Angels are to be our companions in the skies. Nor these alone. People from all worlds will gather there, and we shall be-

hold them, enjoy their society, and gather knowledge from their intercourse. Every age and every clime, every language and every dialect, every creed and every color of earth, will contribute its quota to the heavenly society. There the distinctions of grade and sect, of wealth and poverty, of birth and station, will all be sunk in the higher distinctions of moral and spiritual excellence. How blissful must be that society from which the unholy and vile are forever excluded, and in which are congregated the good of all ages and all worlds! "Therefore are they before the throne of God, and serve him day and night in his temple; and he that sitteth on the throne shall dwell among them. They shall hunger no more, neither thirst any more; neither shall the sun light on them, nor any heat; for the Lamb which is in the midst of the throne shall feed them, and shall lead them unto living fountains of waters; and God shall wipe away all tears from their eyes." (Rev. vii, 16, 17.)

3. *The felicity of heaven.* The two great elements of happiness are found in heaven—an immunity from all evil and the fruition of all good. No physical evil is there, neither pain nor suffering. The presence of all good is there: "With thee there is fullness of joy, and at thy right hand there are pleasures forever more." "Heaven could not be heaven," writes Thomas Brooks, "did it admit of any thing that might interrupt a saint's rest. Heaven is above all wind and weather, the storms and tempests, earthquakes and heartaches; there is nothing to cloud a Christian's joy, or to break in upon his rest. There is joy without sorrow, blessedness without misery, health without sickness, light without darkness, abundance without want, beauty without deformity, honor without disgrace, ease without labor, and peace without interruption. There shall be eyes without tears, hearts without fears, and souls with-

out sin." The sons of immortality, while on earth, longed for this felicity; they looked forward to it as the consummation of all their hopes. Their language was, "Then shall I be satisfied, when I awake with thy likeness.' Now that summit of felicity is reached, and, apart from doubt, or fear, or care, they know the "fullness of joy" which heaven affords.

The sources of the soul's felicity in heaven will be spiritual, as well as material, social and intellectual. To partake of the full measure of bliss in heaven is to rest in God, to sympathize with God, to coöperate with God, to have thoughts of God, to be like God; and, higher and holier than all, to dwell in God. He who is thus enshrined, and thus dwells, has sources of felicity exhaustless as infinity and lasting as eternity. Infinitely varied are those sources of joy, so that they can never pall upon the appetite, but will perpetually awaken and stimulate the noblest aspirations of the soul. Such is heaven.

> "Who, who would live alway, away from his God—
> Away from yon heaven, that blissful abode,
> Where rivers of pleasure flow bright o'er the plains,
> And the noontide of glory eternally reigns?
>
> There saints of all ages in harmony meet,
> Their Savior and brethren transported to greet;
> While anthems of rapture unceasingly roll,
> And the smile of the Lord is the feast of the soul."

4. *Worship in heaven.* There is worship in heaven. The angels worshiped before man or earth was created. They were attendant upon and witnessed the work of creation, and it was then that "the morning stars sang together, and all the sons of God shouted for joy." Before the Majesty of the Divine glory cherubim and seraphim are represented as vailing their faces and bending before the throne. Saints from earth are there also, robed in white, with palms of victory and harps of song; and their swelling notes of

worship resound through all heaven—"Worthy is the Lamb!" St. John says of the four and twenty elders seen in heaven, that they "fall down and worship him that liveth forever and ever." But in that swelling chorus, in which are joined the melodies of both earth and heaven, every rank and order in heaven unite—"Holy, holy, holy, is the Lord of hosts; the whole earth is full of his glory." For aught we know, heaven may have its Sabbaths of worship, as well as earth. If God in heaven rested on the seventh day, and hallowed it, certainly there is no irreverence in presuming that angels and good men in heaven will at fitting times pause in their heavenly avocations, to rest and to worship. Earthly things are the pattern of things in the heavens. And even in the glimpses of the heavenly worship reflected down to earth, we recognize many of our own forms and modes. The heavenly worshipers join in holy convocation; they bow before the throne; they offer "the prayers of the saints" unto God; with golden harps and immortal tongues, they offer thanksgiving and praise; and bowing reverently before the throne, offer ascriptions of honor and adoration: "I heard a great voice of much people in heaven, saying, Alleluia; Salvation, and glory, and honor, and power, unto the Lord our God." And not forgetting the dwellers in their former home, these worshipers in heaven make intercession for the saints in earth. Hence it is no unmeaning expression, when in our worshiping assemblies we sing in the songs of Zion:

> "Come let us join our cheerful songs
> With angels round the throne."

If worship is due to God in heaven, how much more on earth! If it is comforting and elevating to the glorified soul there, how much more to the child of God must it be here! And still more, if the worship of God on earth is but preliminary to the worship of him in heaven, how should we be impressed with the dignity and immortal worth of these temple exercises! On earth, worship is often interrupted by the infirmities of the body or the cares of life; it is too often marred by our worldliness and unspirituality; but, thanks be to God! in heaven, the worshipers around the throne shall send up the incense of a worship pure and perpetual.

"The Church triumphant in thy love,
Their mighty joys we know:
They sing the Lamb in hymns above,
And we in hymns below.

Thee in thy glorious realm they praise,
And bow before thy throne;
We in the kingdom of thy grace:
The kingdoms are but one.

The holy to the holiest leads,
And thence our spirits rise;
For he that in thy statutes treads,
Shall meet thee in the skies."

5. *Work in heaven.* Our Savior says, "My Father worketh hitherto, and I work." Heaven is not to be a place of inactivity. There will be work there. It may not weary as work on earth does, but there will be work there—a tireless, beneficent activity. Dr. Lyman Beecher says: "Excepting exemption from sin, intense, vigorous, untiring action is the greatest pleasure of mind. I could hardly wish to enter heaven did I believe its inhabitants were idly to sit by purling streams, fanned by balmy airs. Heaven, to be a place of happiness, must be a place of activity. Has the far-reaching mind of Newton ceased its profound investigations? Has David hung up his harp, as useless as the dusty arms in Westminster Abbey? Has Paul, glowing with godlike enthusiasm, ceased itinerating the universe of God? Are Peter, and Cyprian, and Edwards mere psalm-singing? Heaven is a place of restless activity, the abode of never-tiring thought. David and

Isaiah will sweep nobler and loftier strains in eternity; and the minds of saints, unclogged by cumbersome clay, will forever feast on the banquet of rich and glorious thought. My young friends, go on, then; you will never get through An eternity of untiring action is before you, and the universe of thought is your field." Thanks be to God for the prospect of "an eternity of untiring action!" We like the idea so beautifully expressed by Isaac Taylor: "This excellent mechanism of matter and mind, which, beyond any other of his works, declares the wisdom of the Creator, and which, under his guidance, is now passing the season of its first preparation, shall stand up anew from the dust of dissolution, and then, with freshened powers, and with a store of hard-earned practical wisdom for its guidance, shall essay new labors—we say not perplexities and perils—in the service of God, who, by such instruments, chooses to accomplish his designs of beneficence. That so prodigious a waste of the highest qualities should take place, as is implied in the notions which many Christians entertain of the future state, is, indeed, hard to imagine. The mind of man, formed, as it is, to be more tenacious of its active habits than even of its moral dispositions, is, in the present state, trained—often at an immense cost of suffering—to the exercise of skill, of forethought, of courage, of patience; and ought it not to be inferred, unless positive evidence contradicts the supposition, that this system of education bears some relation of fitness to the state for which it is an initiation? Shall not the very same qualities, which here are so sedulously fashioned and finished, be actually needed and used in that future world of perfection? Surely, the idea is inadmissible, that an instrument wrought up at so much expense to a polished fitness for service, is destined to be suspended forever on the palace-walls of heaven as a glittering bauble, no more to make proof of its temper."

If the "Father worketh;" and if the Savior could say, "I work;" and if the angels are ministers of his to *do his bidding;* how can it enter into the thoughts of any one, that beings like ourselves, gifted with all the capabilities of usefulness, are to have no mission of usefulness in the future life? Nay, they shall "SERVE him day and night in his temple." What that service will be it is easy, in some degree, to conjecture, when we consider the work for which man is equipped, and the scope of activity that will be afforded in that future world. As their powers and capabilities of service will be indefinitely enlarged and varied by their entrance upon bliss, so shall they find their sphere of activity correspondingly enlarged and varied. "The heavenly life, instead of being a passive, monotonous existence, is a state of intense energy, vast design, and vigorous action; in which to know and do, to love and enjoy, will form a combination of glory, and dignity, and blessedness, far transcending every human conception. To be active, and yet to rest; to be ever employed, and yet to know no weariness; to drink in immortal bliss from all sources and through all the avenues of being, and yet never to be satiated—this is the rest, and this is the glory of heaven!"

6. *Science and knowledge in heaven.* Here "we know in part;" we "see through a glass, darkly." John Angell James has well said that here "our notions are the opinions of children; our discourses are the lispings of children; our controversies the reasonings of children. The prodigious attainments of those luminaries—Bacon, Milton, Boyle, Locke, Newton; and, in the science of theology, of those great divines—Owen, Howe, Charnock, Baxter, Bates, Butler, Hooker—all these are but productions of children, written for the instruction of others less taught than themselves." Every step of our advance in knowledge here is

incumbered with difficulties; our sources of knowledge are limited; our perceptions are blunted and our powers enfeebled; our intercourse is with those whose knowledge is imperfect like our own. Even our explorations into the natural and material world are prosecuted amidst obstacles almost insuperable, and with results far from satisfactory. Many things we would explore, we are unable to reach; and even those reached are found to involve subtile elements inscrutable to the most penetrating intellect. Still more limited and unsatisfactory are our explorations in the vast empire of mind, while the great spiritual realm remains a *terra incognita*, whose boundaries we have barely touched.

In heaven it shall be widely different. The glorified immortal shall be able, with the speed of thought, to traverse the boundless domain of material nature. No sun so burning, no star so high, and no globe so remote even on the very outskirts of creation, but that it may be reached and explored. All his powers shall be immensely enlarged, and his perceptions become intense and piercing to a degree inconceivable in this state. A broad avenue to knowledge will be opened up before him, leading out into all the works and wonders of the created universe. The patriarchs of earth and the sages of other and distant globes shall contribute from the hoarded treasures of unnumbered ages, to increase the storehouse of his knowledge. The records of not only all ages, but of all worlds will be open to his inspection. The problems of mathematics, the subtile combinations of chemistry, the magnificent distances of astronomy, and the limitless realms of mind and of thought will be the play-ground of its research.

Our knowledge there will not be uncertain and doubtful. Even if the truth does not flash upon the mind by intuition, the redeemed spirit will possess the means for the verification of its knowledge in every department of study.

Its mathematical lines, and curves, and measurements, and angles shall be executed with a delicacy and precision admitting of no error; its computations will be definite and certain. The sphere of its knowledge may be bounded, limited; but the outer edge of its horizon will be distinctly marked, and all luminous with the flooding of its light. "The more perfect the sight is," says Richard Baxter, "the more delightful the beautiful object. The more perfect the appetite, the sweeter the food. The more musical the ear, the more pleasant the melody. The more perfect the soul, the more joyous those joys, and the more glorious that glory."

Not only will our knowledge in heaven be free from error, but it will also be connected with practical and beneficent ends, giving higher efficiency and power to the spirit thus endowed, or enabling him to employ that knowledge for the advancement of other beings in knowledge and virtue. And then, too, every advance in knowledge is an appreciable approximation toward the Infinite and Eternal. This approach shall be perpetual. "We have latent powers," says Dr. Price, "which may be the business of eternity to evolve. We are capable of an infinite variety of agreeable perceptions and tendencies, which are now as incomprehensible to us as the enjoyments of a grown man are to an infant in the womb. Our present existence is but the first step in an ascent in dignity and in bliss, which will never come to an end! How amazing and how ecstatic this prospect! What shall we some time or other be?" Here we stand, waiting, and watching, and hoping, in the dimly-lighted vestibule of science; there we shall enter into its very temple, all radiant with the sunlight of eternal day,

> "Where rising floods of knowledge roll
> And pour and pour upon the soul."

7. *Progression in heaven.* We have already anticipated this theme somewhat, and yet its more definite consideration is demanded of us. Unending progression is one of the immutable laws of creation. Man is to increase in all his capabilities of doing good, forever. Fix a limit to the progression of an immortal spirit, and you set bounds to its very felicity. That point reached, its energies would cease to be put forth; it would fall back upon itself; and its very heaven would come to an end. But such is not to be our destiny. The knowledge gained is perpetually to be the stepping-stone to higher knowledge; the power developed is to summon forth still grander power that had hitherto slumbered in the unfathomed depths of an immortal nature; the hights ascended, while they open up broad and extended views, winging the vision afar over the heavenly plains, also reveal loftier summits yet to be scaled in our ascending pathway along the line of eternity. Says a modern writer: "There will come a time when the coldest will have overtaken all the fire of the present Paul, the least loving all the ardent love of the present John; when the stammerer will 'sing a sweeter strain than is now heard from the sweetest singer beneath the throne;' when the feeblest intellect will have 'stretched beyond the capacities of the greatest actual intellect;' and when the lowest saint will be exalted high as the highest now is in 'the kingdom of heaven.'" What a destiny awaits us! Every burden cast aside, every fetter broken off, and every faculty inspired with an unutterable and inconceivable energy, the ransomed immortal shall commence a career in knowledge and in bliss transcending all human conception! No wonder that the Christian breaks forth in sacred song—

"Then shall I see, and hear, and know,
All I desired or wish'd below;
And every hour find sweet employ,
In that eternal world of joy."

8. *The crowning Presence in heaven.* The "vision of God" is the crowning glory of heaven. A heaven without God would be like a solar system without a central sun. For God to be, and yet to be unseen, is to have his saints groping in perpetual darkness—feeling after, yet never attaining unto him. The revelation of the vision of God to mortal eyes would be insupportable, so overwhelming is the Divine glory.

> "Fountain of light, thyself invisible
> Amidst the glorious brightness where thou sitt'st
> Throned, inaccessible but where thou shadest
> The full blaze of thy beams; and through a cloud
> Drawn round about thee like a radiant shrine,
> Dark with excessive bright thy skirts appear,
> Yet dazzle heaven, that brightest seraphim
> Approach not, but with both wings vail their eyes."
> PAR. LOST, b. iii, 372 sqq.

When Moses sought to behold that glory, God said to him, "No man shall see me and live." (Ex. xxxiii, 20.) Thus God has accommodated the revelation of himself to the feebleness of our humanity. He is seen in his works. The countless wonders of creation proclaim him; and when the mind turns in upon itself, we can not fail there to read "the autograph of the invisible God." So God is seen in his Word, reflected as from a mirror, that our darkened humanity might behold the revelation of his glory and admire his beauty. His pathway is marked in that mysterious providence which encircles and pervades all creatures and all movements, whether in the material or the intellectual worlds. There are also spiritual revelations which God makes of himself to the believer. For this spiritual presence there is a longing in the heart of every believer. "Whom have I in heaven but thee? and there is none on earth whom I desire beside thee." (Psa. lxxiii, 25.) "My soul thirsteth for God, for the living God; O when shall I come and appear before him?" (Psa. xlii, 2.) The longing of the earth-worn pilgrim is to "see the King in his beauty," and to become an inhabitant of "the land that is afar off." The prospect cheers him in his pilgrimage, lightens every burden, and sweetens every sorrow. When Job was in the midst of his desolation and agony, he cried out, "O that I knew where I might find him! that I might come even to his seat!" The Divine Presence can light up every valley of gloom, and chase away every night of darkness. Still, these are only twilight revelations, dim foreshadowings of the Divine One. It is a foreshadowing fitted to our earthly state, and such as our humanity can bear.

"In darkest shades, if thou appear,
My dawning is begun;
Thou art my soul's bright morning star,
And thou my rising sun."

"Thy loving-kindness is better than life." The revelation of the Divine glory upon the Mount of the Transfiguration filled the disciples with wonder and joy, so that they exclaimed, "It is good to be here!"

But a more benignant and glorious revelation of the Godhead is reserved for the saints in heaven. "Blessed are the pure in heart, for they shall SEE GOD." "We shall see him as he is." The brightest glory that ever thrilled the heart of the Prince of Israel culminated in that triumphant song, "As for me, I will behold thy face in righteousness!" And Job, amidst the ruins of his earthly fortune and the desolation of his home, finds one bright alleviation: "In my flesh shall I see God; whom I shall see for myself, and mine eyes shall behold, and not another." How God will manifest himself in heaven it is useless for us to inquire. Speculations upon the subject are vain. The glory of our own heavenly nature is beyond our comprehension here. Still less do we know of the Infinite One; how, then, can we even guess the mode and form in which he will manifest himself to the glorified in heaven? But we have this to comfort and assure us—if the dim manifestation of the Divine Presence here is so fraught with heavenly joy, the full blaze of that Presence in the future world must be glorious beyond human conception. "Eye hath not seen, nor ear heard, neither have entered into the heart of man, the things which God hath prepared for them that love him." (1 Cor. ii, 9.) The *beatific vision*—to "see his face"—is the crowning glory of heaven. Thanks be to God, that the blessed Redeemer, bearing up his devoted followers in the arms of his love and power, hath said, "I will that they also whom thou hast given me may be with me where I am, that they may behold my glory which thou hast given me." No wonder that the glorified, worshiping in the presence of an unvailed Deity, in sublime ecstasy cast their crowns at his feet, and reverently bowing low in the Divine Presence, "rest not day and night, saying, Holy, holy, holy, Lord God Almighty!" "Thou art worthy to receive glory, and honor, and power." "Blessing, and honor, and glory, and power be unto him that sitteth upon the throne, and unto the Lamb forever and ever." (Rev. iv, 8, 11; v, 13.)

"Forever with the Lord!
Amen, so let it be!
Life from the dead is in that word,
'T is immortality."

www.ingramcontent.com/pod-product-compliance
Lightning Source LLC
LaVergne TN
LVHW020936110826
845150LV00004B/884

* 9 7 8 1 4 2 5 5 5 2 0 3 9 *